The Magic of the
RED CARPET

The Magic of the
RED CARPET

AJIT MATHEW GEORGE

Magic Dust Press
Wilmington, DE

Copyright © 2019 by Ajit Mathew George

All rights reserved. No part of this publication may be reproduced, distributed, or transmitted in any form or by any means, including photocopying, recording, or other electronic or mechanical methods, without the prior written permission of the publisher, except in the case of brief quotations embodied in critical reviews and certain other noncommercial uses permitted by copyright law. For permission requests, write to the publisher at the address below:

Magic Dust Press

Magic Dust Press, P. O. Box 69, Wilmington, DE 19899
www.ajitmathewgeorge.com
email: ajitgeorge@me.com

ISBN: 978-1-7334181-0-2 (BW paperback)
ISBN: 978-1-7334181-1-9 (full color paperback)
eISBN: 978-1-7334181-2-6 (ebook)

Printed in the United States of America

DEDICATION

I dedicate this book to:

My mother, who named me Ajit, which in Sanskrit means invincible, an impossible name to live up to. She taught me the true meaning of resilience;

The late Chef Matt Haley, who after he won the 2014 James Beard Award persuaded me, against my better judgment, to do "Breaking Bread Behind Bars" inside a prison;

My dear friend and U.S. Senator Chris Coons, who helped me raise the money at "Breaking Bread Behind Bars" to fund a new greenhouse at Baylor Women's Correctional Institution, which seeded the idea for Second Chances Farm;

Delia Cohen, a visionary architect who brings exceptional community leaders into U.S. prisons to work with extraordinary, incarcerated leaders, who attended the TEDxWilmingtonSalon inside Baylor Women's Correctional Institution with the theme, "Second Chances and Redemption," and then invited me to the inaugural TEDxSanQuentin;

Curtis "Wall Street" Carroll, who I met in San Quentin prison, whose TEDx talk entitled, "How I Learned to Read — and Trade Stocks — in Prison," truly inspired me to create Second Chances Farm;

Chris Redlitz and Beverly Parenti, who co-founded The Last Mile, which provides coding and technology training to the incarcerated population across the United States and originated in 2010 at San Quentin State Prison, Calif. The Last Mile serves as my benchmark to measure success for Second Chances Farm;

Saad Soliman, who returned from prison and became the first convicted felon to work for the U.S. Department of Justice and oversee re-entry at the U.S. District Court in Delaware. His TEDx talk was a true testimony to the power of second chances;

Jon Brilliant, whose eloquent TEDx talk on the, "Creation of a Social Impact Fund," served as a catalyst for me to find a for-profit solution to the non-profit problem of recidivism;

Nicole Black, who honored me by becoming one of the first investors in Second Chances Farm, LLC;

Amanda Lemon, who was serving time inside Baylor Women's Correctional Institution, where I first met her at "Breaking Bread Behind Bars," and then gave a TEDx talk on "Second Chances and Redemption" at the TEDxWilmingtonSalon inside Baylor. She has been offered a second chance at Second Chances Farm;

All 490 speakers between 2011 and 2018 who gave 469 TEDx talks at TEDxWilmington for trusting us with their ideas worth spreading and to all members of the TEDxWilmington tribe who volunteered their time and talent to create 32 amazing TEDxWilmington events that showcased all these speakers.

AN AUTHORS' NOTE REGARDING INTELLECTUAL PROPERTY

As an author myself, I respect the intellectual property rights of other authors and creative individuals and entities. The Magic of the Red Carpet makes no claims to affiliations with the third-party trademark or copyright holders described within this book, and all intellectual property is owned by the third parties I talk about and describe. As to the trademarks or copyrights discussed within this book, I have no commercial affiliations, except to the intellectual property owned by the author's recent endeavor, Second Chances Farm, LLC. a Delaware Public Benefit Limited Liability Company (https://www.second-chancesfarm.com).

I have endeavored to adhere to the "fair use" doctrine related to third-party copyright usage, and whenever possible or known, properly attribute the rights of others. I have gained the permission from the TEDxWilmington speakers listed in this book to use their materials on a limited basis, and only for the purpose of criticism and commentary. The trademarks TED® and TEDX® and TED Talks are the property of TED Conferences, LLC. I am no longer affiliated with TEDxWilmington, and any references made regarding specific TED presentations are made from the author's own observations, for teaching purposes only, and are not the views of any other person or entity. However, I earnestly hope that this book will raise the awareness of the TEDx Talks and point the way so others may avail themselves to attending either a TED or TEDx presentation, or even giving a TEDx Talk of their own.

Should any reader feel that your intellectual property has been misused or misattributed in any way, please contact me at ajitgeorge@secondchancesfarm.org, and I will take appropriate measures to either remove your material from this book or work to address your concern. My goal is only to teach and educate, and I am not personally profiting from my book as all the proceeds from the sale of this book, after covering the costs of producing and selling it, will be donated to Peace by Piece, Inc. a 501 (c) (3) organization that helps returning citizens at Second Chances Farm. My book was written only as a reflection of my passion and respect for effective communications and the public speaking that I love so much.

I wish to specifically thank my intellectual property attorney Duane Blake for his assistance in advising me regarding how to best acknowledge and attribute the intellectual property rights of other authors and speakers (www.blakeadvisors.com).

TABLE OF CONTENTS

Foreword xi

Chapter 1: What I Learned from Giving a TEDx Talk 1

Chapter 2: What Do You Do with an Idea Called TEDx? 17

Chapter 3: It is All About the Story By Geoffrey Berwind 44

Chapter 4: Lessons from 168 TEDxWilmington Speakers 49
   By Jake Voorhees

Chapter 5: A Journey Through all 32 TEDxWilmington Events 64
Curated by Elissa Ben-Eli

Chapter 6: Reflections from TEDxWilmington Speakers 235
Curated by Dana Dobson

Chapter 7: Through the TEDxWilmington Process Curated by Alessandra Nicole 288

Chapter 8: It Takes a Village to Produce a TEDxWilmington Event 387
   Curated by Dana Dobson

Chapter 9: Wisdom from Around the World Curated by Dana Dobson 399

Chapter 10: Rehearsal Dinner: Where People Bond, Connect, and 412
Relax Before the Big Day, Reception: Where Speakers Can Exhale
After Giving Their TEDx Talk, By Elissa Ben-Eli

Chapter 11: Life Lessons Learned Directing, Filming, and Live streaming TEDx events 418
   By Matt Urban

Chapter 12: My Journey with TED By Sheryl Winarick 424

Chapter 13: Speakers Resources Curated by Elissa Ben-Eli 427

Chapter 14: Legacy 457

Chapter 15: Second Chances Farm: An Idea Translated into Action 463

Chapter 16: 101 Tips Curated by Evan Bartle, Elissa Ben-Eli, and Dana Dobson 489

Acknowledgments 494

FOREWORD

I first heard about TED in the fall of 2009. I was living in London with my wife, Dr. Sarah Brown, who was assigned to the United Kingdom on a three-year work assignment as a managing director of Accenture, a global consulting company. Dr. Terry Babcock-Lumish and her husband, Brian Babcock-Lumish, had just moved to London from the United States, as Brian was doing his doctoral work at Kings College in London. Sarah and I met first met Terry and Brian at Renaissance Weekend in Hilton Head, South Carolina, several years prior to their move to London. Terry and Brian are among the most erudite and well-connected people we know.

Sarah and I were having dinner at our flat one evening in Westminster with Terry and Brian, having an intellectually stimulating discussion. As always, we were enlightened by the knowledge they shared about one subject after another, when Terry encouraged me to watch some TED talks on the subject material. She told me that most talks were 18 minutes or less, and that I might enjoy watching it.

I was curious about what TED was. I learned that TED started in 1984, five years before the birth of the World Wide Web. It began as a conference in Monterrey, California, organized by architect and iconoclast Richard Saul Wurman. TED was an acronym for **technology, entertainment and design**.

Wurman apparently wanted TED to be the "ultimate dinner party" — with himself as the host — and he chose the speakers from the best and brightest of Silicon Valley, Hollywood and academia. In the early days at TED, groups of brilliant people took the stage and talked about the things that fascinated them. Since it was meant to be the ultimate dinner party, Wurman was right on stage with them, running the show. In fact, if he felt bored, Wurman had apparently no problem sending the speaker off the stage.

The very first TED conference in 1984 featured a demonstration of the compact disc, an e-book reader and a presentation by fractal mathematician Benoit Mandlebrot. Despite the acclaimed speakers, the inaugural conference was apparently a financial flop.

Six years later in 1990, Wurman and his business partner tried again, and the TED Conference took off. TED talks eventually took on their 18-minute format, and the invitation-only event for innovators and power players quickly became one of the most sought-after intellectual tickets of the year.

After Wurman got tired of running the conference, he sold the rights to TED in 2001 to the Sapling Foundation, a nonprofit, nonpartisan foundation run by Chris Anderson. In 2006, a year after YouTube went live, TED made the decision to begin posting videos of select conference talks online. The first six TED talks were posted online on June 27, 2006. By September, these six talks had collectively reached more than one million views. TED talks proved so popular that in 2007, TED›s website was re-launched around them, giving a global audience free access to some of the world›s greatest thinkers, leaders and teachers. From this modest start on June 27, 2006 on YouTube, the number of talks posted on TED's YouTube channel grew to 3,057 TED talks and this channel had 14,016,498 subscribers, as of July 1, 2019. Ironically, the TEDx YouTube channel had more subscribers and talks than TED itself with 19,445,551 subscribers and 137,680 TEDx talks as of July 1, 2019.

On June 15, 2009, TED formally launched the TEDx program to the world. TEDx (where "x" equals an independently organized TED event), is a program to promote local events with the TED spirit. The first TEDx talk presented the biospherian Jane Poynter, who spoke at the TEDxUSC "Ideas Empowered" Conference.

The creation of TEDx in 2009 opened up the TED format to local, independently organized events. TEDx independent events are similar to TED in presentation. They can be organized by anyone who obtains a free license from TED and agrees to follow certain principles. TEDx events are required to be non-profit, but organizers may use an admission fee or commercial sponsorship to cover costs. Speakers are not paid and must also relinquish the copyrights to their materials, which TED may edit and distribute under an Attribution-Noncommercial-NoDerivatives Creative Commons license through TED.com.

TED's mission is all about "ideas worth spreading." According to TED.com:

> "TED is a non-profit devoted to spreading ideas, usually in the form of short, powerful talks (18 minutes or less). TED is a global community, welcoming people from every discipline and culture who seek a deeper understanding of the world. We believe passionately in the power of ideas to change attitudes, lives, and ultimately, the world. On TED.com, we're building a clearinghouse of free knowledge from the world's most inspired thinkers and a community of curious souls to engage with ideas and each other, both online and at TED and TEDx events around the world, all year long. In fact, everything we do — from our Conferences to our TED Talks to the projects sparked by The Audacious

Project, from the global TEDx and TED Translators communities to the TED-Ed lesson series — is driven by this goal: How can we best spread great ideas?"

TED's agenda is to make great ideas accessible and spark conversation and today covers almost all topics — from science to business to global issues — in more than 100 languages.

After I returned to Wilmington, Delaware from London in 2010 and retired as managing director of Nail Bay Resort in Virgin Gorda, British Virgin Islands, I became involved in several ventures, one of which involved Kristofer Younger. Sarah and I first met Kris after we became members of Christ Church Christiana Hundred in 2003. Kris was truly a renaissance man who, after getting a degree in computer science from Purdue University in 1984, became one of the first systems engineers at Sun Microsystem before working directly for Steve Jobs at NeXT Computer. He then went on to build Netscape Communications, one of the most important early internet companies, as vice president, systems engineering from 1994 to 2000. After Netscape was merged with AOL, Kris worked with Marc Andreessen on technology strategy as AOL's new vice president of technology. I recruited Kris in December 2010 to work for one of my clients before he joined my wife's new venture, BookOfYou.com, as its chief technology officer.

Kris was a true fan of TED and TEDx talks and watched more TEDx talks than anyone I knew. In the summer of 2011, Kris suggested I apply for a license from TED to organize TEDxWilmington as a way to showcase ideas worth spreading in our city. Given his amazing background as a thought leader and a forward thinker, I agreed to apply without giving it much serious thought.

On August 14, 2011, I got an email from Lara Stein, director of TEDx, approving my license to organize my first TEDxWilmington event. Each TEDxWilmington event required me to apply for a new license from TED. Between 2011 and 2018, I would be approved to do a total of 32 different TEDxWilmington events, all of which I will cover in some detail in Chapter Five of this book.

By way of background, Wilmington is the largest city in the State of Delaware, with a population estimated by the United State Census Bureau to be 72,846 as of 2017. The population of Delaware was estimated to 967,171 people as of July 1, 2018. Wilmington is about halfway between New York and Washington, D.C. in the middle Atlantic region. Philadelphia is only 27 miles north, while Baltimore is only 60 miles south. Our close proximity to these larger cities is one of our biggest secret advantages.

From: **Lara Stein** lara@ted.com
Subject: TEDxWilmington -- LICENSE APPROVED -- USA (100 attendees maxO
Date: August 14, 2011 at 5:38 PM
To: ajitgeorge@me.com
Cc: **Salome Heusel** salome@ted.com, **Monica Goff** monicag@ted.com, **David Troy** dave@popvox.com, **Lauren Cucinotta** lauren@ted.com, **Edward Rashba** Edward.rashba@verizon.net, **Patrick Smith** patrick@tedxpotomac.com

IMPORTANT: PLEASE READ ALL OF THE ATTACHED DOCUMENTATION. ALL DOCUMENTATION IS ALSO AVAILABLE ON THE TEDxPBWIKI.

Dear Ajit,

Congratulations! I've approved your TEDx event and granted your TEDx license -- you are officially a TEDx organizer! The TED team and I are thrilled to have you aboard the TEDx program.

This license permits you to organize one (1) TEDx event within the next 12 months. After your event, you'll have the remainder of the 12 months to apply to renew your license for the name you've selected, after which the name will be made available for use by other organizers.

Your event: TEDxWilmington

Your event date: TBD (please update your profile page with the date as soon as possible)

Your event type: Standard

Your next steps:

1. Confirm that the information on your event profile is correct. The following items should be updated immediately, and whenever they change:

 - Event date

 - Ticket price

 - Related websites/links

 - Your webcast URL (if you will provide a webcast)

Getting involved in TEDxWilmington was largely an accident of history, but it clearly changed my life in so many different ways that I can never fully fathom. I had no idea when I applied for my first license that I would end up showcasing 490 different speakers who gave a total of 469 TEDx talks at 32 TEDxWilmington events, (which I organized with the help of the TEDxWilmington tribe) that attracted 23,384,106 views worldwide on YouTube as of September 3, 2019. Not bad for a city with a population of 72,846 and a state with a population of 967,171.

When I decided to retire from doing any more TEDxWilmington events to focus on creating Second Chances Farm, I was encouraged by several members of the TEDxWilmington tribe, especially Rhianon Husmann and Alessandra Nicole, to consider writing a book of my TEDx journey. Since so many people participated in helping me creat so many magical moments, I invited some of them to share their insight by writing some of the chapters in this book including Geoffrey Berwind, Jake Voorhees, Elissa Ben-Eli, Dana Dobson, Alessandra Nicole, Matt Urban, Evan Bartle and TED Resident Sheryl Winarick. In addition one hundred and thirty four past TEDxWilmington speakers gave feedback that was incorporated in this book. I am thrilled to share pearls of wisdom from ten TEDx organizers from around the world and ten members of the TEDxWilmington tribe. This book was truly a collaborative effort.

Little did I know what it would take to write this book, but I am grateful to have the opportunity to refresh my memories by revisiting all 32 TEDxWilmington events and looking at pictures from all these events. I hope you enjoy "The Magic of the Red Carpet" by taking this tour of my TEDx journey with me.

Ajit Mathew George
Wilmington, Delaware
September 4, 2019

CHAPTER 1

What I Learned from Giving a TEDx Talk

As a TEDx organizer, you are prohibited from giving a TEDx talk at your own event. It is a very smart rule for many obvious reasons.

Having organized 32 different TEDxWilmington events, and after working with 490 speakers who gave 468 TEDx talks between 2011 and 2018, I had frankly no desire to give a TEDx talk myself. I knew how much work it would be, or at least I thought I knew how much work it would be. For this reason, I never applied, let alone showed any interest, in giving a TEDx talk anywhere, even though I am friends with over 250 TEDx organizers around the world.

I got to know Abigail O'Neal, who everyone calls Abby, when I was managing director of Nail Bay Resort in Virgin Gorda, British Virgin Islands. She not only was the youngest daughter of the Hon. Ralph T. O'Neal, the long time Chief Minister and then Premier of the British Virgin Islands, but she also worked for the BVI Tourist Board. I got to know her well while I was living in London from 2007 to 2010, during which time she was assigned to the London office.

I founded the Virgin Islands Winemakers Dinners in 2008, and soon thereafter I was appointed by the Hon. Premier to the Board of Directors of the BVI Tourist Board. Abby was instrumental in helping me persuade Sir Richard Branson to co-host with me a memorable Winemakers Dinner in July 2009 at Necker Island in the British Virgin Islands, which currently rents for $77,500 a night!

A few years ago, Abby applied and became the organizer of TEDxRoadTown. Road Town is the capital of the British Virgin Islands, a series of small islands in the Atlantic Ocean about 96 miles east of Puerto Rico, 1,200 miles from Miami and adjacent to St. Thomas and St. John, both of which are in the U.S. Virgin Islands. My wife, Sarah Brown and I maintain a small beachfront residence called Sunset Watch in Virgin Gorda, BVI

that got heavily damaged by Hurricane Irma in September 2017. This necessitated my travelling to the BVI even more than normal to oversee its construction.

I was in the BVI on one of these construction trips on November 8th, 2018 when I got a Facebook message from Abby asking if I was available to meet her on this trip. We set up a luncheon meeting on November 12th at Lady Sarah's, a lovely restaurant in Road Town. Abby asked me if I was interested in giving a TEDx talk at the next TEDxRoadtown in late March of 2019.

I knew that my last TEDxWilmington event before I retired was going to be the 3rd Annual TEDxWimingtonWomen Conference on November 30, 2018, and Abby's invitation to give a TEDx talk in March 2019 suddenly seemed very appealing. I asked her if I could give a TEDx talk on giving second chances to men and women returning from prison through the creation of indoor, vertical farms, or "plant factories." Abby thought this would make a great TEDx talk and I told her that I would seriously consider this offer.

On December 2nd, I got a Facebook message from Abby confirming March 23, 2019 as the date for TEDxRoadTown. On January 2nd, I got a formal invitation to give a TEDx talk at the 2019 TEDxRoadtown with the theme, "The Time Is Now." I now had a choice to either accept the invitation or decline it. I made the fateful decision to accept this invitation from Abby, and my journey to be on the red carpet as a speaker began. Little did I know how hard this journey would be.

I was blessed to have several people offer to help me, without whom I could not have delivered this TEDx talk. I quickly learned first-hand the value of having a speaker's coach. Geoffrey Berwind is one of the foremost experts in the world on how to use the power of story to connect, relate, have greater influence, and inspire others. I got to know Geoffrey well when he was coaching some of the past speakers at TEDxWilmington. If you are thinking of giving a TEDx talk or an important presentation, your first step should be hiring an expert storyteller and a speaker's coach like Geoffrey Berwind. I can now see why, as a general rule, speakers who had a speaker's coach did a much better job of getting clear about their idea worth spreading.

While Geoffrey worked very closely with me to develop my idea worth spreading, creating an outline and developing a detailed script, Evan Bartle worked hard to create slides for my PowerPoint presentation. As organizer of TEDxWilmington, I tried hard to discourage speakers from using any audiovisual presentations, but ironically in my case, I found it hard to imagine giving this TEDx talk without any slides. Evan, who was the assistant producer of 11 different TEDxWilmington events, starting from September 19, 2017, had a great sense on presentation design. If you choose to have slides, I strongly encourage you to work with a designer who has prior expertise in producing slides for speakers. Try to make only one point per slide, with as little text as possible.

What makes a good idea for a talk? It is important to challenge a belief, or share something new and surprising. The audience is counting on you to check your facts and use reliable sources. I forced myself to double check all the facts I was reciting. If I could not verify a fact, I discarded it. It is very important as a speaker to continuously ask yourself these three questions:

1. Is my idea new?
2. Is it interesting to my audience?
3. Is it factual and realistic?

Geoffrey was very helpful in developing the structure for my TEDx talk. Here are five useful steps that you might want to use as you work on your own talk:

1. Make your audience care using a compelling story, relatable example or intriguing idea
2. Explain your idea clearly and with conviction
3. Describe your evidence
4. Use a call to action (the how and why of implementing your idea)

5. Reveal the new reality (how the lives of audience members will be affected if they act on your idea)

To help me rehearse, I came up with the idea of embedding the PowerPoint images into my script. I have added at the end of this chapter my final script with the slides for my TEDx talk so you can see what I used and how it was laid out. I wished I had thought of this while I was still organizing TEDxWilmington events, as it would have surely helped many speakers like myself who had trouble memorizing their script. The images embedded in the script helped me remember what the salient point was after that image appeared on the screen.

While I was an excellent student in school, I was never very good at memorizing. My father could recite entire sections of the Greek classics or long verses of Shakespeare. I was not blessed with this gift, and I struggled with memorizing portions of my script. I began to have a greater appreciation for all the speakers who got up on the red carpet and eloquently gave their TEDx talks with grace and no hesitation. I was terrified of becoming one of the speakers who would blank out during their TEDx talk leaving the room sitting in silence. I was mortified by this prospect, but the truth is that this fear did not help me memorize any better.

I advised all the speakers at TEDxWilmington to rehearse over and over again. I advised them to rehearse with people they loved, rehearse with people they feared, rehearse in front of small groups, rehearse in front of large groups, rehearse with peers and rehearse with people who aren't experts in your field. I suggested to my speakers that they accept criticism, learn from it and keep rehearsing. I regret to admit that I failed to follow even my own advice. As I got closer to March 23rd I wanted to ask for a rain check and delay my talk to a future date but I didn't want to let Abby or myself down. I now understood the panic many speakers felt as they got within a week or two of their TEDx talk.

During the period I was a TEDx organizer, I was a stickler for timing and strongly encouraged speakers not to run over their allocated time. Abby was kind enough to give me 18 minutes, which is the maximum time for a TEDx talk. I had trouble getting it under 18 minutes and continued editing the script until the day before to get it to less than 18 minutes during rehearsals. I struggled with getting the timing right every time.

Road Town, Tortola is over 1,600 miles from Wilmington, Del., but I was truly honored to have my wife, Sarah Brown, my colleague, Evan Bartle, and my TEDxWilmington associate producer, Rhianon Husmann, fly down and join me in this journey to the red carpet at TEDxRoadTown.

On Saturday, March 23rd, I woke up and rehearsed my talk several times, but it was clear that I had not rehearsed enough, even though I was very familiar with every word in my script. My inability to memorize 100 percent of my talk was bothering me. I wondered why I accepted Abby's invitation to give this TEDx talk. I wanted to get an extension. I needed more time, but the truth is that I was scheduled to give this talk in a few short hours in front of a community that has been my home away from home since 1982. It was time for me to give my talk, and inhale, and exhale.

I was very fortunate not to have to use a clicker, as Evan advanced the PowerPoint slides as I gave my TEDx talk. I asked Abby if I could Facebook Live my TEDx talk and when she gave me permission, Rhianon was kind enough to Facebook Live my talk that attracted 715 views from around the world with 17 shares and 70 comments in less than 24 hours.

The good news is that I didn't get a mental block, at least not one that was visible to the audience while I was on the red carpet! I finished my talk and got a nice round of applause. I was disappointed that my talk did not come in under 18 minutes, but I gave it my best.

If I were to honestly rate my talk on a scale from 1 to 10, with 10 being perfect, I would rate it between 7.75 and 8. It was good, but could have been much better. I learned that giving a TEDx talk is much harder than I ever imagined, and my appreciation of everyone who has ever given a TEDx talk increased astronomically. My respect for great TEDx speakers grew immensely.

I hope my honesty will not stop you from giving a TEDx talk or a TEDx worthy talk at work, church, or in front of any organization. Just remember to rehearse, rehearse and rehearse more.

Watch my TEDx talk, 'Reducing Recidivism through Second Chances with Vertical Farms,' at https://bit.ly/2ZAWsru.

TEDx speakers at TEDx Roadtown

Second Chances + Vertical Farms = Green Collar Jobs & Compassionate Capitalism

Ajit's TEDx script with PowerPoint Slides

Imagine you have been invited to attend a five-course gourmet farm-to-table dinner prepared by a group of exceptionally talented chefs served outside on a long table on a beautiful evening. Sounds amazing doesn't it.

Just look at these mouth-watering dishes and I am sure you wished you could have joined me on May 14, 2015.

I will give you a couple of hints on the location of this dinner. It was not on a farm. It was not in a fancy restaurant. It was not in a private estate.

As I sat at the table and looked up, I saw the moon rising as the sun was going down. I also saw barbed wires surround the area where this dinner was being held.

These pictures are from a once-in-a-lifetime dinner that I organized called "Breaking Bread Behind Bars," inside Baylor Women's Correctional Institution, the statewide women's prison in Delaware, a small state in the United States, located in the Mid-Atlantic region halfway between New York and Washington D.C.

The 40-plus guests, who paid good money for this experience, sat with the inmates in the prison who helped prepare this meal. This dinner was the brainchild of the late Chef Matt Haley, winner of the 2014 James Beard National Humanitarian of the Year award in 2014. Unfortunately, Matt, who had served time in a prison himself, died in a tragic motorcycle accident in August of 2014, just after proposing the idea of this dinner to me. We decided to host this dinner in Matt's honor.

At the end of this gourmet meal, Prison Warden Wendi Caple got up to thank everyone for attending and mentioned that she would like to see a greenhouse constructed at the prison so that the inmates could grow fresh produce year-round for the prison's culinary program.

I was standing behind the podium with United States Senator, Chris Coons, and Commissioner of Delaware's Department of Corrections, Rob Coupe, and we decided to raise money then and there from the guests in attendance. Since we had a captive audience, we raised all the money we needed to build this prison greenhouse in just two minutes.

My accidental journey to create Second Chances Farm started with this unusual dinner. I began to wonder why, as a society, we are growing prisoners instead of plants.

The Prison Policy Initiative reports there are about 2.3 million people held in prison in the United States.

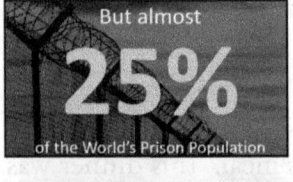

While the United States holds less than 5 percent of the world's population, it has almost 25 percent of the entire world's prison population according to The World Prison Brief. I will not even try to attempt to address in this talk the reasons behind these astonishing statistics. I want to focus on a solution, not the problem.

First, I want you to understand what happens to people after they serve their time in prison and repay their debt to society.

Perhaps I can use an analogy to make this point clear: When you buy a house, you might get a mortgage from a bank securing the property against the default, which is a lien against the property.

It is not unusual in the United States to get a mortgage for 30 years. Assuming you pay the debt on time and in full, at the time the debt is paid off, the bank is obligated to remove the mortgage that secured your house. The deed to your house is then free and clear of any obligation to the bank.

So…wouldn't you be shocked if, after you repaid your debt in full, you got a note from the bank saying that the lien against your house is still there and you are not free of the debt after all?

This is exactly what most people returning from prison experience after they complete their sentence and get released from prison.

In my opinion, when someone is convicted of a crime, served their time in prison, and is released, they have in fact repaid their debt to society — they should get the deed to their life back. This is why I am devoting the next 10 years of my life to giving Second Chances to human beings returning home from prison.

To help make this point, I even organized a TEDx event inside Baylor Women's Correctional Institution in July 2015, with the theme of "Second Chances and Redemption."

Photography by Mobius New Media & Joel Plotkin

What I Learned From Giving a TEDx Talk

Let us look at what happens in the United States to men and women upon release from prison. They are given somewhere between $0 and $200 cash, depending on the prison. Most have no housing to speak of, and many have no real family, or no real friends to help them when they arrive "home," wherever that might be.

Many of the returning citizens have no form of legal identification, like a driver's license or a social security card. Many have large unpaid fees and fines arising from their conviction, which in some states prohibits them from even applying for a driver's license! Most have bad credit or *no credit at all!*

In addition, anyone who has been convicted of a misdemeanor or felony will often find himself or herself automatically excluded from even being considered for many jobs, by virtue of their criminal record, even though they have repaid their debt to society with years of their lives. The deed for a second chance is still burdened by the lien of their time in prison.

It is not surprising to see why so many who are released from prison decide that returning to a life of crime is much easier than getting a legal job. After all, a life of crime requires no legitimate identification and no questions are asked about your background.

It is no wonder why the recidivism rate is so high in The United States. Recidivism is defined as the tendency of a convicted criminal to reoffend.

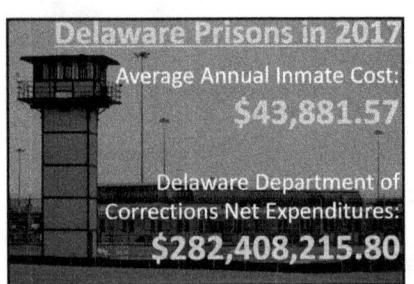

Because I live in Delaware, I will use Delaware to make a point.

According to the 2017 Annual Report published by the Delaware Department of Corrections, it cost more than $43,000 per year to house a prisoner in Delaware. This translated to over 282 million dollars in 2017 that tax-payers paid to keep prisoners incarcerated in Delaware.

If this isn't bad enough, Delaware Criminal Justice Council reports over 70 percent of the inmates released from prison in Delaware will be re-arrested and over 60 percent will be returned to a prison facility within three years. It is a revolving door.

I was invited to go to the infamous San Quentin State Prison in California in January 2016 to join a small group of TEDx organizers from the United States who had organized TEDx events inside a prison to help kickoff TEDxSanQuentin. We were joined by an illustrious group including Robert Rubin, former U.S. Treasury Secretary and Gavin Newsom, who is currently the Governor of California.

I was deeply influenced by a TEDx talk given by Curtis "Wall Street" Carroll who is serving a life sentence in San Quentin.

In his talk, he said: "A financially sound incarcerated person can become a taxpaying citizen, and a financially sound taxpaying citizen can remain one."

This talk made me think what I could do about second chances and redemption. Later that year, I invited two people to give TEDx talks at the 2016 TEDxWilmington Annual Conference, for which I was the organizer. Both of them had served time in prison. One spoke about how vertical farms in urban areas were transforming the organic food industry, while the other one spoke about his journey from prison to being successfully rehabilitated into society.

It was all these TEDx talks that gave *me* the idea and inspired me to create Second Chances Farm. As a former TEDx Organizer from 2011 to 2018 who organized 32 TEDx events and showcased over 480 speakers, I am thrilled to take these ideas worth spreading and turn them into reality. We hope to create a new crop of "Compassionate Capitalists" from these newly free citizens.

Compassionate Capitalism

I've adopted the term "compassionate capitalism" to describe one of the goals of our new venture. This is the idea that a person, even one who has spent years in prison, can begin to make money, pay taxes, and still do social good to make a difference. Wouldn't it be an amazing world if everyone could make money and have a positive social impact too?

Vertical Farming is one industry that has continued to grow in the last 5-10 years, but has not yet fully sprouted. It has recently attracted over $500 Million in venture capital investment.

This quickly evolving market is a source of a new crop of "green collar jobs." "Green collar workers" can become compassionate capitalists one green thumb at a time.

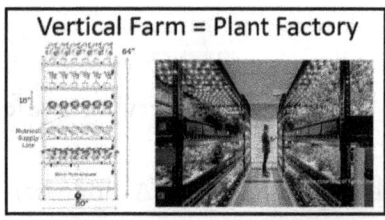

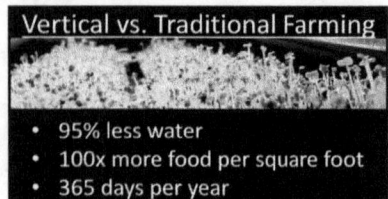

What is a vertical farm? To put it simply, a vertical farm is basically a "plant factory." Seeds are planted indoors, in a facility ranging from a personal basement to a 100,000 square-foot warehouse or more.

These plants spend their *entire life* in a controlled environment, indoors, with every aspect of their growth carefully managed by the farmers. Plants need only light, water, carbon dioxide, and nutrients for photosynthesis, which is the process by which they grow.

In a vertical farm or plant factory all of these elements are artificially constructed and controlled by a group of farmers. And the beauty is, no dirt is needed. The plants are "soilless."

When we install vertical farms in older warehouses or unused office buildings, we are repurposing them and breathing a new life into these old structures. Typically, these buildings are located in communities that are economically depressed.

Humans have been growing plants in water almost as long as they have been growing them in dirt. This is called hydroponics and requires only water, infused with the proper nutrients that may naturally appear in dirt.

This technology was able to grow dramatically in large part due to farmers growing cannabis in Canada, Colorado and California who wanted a more energy efficient system for growing their plants, and worked to design new innovations especially in the field of LED lights

Being indoors, without the use of soil, comes with a slew of incredible benefits like saving more water and producing more food. Hydroponic growers like ZipGrow in Canada claim to use 95 percent less water

than traditional, farming while Bowery Farming in New York has stated they produce 100 times more crops per square foot.

Not only that, but this method of controlled environment agriculture eliminates the need for any pesticides and herbicides. It can be grown 365 days per year, and can be grown locally in your own neighborhood!

Organic produce is a 16.5 billion dollar industry in the United States as reported by the Organic Trade Association. Most of the indoor farming industry grows organic produce without any pesticides or herbicides. This is very beneficial for people like cancer patients who are advised by oncologists to not consume any produce treated with chemicals.

In addition, growing vertically indoors means unaffected by the weather, climate, and natural disasters like hurricanes and droughts.

As long as your farm is in a structurally strong building — or even a shipping container, as I've seen — you can grow the tastiest, freshest, and fastest produce in any location you like, including islands like these British Virgin Islands where most of the produce is shipped in refrigerated shipping containers from Florida which is 1,200 miles away.

Vertical farms allow you to harvest quickly and have that salad or those strawberries on your grocery shelves, in your refrigerator, or on your plate in as little as 24 hours! Not only does this reduce carbon footprints around the world, but also it gives your fresh food a longer shelf-life and a more nutrient-rich product.

One of the ideas I have spoken today about is compassionate capitalism.

Why is this important to me?

I believe capitalism with all its faults is still the best system. As an immigrant to the United States, I have benefitted from it.

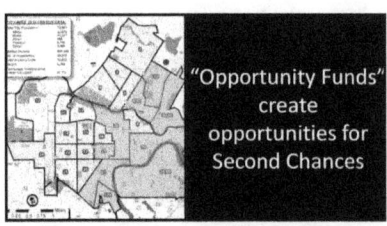

"Opportunity Funds" create opportunities for Second Chances

I want to create a new crop of capitalists in the United States by taking advantage of Opportunity Zones. The **Opportunity Zone** Program is a new community and economic development tool that aims to drive long-term private investment into low-income communities throughout the United States.

How do we plan to do this? If you are in the United States, you can join me by following these seven steps and create your own version of Second Chances Farm. If you live outside the United States you can skip step one.

How Do We Plan to Do This?

Step #1
Raise seed money from Opportunity Zone investors by creating an Opportunity Fund

STEP ONE: Raise seed money from Opportunity Zone Investors by creating an Opportunity Fund.

Step #2
Find an *ugly, unloved* warehouse or office building

STEP TWO: Find an ugly, unloved warehouse or office building

Step #3
Repurpose building to be ready for hydroponic, vertical farming

STEP THREE: Repurpose the building to be ready for a hydroponic vertical farm.

Step #4
Cultivate returning citizens as "Entrepreneurs in Residence"

STEP FOUR: Cultivate returning citizens as "entrepreneurs-in-residence."

Step #5
Grow organic & heirloom crops from seed

STEP FIVE: Grow organic and heirloom plants from seed.

14   The Magic of the Red Carpet

> **Step #6**
> Harvest and Sell Produce

STEP SIX: Harvest and sell produce.

> **Step #7**
> **Turn over** farms to returning citizens, now that they're "Compassionate Capitalists" and "Agri-preneurs"

STEP SEVEN: Turn over farms to returning citizens so that they can become compassionate capitalists and agri-preneurs.

I regard myself as a compassionate capitalist and here is why.

I was born in Kuwait where, at the age of four, I started to work with my mother and father growing a large variety of plants in an arid desert, which was thought to be impossible. My mother was determined to prove that she could grow virtually any flower or vegetable in this barren desert if you nurtured it with love and plenty of brackish water. She even grew an orange tree, and one of my earliest memories was holding the first orange grown in Kuwait on this tree.

Having won three years in a row as the best garden in Kuwait, Sheik Jabber of Kuwait awarded my parents this gold trophy to keep as a memento.

My mother's ability to do something that most people thought impossible is one of the traits of a successful capitalist. She used brackish water in a desert to irrigate her plants. She made beautiful plants grow in a hostile environment and my dream with Second Chances Farm is to allow returning citizens to bloom in a hostile environment.

The legacy I inherited from my mother has inspired me to do the right thing by giving second chances to returning citizens who repaid their debt to have a chance to strike their own green gold by providing turn key opportunities to become compassionate capitalists in the field of vertical farming.

I first met Amanda Lemon, who is pictured here, during the Breaking Bread Behind Bars dinner when she was an inmate at Baylor Women's Correctional Institution. I then invited her to give a TEDx talk in July 2015 on Second Chances and Redemption.

Now that Amanda has repaid her debt to society and has been released from prison, I have invited her to get a Green Collar job, become a vertical farmer and grow into a compassionate capitalist without having any access to capital or credit. This is a good example of why I created Second Chances Farm.

I have grown up with gardens all my life from Kuwait to India, from the United States to my current garden in Virgin Gorda, British Virgin Islands. Won't you join me in growing plants and people, rather than prisoners?

CHAPTER 2

What Do You Do with an Idea Called TEDx?

Before I answer the question, "What do you do with an idea called TEDx?" I wanted to answer some frequently asked questions that I have encountered since I first was granted my license from TED. They are in no particular order:

1. You have to submit an application to TED to get a license to organize a TEDx event in your own community. If TED decides to grant you a license, it is valid for one specific event and the license expires in one year.
2. You have one year from the date you hold your event to renew your license.
3. The license from TED is granted without any charge or fee whatsoever in consideration for, among other things, the organizer agreeing to make no money from organizing your event. I am guessing that there are at any given time over 1,500 TEDx organizers all around the world, all of whom volunteer their time and talent without any financial compensation.
4. The TEDx license is non-transferable to anyone else.
5. Each new event requires an additional license.
6. Speakers are not allowed to pay a fee of any kind to get a speaking slot.
7. No speaker can get any financial compensation for giving a TEDx talk. At TEDxWilmington, we asked our speakers to pay for their travel and accomodations as well.
8. TED has capped the individual ticket price for almost all TEDx events to $100 per person, including any ticketing charges.
9. TED allows an organizer to recruit sponsors to underwrite some or all costs associated under a detailed set of rules.
10. Unless and until you have attended a TED event, which are all by invitation only, you cannot have more than 100 people attend your TEDx event.

11. TED requires each organizer to arrange, at the organizer's expense, to professionally videotape each TEDx talk with no less than three cameras, edit it, and upload it to TED within 30 days of the event.
12. Both the raw footage and the edited videotape are the sole property of TED and cannot be shared with the speaker or anyone else without the prior written approval of TED.

I knew that in order to grow TEDxWilmington, I needed to attend a TED event. The annual TED Conference in Vancouver now costs a minimum of $10,000 per person to attend, excluding travel and accommodations. Even if you are interested, one needs to apply and wait to get an invitation from TED. I was invited by TED to attend the TEDGlobal event in Geneva, Switzerland in December 2015 and the TEDSummit in Banff, Canada in June 2016. I am grateful to TED for offering a partial scholarship to enable me to attend these memorable events. As a result, all TEDxWilmington events starting in 2016 were eligible to have more than 100 attendees. This was a watershed moment for us.

When I attended these TED events, I quickly realized that most TEDx organizers were young idealists who are passionate about ideas worth spreading. I was 61 when I attended the first TED event in Geneva and felt like a fish out of water. Over time, I met a group of more senior TEDx organizers who were veteran TEDx organizers like Randy Bretz from TEDxLincoln, Douglas Coleman from TEDxJacksonville, Gordon Garb from TEDxSunnyvale, Kat Haber from TEDxVail, Edith Howle from TEDxCharleston, Claire Kennedy from TEDxExeter, Mark Lovett from TEDxSanDiego, Mary Reed from TEDxTucson and Mark Sylvester from TEDxSantaBarbara, whose work was a major source of inspiration.

Mark Sylvester is the executive producer of TEDxSantaBarbara. He has been attending TED for over 20 years and started producing his own TEDx in 2010, originally called TEDxAmericanRiviera. He's worked with many organizers, helping them navigate through the hundreds of decisions necessary to create a world-class event.

According to Mark, "'Hacking the Red Circle' is a podcast created for and about TEDx organizers and the TEDx universe. It showcases the many talents required to produce a world-class event worthy of the TEDx brand. If you're thinking of producing a TEDx or have been involved with one and want to learn more, this is the show for you. If you've been involved with a TEDx event and are now stepping into a leadership role, you'll enjoy our guest's unique perspective of what it takes to be successful. We interview organizers before and after their events, talk to them about what makes the event specific to their locale as well as what particular talents they bring to the organization. Some are great at managing, curating, building partnerships, rallying the volunteers and creating compelling user experiences. We bring it all to you, in their voice. We interview TEDx speakers and those who provide services to the TEDx ecosystem, to talk about their experience with TEDx. Seeing the event from their point of view is often illuminating. Seeing TEDx from the outside in provides a unique perspective not usually heard."

If you were ever curious about organizing your own TEDx event, I encourage you to sign up and listen to a series of podcasts at "Hacking The Red Circle," hosted by Mark Sylvester from TEDxSantaBarbara. Here is the podcast interview with me: https://hackingtheredcircle.com/tedxwilmington-ajit-mathew-george-organizer/

I am often asked why I organized 32 TEDxWilmington events between 2011 and 2018 when I could not financially benefit from this endeavor. I am not sure I can explain well why I spent so much time helping 490 speakers share their ideas with the help of 70 plus TEDx tribe members. All I can say is it was an emotionally satisfying experience that enriched me in so many ways other than monetarily that I could not imagine *not* having done it.

Perhaps the most satisfying reward that cannot be measured in dollars and cents is the feedback I received from the speakers, our audience and members of the TEDx tribe. Here is one thank you note from Cyrus Rosen, who at the age of 15 gave a powerful TEDx talk at the 32nd and final TEDxWilmington event that I organized on November 30, 2018. The value of this note to me is priceless:

Dear Ajit,   December 3, 2018

I want to thank you for welcoming me to the TEDx Tribe and having confidence in me even though I'm a 15-year-old kid. Thank you for taking me under your wing and inviting me into your home and taking the extra time to give me feedback directly, instead of over email. That extra step allowed me to apply the variation to my tonality and gave me confidence in my material. I had a lot of help from Geoffrey and the TEDx Tribe, who collaborated with me to bring my idea to its fullest potential. I want to thank you for connecting me and being appart of that support network.

I'm afraid I neglected to say goodbye to you after the TEDx event. My friend whisked me away to a celebration party. I am sorry I didn't thank you in person.

Just before taking the stage, my anxiety was building to a fever pitch. Even though I'd practiced my talk many times, I almost passed out backstage. When you introduced me, I heard how much you believe in me. You saying I was your favorite speaker caused my anxiety to dissipate, and gave me the confidence to walk on stage with a smile and a wave.

I also want to thank you for acknowledging my late grandparents. Hearing the dedication also calmed me down. My late grandparents were an inspiration to my entire family. My grandfather inspired my Dad to give his first TEDx talk, and inspired me to give mine. When my mom arrived at the TEDx event, she gave me an engraved silver card holder of my grandfather's and my grandmother's golden locket for good luck. My grandparents were on stage with me. Your kind words meant a lot to both myself and my family.

I can't thank you enough for your guidance and support throughout this entire process. I will take the lessons I've learned with me for the rest of my life. Not every 15-year-old gets such a valuable experience. The TEDx talk has prepared me for my future and given me the tools, confidence, and ability to speak in front of people and share my ideas in a meaningful, passionate way.

I'm looking forward to our next dinner and pool party with you, Sarah, and HRH Maharani. Thank you for everything.

Sincerely,
Cyrus

I will share below an email I received on September 22, 2017 from Janine Driver, an executive consultant, *New York Times* Best Selling Author and award-winning keynote speaker. Her words were worth the price of gold:

> "Yesterday, I was on NBC's TODAY show for the last time in the 9:00 a.m. hour. I've been going on that 9:00 to 10:00 a.m. segment six times a year for the past 14 years. Al Roker will no longer host the 9:00 a.m. hour, as Megan Kelly is taking over the slot with a talk show starting Monday. I am sad because I love Al and think he is one of the funniest hosts I've ever met.
>
> "So, why do I start my blog about TEDxWilmington with a TODAY Show update? Because anytime I'm lucky enough to get a slot on live national TV, I very rarely plug something else happening in my life. As you might imagine, if I did that all the time, I would never be invited back. However, yesterday, I felt like I had nothing to lose (and everything for the public to gain) since the 9:00 a.m.

Al Roker hour, is devastatingly over, so I not only shared a tip from my recent TEDxtalk, "The Cooperation Paradigm," I also mentioned TEDxWilmington.

https://www.today.com/video/body-language-tricks-grab-your-chin-to-win-and-more-1050744899953

"Why take the risk and plug TEDxWilmington? Because there's something magical that happens on Wilmington's TEDx stage! I've been to other TEDx talks and they slightly lack the magic Wilmington brings to life. Ajit, the TEDx organizer, and his rock star team of volunteers, somehow attract remarkable people from around the world to share their ideas. And I want the world to watch *all* their talks, which were given in August in Wilmington, because I believe, in my heart, they *will* change lives, and in some cases, save lives.

"I can testify firsthand that I'm a completely different person because of the other speakers. One person, Dr. Melissa Root, shared a technique, video self-monitoring, which is now helping my 12-year old son, who has dyslexia, read more easily. Another presenter, Clint Rogers, inspired me to push a spot on my right pointy finger, six-times, to rebalance myself (among other health tips), and man, does it work. A husband and wife shared firsthand stories about refugees, and my heart sank. Imagine being held by gunpoint and being given the choice to, 'be raped or killed.' Terrifying. I learned about proper meal etiquette, and discovered that outside the boardroom most decisions are made over a meal by Michele Pollard Patrick. I witnessed a young boy share his story about labeling children, two other young teens playing their hearts out on banjos (my right foot was tapping away), and I learned about the importance of the 'Contribution Code,' by Valerie Biden Owens, the former Vice President Joe Biden's sister, best friend, and campaign manager. I could go on and on, however, wouldn't you rather just connect with TEDxWilmington so you can see the talks for yourself?

"As I wrap up this post, I'd like to share with you that this was my second time getting to play with the TEDxWilmington team and something magical happened for me thanks to the coaching of Ajit George. Because he prepared me through meeting deadlines for blogs and practice videos, and chatted with me on the phone when I had questions, on the big day, I was able to focus less on me and more on the others presenters, the TEDxWilmington A-team, and the audience!

"When the day came to a close, I left the gorgeous theater in Wilmington, DE, touched, moved, and inspired.

"I'll be back to cheer on the women at the upcoming TEDxWomen Conference on November 2nd. Anyone want to join me at my table? Get this — while at a dinner the night before our TEDx event in August, I met a couple of the future female speakers, including a Hollywood producer, a life coach, and the modest woman who created the AMBER Alert. Yes, *the* AMBER Alert! She literally said, 'I may have created it, but you all make it work.'

"Thank you, TEDxWilmington, for all that I know you did for the other speakers and me, and thank you for all you did for us that we will never know you did! You rock! See you all on November 2nd. I'll be the one cheering louder then anyone else!

On March 3, 2019, I got this email from Nicole Black, a motivational speaker, corporate trainer, author, and entrepreneur who had given a TEDx talk at the 3rd Annual TEDxWilmingtonWomen Conference in November 2018. Nicole had seen a Facebook posting I had made in February 2019 about an article in *Delaware Business Times* about Second Chances Farm and had on her own volition contacted Jon Brilliant, who is my fellow managing member and CFO of Second Chances Farm, expressing her interest in being part of Second Chances Farm. I will treasure this kind note from Nicole, which references three TEDx talks that you might want to watch also:

1) "Taste of the World — Adventurous Business" | Matt Haley: https://youtu.be/i_WsTFtXmoA
2) "How I Learned to Read — and Trade Stocks — in Prison" | Curtis "Wall Street" Carroll: https://www.youtube.com/watch?v=F89eycANUrQ
3) "Redemption Song" | John Legend & James Cavitt: https://www.youtube.com/watch?v=Znc6TJAAXFU

Dear Ajit,

Thank you for sharing your journey and vision with me! You are one of the best storytellers I have ever met.

I watched Matt's talk and was so blown away by so many things he said, the world truly lost a bright light when he passed away. I see so much of my own philosophy in him and his work. To quote him: nothing happens to me, everything happens for me.

Curtis's talk was incredibly inspiring. That man has a wonderful stage presence and he's funny! Here is where you are (2:43; 3:17; 6:06 and 10:58) it was pretty neat to see you there in the audience. John Legends talk / singing blew me away and I also really enjoyed Jon Brilliant's talk. I agree with him, having a social mission is critical; having the dots make the word nurture was brilliant. The two of you together are a force to be reckoned with; in short I am willing to bet it's going to be even bigger than you can imagine.

Overall, I know this is a million-dollar opportunity and I would be honored to be a part of Second Chances as well as be on your advisory committee.

Looking forward to talking to you soon,

Nicole

Little did I did know when I applied in 2011 to get my first of 32 TEDxWilmington licenses what a profound impact TEDxWilmington would have on me. To say it has been a life-changing journey for me is an understatement. I never anticipated TEDxWilmington would become part of my identity. I am often introduced as the person who brought TEDx to Wilmington. It was like I had done nothing before TEDxWilmington. Even though this was an unpaid venture, my TEDx journey would define me in ways I could never have imagined. On my 65th birthday in 2019, I formally announced my retirement as the organizer of TEDxWilmington so that I could invest all my time and talent in developing Second Chances Farm, which would never have happened without my involvement in TEDxWilmington.

All TEDx talks are about one idea worth spreading. A good TEDx organizer is eager to consider ideas that:

- Are radically new
- Showcase fresh approaches to enduring problems
- Challenge our conceptions about what's possible
- Expose us to cutting-edge research, technology or design
- Energetically redefine the human experience

In my mind, the greatest challenge that a potential TEDx speaker faces is focusing their TEDx talk on one idea. There is a great tendency on the part of potential speakers to try to incorporate multiple ideas into one TEDx talk that, as a general rule, cannot exceed 18 minutes. Very few TEDx speakers are successful in keeping the attention span of their audience when they cram multiple ideas into one TEDx talk.

A good TEDx speaker features a TEDx talk with a single core idea. The speaker then takes a deep dive into the single idea by using stories, examples, research, and/or studies that all reinforce the main idea. At TEDxWilmington, we called this concept the throughline, which is described in more detail in Chapter 4 of "TED Talks: The Official TED Guide to Public Speaking" by Chris Anderson.

Tamsen Webster, a professional "idea whisperer" who created The Red Thread®, the former executive producer of TEDxCambridge, and a TEDxWilmington speaker, makes the following point better than I could:

> To get a TEDx, you have to be able to state that big idea clearly, cleanly and quickly. That's why the next question is, "Does it fit in 140?" where 140 is the number of characters. This is a very good pressure test of your idea into a space that small requires you understand your idea well enough to make it that small. Also, some version of this question is on just about every TEDx application I've seen. The trick is that you have to create that sentence using words people understand. This is not your title or tagline, so you can't use any proprietary terms or words that need more explanation. If you can't say "yes" to both questions, you need to keep working until you do. Test it with people who don't know you or your idea already.

Do you have an idea worth spreading? It might be useful to answer a few of these questions. Why you? Why now? Is it a really big idea? Why would viewers of your TEDx talk care? Are you prepared to invest 90 hours to prepare and rehearse before you give your TEDx talk? Do you have credible proof to support your idea? If you answered yes, then please browse to see what other TEDx talks exist at https://www.ted.com/watch/tedx-talks on your idea and how you can add something new or in an unexpected way.

As part of its video review and approval process, TED is now requiring organizers in certain instances to share the speaker's credentials including degrees, certifications, affiliated institutions, and/or organizations. In addition, TED is requesting organizers provide a full reference list for certain speaker's talk, including peer-reviewed journal articles and publications, books, and links to accredited scientific organizations. Please be prepared to share this information upon request.

While a TEDx talk should not exceed 18 minutes, my recommendation after working with 490 speakers is to aim for 10 minutes in length. According to various neuroscience studies, humans have an attention stopwatch that ends around the 10-minute mark. I found it interesting that Apple announced in 2018 that their product launch presentations would no longer exceed 10 minutes.

Here is the best advice I found on using slides in your presentation. Carmine Gallo in an article in *Inc.* entitled, "Guy Kawasaki Explains Why Steve Jobs Used 190-Point Text on Presentation Slides," makes the point about making the type size on your slides bigger. Carmine wrote:

> Former Apple Macintosh evangelist and author Guy Kawasaki has given at least 2,000 speeches since 1987. Many of the presentation techniques he uses to captivate an audience he learned from the most influential boss he's ever had — Steve Jobs.
>
> I recently had an opportunity to sit down with Kawasaki at his Silicon Valley house to talk about his new book, 'Wise Guy.' Specifically, we talked about public speaking strategies that all entrepreneurs and leaders should follow if they want to give presentations that stand out.
>
> One strategy in particular sounds simple — and it is — but the reason behind using it is profound.
>
> "Make the type size on your slides bigger," says Kawasaki. While Kawasaki suggests using 30-point text at a minimum, he reveals that Jobs used 190-point text. Why? The simple answer, according to Kawasaki: "Bigger text is easier to read." Duh!
>
> "The strategic reason is that larger text forces you to use fewer words on a slide. Creatively, it's a good exercise, because it requires the speaker to be more thoughtful with the words they use. Also, fewer words means the audience's attention is on the speaker, not on the words on the slides.
>
> When I was writing, "The Presentation Secrets of Steve Jobs," I spoke to Apple designers who created Jobs's slides. They told me that while most presenters try to put as many words as possible on a slide — Jobs did the opposite. He removed and removed and removed through every iteration. The result was strikingly simple, often just one word on a slide.
>
> The average presentation slide is said to have about 40 words. When I first learned that statistic, I examined some of Jobs's most famous presentations,

notably the iPhone launch of 2007. I discovered that Jobs didn't reach 40 words until the 10th slide or so.

According to cognitive biologists, the human brain is far more capable of recalling information when it's presented as pictures with few words — one or two words to accompany the photo. If you take a look at some of Jobs's presentations, you'll see he followed the guideline.

For example: When Jobs was talking about the weakness of Apple's competitors in the smartphone category, one slide simply read: Smartphone. The next slide showed photos of the competitors with no text. When Jobs revealed the new touchscreen user interface, his slide simply read: Revolutionary U.I. The next slides showed photographs of the phone with a finger touching it.

If you go this route — less text, bigger font — keep one thing in mind. You'll need to practice a lot. Jobs rehearsed relentlessly. "He really practiced," Kawasaki says. "He made it look easy because he practiced for weeks."

It might sound counterintuitive, but putting only a few words on a slide will force your audience to listen to your idea more attentively. Go bigger. Your ideas deserve to be heard.

During our rehearsal with the speakers, I would remind our speakers to start with a compelling story. I remind them about the three types of audience they need to inspire when they give their TEDx talk:

1. **The audience that is sitting in the seats in the room where you are giving your TEDx talk.** Assuming most of the guests bought their tickets, they are expecting you to share with them an exciting idea worth spreading. Without these paid guests, it is likely that this TEDx event would *not* have materialized and you wouldn't have the opportunity to give a TEDx talk. While you should not take the audience in this room for granted, it is unlikely this is your primary audience.
2. **Many TEDx events are live streamed on the Internet or broadcast via Facebook Live.** More often than not, the number of viewers are larger than the audience in the room where you are giving your TEDx talk. Most of the people are watching this talk on a smart phone and not on a big screen. Think how you are keeping this virtual audience engaged during your talk. Take pauses often. It gives people viewing your talk elsewhere a chance to catch up with your ideas worth spreading.

3. **TED requires every organizer to tape, edit and upload all TEDx talks to TED's specifications for their review, and hopefully, approval.** When an organizer uploads each talk, they also must put in the title of their TEDx talk a short description and key words so that the talk is searchable on YouTube once it is approved and posted by TED. A great title is a key differentiator of whether or not your talk is found on YouTube. Having a number of appropriate key words is equally important. It is very important to recognize the global nature of the audience that watches TEDx talks on YouTube. I often told the speakers at TEDxWilmington that someone in Brazil, South Sudan, or Vietnam might be watching your TEDx talk on YouTube and it is very important to acknowledge that English is often the second or third language for most of these viewers. Speaking slower than usual and pausing regularly will help your worldwide audience follow your idea much better. It is even more important to focus on one idea to keep a viewer's interest. I always remind speakers to ensure that not everyone knows where certain cities in the United States are. For example, if you are talking about Wilmington, here is the right way to describe Wilmington from a geographical point of view: Wilmington is the largest city in a small state called Delaware, which is located half way between New York and Washington in the mid-Atlantic region of the United States.

It is important to start any TEDx talk with something powerful that will get the audience's attention in the first 30 seconds. The sixth Toastmasters speech project encourages all speakers to plan around the 4 P's: Pace, Pitch, Power, and Pauses. Be conscious of all four major vocal variables, and work all of them into your speech.

1. Pace — One of the easiest ways to incorporate variable pace is to slow down through key statements.
2. Pitch — A convenient way to hit different pitch points is to play with different emotional content. A sad voice takes on a different pitch than a content voice, which is distinct from an excited voice, and so on. Stories are good speech building blocks for many reasons, including how they bring a speaker's voice alive through different emotions.
3. Power (Volume) — Don't overdo it with changes in volume. Again, align your variations in volume with emotional content. Anger or joy tends to bring out a loud voice. Fear or sadness calls for a quiet voice.

4. Pauses — There are a multitude of ways to incorporate pauses in a meaningful way. For this speech, keep it straightforward. Make sure you've got short pauses following every sentence, and longer pauses at the ends of paragraphs or transitions within your speech.

These tips from Toastmasters are perfect for any presentation including TEDx talks. I am also a great believer in using humor to make your audience smile or laugh during your talk. I am also an advocate of giving your audience goose bumps and ending strong with a compelling call to action.

What makes TEDx talks remarkable is the potential to get a much larger worldwide audience than any theatre, meeting room or facility can handle. None of the venues where we held TEDxWilmington events could accommodate anything close to 500 people.

It is mind blowing to me that 106 TEDx talks given at TEDxWilmington had each attracted over 100,000 views as of June 30, 2019, with five TEDx talks from TEDxWilmington each attracting well over one million views. In fact one TEDx talk attracted over three million views. An itemized playlist of the top 100 TEDx talks given at TEDxWilmington as of June 30, 2019 is published at the end of this chapter. You are encouraged to watch all of them in a TEDx marathon viewing party and share your recommendations with your friends and family members.

I somewhat joke that the best way to measure the success of a TEDx talk is by the number of views it accumulates on YouTube. The total number of views is the currency of record for each TEDx talk on YouTube. After all, an idea worth spreading has relatively limited value if only 100 people see it, but if it impacts just one person somewhere in the world, it is well worth it.

It used to be that if you wanted your TEDx talk to get a lot of views, the best way to achieve that is for TED to select your TEDx talk and publish it on the TED website. While every TEDx organizer would love to have one of their TEDx talks chosen by TED, this happens infrequently. I was not one of the organizers who was fortunate enough to have a TEDx talk selected for TED.com.

As of July 1, 2019, there were 3,057 TED talks listed on the TED YouTube channel, which had 14,016,498 subscribers. By way of contrast, the TEDx YouTube channel had more subscribers and talks than TED itself, with 19,445,551 subscribers and 137,680 TEDx talks. Billions of people around the world have watched both TED and TEDx talks.

By way of illustration, one of the 3,057 TED talks was given by Jeff Bezos, the founder of Amazon, which as of June 30, 2019 attracted 1,268,082 views. Another one of the

3,057 TED talks was given by Sergey Brin and Larry Page, the founders of Google, which owns YouTube, and as of June 30, 2019 attracted 1,618,746 views. It can be argued that it would be hard to attract more views than Jeff Bezos, Sergey Brin and Larry Page, but we have proved that three TEDx talks given at TEDxWilmington did very well compared to this distinguished trio. Galit Goldfarb's TEDx talk attracted 3,017,349 views, while Yvonne Orji's TEDx talk attracted 1,532,809 views and Dr. Clint Rogers' TEDx talk attracted 1,452,595 views, as of June 30, 2019.

When I first became an organizer of TEDxWilmington, I hoped that one day our TEDx talks would collectively reach 100,000 views on YouTube. The first TEDxWilmington talk that broke the 100,000 view mark was Yasser's Payne's impassioned TEDx talk given on August 6, 2014 entitled, "Walk With Me: Organizing Those from the Streets, a Community Development Effort."

As of February 22, 2016, our total view count of the talks given to date was a staggering 421,408. I suddenly realized people around the world were watching our TEDx talks from Wilmington and they were having a real impact. Almost a year later, on February 5, 2017, our total view count of the 189 talks given to date was 998,207 and we were closing on a total of a million views. On May 29, 2017, we exceeded over two million views, with 210 talks. In two months, on July 31, 2017, we had grown to 3,100,000 views, with 218 talks.

On September 30, 2017, we exceeded 3,500,000 views for the 278 talks that were given at TEDxWilmington. We hit 5,656,501 views on February 8, 2018, with 352 TEDx talks. Then we suddenly hit 7,605,586 views as of April 22, 2018, with 375 talks. The tipping point came when we realized that we had 13,771,743 views on September 19, 2018, with 410 TEDx talks. Just prior to our final TEDxWilmington event, we had over 15 million views from 439 TEDx talks on November 26, 2018.

If TEDxWilmington were a business, which it never was, and views on YouTube were the currency of the realm, we were truly like a very successful dot.com in real life! From 998,207 views on February 5, 2017, we grew in one year to 5,656,501 views, which is an increase of 4,658,294 views in one year. A year later, on February 5, 2019, the number of views increased to 17,057,178 views, which is an increase of 11,499,677 views in one year, and 16,058,971 views in two years. As of August 4, 2019, the number of views had grown to an astounding 22, 514, 459 views.

I have never been associated with the number 22 million in any venture I have been associated with. Even though I will never organize another TEDx event anywhere, I will rely on the amazing algorithm of YouTube to showcase the 469 talks on an on-going basis so that the ideas worth spreading at TEDxWilmington between 2011 and 2018 attract new views.

One of my goals at TEDxWilmington was to bring great ideas worth spreading from around the world to Wilmington, while at the same time share great ideas worth spreading from Wilmington to the world via TEDx talks. At the risk of bragging, I can safely argue that I achieved this goal. With TEDx speakers from 12 countries, including United Kingdom, Sweden, South Africa, Papua New Guinea, Mexico, Kenya, Israel, India, Hong Kong, Canada, British Virgin Islands and even Australia, we had ideas from around the globe. We had TEDx speakers from 30 states throughout the United States including Alaska, Arizona, California, Colorado, Connecticut, Delaware, Florida, Georgia, Idaho, Illinois, Maine, Maryland, Massachusetts, Michigan, Minnesota, Mississippi, Nevada, New Hampshire, New Jersey, New Mexico, New York, North Carolina, Oregon, Pennsylvania, Rhode Island, Tennessee, Texas, Virginia, Washington and Wisconsin.

While I was not financially enriched by my TEDxWilmington experience, I was enriched in an unimaginable way by connecting in person with each of the 490 speakers from 12 countries and 30 states and getting feedback in writing or in person from the audience who typically paid $100 per ticket to attend one of our 32 TEDxWilmington events. I would not trade this set of experiences for anything else.

The high water mark of TEDxWilmington was 2017 when we organized 12 different events. This graphic captures what truly was an epic year, with 172 speakers who gave 164 talks.

Icing On the Cake

It is wonderful when one of our speakers gets coverage in national media where their TEDx talk is highlighted. Here are three TEDxWilmington speakers and a TEDxYouth@UrsulineAcademy speaker, who got this well deserved coverage between December 2018 and April 2019.

1. On April 18, 2019, Yvonne Orji got interviewed on the TODAY show on her role in HBO series, "Insecure," and discusses her TEDxWilmington talk that she gave in February 2017 entitled "The Wait is Sexy."
2. *People* magazine featured Kalliope Barlis on February 13, 2019 and highlighted her TEDx talk from 2017 which was entitled, "Phobia Relief: From Fear to Freedom."
3. The *Washington Post* featured an article by Joan DelFattore on December 3, 2018 titled, "If You're Single with Cancer, You May Get Less Aggressive Treatment than a Married Person." There was a hyper link at the end of the article to Joan's TEDxWilmington talk, "Sick While Single? Don't Die of Discrimination."
4. On April 23, 2019, the *New York Times* interviewed Joyce Short about her efforts to pass a law on consent and assent and referenced her TEDx talk in May 2018 entitled, "When 'Yes' Means 'No:' the Truth about Consent."

Celebrate a Miracle!

Marie White gave a TEDx talk in the spring of 2018 entitled, "My Child Was Abducted: How Branding Helped My Family Heal." On April 1, 2019, her child was returned to Marie safely after a 4 ½-year absence. This is what Marie shared with me in an email in late April 2019:

> "TEDxWilmington speaker Marie White shared her pain and entrepreneurial techniques in the talk, 'My Child Was Abducted: How Branding Helped Heal Our Family.' This month, on April 1st, her child was returned to her safely, after 4 ½ years! And another miracle is that she found her child had searched for Marie's name on YouTube and heard Marie's TEDx talk."

The power of an idea worth spreading through a TEDx talk can never be underestimated.

Here are some of the innovative practices we adopted at TEDxWilmington, which may not be found at many other TEDx communities in the world.

1. At every event, beginning with our event number eight on October 28, 2015, we had a person designated as our "speaker angel." The speaker angel served as the primary liaison with all the speakers on the day of the event, including keeping track of them and ensuring that they were ready to get on stage and dealing with all last minute emergencies. I will be forever grateful to Denise Angeli-Desiderio, who was the lead speaker angel and did an amazing job making each and every speaker feel very special.

2. At every major TEDxWilmington starting in 2015, we retained at our expense a very talented make up artist, who rendered her services at a discounted price. For most of these events, Linda Yenshaw served this role with distinction.

3. One of the smartest things I did was to require speakers to write initially two blogs starting, with our first event in 2016. The first blog was due soon after they accepted our invitation, and the second blog was due before they gave their TEDx talk. Starting in 2017, we required three blogs, with the first blog due soon after they accepted our invitation, the second blog due before they gave their TEDx talk, and the final blog due after they gave their TEDx talk. These blogs gave the curating team at TEDxWilmington valuable insight into what speakers were experiencing through this whole process giving

us an opportunity, if appropriate, to help them. All the blogs were posted publicly on our web sites and shared on our social media pages. I also wanted the blogs to be read by prospective speakers so that they could get some insight on how rigorous the process it was to give a TEDx talk at TEDxWilmington after they applied, received a formal invitation and accepted our invitation by signing an even more formal agreement. I saw the blogs the equivalent of our own version of a Rorschach test. Please check out these blogs on our web site.

4. As the cohort of alumni speakers grew to well over 300, it became important to find a way to keep connected with them. This cohort of alumni speakers became a major source of referring potential speakers to TEDxWilmington, providing us with a rich pool of talent to choose from. We created a TEDxWilmington Tribe group on Facebook which all TEDxWilmington speakers and tribe members were invited to join. Many of the speakers have become connected on LinkedIn and Facebook, also creating a brand new community.

5. In the summer of 2017, I was invited to apply for a Public Ally to help me with TEDxWilmington and Second Chances Farm. Public Allies Delaware is a program of the University of Delaware Center for Community Research and Service, and a member of the AmeriCorps national service network. Their program is made possible through funding of the Corporation for National and Community Service. Each Public Ally gets a stipend from the organization that they are assigned to and they work four days a week for 10 months from mid-September to the end of June. Evan Bartle joined me as the first Public Ally of TEDxWilmington in mid-September 2017 and served as the first speaker ambassador. I got an unanticipated opportunity to add a second Public Ally in December 2017, when Kelsey Guinnup joined us, freeing Evan to work more closely on Second Chances Farm. Kelsey did a fantastic job of continuing the role of speaker ambassador. Evan finished his term as a Public Ally on June 30, 2018, after which he continued to work on Second Chances Farm full time, and Kelsey's term ended on September 30, 2018, leading to her accepting a job for an events company in Philadelphia, Pa. Our third and final Public Ally was Elissa Ben-Eli, who joined us in mid-September 2018 and her term ended on June 30, 2019. Elissa also did a great job as a speaker ambassador and helped produce the final events of TEDxWilmington. All three Public Allies also served as assistant producers of TEDxWilmington and took over all day-to-day logistics of

organizing all TEDxWilmington events from October 2017 onward. They managed all of the marketing and promotions, including publishing our newsletter and posting on social media. In addition, they worked with the TEDxWilmington tribe to provide feedback to speakers on their upcoming TEDx talks and handled all the day-to-day communication with potential and confirmed speakers, venues, volunteers, and more. I cannot imagine what my life would have been like without the help of Evan, Kelsey and Elissa. The success and growth of TEDxWilmington can be directly attributed to their leadership roles at TEDxWilmington.

6. As the cohort of alumni speakers grew, many of them offered to help new speakers as they prepared for their upcoming TEDx talks. We were asked by TEDxYouth@Ursuline Academy if we could recruit some of our alumni speakers to mentor and help each of their 25 speakers. I sent a note to our cohort of alumni speakers asking for their help, and much to my surprise, over 85 TEDxWilmington alumni speakers volunteered their time and talent to help the 25 speakers at the 2019 TEDxYouth@Ursuline Academy.

7. For all-day TEDxWilmington events, we began to do rehearsals in 2015. Whenever possible, we did rehearsals for all half-day events. As a general rule, I hosted a dinner for all speakers immediately after rehearsal, where I invited some members of the TEDxWilmington tribe to join us. These rehearsal dinners almost became the highlight of our TEDxWilmington events. It became an opportunity for speakers, most of whom did not know each other, to get better acquainted and serve as relief value before the actual event next day. I will miss hosting these very special dinners that truly created a sense of community with our speakers and the TEDxWilmington tribe.

8. My wife and I hosted at our house a number of dinners immediately after some of our all-day TEDxWilmington events in honor of our out-of-town speakers. Everyone was truly exhausted, including me, but it gave everyone an opportunity to decompress in a safe environment. I found them therapeutic.

All good things must come to an end, and I am glad to share the "Magic of the Red Carpet" with you. I wanted to share some pictures from our 32 events showcasing some of our amazing venues. When I was hosting a TEDx event, I tried to wear something different, although I quickly ran out of outfits!

I was pleased to share the red carpet with three of my favorite pups — HRH Maharani, Harry the Dog and Wellington Doodle. HRH Maharani is my red standard poodle and Harry the Dog is her best friend. Wellington Doodle introduced me to Pina Anna-Grace De Rosa from Los Angeles, who gave a TEDx talk at the 5th Annual TEDxWilmington Conference on, "Sniffing Out Cancer: the Making of a Groundbreaking Documentary about Early Cancer Detection." Wellington unfortunately died within 12 months of this appearance, but his spirit continues at http://www.treatsforpups.com.

(left) Ajit, Linda Tucker, and HRH Maharani
(above) Ajit and Harry

Ajit and Wellington Doodle

Delaware Art Museum

World Café Live at the Queen

Gold Ballroom, Hotel Du Pont

Baylor Women's Correctional Institution

Wilmington Public Library

Nemours Alfred I. duPont Hospital for Children

Nemours Alfred I. duPont Hospital for Children

The Soda House, Hagley

Ursuline Academy

The Mill Auditorium, Nemours Building
Mark Lovett, TEDx Organizer for TEDxSanDiego, attending a TEDxWilmington event

Route 9 Library and Innovation Center

Route 9 Library and Innovation Center

The Delaware Historical Society
Geoffrey Berwind

The Delaware Historical Society

Friends School

Figure 8 Barn, Bellevue State Park

Baylor Women's Correctional Institution
Second Lady of United States, Jill Biden,
Amanda Lemon, and Sarah Brown

Ajit and U.S. Senator Chris Coons

Top 100 Playlist for TEDxWilmington Talks Viewed on YouTube as of June 30, 2019

1. Galit Goldfarb
"The Ideal Diet for Humans"
3,017,349

2. Yvonne Orji
"The Wait is Sexy"
1,532,809

3. Dr. Clint Rogers
"Ancient Secrets of a Master Healer: Deeper Healing Solutions"
1,452,595

4. John Livesay
"Be The Lifeguard of Your Own Life"
1,120,653

5. Jill Sherer Murray
"The Unstoppable Power of Letting Go"
1,103,578

6. Sharon Livingston
"8 Signs of a Toxic Friendship"
905,998

7. Teresa Rodriguez
"Owning Alone: Conquering Your Fear of Being Solo"
889,706

8. Dr. Lani Nelson Zlupko
"Staying Stuck or Moving Forward"
763,334

9. Susan Heitler
"Lift Depression with These 3 Prescriptions..."
762,587

10. Annie White
"Why Ms. Independent Can't Find Mr. Right"
687,200

11. Rita Wilkins
"Downsize Your Life: Why Less is More"
593,866

12. Kevin Carr
"Dating is Dead"
528,659

13. Mary Morrissey
"The Hidden Code For Transforming Dreams Into Reality"
477,962

14. Sheryl Ziegler
"Why Moms Are Miserable"
445,478

15. Kalliope Barlis
"Phobia Relief: From Fear to Freedom"
421,093

16. Steve Harrison
"How to Sell Without Selling Your Soul"
401,911

17. Tony Jeton Selimi
"Technological Armageddon: A Wake-Up Call"
389,027

18. Suzanne Eder
"The Dark Side of Self Improvement"
364,227

19. Michael Phillips
"When Kids Learn on Broken Chairs"
249,592

20. Dr. Debra Laino
"Low libido prime your pump ladies"
238,571

21. Yasser Payne
""Walk with me" – a community development effort"
209,206

22. Joseph Geraci
"The near-death phenomenon"
181,543

23. Vicky Kelly
"The paradox of trauma-informed care"
179,745

24. Brooke Miles
"The Magnificent Milk Myth: Debunked"
178,291

25. Mary Schaefer
"Putting the human back into human resources"
165,789

26. Julie Wei
"The Hidden Dangers of the 'Milk and Cookie Disease'"
128,949

27. Pritika Mehta
"5 Ways to Fail in 21st Century"
126,310

28. Jennifer Simonetti-Bryan
"Unlocking the Hidden Power of the Palate"
124,589

29. Soraya Morgan Gutman
"How to Connect to Anyone"
118,201

30. Marianne Ryan
"What Your Momma Never Told You About Childbirth"
115,929

31. Renée Jones
"Lose Weight AND Keep It Off: Emotional Eating"
114,961

32. Chris Grundner
"Modern Nonprofit Board Governance – Passion is not Enough!"
109,059

33. Karina Funk
"Sustainable Investing: What You Didn't Know Could Make You Money"
102,015

34. Nicole Black
"Conscious Uncoupling: How to Have a Mindful Divorce"
91,189

35. Allan Ting
"How to Bounce Back from Burnout in 3 Simple Steps"
87,792

36. Karen Mayo
"Mindful Eating with Mayo"
86,805

37. Colleen O'Grady
"Ticked-Off Teen Daughters & Stressed-Out Moms: 3 Keys"
81,229

38. Lena Sisco
"My Secret to Breaking Terrorists: Detecting Deception & Rapport"
79,469

39. Dr. Daniel Z. Lieberman
"Dopamine: Driving Your Brain into the Future"
78,297

40. Dr. Paul Rosen
The Next Revolution in Health Care? Empathy"
74,145

41. Michael Keriakos
"Why Luxury Hotels & Publishers Will Change Their Relationship"
69,999

42. Rachel Hutchisson
"The Era of Corporate Social Responsibility is Ending
68,252

43. Chris Largent
"The Secret Skills Gap Between Men and Women"
63,717

44. Janine Marie Driver
"How To See Past What Drives You Nuts"
63,443

45. Bashar Wali
"A Hotel is Just a Building"
62,717

46. Yolanda Schlabach
"Sex Trafficking in the U.S.: Young Lives, Insane Profit"
61,398

47. Peter Atwater
"Confidence-Driven Decision Making"
60,030

48. Jason Treu
"How to Get CoWorkers to Like Each Other"
54,210

49. Joan Ranquet
"The Rainbow Bridge, Animals in Transition"
43,670

50. Andrew Gomory
"Lost Words — Finding Hope for
Aphasia Through Technology"
42,962

51. Cyndi O'Meara
"What's with Wheat?"
38,987

52. Jen Kluczkowski
"Can Mindfulness Save the Earth?"
35,612

53. Sadhana Pasricha
"Social Capital — The Critical Assets for Success"
35,565

54. Alex Cabañas
"The Bar is So Low- The Realities
of Memorable Service"
34,574

55. Peter Ward
"Volcanoes: A Forge for Climate Change"
34,473

56. Sarah E. Brown
"What My Job Taught Me About Finding
a Romantic Relationship"
33,239

57. Jerry Inzerillo
"Global Trends In Luxury Hospitality"
33,050

58. Clancy Cash Harrison
"The Shocking Truth About Food Insecurity"
32,582

59. Mikki Williams
"From Bucket List to Experience List:
How to manifest your dreams"
32,350

60. Allison Ford
"Why Strong People Finish Last"
31,274

61. Janine Driver
"The Cooperation Paradigm: How to
Get People to Listen & Cooperate"
31,121

62. Dr. Debra Laino
"Technology & the Extinction of
Romance: Dissecting Love"
29,077

63. Arthur Brodsky
"Immunotherapy: Conquering
Cancer from the Inside"
28,869

64. Dr. Michelle Yep Martin
"Moving from Porn to
Meaningful Connections"
28,668

65. Dr. Kien Vuu
"The Unconventional Prescription:
YOU are your Best Medicine"
27,421

66. Robin Burk
"Countering Collapse of Out Interconnected,
Interdependent World"
26,701

67. Lu Ann Cahn
"Why We Must Do New Things
to Live a Happier Life"
25,539

68. Sunil Robert
"Comeback – Rebound when
Adversity Knocks You Down"
25,023

69. Jack A. Daniels
"The Power of Your Love Story"
24,752

70. Bill Walshe
"Business Ideology: A Roadmap Of Pride"
23,652

71. Dominick Quartuccio
"The Bold Journey Women Want Men to Take"
22,894

72. Claudia Six, PhD
"Performance Anxiety, it's not just for men"
21,430

73. Mark Harmon
"The Soul of a Hotel"
21,034

74. David Silver
"How Self-Driving Cars Work"
20,806

75. Myra Godfrey
"Is Living Your Purpose the Key
to Health and Wellness?"
19,939

76. Myra Salzer
"Wealth Prejudice: How It Affects Us"
19,314

77. Renae Baker
"Can Caroling Lead to World Peace?"
16,885

78. Kevin Rose
"Can Tigers Tame Your Stress?"
16,657

79. Jane Shure
"Boost Resilience: Take Charge of the Inner Critic & Inner Worrier"
16,127

80. Sean Douglas
"Hack Your Brain For Success"
15,336

81. John Ellis
"Advertisers Shape Technology — What that Means for 'Smart' Cars
15,121

82. Susanne Birgersdotter
"Pivotal Moments"
15,104

83. Tony Allen
"Fix Poverty, Fix Education or Fix Nothing"
15,049

84. Melissa Escaro
"Modern Mindfulness for Today's Busy World: The Power of Intention"
14,808

85. Liane Hansen
"Reflections from a Functional Depressive"
14,765

86. Pina De Rosa & Adriana LaCorte
"Sniffing out Cancer"
14,613

87. Deirdre Mylod
"Improving Patient Experience Means Reducing Suffering"
14,560

88. Jim Lee
"Why the Millennial Generation isn't Broken
14,394

89. David Tuttleman
"Coincidence, Charisma, and Cannabis"
14,032

90. Mindy Tatz Chernoff
"How Horses Heal, Transform and Empower"
13,955

91. Doug Lipman
"What Can Storytelling Teach Us About Creating Connection?"
13,393

92. Dr. Rose G. Maina
"Could There Be a Pedophile Hiding in Your Family Tree?"
13,013

93. Simon Mikhailovich
"Safeguarding Your Money in Uncertain Times"
12,927

94. Gerald Leonard
"What if Practice is the Performance: Falling In Love with Practice"
12,105

95. Jane Krukiel
"The Power of Depression in Shaping our Lives"
11,996

96. Jan Ting
"Some thoughts on Immigration"
11,957

97. Mary Beth Minton
"Unplug to Play — Letting Kids be Kids"
11,776

98. Sam Calagione
"Growing Up: A Business"
11,741

99. Bahira Trask
"Globalization and Families"
10,865

100. Will Latif Little
"How to Become the Best Version of Yourself"
10,445

CHAPTER 3
It is All About the Story

By Geoffrey Berwind

What was the first TED or TEDx talk you ever experienced? Or, more specifically, what was the first TED talk when you realized you had just watched something very special?

My TED talk epiphany was years ago when I stumbled on a talk called, "The Mothers Who Found Forgiveness, Friendship," given by two women, Phyllis Rodriguez and Aicha el-Wafi. Someone had recently told me about TED talks, so one night, as I'm sitting in front of my laptop surfing the internet and not finding anything interesting, I decided to google TED talks. The first video that popped up was this one. Ten minutes in length? I decided I could spend the time.

Those 10 minutes changed my life. I saw three women on stage. One woman was in regular Western American attire. She was holding the hand of a woman on her left who was dressed in black, in clearly middle Eastern attire. Off to the side, a third woman whispered in this woman's ear.

The American woman was Phyllis Rodriguez, and she spoke first:

"I first learned that my son had been in the World Trade Center on the morning of September 11th, 2001. We didn't know if he had perished yet until 36 hours later — and a couple of weeks later, when Zacarias Moussaoui was indicted on six counts of conspiracy to commit terrorism, and the U.S. government called for a death penalty for him, if convicted, my husband and I spoke out in opposition to that, publicly. Through that and through human rights groups, we were brought together with several other victims' families.

"When I saw Aicha in the media, coming over when her son was indicted, and I thought, 'What a brave woman. Someday I want to meet that woman when I'm stronger.' I was still in deep grief; I knew I didn't have the strength. I knew I would find her someday, or we would find each other. Because, when people heard that my son was a victim, I got immediate sympathy. But when people learned what her son was accused of, she didn't get that sympathy. But her suffering is equal to mine."

While Phyllis unfolded her part of the story, she tightly clasped Aicha's hand while the third woman translated for her.

This is where Aicha took over the story:

"I am the mother of Zacarias Moussaoui. And I asked the Organization of Human Rights to put me in touch with the parents of the victims. So, they introduced me to five families. And I saw Phyllis, and I watched her. She was the only mother in the group, and I saw in her eyes that she was a mother, just like me.

"I was married when I was 14. I lost a child when I was 15, and a second child when I was 16. So, the story with Zacarias was too much, really. And I still suffer, because my son is like he's buried alive. I know she [Phyllis] really cried for her son. But she knows where he is. My son, I don't know where he is. I don't know if he's alive; don't know what happened to him.

"So that's why I decided to tell my story, so that my suffering is something positive for other women."

These two mothers, who shared two sides of the same tragedy, had found each other, reconciled, formed a friendship and were now on a mission to share the importance of forgiveness.

Wow. I fell in love with TED talks right then and have never looked back.

By profession, I help individuals, companies and non-profits use the power of real-life storytelling to connect to their audiences. I first began this work as the co-creator of Once Upon A Nation, a unique storytelling project that Historic Philadelphia, Inc. launched in 2005. I was their storytelling director for seven years, and during that time helped to create a signature style of conveying dry historical information through storytelling. I witnessed countless interactions between our trained storytellers and the public, and then eventually took my observations and techniques to other organizations. (You can see me at www.storytellingsuccess.com)

What is it about storytelling that is so compelling? Why is it needed now more than ever? And, why do the best TED speakers know to make their ideas come to life by sharing stories?

Stories — and I am focusing in on real-life stories — are compelling, because you and I are hard-wired and conditioned to process life through stories. As long as there have been humans, we have told each other stories. I like to say that stories bring us back around the "primal campfire."

You can google "brain science of storytelling" and find all sorts of articles and studies. You'll read about neural coupling, mirroring and dopamine. So, when you tell or listen to stories, your brain lights up and goes to a uniquely happy place.

And we are conditioned for stories as well. Most of us were read bedtime stories. We acted out all sorts of pretend stories as kids, and I'd suggest that day-to-day, as adults, you and I are constantly telling ourselves stories, both positive and negative.

Fundamentally, when we share stories (I prefer you become a "story sharer" and a "story listener" — so much closer to the ideal than being a "storyteller"), what we're experiencing on a deep level is connection. Your brain, heart and soul naturally want to connect to other people. This is how you and I are wired.

I suggest that stories are *doors* and *bridges*. They are doors to a greater world than our own individual lives; they are bridges connecting us to each other. You, at the deepest level, want and need community, and I believe the way to get there is through the sharing of stories. We need this today more than ever.

The internet and technology are incredible tools; however, there is a cost to them. We are awash in information due to the internet. It's great to have most of human knowledge at my fingertips, but I also feel brain weary because it can be just too much. And I believe that technology, whether phones or social media, simultaneously connects (on a surface level) and disconnects us (on a soul level). The worldwide rise of worry, anxiety, depression and suicide is evidence that a huge price is being paid for this disconnecting.

So, stories are those *doors* and *bridges* to share our universal human experiences. This is why your ability to share stories is so vital — it's about connection!

I want to share with you just a few of my favorite techniques about how to craft stories:

1. Use stories to convey your "why" behind your idea. Watch TED speaker Bryan Stevenson as he talks about injustice and how it all started with his grandmother. Bryan starts with his story and then shifts into his idea worth spreading. If you have an idea worth spreading, an aspect of this is you being clear on *why it matters*. Why does it matter to you, to others and to the world?

2. Use your "why" story to establish an emotional connection with your audience. As a speaker, you are expected to convey ideas, information and solutions, but you also want to inspire people so that they realize the purpose and passion behind your idea. Don't you want other people to get behind your idea? Make sure you reveal the heart behind it all.

3. In a story, avoid anything that interrupts your story. Remember, stories inhabit an ancient part of our brains, so no digressions, please! Don't teach, don't go off onto tangents or detours and avoid commenting on your story from the future. When you launch a story, you're taking your listeners back in time, and if you do this right, they will forget that you're in the room with them.

4. Focus your story on ah-hah, light bulb moments — these are epiphanies, by definition a "sudden revelation or insight." If you think about the metaphor of a light bulb turning on, this is most compelling when the light bulb illuminates the darkness. When did you first realize something? Or maybe make a new

decision, take a new direction, come up with an idea? Epiphanies are the heart of great stories.

5. And finally, my favorite. Bring your epiphanies to life by transporting your audience back there with you. Create scenes where you describe where you were and when you were.

Descriptive language is powerful because it taps our imagination. Think of the root word of imagination: image!

Paint pictures in your audiences' brains and watch what happens. You will probably observe people leaning forward, eyes sparkling, and at intense moments, hear "a pin drop." This is because you have taken everyone to a sacred moment with you, and in that brief stillness, all those individuals in the audience — just for a moment — became as one.

If that's not community, I don't know what is!

So, what's your big idea? Then, how will you make your idea happen? It's good — very good — to know your "what" and your "how." Just make sure you use your stories to communicate your "who" and your "why." When you do that, I believe your idea will light up the world.

CHAPTER 4

Lessons from 168 TEDxWilmington Speakers

By Jake Voorhees

In early 2017, I sent an email to a pair of individuals I had never met before. With names like Ajit and Rhianon, it felt like I was entering some sort of fairytale story. Two years later, I now realize it was exactly what was beginning to happen.

From 2013-2017, I lived in Vancouver, British Columbia, Canada, one of the most beautiful cities in the world. Home to the 2010 Winter Olympics and over 500 feature films, it is no surprise that Vancouver is the home of the annual TED Conference. I aspired to join the TED volunteer team, and tried for a while, but it never happened. Imagine the waitlist to support an event that costs $10,000 for attendees?

Later, while planning to return to the east coast, I discovered that TEDxWilmington had emerged in the eight years I was away. That is when I sent the email to Ajit and Rhianon. Rhianon excitedly replied, and in May 2017, when I actually returned, she conducted essentially a job interview to decide if I was the right fit. An interview!

We began my TEDxWilmington tribe journey with a plan to make promotional videos for our events, and this vision evolved into so much more. Ajit had a magical idea to interview speakers the minute they stepped off the red carpet stage. I said "sure." What I did not realize is how TEDx would leave such an impression on my life.

Two years later, the project ballooned into 168 speaker interviews from 10 different events. The intent was to capture the experience of being a speaker. This included asking questions around their emotions as they stepped off stage, connection to the audience, what made them want to give a TEDx Talk, and advice for future speakers.

Bigger Than Expected

After applying and being accepted, speakers typically did not fully understand or expect what was ahead. They did not foresee our TEDx team deadlines to be so demanding and frequent. They did not anticipate the time requirement for content evolution and talk rehearsal. And they certainly did not expect their own internal pressure to reach the heightened point it usually did.

Even for speakers who travel the world and command huge keynote fees, most of them said TEDx was the hardest thing they have ever done. They put more pressure on themselves and were more nervous for this talk than anyone before. Jeff Patnaude said, "I did Firewalk with Tony Robbins, and this was much harder."

After months of preparation, iteration after iteration of their talk, several blog entries, outlines, video submissions, hundreds of practice sessions, usually listening to themselves on audio, and then a full-day, before-event rehearsal, it was now time for their big moment time for the speaker to walk onto the red carpet and share their idea worth spreading.

They enter the circle, deliver the talk, and in what feels like an instant, it is all over. Then immediately upon exiting the stage, I would escort them into a green room, hallway, or broom closet to conduct a 10-minute interview.

They would collapse onto the couch or chair. The analogy that fits best is to imagine you have been on a journey, lost at sea and preparing for this one moment, for months. There was so much anticipation, and so much preparation (usually 100 hours of work). They remember the blogs. The submissions. The deadlines. The structure, the coaching, the rules. It only makes sense to them now, as they are finished. And then we share an intimate moment together.

They usually poured their hearts out.

I was surprised to hear what made TEDx such a big deal to our speakers. It is not the event itself being a TEDx speaker. It is not the TEDx audience. It is not the fact that there is a circular piece of red carpet and you get to give the talk of your life. Joia Jefferson Nuri said it best: "TEDx is a precious space. Not every good idea is a TEDx idea." What makes it such a big stage is the opportunity for your unique TEDx idea and video to be shared with potentially millions. It's an opportunity for you to deliver something bigger than yourself a concept for most speakers that is a once-in-a-lifetime opportunity.

Janine Driver said, "People do this in order to change the world. The speaker is not the hero. The audience is the hero." You as a speaker are empowering the audience with your idea so that together, collectively, you can change the world.

This was the primary takeaway for most speakers. Only when they exited the stage did they understand what TEDx represented to themselves and the greater TEDx community. They saw that they were the conduits to deliver an idea that has the potential to spread throughout the globe and literally change the world. Our interview was their first opportunity to reflect on all of this.

It Is About The IDEA!

There are some speakers who apply to TEDx who are absolute junkies. They know the differences between TED and TEDx. They know all about Chris Anderson already. They know what makes a TEDx Talk different from any other conference.

But these people are rare.

Most speakers do not have a true epiphany around their idea until far into the preparation process. They may iterate their talk, over and over, and may even develop three, four, or five talks between invitation and the day of their event.

Tatiana Poladko advises speakers to avoid what she did. "I went through several iterations of my talk and was iterating until the very end. Lean into early drafts. Get more eyes on the versions early so you have more time to prepare."

Many speakers did not take the time to develop their idea early in order to provide ample time for preparation and rehearsal of the performance.

What 80 percent of speakers said about their intent for giving a TEDx talk was that you must be passionate about the topic. You have to want the idea to spread so badly that you are willing to give blood, sweat, and tears to make it happen. Otherwise, you will quit, because it is just too hard. So figure out the idea that means the most to you, and give your TEDx talk about that.

Emotion, Relief, and Blackouts

Many speakers cried. They said how good they felt that it was over. Often, their first words were "amazing" or "awesome" or "fun," or you could be like Terri Levine and say all three of those words first, and in that order! A few speakers, like Delaware Department of Transportation Secretary Jennifer Cohan said, "That was so much fun I am ready to do it again right now!" Whether it was relief or pure joy, most experienced a tidal wave of emotion.

They were mostly happy and relieved it was over. Some were sad that it was over. But most were relieved. Even some speakers, who we knew would be great, like Marla Blunt-Carter, said during her interview, "Wow I did it. I actually did it." Concise powerful phrases like this show what an accomplishment it was to speakers.

Many speakers said they blacked out on stage. Some would actually say, "I don't know what just happened." That they had an out-of-body experience, like Bill Haley expressed: "Now that I am thinking about it, I hope I covered all my points." This was common. They could not remember exactly how it went and if they said everything they wanted to say. Many expressed an eagerness to watch the video as soon as possible to answer their questions. This is exactly why we have speakers rehearse so much. So that no matter what happens on stage they perform the talk that was meant to be delivered.

Attitude

Another core suggestion was to enter TEDx speakership with an open mind. In the end, speakers were able to look back at how much their content evolved. They had a better understanding of how to take feedback; to take advice from the core tribe, speaker coaches, and friends/family; and have it guide their idea worth spreading. Regardless of what the idea was when they started, it was never the same idea at the end.

Another example of attitude is being open-minded about talk structure. Speakers have a tendency to make simple content order mistakes. They do not start with a story. They do not adequately describe their major low moment so the listeners can experience their pain. Another issue in general was trying to say too much. TEDx talks should be lean, with no excess content besides the absolute necessities. Developing a good talk is like being a sculptor — you trim away everything unneeded besides the most masterful pieces.

This open-mindedness extends outside of speaking and into an observer perspective as well. Jennifer Simonetti-Bryan advised, "Don't pre-judge TEDx topics. Things you may not have been interested in can become something that blows your mind."

Storytelling

Lots of speakers said they viewed their talk as an opportunity to incorporate their personal story or life journey into the message. This is particularly true for academics or corporate leaders who feel like they normally do not have permission to do so. These speakers often left the stage, and like Gustavo Grodnitzky said, "Telling stories felt good. I'll be doing more of that in my future talks."

And not just *any* story, tell *your* story. Telling your personal story as a part of your TEDx talk is essential for success. It makes your talk unique. Plus, stories are the only true ways we learn as human beings. We have been evolutionarily designed for telling and listening to stories. You are alive today because your ancestors were good storytellers and good listeners.

Remember this during your next presentation, TEDx or not. Tell your story. You will find the audience attentiveness is so much higher during a story. It activates both sides of the brain, and stories can release dopamine/oxytocin/endorphins, and allows humans to transfer emotions. That is why you cry when a speaker cries, you feel anxious when they are on stage, and feel happy for them when they finally slay the dragon in their story.

Steve Harrison knows about storytelling and has changed the world through story. He has helped thousands of authors sell millions of books, including Jack Canfield's "Chicken Soup For The Soul" (500 million copies). He has them use stories to help deliver their message. Steve advised, "Try to have a story for every point. It makes it more memorable and helps you memorize your talk."

Talk Duration

Even with a unique idea, great stories, and the necessary preparation, there is a golden zone for the right length of a TEDx talk. Many speakers, who selected a long talk duration, 15 to 18 minutes, were filled with regret during our interview. They would have done 10 minutes rather than 18, and most communicated their struggle in memorizing a longer talk. Eighteen-minute speakers also lost their way more often than with shorter talks, and this is to be avoided.

Reducing content to reach a 10- to 12-minute talk is a major challenge for speakers. While developing their talks, they are usually summarizing another piece of content and formatting it for the TEDx stage. This could mean a 90-minute keynote into a 10-minute version, or worse, a 350-page book into a 10-minute talk.

It pains them to think some of their words go unnoticed. "How can I possibly cut it to this length?" But in the end, speakers have an epiphany about this. While on any public speaking stage, particularly the TEDx stage, the goal is not for more words to be said it is for more words to be heard. That usually means saying fewer words.

Michelle DiFebo Freeman said to, "Cut cut cut! And then you have the opportunity to add back good parts if you like."

Practice

During our interviews, every single speaker mentioned how much they practiced. Many had positive remarks about rehearsing it to as many live victims as possible. Family and close friends would jokingly complain about how much they heard the talk, over and over and over again. Speakers said practicing the talk to different audiences is key. Do not rehearse for people in your industry or family who already know about the idea. Perform it for people who have no clue what you are talking about. You will know what vital pieces you are omitting, or where you are confusing people.

Many speakers recorded themselves while rehearsing and play it in their earphones on repeat. The same technique applies for video recording of your rehearsals. There is no better way to identify body language and movement patterns you are making than by watching yourself on video

I love Mindy Tatz Chernoff's practice tactic. She had a friend read her three random lines of the talk script, and Mindy would have to pick up where they left off. She was the kick-off speaker for two of our events, and absolutely knows how to ignite a TEDx audience!

Slides or No Slides?

Another fork in the road for speakers is the slides vs. no slides dilemma. The TED/TEDx rule of thumb is as follows: In order to use slides, a speaker had better have a valid requirement for them, and they must be beautifully designed. The reality of slides is that it takes attention away from you as a speaker. Sometimes you absolutely need slides, and there is no better way to demonstrate a concept than with a simple visual. But through storytelling and adding appropriate detail, speakers usually do not need slides.

Sometimes speakers want to use keywords from their talk to show a reinforcing phrase that keeps them on track within their content. This is a horrible use of slides. Slides are not to be used as a crutch or as a content reminder. Remember the two rules! Valid requirement and beautifully designed!

Hire a Coach?

Most TEDx speakers are given guidance by the organizing team that invited them to speak. Ideally, the organizers require outlines, scripted drafts, and even video submissions during their journey to the red carpet. The amount of support varies tremendously from event to event. Some events dedicate a team member to be a one-on-one coach for each speaker. Some provide almost no support, and when we travel to neighboring TEDx events, we see weird things happen on stage. "Morning! Some weather out there today huh?" Ouch!

While getting to know hundreds of TEDx speakers over the years, I have learned how many hire a professional coach on top of the organizer support. A TEDx team generally has idea generation/uniqueness and TEDx content formatting covered for their speakers. However, there are other crucial things a speaker coach can help with.

Storytelling, joke delivery, body language, cadence, pause, stage positioning, etc. — these are all things a professional speaker coach can help you with. They are vital for a great stage performance, or the best TEDx talk of your life. I built an entire website with speaker tips and this type of information at www.SpeakerAngel.com/blog.

Dress Rehearsal

Not all TEDx events have a full dress rehearsal the day before the actual live event. The ones who do not are making a big mistake and are doing their speakers a disservice in the process.

Most speakers said they were more nervous during the rehearsal the day before than they were during the day of the event. There is something about the dress rehearsal's intimate environment that makes it more nerve-racking. There is nothing but organizers, speakers and coaches in the audience the day before, so it is intimidating for the speakers. We have seen several speakers bomb during rehearsal, collect themselves over the next 24 hours, take the stage the next day with ease, and crush it.

Performance

One thing we emphasize for the day of performance is to have fun. Smile. Enjoy it up there. It is over in a flash, so make sure to have a great red carpet experience. Allington Gumption Creque said his experience was, "Incredible. Fun. Inspiring." Speakers sometimes show too much concern and worry, and this makes it more challenging for the crowd to engage with them.

Michelle Yep Martin reminded us that even with a controversial topic that no one wants to discuss, "You have to find a way to have fun with the process. You have to be your authentic self. Be yourself on stage."

Being in a fun mindset allows you to go off script if needed. It gives you the confidence to recover if you lose your place you know you are going to be fine no matter what.

Take time to connect with people while on stage. Finish a full sentence while making eye contact with someone in the audience. Find the people who are radiating the most energy back at you. Find the head nods and "amens" in the audience, and they will help you push through.

Sometimes audience engagement works very well. I have never seen another speaker do it like Renae Baker. Towards the end of her talk, she invited the audience to join her in song. And not just to join, but she split the audience into four imaginary sections where they were responsible for a certain note. And it worked great! She created a more memorable experience through audience engagement.

Regardless of the method for you, make sure you bring the energy that is the right fit for your talk. Will Latif Little said, "Energy transcends. It's invisible, but once you set the tone for that energy, their mind is open now. You've opened them up to new possibilities new ways of thinking."

Trust the Process

For even the most seasoned of speakers, there are many things about TEDx that is different. There were things about our TEDxWilmington process that was vastly different than other TEDx events. Like mentioned previously, most speakers did not appreciate these intricacies until the end.

Linda Tucker, founder of the Global White Lion Protection Trust, pointed out what made us different: "I am going to use a word now, a lion word. There was a ruthless professionalism around your team, and nevertheless, you have the hearts of lions. Loving, supportive, encouraging, you call yourselves a tribe, but I would call you a pride."

We had to be ruthless with our expectations and processes in order to guarantee speaker success. It was in the best interests of our speakers, of the TEDx platform, and of the audience.

Overcoming TEDx fear is one of the first processes you must trust. Fear/anxiety/nerves is mostly an interpretation of signals from your brain. You have to balance the combination of fear/excitement and know that you have a greatness ahead of you.

David Raymond said, "It's so hard to explain, but it's this mixture of complete and utter fear, but also incredible excitement. Which is the opportunity. That's the excitement. But then there comes more fear, because it's such a big opportunity."

Another one of the larger challenges for speakers is forcing themselves to memorize their content. The stage is too serious for things to be left to chance. Like Shane Coen said, "This is TEDx, so you're not winging it." Speakers must script out their content and memorize it. They must know it so well that they can then go off script and speak freely without recalling specific words.

This preparation process is often eye opening to speakers. Cari Feiler Bender said, "The process has changed how I will give speeches in the future. Memorizing gave me a chance to play with more options, lines, and tone."

Chris Buccini said, "It's a lot of work. Embrace it. Give yourself time. Don't stress. Trust the process. Be passionate. Write, rewrite, and start remembering it. It was all worth it!

Follow Bonnie St. John's advice, which said, "[Before your talk] go to a TEDx event. Meet the people. Show up. Experience it. I didn't really understand what was happening and how it is organized."

Marketing the TEDx Video!

In seven years and 490 speakers, we have had just four videos garner over one million views. Here are some observations about the success of their videos.

Yvonne Orji — The Wait Is Sexy — 1.53 million views

Yvonne is an actress and HBO star who has a significant social media following 670,000 followers on Instagram during the creation of this chapter. The success of a TEDx talk is no different than the success of a great book or great product. It is all in the marketing. Speakers who have existing personal brands and online followings (email opt-ins, website viewers, social media followings, online group members, etc.) are far more likely to see early success with their TEDx video.

Galit Goldfarb — The Ideal Diet for Humans — 2.90 million views

Upon the release of her video, Galit did not have as much of an online following as Yvonne. In fact, she trailed Yvonne in views for a while, and at some point, passed her in dramatic fashion. As someone who has deeply invested in understanding the YouTube algorithm, with over 1.5 million channel views and 43,000 subscribers, my finding is that it is all about the title! Galit chose a title that people actually type into the search engine that is YouTube. Besides its parent engine, Google, more searches occur on YouTube everyday than any other search engine in the world. Take the time to invest in learning YouTube Search Engine Optimization and discover the keywords you should be using for your talk title.

Dr. Clint Rogers — Ancient Secrets of a Master Healer — 1.33 million views

I had the privilege to travel with Dr. Clint after his TEDx talk. While we were in Europe for a month, I would interview his patients, and we witnessed his talk explode from 5,000 views to 500,000 in less than 30 days. In this case, it was not a social following or a catchy title.

The success of Dr. Clint's talk was due to his genuine story. You can see the emotion pouring out of him while he tells the story of his father, and how Dr. Clint's future mentor Dr. Naram, helped him. If you were an early adopter of his TEDx video, you probably shared it with a friend because you were moved by the story. Dr. Clint says, "After watching me share some of those secrets, people would fly from all over the world to meet us. Sometimes with tears in their eyes they shared how much it changed their life. Needless to say, it changed my life too, and I was so grateful Jake was there to capture so much of it on video."

John Livesay — Be the Lifeguard Of Your Own Life — 1.12 million

While writing this chapter, I gave John a call to ask about marketing for his video. John is a startup co-founder and master marketer, so I am not surprised he is one of our four, one million view videos. John's video success is based on his overall TEDx performance as well as his marketing strategy.

John says, "The first key to a successful talk is to come up with an idea worth spreading and position it for universal appeal. When people can see themselves in the story and want to share it, you know you've nailed it!"

Secondly, you have to be great. Practice more than you think. John suggested, "10 hours for each minute of content. I rehearsed over 100 hours for my 11-minute talk." And thirdly, you need a promotion plan. John has a TEDx video pop-up on his website www.JohnLivesay.com. He sent the link to his email list, was featured on several radio/TV shows that referenced the talk, and ran Facebook ads with video clips of him on the TEDx stage.

Gratitude

During our interviews, I heard many grateful remarks from speakers. They were thankful to have survived the journey and were always so appreciative of the tribe and volunteers for making the event possible. Many speakers expressed specific gratitude towards Ajit, as he helped them through the process that changed their life. Rani St. Pucci said, "I commend Ajit for putting on such an event. I will forever owe him for this experience."

Nicole Black said that TEDx was her top priority during the nine weeks leading up to the event. She was able to be in a good headspace during the grand finale. Nicole said, "The rehearsal felt natural, and then during the actual event, I took a moment to savor how far I had come before I started the talk. I was amazed and humbled beyond belief." Don't forget to smell the roses!

James Barnes said, "Giving a TEDx talk was one of the most meaningful things I have ever done. I am so grateful to Ajit, his TEDx Wilmington Tribe, and Geoffrey Berwind for making that possible through their hard work and encouragement."

There were even moments of gratitude while they were on stage — memories that will last forever. Michael Hankin, CEO of Brown Advisory, said, "I could see Ajit in the crowd. He encouraged me to smile on stage. I was smiling, and then I saw him smiling, and it made me smile more."

Creating Impossible Encounters

I think it is important for speakers to remember why they are doing this. At the very end of the journey, speakers finally realized what it means to be a part of this global community that is TEDx, that they really do have the ability to share an idea worth spreading with the world and have the potential to leave their impression on the planet forever.

In the TEDx organizer community, we call this effect, "Creating Impossible Encounters." A TEDx speaker is provided with a platform that enables their voice and their idea to reach potentially millions of people who may never have been exposed to you otherwise, and one day, your TEDx video could end up on their screen.

Sometimes it is not creating an impossible encounter online through your TEDx video, but having someone in your local community look at your topic in a different way. Stephanie Diggins said, "I wanted to give a TEDx talk for my students to show them there is a platform for their voice, too."

Impossible encounters happen not only from the speaker's ideas, but also for the speakers themselves. Usually, what happens for our speakers is that someone unexpected finds their video and reaches out. This can spark a new partnership, collaboration, funding support, client, whatever you name it. But most speakers have something happen to them and their career after TEDx that normally would not have happened otherwise. Something transformative for their lives.

And finally, when the thought leaders meet in the audience during an event, magical things can happen. There will be people in the crowd who are working on solving the same things as one another the same things as certain speakers all in your local community. These people find one another after the talks, have lunch, exchange information, and afterwards, can support and amplify one another's projects. You never know what can happen, as Richard Lackey, founder and CEO of the World Food Bank, so beautifully put it, "We are in a dynamic in the world now where I believe we have the tools and technologies for most challenges. We just need the formula to get them done." The audience awaits your formula.

TEDx Changes Lives

What this entire TEDx journey and interview project has taught me is the power of connection. Connecting people with first great ideas, yes. But what has impacted me personally is the human connection that TEDx has provided. Most of the exciting things in my life today — relationships, collaborations, opportunities, projects — all came in the door through TEDxWilmington.

Ajit has been an unbelievable mentor, friend, and guide for me personally as well as entrepreneurially. I left my corporate engineering career behind in May 2018, and no one has helped me more than Ajit. He has been there for me during the low moments, cheered me on during the highs, and connected me to lots of amazing people and opportunities. I am forever grateful to have someone like him in my corner. Thank you Ajit, from the bottom of my heart.

The TEDxWilmington team, our tribe, has been such a supportive group of friends. Rhianon, Alessandra, Evan, Alex, Dana, Bob, Ken, Megan, Terry, Julie, and of course, Denise :) A few of us, including Rhianon, Alessandra, Evan and myself, travelled to events around the east coast: TEDxMidAtlantic, TEDxBethesda, TEDxPittsburgh, TEDxBeaconStreet in Boston, and even TEDFest. TEDFest featured 600 TEDx organizers from 60 different countries who all came together for a week of activities in Brooklyn. It is a powerful feeling to have TEDx friends around the world. We forged such awesome bonds with these excursions, ideas, and memories.

I am so grateful that the "job interview" with Rhianon went great two years ago. We specifically have spent a lot of time together, masterminding TEDx things, usually making plans for her event, which is TEDxYouth@UrsulineAcademy. Whether it was weekly meetings, mentoring students, making videos, speaker coaching, or prepping for my emcee role, we are usually talking TEDx in some fashion. We joke about once you have TEDx friends, you cannot really make just "regular friends" anymore. I am thrilled to see where her TEDx event goes in the future.

I strengthened my relationship with my business partner, Markevis Gideon, during his journey to the red carpet in September 2018. His TEDx epiphany happened when he stepped off stage. "Someone I never met before came to me after my talk, crying, and she said that my talk spoke right to her. She had experienced similar things. I am so glad to help people."

Together, Markevis and I are growing our marketing agency, specifically the arm that works with speakers via coaching/marketing consulting, www.SpeakerAngel.com. We help speakers focus their message, land more stages, and leverage speaker content to amplify their businesses.

The original "speaker angel" concept, originated by Ajit, was a tribe member role that was vital during rehearsals and the days of events. Speakers are often in panic-mode the day before and day of their TEDx talk. They usually have a million questions, do not know where they need to be and when, etc. They often need little things like water, snacks, help with their face microphone, and a bunch of high fives and "you got this!" type of hype. The person who did this role masterfully was Denise Angeli-Desiderio. Denise would literally dress in a full-sized angel outfit — wings and halo and all, so that speakers could find her from across the venue. She was the perfect "Speaker Angel" by being such a warm, friendly face, and who was a guide and savior to speakers for whatever they needed.

Another amazing life-impacting event that TEDxWilmington created was meeting Dr. Clint Rogers. He invited me to this crazy European tour where we travelled to 10 cities in 30 days, and everywhere we went, people were booking appointments with him and Dr. Naram because of his TEDx video. Dr. Clint says, "The whole thing feels like such a surreal experience. Now that my TEDx talk has crossed one million views and I have met thousands who have said their lives are changed because of it. Now I know more than ever how important it is to go outside of your comfort zone." I'll visit India soon, Dr. Clint!

I have been to Kenya with a speaker, Joyce Tannian, who founded Water Is Life Kenya with her co-founder Joseph Larasha, who is also a TEDx speaker. Joyce and Larasha used their personal journeys, lessons from singing or from lions, respectively, to share their ideas worth spreading about their nonprofit efforts. Cannot wait to see you both in Kenya again!

Geoffrey Berwind has also become a mentor of mine and remains the best storyteller I have ever met. He co-organized a TEDxWilmington Fireside event with us, which featured 10 expert storytellers during the Winter Solstice of 2018. I appreciate any opportunity to learn from him and his network and hope to continue to study and collaborate with Geoffrey in the future.

Bill Haley has been full of great advice for me, and a mentor on my entrepreneurial journey. As someone who started a media company over 20 years ago and is today trailblazing the personalized video market, Bill wants young video/marketing entrepreneurs to succeed. We have had many conversations about choosing the right life direction. Bill, you are the best.

Sunil Robert is someone who has provided valuable insights to me as well. Thank you for all of your kind words. Sunil and I met during our final TEDxWilmington event when I had an employer. He was so encouraging during the speaker dinner, during our interview, and even afterwards. We have reunited several times at other events, and he is just so positive about my future. What great energy someone can transfer to others! Thank you, Sunil.

I want to give a big shout out to Sara Crawford Jones, who was one of the original speakers I collaborated with after their talk. She was the first speaker to ask me about video, and the first paid gig I did in Delaware. She also taught something about connection. Sara and her Mom adopted another speaker on the day of his talk, saying, "Oh, your family isn't here today? We will be your family!"

Through Ajit, the TEDxWilmington tribe, 168 speaker interviews, helping with Rhianon's TEDxYouth@UrsulineAcademy event, meeting organizers and speakers from all over the world, and experiencing thousands of ideas worth spreading what TEDx means to me most is the power of connection.

I was able to connect with 168 speakers during their vulnerable moments. After such a stressful journey, they were given a safe space to release their emotions. We shared those beautiful moments and afterwards, I was a unique memory within their TEDx journey.

You now understand my love for TEDx and how it has changed my life. What is stopping you from allowing it to change yours? Get involved. Attend your local TEDx events. Join a tribe. Share an idea with the world! You will be happier afterwards.

See more about the TEDx Interview project series and watch TEDxWilmington interviews here http://bit.ly/TribeInterviews.

Say hello! Jake@SpeakerAngel.com

CHAPTER 5

A Journey Through all 32 TEDxWilmington Events

I got involved in TEDxWilmington in 2011. I was granted 32 TEDx licenses from TED from 2011 to 2018. I produced 32 events in total. This includes: two TEDxWilmingtonLive events, one being a simulcast of TED2012, seven Annual TEDxWilmington Conferences, three TEDxWilmingtonWomen Conferences, 18 TEDxWilmingtonSalons, one TEDxYouth@Wilmington event, and one TEDxWilmingtonED event.

This chapter will showcase the 32 events produced by TEDxWilmington in the order the events were held, as well as, the 490 speakers' names alphabetically in each event, with the 469 talks and their links included.

At the end of each event there are comments from attendees. TED emails a survey to every attendee from that event with one question, "How likely are you to recommend this TEDx event to a friend or colleague?"

The score is based off of a Net Promoter Scale. Attendees give a rating between 0 (not at all likely) and 10 (extremely likely) and, depending on their response, attendees fall into one of three categories to establish an NPS score:

- **Promoters** respond with a score of nine or 10 and are typically loyal and enthusiastic.
- **Passives** respond with a score of seven or eight. They are satisfied but not happy enough to be considered promoters.
- **Detractors** respond with a score of zero to six. These are unhappy attendees who are unlikely to come to another event and may even discourage others.
- Although TED asks one question, people can respond based on event, location, food, speakers, volunteers, networking, etc.

Event Index

Event #1: TEDxWilmingtonLive
Simulcast of TED2012
February 29, 2012

Event #2: 1st Annual TEDxWilmington Conference
Theme: Resilience
August 9, 2012

Event #3: 2nd Annual TEDxWilmington Conference
August 7, 2013

Event #4: 3rd Annual TEDxWilmington Conference
Theme: Roots of Change
August 6, 2014

Event #5: TEDxWilmingtonSalon
Theme: Invest in the Future
November 19, 2014

Event #6: TEDxWilmingtonSalon
March 13, 2015

Event #7: TEDxWilmingtonSalon
Theme: Second Chances & Redemption
July 31, 2015

Event #8: 4th Annual TEDxWilmington Conference
Theme: Pioneering and Innovating
October 28, 2015

Event #9: TEDxWilmingtonSalon
Theme: Living the Good Life: Religion, Human Flourishing, and the Common Good
April 30, 2016

Event #10: TEDxWilmingtonSalon
Theme: Wilmington World Class: Expanding Employment in Wilmington
July 21, 2016

Event #11: TEDxWilmingtonSalon
Theme: Whistleblowers & the First Amendment
July 30, 2016

Event #12: 5th Annual TEDxWilmington Conference
Theme: Kinetic Ideas with Energy
August 24, 2016

Event #13: TEDxWilmingtonSalon
Theme: Innovation in Healthcare
October 18, 2016

Event #14: 1st Annual TEDxWilmingtonWomen
Theme: It's About Time
October 27, 2016

Event #15: TEDxWilmingtonSalon
Theme: Information is Power
November 17, 2016

Event #16: TEDxWilmingtonSalon
Theme: Investing in Opportunity
December 6, 2016

Event #17: TEDxWilmingtonSalon
Theme: Swipe Left: Love, Dating & Situationships
February 16, 2017

Event #18: TEDxYouth@Wilmington
Theme: Agents of Change
April 2, 2017

Event #19: TEDxWilmingtonSalon
Theme: Lust for Life: Adventure, Travel, Hospitality
June 7, 2017

Event #20: 6th Annual TEDxWilmington Conference
Theme: Limitless: Ideas Beyond Borders
August 16, 2017

Event #21: TEDxWilmingtonSalon
Theme: Personal Finance. Community Results. A Summit on Financial Empowerment
September 12, 2017

Event #22: TEDxWilmingtonSalon
Theme: Adulting 101: Your Path. Your Purpose.
September 19, 2017

Event #23: TEDxWilmingtonSalon
Theme: Who's in the Driver's Seat: The Transformation of Transportation
October 17, 2017

Event #24: 2nd Annual TEDxWilmingtonWomen
Theme: Bridge Builder
November 2, 2017

Event #25: TEDxWilmingtonSalon
Theme: Technology and Innovation
November 28, 2017

Event #26: TEDxWilmingtonSalon
Theme: The Meaning of Leadership
December 5, 2017

Event #27: TEDxWilmingtonSalon
Theme: Bridging Communities Through Innovation
December 14, 2017

Event #28: TEDxWilmingtonSalon
Theme: Fireside: Illuminate the World
December 21, 2017

Event #29: TEDxWilmingtonED
Theme: Education Possible
February 9, 2018

Event #30: TEDxWilmingtonLive
Theme: The Age of Amazement
April 28, 2018

Event #31: 7th Annual TEDxWilmington Conference
Theme: Now What?
September 27, 2018

Event #32: 3rd Annual TEDxWilmingtonWomen
Theme: Showing Up
November 30, 2018

TEDxWilmington Event #1

TEDxWilmingtonLive
Simulcast of TED2012
February 29, 2012

Delaware Art Museum

After my application to organize a TEDx event was granted by TED on August 14, 2011, I ended up getting very sick with a mysterious illness and was hospitalized in October 2011 for almost 10 days. I was diagnosed with a severe case of endocarditis, which almost destroyed the mitral valve in my heart. After I was released from the hospital, I was treated for six weeks with a heavy dosage of antibiotics, administered intravenously every day. I went to the Cleveland Clinic in early December 2011 to get a second opinion, and finally decided to have open-heart surgery on January 13, 2012.

While I was in the hospital and or recovering from all these treatments, I had made a mental decision to abandon my TEDx license, even though I had until August 2012 to do my first event with speakers. I was tired, both mentally and physically, and did not think I had the energy to do anything new. In early February 2012, TED offered me the opportunity to host my first TEDx event by doing a simulcast from TED2012.

On or about February 17th, TED approved my application for a license to do a live stream of TED talks given at TED2012 on February 29, 2011. I persuaded Delaware Art Museum to host our first TEDxWilmington event, which was called TEDxWilmingtonLive. Without any money for any promotion, or having a database for past TEDx events, we had 70 people attend this inaugural event.

Reflecting back on how close I came to walking away from being involved with TEDxWilmington in early 2012, I am grateful to Kris Younger and Gretchen Kennedy for making sure I did not walk away from what become a life changing experience. Thank you, Kris and Gretchen.

Here was the program as was listed on https://www.eventbrite.com when guests registered for tickets:

> The TED talks feature a diverse, world-class lineup of innovators and experts in their fields, presenting wildly interesting ideas and paradigm-shattering discoveries to an invitation-only audience. Each talk may last no longer than 18 minutes, and some only last for five, but each one will be highly thought provoking, jaw dropping and entertaining. This TEDxLive event enables TED enthusiasts in the Brandywine Valley to experience simulcast sessions of the TED Conference in a similar group setting, for free!

The schedule for the February 29 live streaming is as follows:

11:30 — 1:15   Session 4: The Lab
Henrik Schärfe, Roboticist
Regina Dugan, Director of DARPA
Jack Choi, Technologist
Marco Tempest, Techno-illusionist
Donald Sadoway, Materials engineer
Julie Burstein, Writer and radio producer

2:00 — 3:45   Session 5: The Earth
Karen Bass, Civilians Investigative Theater
Sharon Beals, Natural history filmmaker
Wade Davis, Photographer
James Hansen, Anthropologist, ethnobotanist
T. Boone Pickens, Entrepreneur and energy theorist

5:15 — 7:00   Session 6: The Crowd
Cameron Carpenter, Social entrepreneur
Reid Hoffman, Organist
Lior Zoref, Crowdsourcing advocate
Jen Pahlka, Code activist
Frank Warren, Secret keeper
Reggie Watts, Vocalist, beatboxer, comedian

TEDxWilmington
Event #2

1st Annual TEDxWilmington Conference
Theme: Resilience
August 9, 2012
Delaware Art Museum

I had until August 13, 2012 to organize the first TEDxWilmington Conference, pursuant to the license that was issued on August 14, 2011, which was valid for one year. I was still recovering from my open-heart surgery in January, and slowly gaining my strength.

I was chairman of Strongpoint Atlantic, a marketing company that was established in 2011, and I was also serving as chairman of the MidAtlantic Wine & Food Festival. I was still not sure why I would want to invest time and talent into TEDxWilmington when I could not make any money, or worse, lose money if there were not enough ticket sales or sponsors to underwrite the expenses.

Just when I had almost decided to "surrender" my TEDxWilmington license, Laura Stimson, who had just joined the Strongpoint team, and Rachel Dance, who was an intern at Strongpoint, persuaded me that it would not take a lot of work to pull off our first TEDxWilmington Conference.

We limited the number of speakers to just six people and kept the program to two sessions. With a great deal of help from Kris Younger, Matt Sullivan, Laura Stimson, Rachel Dance, Jim Donahue and the team from Mobius New Media, who videotaped the speakers at no cost, we pulled this event off just a few days before the license expired. Special thanks to Kris Younger for moderating and introducing the speakers. Resilience was an appropriate theme for this event.

There were six speakers at this event. Below are the speakers' names and TEDx talk titles.

Eric Aber
Title: *Finding very local food*

Andrew Vogts
Title: Fiddle Performance

Kathleen Koch
Title: *Resilience*

Dr. Ashok Gangadean
Title: Global Philosophy

David Reese
Title: *Democratization of Space*

Dr. Bahira Sherif Trask
Title: *Globalization and Families*

TEDxWilmington Event #3

2nd Annual TEDxWilmington
Conference
August 7, 2013
World Café Live at the Queen

I made a decision to make the annual TEDxWilmington Conference in 2013 into a full-day event and have it at a major venue. By signing a contract for the World Café Live at the Queen, I was making a commitment to invest a significant financial investment, as well as time into making TEDxWilmington into a significant event.

We started looking far and wide for speakers with ideas worth spreading, and we ended up with a truly diverse group of speakers, including a band and a remarkable variety of topics. I was especially honored to have my long-time friend, Liane Hansen, the long-time co-host of Weekend Edition of NPR's All Things Considered, give a highly personal talk entitled "Reflections From a Functional Depressive."

I asked Kathleen Koch, a former CNN correspondent who gave a TEDx talk at the 2012 TEDxWilmington Conference, to host this event and introduce the 24 speakers. Laura Stimson produced a beautiful printed program guide. We sold out every ticket and had a waiting list. This was the turning point of my TEDx "career," and I never seriously questioned the benefits of being the organizer of TEDxWilmington.

Teresa Rodriguez's TEDx talk attracted over 878,000 views, while Joseph Geraci's talk has attracted over 155,000 views.

There were 24 speakers at this event. Below are the speakers' names and TEDx talk titles.

Jamie Kleman
Title: **Pass It On: How To Make a Monster Difference and Share it with the World**

Andrew Gomory
Title: **Lost Words: Finding Hope for Aphasia Through Technology**

Steven Grasse
Title: **The Spirituality of Booze: Transcendentalism and the Art of Making Craft Spirits**

Neil Izenberg
Title: **Stories We Tell Ourselves**

Steve Boyden
Title: **It's Not About The Honey: Adventures of an Accidental Bee Keeper**

Robert Lhulier
Title: **Culinary Collaboration: Getting the Most Creativity Out of Cooks Through Kitchen Alliances**

Rob Prestowitz
Title: *All in the Family: Skinheads, Crackheads and the Angels of Our Better Nature*

Ganesh Vaidyanathan
Title: *Transforming the Art of Analysis Into the Magic of Discovery — Realizing the AHA Moment*

Jim Kelly
Title: *Financial Literacy for the Ages*

Chris Ungermann
Title: *The Environment: Germs & Chemistry*

New Sweden
Title: *The Complexities of Writing and Performing Music in Real Time*

Jordana Wright
Title: *Google+ and the Artistic Revolution*

Silvio Santino
Title: *A Brief History of Modern Wall Street and How to Manage Your Personal Finances in the Post Credit Crisis World*

H. Avery Jones
Title: **BLACK BROWN & BLUE**

Sarah E. Brown
Title: *How to be Happy, Successful, and Understood*

Teresa Rodriguez
Title: *Owning Alone: Conquering Your Fears of Being Solo in 7 Easy Steps*

Chris Largent
Title: *The Secret Skills Gap between Men and Women*

Peter Atwater
Title: *Confidence-Driven Decision Making*

Joseph B. Geraci
Title: *The Near Death Phenomenon*

Liane Hansen
Title: *Reflections from a Functional Depressive*

Jim Lee
Title: *Why the Millennial Generation Isn't Broken*

U.S. Senator Chris Coons
Title: *Nurturing Innovation in an Era of Political Gridlock and Policy Stagnation*

Dr. Debra Laino
Title: *Low Libido? Prime Your Pump Ladies*

Phil Spampinato
Title: *Space Suit Design, Manufacturing and Culture*

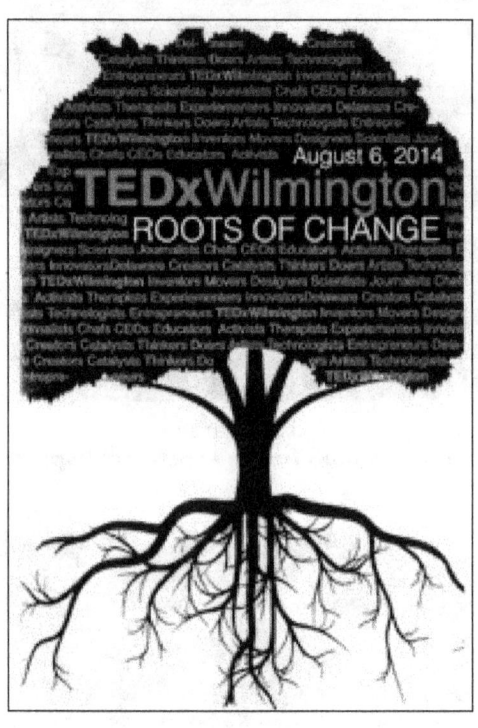

TEDxWilmington Event #4

3rd Annual TEDxWilmington Conference
Theme: The Roots of Change
August 6, 2014
World Café Live at the Queen

Following on the heels of a very successful TEDxWilmington Conference in 2013, we booked the World Café Live at the Queen for the 3rd Annual TEDxWilmington Conference in 2014, with the theme, "The Roots of Change."

We invited proposals from prospective speakers who wanted to give a TEDx talk, and invited some speakers to give a TEDx talk. While our selection process was very informal, we wanted to be thought provoking. We had 18 speakers. Yasser Payne's powerful TEDx talk at this event was the first TEDx talk given at TEDxWilmington that crossed the threshold of 100,000 views on YouTube, and was for a couple of years our most popular TEDx talk.

We were honored to have Chef Matt Haley, who had just won the 2014 James Beard Humanitarian of the Year Award, give a heartfelt TEDx talk. Unfortunately, Matt died less than two weeks later in a tragic motorcycle accident in India, but his TEDx talk sowed the seeds for my inspiration to create Second Chances Farm (read more in the final chapter of this book). This event was sold out with a waiting list and the response from the attendees was overwhelmingly positive.

The TEDx talks by the following five speakers each attracted well over 100,000 views, and in some cases, well over 200,000 views.

1. Chris Grundner
2. Vicky Kelly
3. Dr. Lani Nelson Zlupko
4. Yasser Payne
5. Mary Schaefer

There were 18 speakers at this event. Below are the speakers' names and TEDx talk titles.

Eric Miller
Title: **Virtual Winemaking**

Mary Schaefer
Title: **Putting the Human Back into Human Resources**

A Journey Through All 32 TEDxWilmington Events

Paul Herdman
Title: *What Will It Take for America's Kids to Compete at a Global Level?*

Anthony Armstrong
Title: *Happiness Education*

Patrick Lloyd
Title: *Share the Goodness*

Jason Ingle
Title: *Co-Founder of Greener Partners*

Yasser Payne
Title: *Walk With Me: Organizing those from The Streets, A Community Development Effort*

John Moore
Title: *The Enercosm: The Invisible Driver of Our Coming Prosperity*

Sadhana Pasricha
Title: *Social Capital: The Critical Assets for Success*

Chris Grundner
Title: *Modern Nonprofit Board Governance — Passion Is Not Enough!*

Jan C. Ting
Title: *Some Thoughts on Immigration and Why It's Always a Problem, a Controversy, and a Political Issue*

Dr. Paul Rosen
Title: *The Next Revolution in Health Care? Empathy*

Brendan Cooke
Title: *Delaware, Home of Single-A Baseball and AAA Opera*

Mary Beth Minton
Title: *Unplug to Play: Letting Kids Be Kids*

Matt Haley
Title: *Taste of the World: Adventurous Business*

Chef Otto
Title: *Be Persistent, Be Present, & Use Your Gift*

Dr. Lani Nelson-Zlupko
Title: *Staying Stuck or Moving Forward: How to Effectively Manage Mood, Thoughts and Problems*

Vicky Kelly
Title: *The Paradox of Trauma-Informed Care*

TEDxWilmington Event #5

TEDxWilmingtonSalon
Theme: Invest In The Future
November 19, 2014
Opera Delaware

The popularity of TEDxWilmington events resulted in my being approached by numerous people to organize more TEDx events. I applied for and received approval to organize three TEDxWilmingtonSalons. A Salon was limited to no more than two, 90-minute sessions, and was meant to be a much more intimate event with a narrower focus than the annual event.

I was approached by Bill Dugdale and Porter Schutt about sponsoring a TEDxWilmington event that focused on the theme of, "Invest In The Future." Our first Salon was a by-invitation event at the Opera Delaware Studios, and this event featured three very talented speakers who attracted a full house of guests. It was because of this TEDx event that I first met Jon Brilliant, who gave a TEDx talk entitled "The Creation of a Social Impact Fund: A 'Connect the Dots' Story." Jon's TEDx talk sowed more seeds for my inspiration to create Second Chances Farm (read more in the final chapter of this book). Jon and I became friends and he has now become my partner and CFO of Second Chances Farm, LLC.

Below are the speakers' names and TEDx talk titles.

Josh Wolfe
Title: *Contrarion Investing and Inventing the Future*

Suzanne Clough
Title: *Stop the Clock: Bending the Paradigm of the 12-Minute Doctor Visit*

Jon Brilliant
Title: *The Creation of a Social Impact Fund: A "Connect the Dots" Story*

TEDxWilmington Event #6

TEDxWilmingtonSalon
March 13, 2015
Winterthur, Delaware

Richard I. G. Jones, Jr., executive director of The Nature Conservancy in Delaware, attended the first TEDxWilmingtonSalon on November 19, 2014. The Nature Conservancy is the largest science-based conservation organization in the world. The Nature Conservancy in Delaware was celebrating its 25th anniversary in 2015. Rather than do a black-tie gala, Richie asked me if I would organize a TEDxSalon to showcase global thought leaders, who would discuss innovative and inspiring ideas about the health of our planet for future generations at Winterthur Museum, Garden and Library on Friday evening, March 13, 2015. It was an offer I couldn't refuse, and this by invitation only event was a great success.

There were three speakers at this event. Below are the speakers' names and TEDx talk titles.

James C. Borel
Title: *From Farm Gate to Dinner Plate: Feeding a Growing Population of 10 Billion*

Sam Calagione
Title: *Growing Up: A Business.
Competition versus Competition*

Peter Kareiva
Title: *How Conservation Can Succeed
in a World of 10 Billion*

TEDxWilmington Event #7

TEDxWilmingtonSalon
Theme: Second Chances & Redemption
July 31, 2015
Baylor Women's Correctional Institution
NPS: 86

I had no idea that this TEDx event would be such a watershed moment in my life. It began a journey that has culminated in my founding Second Chances Farm, which I describe in more detail in one of the last chapters in my book.

This event was inspired by an event I organized in May 2015 within Baylor Women's Correction Institution called, "Breaking Bread Behind Bars," an elegant five-course dinner, as part of the 2015 MidAtlantic Wine and Food Festival.

With the strong support of Rob Coupe, the then commissioner of the Delaware Department of Corrections, and Wendi Caple, the then warden of Baylor Women's Correction Institution, we organized this sold out event in less than 60 days with the theme "Second Chances and Redemption."

Warden Caple nominated a group of inmates who might have an interest in giving a TEDx talk, even though most of them had never heard of or seen a TED or TEDx talk. I recruited my friend, Steve Boyden, who had given a TEDx talk at the 2013 TEDxWilmington Conference, to help select the women who would give a TEDx talk and then meet with them regularly inside the prison and coach them. Steve selected six women inmates, and I selected six speakers from outside the prison system.

I must acknowledge the tremendous help I got from Meera Gandhi, who served as an intern while we prepared for this event. I will be eternally grateful to Steve for investing so much time and talent to coach the six inmates who gave TEDx talks. I will remember this event also because it was indeed Rhianon Husmann's first event, volunteering to run the audiovisual presentation for this event. Rhianon, who became the first official member of our TEDxWilmington tribe that grew to over 70 people by the end of 2018, became our associate producer and my right hand at TEDxWilmington.

There were three inmates that stood out to me:

1. Trudy Downs, who was serving a long sentence that started before YouTube, TEDx and smart phones existed. Just before she went on stage, I had persuaded her to use my iPhone (which I was legally permitted to bring into the prison) to take a few selfies of herself, thus bringing her up to date with technology;
2. Lakisha Short A few days before this TEDx event, there was an article on Lakisha which read in part as follows: "What's in a name?" This is a loaded question for Lakisha Lavette Short. Serving a 55-year prison sentence for robbery and weapons charges, Short knows his name is one of the few things he can control. He hates Lakisha; it never suited him. Born as a female, he always identified as a male. The feeling went deeper than the baggy T-shirts and bandages he wore to flatten his breasts, deeper than the sneering demon tattooed on his neck, and lines shaved into his eyebrow or chin stubble. "I've always gotten who I was," he says, "but I just had to put on a mask." After a two-year legal fight, Short recently became Delaware's first transgender inmate to be granted the right to change his name. (While Short has not undergone gender reassignment surgery, this article identifies him as male based on his gender identity.) My wife, Dr. Sarah Brown, who moderated this TEDx event, also now volunteers inside the prison and has kept in touch with Lakisha, who has sent us many thank you notes on an annual basis;
3. Amanda Lemon, who was part of the culinary team at Baylor who participated in the "Breaking Bread Behind the Bars" dinner in May 2015, gave an inspirational TEDx talk. She has now completed her sentence and is out of prison, and I have invited her to become part of the team at Second Chances Farm.

One of the guests who purchased a $100 ticket to this event and who travelled from California to attend this event was Delia Cohen, whose LinkedIn profile reads as follows:

"Bringing exceptional community leaders into U.S. prisons to work with extraordinary incarcerated leaders." Delia and I became good friends and she invited me to join a handful of other TEDx organizers who had organized a TEDx event inside prisons to join former Treasury Secretary Robert Rubin and others to kick off the inaugural TEDxSanQuentin in January 2016.

Last, but not least, the biggest surprise was when I got a call from the White House a few days before the event informing me that Jill Biden, the then Second Lady of the United States, would be attending this event, and asking me to meet with the Secret Service and coordinate the logistics of her presence with both Delaware State Police and the prison security system. This added an extra level of challenges to what was already a very complex event to organize, but everything went smoothly. The Second Lady was kind enough to pose with all the speakers for pictures, and we created a photo book for each speaker that she personally autographed. Special thanks to Ashley Biden, former Executive Director of the Delaware Center for Justice, for arranging for her mother to sign these photo books.

There were 12 speakers at this event. Below are the speakers' names and TEDx talk titles.

Sarah Brown, Dan Gottlieb, and Jill Biden
Dan Gottlieb Title: *Roadblocks That Prevent Us From Loving and Being Loved*

Chris Darling
Title: *Let's Talk About Mental Illness*

Trudy Downs
Title: *Second Chances and Redemption*

Jill Biden, Ami Temple, and Sarah Brown Ami Temple
Title: *Second Chances and Redemption*

Sharon Kelly Hake
Title: *Discover your inner leader*

Michael Kalmbach
Title: *The Story of The Creative Vision Factory*

Melissa Hutchison
Title: *Second Chances and Redemption*

Patricia Beebe
Title: *Second chances shouldn't be a privilege*

Latoya Mcduffie
Title: *Second Chances and Redemption*

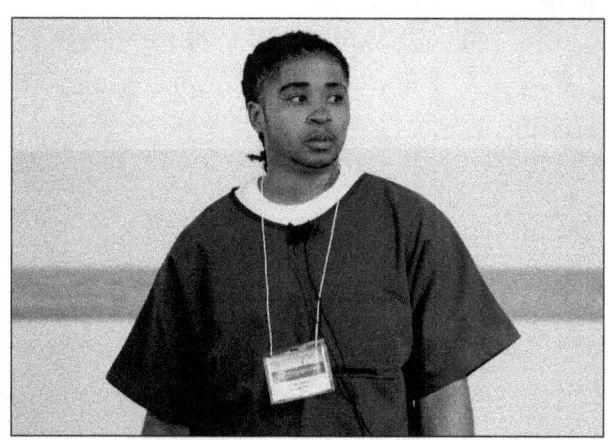

Lakisha Short
Title: *Second Chances and Redemption*

Amanda Lemon
Title: *Second Chances and Redemption*

Joe del Tufo
Title: *Exercise Curiosity: The Wonder Right Under Your Nose*

All attendees at each event get a survey from TED via email after the event. Each event gets a score based on the Net Promoter Score. This event received a score of 86 — one passive, 32 promoters and two detractors.

Below are some of the comments from audience members from this event and the score they gave.

10: I learned so much. It challenged me.

10: What a fantastic group of speakers, especially the six inmates.

10: I chose 10 because the environment, the prison, offers an opportunity to affect and transform the lives of not just the general population via TEDx Talks online, but to also affect the lives of the inmates. I find that truly inspiring and the possibility to change their lives is exciting to me!

TEDxWilmington Event #8

4th Annual TEDxWilmington Conference
Theme: Pioneering and Innovating
October 28, 2015
World Café Live at the Queen

Having done seven previous events, including three annual TEDxWilmington Conferences, we started to attract a lot of attention from potential TEDx speakers. We chose the theme "Pioneering and Innovating," and invited 31 speakers to the TEDxWilmington red carpet to give TEDx talks on a wide range of topics. Listening to all theses ideas worth spreading from the stage at the World Café Live at the Queen made me fully appreciate how TEDxWilmington was doing its part to bring ideas from around the world to Wilmington, and at the same time, share ideas from around our region with the whole world using the TEDx platform.

The TEDx talks by the following four speakers each attracted well over 100,000 views, and in some cases, well over 200,000 views.

1. Suzanne Eder
2. Brooke Miles
3. Julie Wei
4. Karina Funk

There were 31 speakers at this event. Below are the speakers' names and TEDx talk titles.

Hari Cameron
Title: The Pursuit Of Happiness, Creativity, & Excellence, Both In Life & In The Kitchen

Theresa Del Tufo
Title: *The Fullness of Nothing: Discover the Hidden Joy that Surrounds You*

Arreon Harley
Title: *How Choirs Have the Capcity to Change Lives*

Ashley Jansen
Title: *That Fierce Embrace: Mental Illness and Mysticism*

Allison Moore
Title: *I Was I Am: How to Move Beyond Your Past and Create an Extraordinary Life*

Greg Snyder
Title: *Patient Doctors as Physician Leaders*

Jose Somalo
Title: *Hispanics in Delaware: You think you don't know much about us? Don't worry, we don't even know about ourselves either!*

Suzanne Eder
Title: *The Dark Side of Self Improvement*

Peggy Raley
Title: *Don't say it can't be done if no one has ever tried*

Mac Nagaswami
Title: *The Golden Domain Name*

Julie Wei
Title: *The Hidden Dangers of the "Milk and Cookie Disease"*

Brooke Miles
Title: *The Magnificent Milk Myth ... Debunked*

Tony Allen
Title: **Fix Poverty, Fix Education or Fix Nothing**

Peter Ward
Title: **Volcanoes: A Forge for Climate Change**

Vikram Dewan
Title: **When you change the way you see the world you change the world you see**

Lena Sisco
Title: **My Secret to Breaking Terrorists: Detecting Deception & Rapport**

Linda Farquhar
Title: **Dropped Change: Insiders' Tendency to Reject Innovation**

Melissa Escaro
Title: **Modern Mindfulness For Today's Busy World: 3 Keys to Creating a Phenomenal Life**

Karen Mayo
Title: **Mindful Eating with Mayo**

Anisha Abraham
Title: **Demystifying Teens**

Kris Younger
Title: **Why I Need Many Grandmothers**

Nick Gianoulis
Title: **Fun as a competitive advantage**

Greg Plum
Title: **Get Your Head in the Cloud — Make Technology Work for You**

Therese Jornlin
Title: **Reclaiming the Wisdom of Female Biology**

Mindy Tatz Chernoff
Title: *How Horses Heal, Transform, and Empower*

Mikki Williams
Title: *From Bucket List to Experience List: How to manifest your dreams!*

Martin Rayala
Title: *Blowing the Roof Off of Education*

Karina Funk
Title: *Sustainable Investing: What you didn't know could make you money*

Annie Norman
Title: *Libraries and the American Dream*

Jim Matheson
Title: *Winning the Sustainability War*

Larry Selzer
Title: **CONVERGANCE**

TEDxWilmington Event #9

TEDxWilmingtonSalon
Theme: Living The Good Life:
Religion, Human Flourishing,
and The Common Good
April 30, 2016
Christ Church Christiana Hundred
NPS: 87

The year 2016 marked a turning point in the number of events we organized in any given year. We had sent an email to all previous attendees of TEDxWilmington events and invited interested people to join us on Monday, February 29th to learn how they could become part of the TEDxWilmington tribe. We had such a tremendous response and we had a standing-room- only turnout. Our TEDxWilmington tribe grew leaps and bounds, and we had enough people volunteer to help us and with whom we organized eight separate TEDxWilmington events in 2016.

The first event was the brainchild of the Rev. Stephen Setzer, who was the new associate minister of Christ Church Christiana Hundred, the Episcopal Church to which I belong. He suggested we feature two speakers who had been in the news recently, one for holding Muslim prayers, and the other who was a Christian who was suspended by her academic institution for wearing a hijab in sympathy of Muslim women. I thought that the theme of, "Living The Good Life: Religion, Human Flourishing, and The Common Good," was perfect for a TEDxWilmington event.

This event almost didn't happen, because I got a call from Will Davis from TED Headquarters one day. I had previously never talked to anyone at TED before this and was surprised to get a call from an unlisted number questioning this TEDx event, because it could be seen as promoting religious beliefs. After much discussion, we decided to proceed with this event exactly as planned. We held our breath until the video of these three talks were approved by TED and posted on YouTube.

There were three speakers at this event. Below are the speakers' names and TEDx talk titles.

Dr. Larycia Hawkins
Title: **The Gospel and The Meaning of Embodied Solidarity**

Miroslav Volf
Title: **Why We Need Religion in a Globalized World**

Adeel Zeb
Title: **Can Interfaith Restore Humanity?**

All attendees at each event get a survey from TED via email after the event. Each event gets a score based on the Net Promoter Score. This event received a score of 87 — three passives, 35 promoters, one detractor.

Below are some of the comments from audience members from this event and the score they gave.

10: I enjoy the personal feel of the event.

10: This felt like a collegial event. I was able to network with many wonderful people and it was good, wholesome fun. I watch TED videos and listen to TED radio, so I am a fan already. Having events within driving distance is an elevating experience. I will attend many more. Thank you for all the work that went into organizing this event, for the people who hosted the event, for the people that gave us something to think about, and for all the people who attended the event. Fabulous.

10: I went in with high expectations, those expectations were exceeded on all levels. I have been processing the thoughts and ideas presented for the past few days.

10: The environment was pleasant, the staff was hospitable, the speakers were passionate about their topics and informative, and we got an opportunity to meet speakers afterward and share a simple meal with attendees. I was gratified to see that youth were included in the running of the program and were acknowledged. It was a community-building event that brought people together from different walks of life.

TEDxWilmington Event #10

TEDxWilmingtonSalon
Theme: Wilmington as a World Class City:
Expanding Employment in Wilmington
July 21, 2016
Gold Ballroom, Hotel Du Pont
NPS: 53

I am a member of the Rotary Club of Wilmington, which was granted its charter in 1915, making it the 148th club to join Rotary International that numbers over 35,000 clubs worldwide. After celebrating its 100th anniversary, this club decided to make its focus for the next 100 years on how to make Wilmington a World Class City. A critical component of this strategy was expanding employment in Wilmington. This TEDxWilmingtonSalon attracted a packed audience in the glittering Gold Ballroom of the Hotel Du Pont, where the 200 members of Rotary Club of Wilmington typically have met every Thursday for almost 100 years. Dr. Sarah Brown moderated this Salon.

There were four speakers at this event. Below are the speakers' names and TEDx talk titles.

Sebastian Kretschmer
Title: *Green Prison Reentry: Growing New Farmers*

Bryan Tracy
Title: *Sustainable Strategies to Re-Employ Delaware's Capital*

Harold DeZell Lathon
Title: *Self-Sufficient Economic Empowerment*

Marzuwq Muhammad
Title: *Blazing a Trail: The Road Less Travelled*

All attendees at each event get a survey from TED via email after the event. Each event gets a score based on the Net Promoter Score. This event received a score of 53 — 10 passives, 37 promoters and eight detractors.

Below are some of the comments from audience members from this event and the score they gave.

6: Slides were not easily visible at the back of the Gold Ballroom. It was hard to understand the speaker. I didn't understand the messages of some of the speakers. Flag obscured part of the screen for those sitting near one side of the room.

10: The talks were compelling and informative. The presenters' delivery kept my attention and stimulated my interest and passion towards the subject. What a great way to advocate for change!

10: Very informative, great setting, well run and worth every penny.

TEDxWilmington Event #11

TEDxWilmingtonSalon
Theme: Whistleblowers
July 30, 2016
Wilmington Public Library
NPS: 85

I first met Michael McCray at a conference in Philadelphia and found out that he was a whistleblower. This casual encounter resulted in my organizing a TEDxWilmingtonSalon on whistleblowers. I was frankly ignorant of how much courage it takes to be a whistleblower until I began to organize this event.

Michael introduced me to a community of whistleblowers, public interest groups who were interested getting the public involved in whistleblowing and lawyers who acted on behalf of whistleblowers, who invariably get victimized after they blow a whistle on wrongdoing.

We decided to hold this event in the Wilmington Public Library, in part because the First Amendment protected the freedom of speech and librarians are essential in providing information to the population at large. Ken Grant was the moderator of this Salon, which featured seven powerful ideas worth spreading.

Below are the speakers' names and TEDx talk titles.

Marcel Vivian Reid
Title: *Whistle-Blowing: An Extension of Hope*

Louis Alan Clark
Title: Getting the Public Involved in Whistle-Blowing

A Journey Through All 32 TEDxWilmington Events

Stephen Kohn
Title: *The Untold Stories of the Whistleblowers of 1777*

Arthuretta Martin
Title: *Blowing the Whistle While Black*

Tom Devine
Title: *Whistle-Blower Protection and the Truth: Intimately Linked*

Michael McCray
Title: *We the People: Citizens Must Fix Our Broken Justice System*

Ken E. Williams
Title: *Follow-up to Ferguson*

All attendees at each event get a survey from TED via email after the event. Each event gets a score based on the Net Promoter Score. This event received a score of 85 — four passives, 22 promoters and zero detractors.

Below are some of the comments from audience members from this event and the score they gave.

8: I really enjoyed the diversity in speakers. I actually walked away with new ideas about how to address pressing social issues.

10: I tell people about TEDx ALL the time. Just this morning a woman told me she volunteered to help out TEDxWilmington because of a conversation we had.

TEDxWilmington Event #12

5th Annual TEDxWilmington Conference
Theme: Kinetic Ideas with Energy
August 24, 2016
World Café Live at the Queen
NPS: 90

The 5th Annual TEDxWilmington Conference profoundly affected me. While there were a record 38 speakers at this "all-day" event, there are two TEDx talks in particular that changed the direction of my life. These two talks were given by Saad Soliman, on the "The Abstracts of Justice," and Jack Griffin's TEDx talk was entitled, "Building the World's First Vertical Farming City."

I had never heard of vertical farming until I learned about Jack's efforts to create a vertical farm in Philadelphia. Saad Soliman had served over 10 years in prison, and his talk was about getting several second chances after he was released, resulting in his being one of the first felons ever hired by the U.S. Department of Justice, and heading re-entry for the US District Court in Delaware. After visiting Jack's vertical farm that he used to be associated with, I came up with the idea of creating indoor vertical farms and exclusively hiring returning citizens and giving them an opportunity to become partial equity owners of the vertical farms they are involved in. These two TEDx talks were instrumental in my creating Second Chances Farm, LLC. More on this at the end of this book.

At the risk of alienating speakers I don't mention, I need to acknowledge a few truly amazing speakers who were part of this magical event.

a) In 2013 at the age of nine, Braeden Mannering started 3B: Brae's Brown Bags, which provides bags of healthy food and clean water to homeless and low-income populations in need. At age 12, he became one of our youngest speakers to give a powerful TEDx talk.

(b) I met Galit Goldfarb, who lives in Israel, at a gathering in New York. Little did I realize her TEDx talk, entitled, "The Ideal Diet for Humans," would end up being the number one TEDx talk ever given at TEDxWilmington, with over 3 million views as of August 3, 2019. Very few TED or TEDx talks exceed the one million-view count, and for this reason this is quite an achievement.

(c) Special thanks to my dear friend and U.S. Senator Chris Coons for giving a second TEDx talk at TEDxWilmington entitled "Why Would Any Rational Person Run for Congress?"

(d) One of my favorite pictures on the TEDxWilmington red carpet is with Wellington Doodle, who joined his human, Pina DeRosa, on the red carpet to give a TEDx talk on, "Sniffing Out Cancer," the groundbreaking documentary about how dogs can help with early cancer detection.

(e) I invited Alington Gumption Creque from the British Virgin Islands to give a TEDx talk. He had practiced his TEDx talk in front of Sir Richard Branson, and just before he went on the magical red carpet, Sir Richard sent words of encouragement via Twitter that we posted on the big screen. What special talk this has turned out to be. Gumption has become a dear friend.

(f) Dr. Susan Heitler's TEDx talk, entitled, "Lift Depression with These Three Prescriptions — Without Pills," attracted over 738,000 views and should be watched by anyone fighting depression.

(g) If I had to pick one TEDx talk that I am exceptionally proud to be associated with, it is Yolanda Schlabach's TEDx talk entitled, "Sex Trafficking in the U.S: Young Lives, Insane Profit." Yolanda had tried for several years to get the attention of the Governor's Office to help address this problem, without any success. By pure coincidence, Drew Fennell, the Governor's chief of staff, was in the audience seated in the front row. In less than 24 hours, Drew reached out to me and asked how she could reach Yolanda. As a result of this TEDx talk, Yolanda met with the Governor's Office in less than a week. This is how ideas worth spreading truly matter.

Below are the speakers' names and TEDx talk titles.

112   The Magic of the Red Carpet

Donna Chicone
Title: *Super Pet Parents Save Dogs Lives*

U.S. Senator Chris Coons
Title: *Why would any rational person run for Congress?*

A. Kimberly Hoffman
Title: *Yes, In My Back Yard: Delaware Can Thrive in a New YIMBY Culture*

Walter Durant
Title: *From Pawns to Kings: Chess Champions of Murder Town USA*

Jack Griffin
Title: *Building the World's First Vertical Farming City*

Kaamilah Diabate
Title: *The Y in AYR*

Heather Huddleston
Title: *Life Beyond PTSD: How Something Called Nia Gave Me My Body Back*

Ian Khan
Title: *Would you Change Your Childhood?*

Lindsay Hoffman
Title: *A New Algorithm for Civic Life*

John Jenkins
Title: *The Power and Pitfalls of Labels*

Braeden Mannering
Title: *A boy, a brownbag and a tidal wave of change*

Thianda Manzara
Title: *Veggie-cate the First State: Using school vegetable gardens to improve learning and health*

Karissa Thacker
Title: **Why Authenticity Matters**

Gregory Lloyd Morris
Title: **Street Participatory Acting: Put the STREETS on STAGE!**

Saad Soliman
Title: **The Abstracts of Justice: How one man's contribution is creating a way out for others**

Nicole Hibbert
Title: **Our Subconscious is a Symphony**

Mary Dupont
Title: **Stand by Me**

Joe Sielski
Title: **Forecasting Forgiveness: "How Nature's Storms Help us Calm our Inner Storms"**

Nnamdi Chukwuocha and Al Mills
Title: *Two Poets, One Vision: The Art of the Spoken Word*

Nelson Emokpae
Title: *The Art of Winning over a crowd*

Yolanda Schlabach
Title: *Sex Trafficking in the U.S.: Young Lives, Insane Profit*

Myra Salzer
Title: *Wealth Prejudice: How It Affects Us*

David Tuttleman
Title: *Coincidence, Charisma and Cannabis: How making connections has changed my life and is allowing me to be part of changing the world*

Allington Gumption Creque
Title: *(9 no's one yes) How not quitting my dreams changed my life to help change others*

Kathy Abusow
Title: *Hugging the forest, rather than the trees – How responsible forestry does more than stop deforestation*

Pina DeRosa and Adriana LaCorte
Title: *Sniffing Out Cancer: the making of a groundbreaking documentary about early cancer detection*

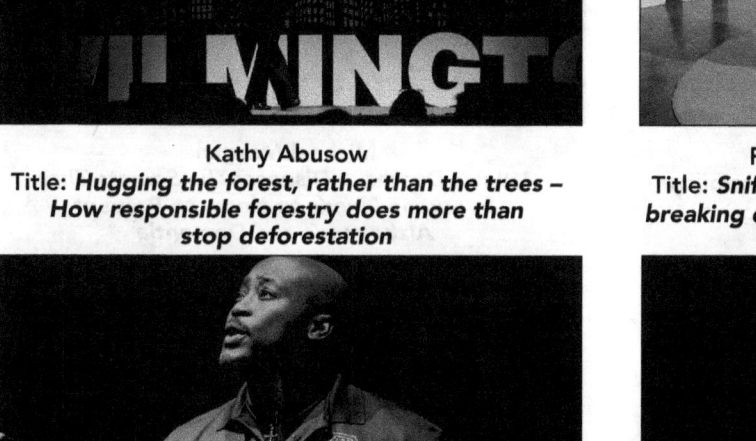

Cornelius "Nippy" Betz III
Title: *How to graduate from college debt-free!*

Galit Goldfarb
Title: *The Ideal Diet For Humans*

Susan Heitler
Title: *Lift Depression With These 3 Prescriptions-Without-Pills*

Janine Driver
Title: *HOW TO SEE PAST WHAT DRIVES YOU NUTS*

Rachel Hutchisson
Title: *The Era of Corporate Social Responsibility is Ending: Why that's a Good Thing*

Michael Morgan
Title: *2 Deaths, 1 Disease: The Secrets That Everyone Needs to Know to Prevent Alzheimer's and Dementia*

Claudia Six, PhD
Title: *Performance anxiety – it's not just for men*

Robert (Dusty) Staub
Title: *Daily Acts of Courage: Developing the Cardiovascular System of the Soul*

Hudson Taylor
Title: *How Rethinking Sex-Segregation in Sports is the Key to Equality*

Kevin Rose
Title: *Can Tigers Tame Your Stress?*

All attendees at each event get a survey from TED via email after the event. Each event gets a score based on the Net Promoter Score. This event received a score of 90 — 10 passives, 93 promoters and zero detractors.

Below are some of the comments from audience members from this event and the score they gave.

10: I cried (several times). I laughed. I had very deep conversations with strangers and reconnected with old friends. I left wholly uplifted and inspired by the beauty and brilliance of humanity. TEDxWilmington proved to me that my heart is right we are moving toward unity and compassion, not fear and discord. Bravo.

10: Everything was so well organized at TEDxWilmington and the speakers were so diverse and interesting. All of the talks were informative and inspiring. I will definitely return for more TEDx events as well as recommend them to others!

10: Lots of variety in speakers all with great messages. Everyone can benefit from the experience regardless of age.

10: The whole day was amazing, with ideas that have the potential of changing the world for the better.

10: I think it is a safe and supportive opportunity to allow people to share their ideas. From the organizer to the volunteer staff to the fellow presenters and the audience, the experience was top notch in every way!

TEDxWilmington Event #13

TEDxWilmingtonSalon
Theme: Innovation in Healthcare
October 18, 2016
Nemours Alfred I. duPont
Hospital for Children
NPS: 93

I first met Dr. Paul Rosen when he gave his first TEDx talk at the 2014 TEDxWilmington Conference. We became friends, and I encouraged him to do a TEDxWilmingtonSalon with the theme, "Innovation in Healthcare." He persuaded the famous Nemours Alfred I. duPont Hospital for Children, where he worked, to host this event. Following this event, we had a once-in-a-lifetime reception inside the beautiful Nemours Mansion. It was truly a magical day for which I am very grateful to Dr. Rosen.

There were 11 speakers at this event. Below are the speakers' names and TEDx talk titles.

Brendan Cooke
Title: *Opera in Unlikely Places: the Healing Power of the Human Voice*

Timothy Mix
Title: *Opera in Unlikely Places: the Healing Power of the Human Voice*

Aurelien Eulert
Title: *Opera in Unlikely Places: the Healing Power of the Human Voice*

Dr. Bon Ku
Title: *Using Design Thinking to Create the Doctor of the Future*

Dr. Paul Rosen
Title: *Opera in Unlikely Places: the Healing Power of the Human Voice*

Arthur Brodsky
Title: *Immunotherapy: Conquering Cancer from the Inside*

Dr. Stephen Lawless
Title: *Alarms in Hospitals — Are We Really Addressing?*

Dr. David Hindin
Title: *Why Your Doctor Should Daydream: the Importance of Creativity in Medicine*

Deirdre Mylod
Title: *Improving Patient Experience Means Reducing Suffering*

Shahid N. Shah
Title: *Leaders Find Ways to Say Yes*

Wayne Kimmel
Title: *Entrepreneurs will change health care*

All attendees at each event get a survey from TED via email after the event. Each event gets a score based on the Net Promoter Score. This event received a score of 93 — two passives, 25 promoters and zero detractors.

Below are some of the comments from audience members from this event and the score they gave.

10: I thought the topics were thought provoking, the way it was presented was professional, and the venue was top notch.

10: It was very well put together, and I enjoyed all the speakers I saw. Would highly recommend!

10: Ajit's ability to curate and optimize raw talent into high caliber talks is the best-kept secret in Delaware. Amazing to see folks from all walks of life — physicians, CEOs, VC funders, Senators — all working so diligently on their TEDx talks.

TEDxWilmington Event #14

1st Annual TEDxWilmingtonWomen
Theme: It's About Time
October 27, 2016
World Café Live at the Queen
NPS: 81

When TED invited organizers to apply for licenses to organize TEDxWomen events, I jumped at the chance to do this type of event. We were required to do our event in conjunction with the TEDWomen event, and simulcast one session live. I made the decision to have just women as speakers at this event, and I was thrilled to have 25 women speakers give TEDx talks. The diversity of women who gave TEDx talks at this event was simply amazing. I was particularly honored to have one of my mentors, Mary Morrissey, accept my invitation to give a TEDx talk. We were grateful to have Anne Barry Jolles install The Grace Tail at the World Café Live at the Queen so guests could experience it firsthand.

I would be remiss if I didn't mention Jill Sherer Murray, whose TEDx talk is one of five TEDx talks that broke the one million-view mark when this book went to print. I encourage you to watch each and every one of these TEDx talks. In addition, Sharon Livingston's TEDx talk has exceeded 880,000 views, while Mary Morrissey's TEDx talk exceeded 439,000 views. Soraya Morgan Gutman's TEDx talk attracted over 115,000 views, while Pritika Mehta's talk attracted over 125,000 views.

There were 25 speakers at this event. Below are the speakers' names and TEDx talk titles.

Tahira Akua
Title: *Life Legacy: The Story You Leave Behind*

Pritika Mehta
Title: *5 Ways to Fail in the 21st Century*

Soraya Gutman
Title: *How to Connect to Anyone*

Lu Ann Cahn
Title: *Why We Must Do New Things to Live a Happier Life*

Clancy Cash Harrison
Title: *The Shocking Truth About Food Insecurity*

Dr. Bahira Sherif Trask
Title: *Blending Work and Family. You Are Not Alone.*

Latisha Bracy
Title: *What Color Is Your Fence?*

Susan Bradley
Title: *Change Launches Your Next Chapter*

Mary Lavelle Cairns
Title: *Gender Freedom in Rural India*

Kim Castellano
Title: Life: *What Could Possibly Go Wrong?*

Avid Jones-DeWeever
Title: *Why Gender Equality Is Not Enough*

Jessica Gibson
Title: *The Diamond Polisher Revealed*

Krupa Jhaveri
Title: *Art As a Mirror*

Ajit George and Danielle Martin Moffett
Title: *Resurging Hope: The Power to Rise Again*

Susan Sandler
Title: *Punch Fear in the Face and Claim Your Life*

Dr. Robyn Odegaard
Title: *Creating Success Out of Chaos*

Diane Capaldi
Title: *Cultural Collision*

Dr. Stephanie Barnes Taylor
Title: *How Gendered Discourse Perpetuates Bias*

Donna Marie Duffy
Title: *Kairos Living in a Chronos World*

Anne Barry Jolles
Title: *Cracking the Grace Code*

Sharon Livingston
Title: *8 Signs of a Toxic Friendship*

Mary Morrissey
Title: *The Hidden Code for Transforming*

Jill Sherer Murray
Title: *The Unstoppable Power of Letting Go*

Arianne Missimer
Title: *Challenge Accepted*

Alisa Morkides
Title: *Was There Life Before Coffee?*

All attendees at each event get a survey from TED via email after the event. Each event gets a score based on the Net Promoter Score. This event received a score of 81 — 12 passives, 81 promoters and three detractors.

Below are some of the comments from audience members from this event and the score they gave.

10: The interesting topics, the quality and variety of the speakers, the location, the venue, the structure and organization. Oh, and the moderator, Ajit Mathew George, does an excellent job of keeping everything on track.

10: Quite simply, it was magnetic!

10: I believe we all have a story to tell. These women were given a platform to share their stories in an authentic, personal way. Listening to others' journeys in this way creates an enriching learning experience. Thank you.

10: We loved the format with breaks in the live talks, and the opportunity to see the live stream TED talks. The Grace Trail was fun and thought provoking! The other reason is the diversity of the speakers, including topics and backgrounds. The topics were of high interest, and YES, my best friend from childhood was a speaker. Lastly, the venue was awesome. It had a great feel and was a perfect place to host a TEDx event.

2: I was bored by it and the headliners were all at the end of the day and the talks for me were boring and not exciting.

TEDxWilmington Event #15

TEDxWilmingtonSalon
Theme: Information is Power
November 17, 2016
Wilmington Public Library
NPS: 96

It was Dr. Annie Norman, the State Librarian for Delaware, who inspired me to organize this TEDxWilmingtonSalon with the theme, "Information is Power," and hold it inside a library. Annie has previously given a TEDx talk at TEDxWilmington, and she believed in ideas worth spreading.

Marianne Ryan's TEDx talk on "What Your Momma Never Told You About Childbirth" attracted over 114,000 views.

There were eight speakers at this event. Below are the speakers' names and TEDx talk titles.

Peter L. Levin
Title: *Data Fracking Is Good for Your Health*

Shahid Shah
Title: *Data Liberation Does for Science What Social Media Did for the News*

Lozetta Hayden
Title: *Supporting and Motivating Our Youth Through Telementoring*

Anita Foeman, PhD and Bessie Lawton, PhD
Title: *Our Common Core: Ancestry DNA — Hope for Humanity*

Vincent James
Title: *3 Trends that Are Killing the Future of Music*

Jane Shure
Title: *Boost Resilience: Take Charge of the Inner Critic and Inner Worrier*

Marianne Ryan
Title: *What Your Momma Never Told You About Childbirth*

All attendees at each event get a survey from TED via email after the event. Each event gets a score based on the Net Promoter Score. This event received a score of 96 — one passive, 25 promoters and zero detractors.

Below are some of the comments from audience members from this event and the score they gave.

10: I really thought that the speakers were spectacular.

10: The value of having an expert share their knowledge, passion, and expertise is a gem and it was accessible.

8: Some great talks, but a few too many videos. The conference would be better served by using updated equipment — an LED screen — rather than a projection screen.

TEDxWilmington Event #16

TEDxWilmingtonSalon
Theme: Investing in Opportunity
December 6, 2016
The Soda House, Hagley
NPS: 82

Doing eight TEDx events in one year can be exhausting, but having three great speakers to work with to end a year can be a great joy. It was like an early Christmas gift to work with the following speakers, who shared thought provoking ideas worth spreading to a capacity audience.

Below are the speakers' names and TEDx talk titles.

Atnre Alleyne
Title: *Why Investing in Public Education Is So Risky*

Dune Thorne
Title: *Jump to the S Curve: Unleash the Power of Inclusion*

Dr. Janice Nevin
Title: *Better Health, Lower Cost — Absolutely!*

All attendees at each event get a survey from TED via email after the event. Each event gets a score based on the Net Promoter Score. This event received a score of 82 — zero passives, 10 promoters, one detractor.

Below are some of the comments from audience members from this event and the score they gave.

10: I learn so much at each TEDx I attend. This one felt informative and inspiring.

10: Great experience. Very insightful and thoughtful.

TEDxWilmington Event #17

TEDxWilmingtonSalon
Theme: Swipe Left: Love, Dating, & Situationships
February 16, 2017
NPS: 81

In 2017, I organized 12 separate TEDxWilmington events. I was blessed to have over 50 people volunteer to be part of the TEDxWilmington tribe, including Kia Ervin Wiliams and Leah Coles. I am grateful to Kia and Leah for approaching me with the idea for organizing two TEDxWilmingtonSalons showcasing TEDx talks that appealed to milennials. They helped identify topics that would attract millennials, and more importantly, speakers who would appeal to this generation. The theme "Swipe Left: Love, Dating, & Situationships," attracted a sold out crowd just two days after Valentine's Day.

Kia has an amazing Rolodex, and she persuaded Yvonne Orji to give a TEDx talk that now ranks as the number two TEDx talk at TEDxWilmington, with over 1.5 million views. Yvonne Orji is a Nigerian-American actress, comedienne and writer who continues to display her versatility and passion with each project she takes on. On television, she stars in HBO's new comedy series "Insecure." In addition, Kevin Carr's TEDx talk entitled, "Dating is Dead," attracted over half a million views.

There were four speakers at this event. Below are the speakers' names and TEDx talk titles.

A Journey Through All 32 TEDxWilmington Events

Kevin Carr
Title: **Dating Is Dead**

Yvonne Orji
Title: **The Wait Is Sexy**

Jack A. Daniels
Title: **The Power of Your Love Story**

Dr. Debra Laino
Title: **Technology & the Extinction of Romance: Dissecting Love**

All attendees at each event get a survey from TED via email after the event. Each event gets a score based on the Net Promoter Score. This event received a score of 81 — nine passives, 49 promoters, one detractor.

Below are some of the comments from audience members from this event and the score they gave.

10: It was very informative as well as humorous. Worth the time, indeed.

7: The event was great, but one thing that was a letdown was the fact that there was no food at the venue. Coming to an event at a "happy hour" time, I felt like there should have been some small plate food options. Again, the event itself was GREAT, the speakers were PHENOMENAL, would surely attend another.

10: It was a great event for millennial, and it provided an affordable and accessible fun outing.

TEDxWilmington Event #18

TEDxYouth@Wilmington
Theme: Agents of Change
April 2, 2017
Ursuline Academy
NPS: 86

In the fall of 2016, I received an email from Sue Manelski Kampert, a teacher at Ursuline Academy, an independent, all girls Catholic school in Wilmington. Even though I'd lived two blocks from this school for over 20 years, I had no contact whatsoever with this school.

In her email, Sue asked if she could bring a group of the students in her leadership class to the 1st Annual TEDxWilmingtonWomen Conference that we held on October 27th, 2016, and if I could offer a discounted ticket price for these students. Thanks to a generous gift from Mary Morrissey, who agreed to underwrite the bulk of the $100 ticket price, we were able to offer 22 scholarship tickets to Ursuline students and faculty. I was able to introduce this group of students to Mary Morrissey and get a group picture with Mary on the red carpet.

After this event, Sue invited me to meet her and two of her students, Areeba Khan and Yara Awad, to discuss the possibility of organizing a TEDxWilmington event at Ursuline Academy. I then applied and got a license to hold TEDxYouth@Wilmington at Ursuline Academy. We decided to meet weekly beginning in January 2017 at Ursuline to organize this event. I had slipped on ice in the first week of January 2017 and fractured my shoulder, which required not only surgery but also extensive physical therapy that would last all through 2017. These weekly meetings at Ursuline were the highlight of my week while I recuperated.

I was inspired by Sue and the students at Ursuline. Along the way, I invited TeenSHARP to join us in planning this event and recruiting talented students from outside Ursuline. It was unusual, at least for me, to see two Muslim girls attend this prestigious Catholic school, and both Areeba Khan, whose TEDx talk was entitled, "Muslim, American, Female: America's Future," and Yara Awad, whose TEDx talk entitled, "Does the American Dream Exist for a Girl Like Me?" gave powerful presentations. Jane Krukiel's highly personal and vulnerable talk entitled, "The Power of Depression in Shaping Our Lives," wound up being used in Brandywine School District as part of a mental health curriculum. Elijah Jones stole the day with his powerful TEDx talk entitled, "Diverse Education for a Student in the Education System: Fact or Fiction," while Chase Reid's talk, entitled, "Will They Replace Us or Enhance US," was truly an idea worth spreading. The success of this event resulted in my encouraging Rhianon Husmann to apply for a freestanding license from TED to organize TEDxYouth@Ursuline Academy in 2018 and 2019.

There were 18 speakers at this event. Below are the speakers' names and TEDx talk titles.

Erin McNichol
Title: Animal Sounds and Other Tales that Teach

Grace Nordmeyer
Title: Beyond the A+

Alcia Francis
Title: An Unexpected Ripple

Amy Xu
Title: The Power of Each Person's Story

Yara Awad
Title: Does the American Dream Exist for a Girl like Me?

Maya Showell and Morgan Thornton
Title: The Black Girls that are not "Black Enough"

Chase Reid
Title: Will They Replace Us or Enhance Us

Carly Palkon
Title: *The Cost of Silence: Defending Music Education*

Jane Lyons
Title: *Second Chances To Save Our Community*

Areeba Khan
Title: *Muslim, American, Female: America's Future*

Jessica Falasco
Title: *Solve the Cube, Solve Your Life*

Molly Clark
Title: *Stand by Your Sisters*

Emountey White
Title: *Get comfortable with discomfort: You made a mistake? Great Job!*

Elijah Jones
Title: Diverse Education for a Student in the Education System: Fact or Fiction

Jane Krukiel
Title: The Power of Depression in Shaping Our Lives

Abby Larmore
Title: The Shirtless Man

Alphina Kamara
Title: Age Ain't Nothing but a Number

All attendees at each event get a survey from TED via email after the event. Each event gets a score based on the Net Promoter Score. This event received a score of 86 — nine passives, 69 promoters, one detractor.

Below are some of the comments from audience members from this event and the score they gave.

10: My experience was amazing. This was the first time I attended TEDx. Very interesting, informative, meaningful and with a message. It had a lot of different topics. I enjoyed the whole event. Everyone worked so hard and the entire program was very pleasant. The host was amazing, the way Ajit introduced speakers and hosted the event was wonderful. Management was very good. Lighting, sound system was super, especially the live music and the singer was amazing. I hope we will have more TEDx events like this in the future.

10: It was an amazing experience for my daughter. The commitment and preparation they gave to the students was incredible. Everyone at TEDx wanted them to succeed.

10: It was inspiring to see all these adolescents have all these great thoughts, that made me feel that our future is going to be great. The ideas that they brought up were eye opening to all of us to think deeply about.

10: Talks were not only inspiring but also informative. Was nice to hear directly from the youth of today about their struggles and passions.

TEDxWilmington Event #19

TEDxWilmingtonSalon
Theme: Lust for Life:
Adventure, Travel, Hospitality
June 7, 2017
The Queen
NPS: 89

I had spent the better part of 40 years in the real estate and hospitality industry, with a significant portion of this time as managing director of Nail Bay Resort, a luxury real estate development in Virgin Gorda, British Virgin Islands. It was therefore natural for me to organize a TEDxWilmingtonSalon with the theme, "Lust for Life: Adventure, Travel, Hospitality." I am grateful to Andrew Benioff, whose Rolodex in the hospitality industry is extensive, for helping me recruit a true galaxy of eight distinguished speakers from around the world who could speak eloquently on this theme.

Below are the speakers' names and TEDx talk titles.

Joe Diaz
Title: *From Fear to Fearless: The Transformational Power of Travel*

Gerard Greene
Title: *Society: Building Flourishing Co Living*

Mark Harmon
Title: *The Soul of a Hotel*

Jerry Inzerillo
Title: *Global Trends In Luxury Hospitality*

Michael Keriakos
Title: *Why Luxury Hotels & Publishers Will Change Their Relationship*

Alex Cabañas
Title: *The Bar is So Low — The Realities of Memorable Service*

Bill Walshe
Title: *Business Ideology — A Roadmap Of Pride*

Bashar Wali
Title: *A Hotel is Just a Building*

All attendees at each event get a survey from TED via email after the event. Each event gets a score based on the Net Promoter Score. This event received a score of 89 — zero passives, 35 promoters and two detractors.

Below are some of the comments from audience members from this event and the scores they gave.

0: I did not think any of the talks were particularly enlightening or had anything much new to say. Some of the talks were downright disorganized and poorly done.

10: Amazing event! Great speakers! Excellent venue! Yummy lunch! Plenty of time to network! I thoroughly enjoyed it and have already recommended it to my colleagues.

4: The program was very well organized, despite a turnover of the ownership of the building the day before. The talks were interesting, and the pacing was just right.

9: I loved it and the only issue was Wilmington is not Philly or NYC where I can do more business aside while I make a trip. If it were in Philly, I'd have given it a 10. No offence Wilmington!

10: It was a more intimate and hip setting than most conferences or networking events; all of the talks were interesting and well presented; better opportunity to meet people in the same industry without it feeling forced; very well organized!

TEDxWilmington Event #20

6th Annual TEDxWilmington Conference
Theme: Limitless
August 16, 2017
The Queen
NPS: 85

We attracted literally hundreds of applications from around the world from potential speakers who wanted to give a TEDx talk at TEDxWilmington. Many were referred by past speakers or attendees. The process of choosing who to invite to give a TEDx talk at our 6th Annual TEDxWilmington Conference became much more formal and complicated than I ever imagined. We had a large group of TEDxWilmington tribe members to vet each application and watch the videos that were submitted with each application. At the end, we had so many interesting applicants that it was impossible to find a way to be totally objective, but we selected a collection of 35 speakers from as far away as Australia and throughout the United States.

To mention only 11 speakers is very dangerous, but I must take that risk and highlight the following speakers:

1. Marla Blunt-Carter spoke for less than six minutes, but anyone who sees her TEDx talk will never forget the message. Marla's sister and Delaware's lone member of Congress, the Hon. Lisa Blunt Rochester, was in the audience together with their parents to witness this deeply personal talk.
2. When I first met Shane Coen, I was totally blown away by his passion for his work as a landscape architect, and reached out to ask him if he had ever given a

TEDx talk. When I found he had not given a TEDx talk, I invited him on the spot and he did not disappoint.
3. Michael Martin's TEDx talk on how RapidSOS is working to provide life-saving health information for every 911 call is perhaps one of the best examples of an Idea Worth Spreading.
4. Cyndi O'Meara came from Australia to share her message about, "What's with Wheat?"
5. John Quinlan shared his journeys and lessons learned from being a rainforest CEO in Papua New Guinea.
6. Jennifer Simonetti-Bryan is among a small number of people to have received the highest credentials in the wine and spirits industry. She is one of only a few hundred people in the world to have achieved the Master of Wine (M.W.) title from The Institute of Masters of Wine in London, England, the highest and most difficult title to achieve in the industry. She did a blind tasting on stage with volunteers from the audience during her TEDx talk, which has attracted over 124,000 views.
7. Until John Legaré Williams gave his TEDx talk about Series LLC entities, I had no idea what they were. Now I am a big fan, and as a result Second Chances Farms is a Delaware Series LLC.
8. Andrew Wilson shared how Delawareans can shape worldwide care through telemedicine.
9. Tony Jeton Selimi came from London to give his TEDx talk, which has attracted over 388,000 views.
10. I will never forget Broadway star Glory Crampton, who shared her story of facing and overcoming overwhelming stage fright.
11. Vice President Joe Biden's only sister, Valerie Biden Owens, was a great storyteller.
12. Clint Rogers spoke about the, "Ancient Secrets of a Master Healer," and his TEDx talk has become number three in the number of views of all TEDxWilmington talks, with over 1.3 million views.

There were 35 speakers at this event. Below are the speakers' names and TEDx talk titles.

Michael Martin
Title: The Future of Data: Predicting & Preventing Emergencies *oul of a Hotel*

Michael Goergen
Title: *Using tiny bits of trees to save the forest*

Sara Crawford Jones
Title: *A Signature Pigment*

Tyrek Traylor
Title: *The Center*

Melissa Root
Title: *Eliminate Self-Doubt: Tap Your Root Response*

Dr. Edward Van Gieson
Title: *Create Like Einstein: Gratitude, Music & Meditation*

Dr. Clint Rogers
Title: *Ancient Secrets of a Master Healer: Deeper Healing Solutions from an Ancient Science*

Cory Budischak
Title: *Electricity in Self-Driving Vehicles Should Flow Both Ways*

Daniel Farber Huang and Theresa Menders
Title: *The Power of Faces: Looking at the Global Refugee Crisis*

Mason Jeffers
Title: *Limiting Labels*

John Legaré Williams
Title: *Series LLC: Stretching the Boundaries of Business Entity Innovation*

Bill Haley
Title: *Personalized Video- A Better Way to Engage with Your World*

Andrew Wilson
Title: *Telemedicine: How Delawareans Can Shape Worldwide Care*

Gustavo Grodnitsky
Title: *Culture Trumps Everything*

Glory Crampton
Title: *RELEASE STAGE FRIGHT — IGNITE UNLIMITED POSSIBILITIES*

Shane Coen
Title: *Contextual Design; Creating Connection and Calm*

Alton Bertie
Title: *How to Create an Industry*

Cyndi O'Meara
Title: *What's With Wheat*

Joia Jefferson Nuri
Title: *A Reimagined Fourth Estate*

Jennifer Simonetti-Bryan
Title: *Unlocking the Hidden Power of the Palate*

Rani St. Pucchi
Title: *Is Your Body Image Holding You Back*

Amanda Kemp
Title: *How to Have a Voice and Lean in to Conversations about Race and Racism*

Simon Mikhailovich
Title: *Safeguarding your money in uncertain times*

Andrew Vogts and Victor Furtado
Title: *An Innovative Twist On Appalachian Old Time Music*

Michele Pollard Patrick
Title: *Leveling the Playing Field — One Utensil at a Time*

Tony Jeton Selimi
Title: *Technological Armageddon: A Wake-Up Call*

Dinette Rivera
Title: *The Life-Saving Gift of Entrepreneurship*

Jason Treu
Title: *How to Get CoWorkers to Like Each Other*

Marla Blunt-Carter
Title: *The Importance of Being Color-Full: A Journey in Black & White*

Colleen O'Grady
Title: *Ticked-Off Teen Daughters & Stressed-Out Moms: 3 Keys to Dial Down the Drama*

John Quinlan
Title: *JOURNEY INTO VULNERABILITY — LESSONS FROM A RAINFOREST CEO*

Valerie Biden Owens
Title: *The Contribution Code: Three B's That Make All the Difference*

Janine Driver
Title: *THE COOPERATION PARADIGM — How talking like a hostage negotiator makes life easier for everyone*

All attendees at each event get a survey from TED via email after the event. Each event gets a score based on the Net Promoter Score. This event received a score of 85 — 70 passives, six promoters and three detractors.

Below are some of the comments from audience members at this event and the score they gave.

8: I liked it. It was informative and entertaining. It was an uplifting vibe.

0: Many topics not of interest.

10: The session was extremely well organized, allowing flexibility coming and going, along with a fairly diverse set of ideas. Very educational and entertaining.

5: Too long. Not sure enough time or space to actually talk to speakers. Expensive event to be seated in balcony.

10: Absolutely one of the interesting, informative and uplifting days that I can remember. I honestly think I learned more in one day than in years of other endeavors. Thank you for TEDxWilmington.

TEDxWilmington Event #21

TEDxWilmingtonSalon
Theme: Personal Finance. Community Results.
September 12, 2017
Gold Ballroom, Hotel DuPont
NPS:78

Anyone who has met Mary Dupont, who founded $tand By Me, knows she is a force to be reckoned with. After she gave a TEDx talk at the 5th Annual TEDxWilmington Conference, we became friends. With her help, I organized a TEDxWilmingtonSalon with the theme, "Personal Finance. Community Results," that covered a wide variety of subjects involving finances and wealth. I was proud to be associated with this event.

There were 13 speakers at this event. Below are the speakers' names and TEDx talk titles.

Alexandra Bastien
Title: *Courage Vs. Racial Wealth Gap*

Susan Getman and Anna Maria Chávez
Title: *No More Grandmas Eating Catfood*

Denise Freeman
Title: *Financial Empowerment Leading to Homeownership*

Luke Rhine and Shana Payne
Title: *Building Delaware's Talent Pipeline*

Kevin Gilmore
Title: *Financial Empowerment and Neighborhood Revitalization*

Jonathan Morduch
Title: *Steady Jobs Don't Mean Steady Pay*

Secretary Kara Odom Walker
Title: *Financial Health is Public Health*

Javier G. Torrijos
Title: *Latinos Overcoming Barriers Toward Financial Empowerment*

Whitney Williams and Irene Lee
Title: *The 3 C's of Financial Grit*

Mark LoGiudice
Title: *Financial Wellness Use of a Financial Coach*

All attendees at each event get a survey from TED via email after the event. Each event gets a score based on the Net Promoter Score. This event received a score of 78 — 47 passives, nine promoters and two detractors.

Below are some of the comments from audience members from this event and the score they gave.

10: TEDxWilmingtonSalon gave very informative and empowering information to all in attendance. I think anyone who participates in TEDx will leave with very valuable information.

10: It was great to hear local professionals share their stories. I didn't care for watching the recorded videos — doesn't seem like a good use of time in person, but totally enjoyed the presentations. We should showcase the good work of our state/city more often!

10: Presentations made me think outside of my normal routine. I not only enjoyed the talks, but I want to investigate topics in more detail and use the information provided in my work.

TEDxWilmington Event #22

TEDxWilmingtonSalon
Theme: Adulting 101: Your Path. Your Purpose.
September 19, 2017
The Mill Auditorium, Nemours Building
NPS:91

Kia Ervin Wiliams and Leah Coles had approached me with the idea for organizing two TEDxWilmingtonSalons showcasing TEDx talks that appealed to millennials. They helped identify topics that would attract millennials, and more importantly, speakers who would appeal to this generation. The first of these events was held in February and this was the second Salon that focused on talks that were geared to millennials.

There were five speakers at this event. Below are the speakers' names and TEDx talk titles.

Jullien Gordon
Title: *Mastermind Groups*

Dr. Myla Bennett
Title: *When Your Intuition Tells You that Enough is Not Enough*

Johniece Ray
Title: *#52weeksof30*

Wes Gay
Title: *Great Workplaces Look Like a Church, Not a Company*

Marcella Barker
Title: *The Transformative Power of Making*

All attendees at each event get a survey from TED via email after the event. Each event gets a score based on the Net Promoter Score. This event received a score of 91 — three passives, 32 promoters and zero detractors.

Below are some of the comments from audience members from this event and the score they gave.

10: Great speakers, inspiring content, well-organized program, cool venue.

10: I felt as if I was able to relate a lot to the speakers. What they said during their stories helped me understand some of the things that I am currently going through in my own life. I believe that everyone can gain something out of these talks.

TEDxWilmington
Event #23

TEDxWilmingtonSalon
Theme: Who's in the Driver's Seat:
The Transformation of Transportation
October 17, 2017
The Queen Wilmington
NPS: 83

Ken Grant is one of the most active members of the TEDxWilmington tribe and a well-respected member of our local community. When Ken approached me with the idea of doing a TEDxWilmingtonSalon centered on transportation, it was impossible to say no. I for one am intrigued by the notion of self-driving cars, and the majority of speakers spoke about various aspects of self driving cars, or smart cars. I was intrigued by David Woessner's talk about building cars locally and customizing them for each buyer.

What I have learned so far from organizing 23 TEDxWilmington events is that need to remain open-minded to new ideas that I have never heard of or ones that challenge all my fundamental assumptions. I now am looking forward to getting a self-driving car where I can nap, have a glass of wine or work without having to worry about driving anywhere. Let me know when this car is ready for pick up!

There were 13 speakers at this event. Below are the speakers' names and TEDx talk titles.

James Koenig
Title: **Navigating Privacy to Realize the Promise of Connected Cars**

Andreas Mai
Title: **A $5 Trillion Ticket: Funding the Future of Transportation**

Elan Nyer
Title: **Moving Towards a Connected and Safer Future**

Anya Babbitt and Yale Zhang
Title: **Getting there together —
Why Sharing is the Future**

Maureen Ohlhausen
Title: **Should Government Regulate Connected Cars**

Jennifer Cohan
Title: **Future Transportation Requires
a Governmental Leap of Faith**

Dr. Tom Dingus
Title: **Automated Vehicle (R)evolution**

John Ellis
Title: **Advertisers shape technology —
what that means for "smart" cars**

John Nielsen
Title: *Self Driving Cars, why we can't leave the driver behind*

Lauren Smith
Title: *What's Driving the Connected Cars*

David Silver
Title: *How Self-Driving Cars Work*

David C. Woessner
Title: *New Mobility: The Efficient Frontier?*

All attendees at each event get a survey from TED via email after the event. Each event gets a score based on the Net Promoter Score. This event received a score of 83 — 81 passives, 12 promoters and two detractors.

Below are some of the comments from audience members from this event and the score they gave.

10: It was a great event. The presentations were excellent. The crowd was engaged. The event was well organized and well run.

10: TEDxWilmington is an amazing opportunity to share ideas worth spreading in our local communities around the world. I have learned so much from watching TEDx talks. TEDxWilmington is the perfect stage for bringing great ideas to Wilmington as well as sharing Wilmington with the world!

5: The topic covered in transportation seemed to overlap tremendously about autonomous vehicles. There are so many aspects of vehicle autonomy that did not get discussed. Delivery vehicles right now in Colorado, taxi service in Pittsburgh, Pa. — these are where autonomy is going to be introduced to the masses and gain acceptance. It won't be pushed through purchasing autonomous vehicles. Where is the discussion on traffic and autonomous-only driving lanes? How does this impact the elderly and disabled community that needs assistance in and out of vehicles?

1: Way too lightweight. Sessions so short barely got much info.

TEDxWilmington Event #24

2nd Annual TEDxWilmingtonWomen
Theme: Bridge Builder
November 2, 2017
The Mill Auditorium, Nemours Building
NPS: 78

TED invited organizers to apply for a license to organize another TEDxWomen event, and when my application was approved, I decided to add three men to the roster of speakers. We had an overwhelming number of applications from a large list of potential speakers for this event, and we choose less than 15 percent of all the applicants.

I will highlight some of the 36 speakers below:

I learned about the amazing work that Joy McBrien was doing with Fair Anita, which was built on her vision where women and girls can grow up feeling safe, respected, and valued no matter their geography. In 2009, Joy set out to learn about violence against women in Peru, which has one of the highest rates of reported domestic violence in the world. During the months she spent building a women's shelter in Chimbote, Peru, Joy met many survivors of domestic violence and learned about their stories of survival and resilience. Each of these women expressed that jobs are the single most important resource for women experiencing domestic violence, knowing that sustainable income would help empower them to leave an abusive partner. Joy founded Fair Anita from the lessons she learned in Chimbote, and to this day her work remains grounded in supporting women's resilience through responsive business relationships. Please support their mission by buying products from Fair Anita and watch Joy's TEDx talk.

Margaret Joyce Tannian is another powerful woman who I have gotten to know well. She co-founded "Water Is Life Kenya" (WILK) about 11 years ago. She helps remote villages in Southern Kenya bring water close to home. WILK trains women and men how to benefit from their skills in raising cattle. They have a beaded handicraft division that helps artisans and their families immediately, and the profits go back into water projects. I encourage you to buy their beaded handicrafts at www.waterislifebeads.com and listen to Joyce sing Amazing Grace as she starts her TEDx talk.

A speaker who did not expect to get a standing ovation at the end of his talk was Erik Younger, whose powerful talk, entitled "Operation PTSD: Veterans Healing Themselves Through Meditation," left not a single dry eye in the room.

My red standard poodle HRH Maharani's favorite speaker was Joan Ranquet, whose talk entitled, "The Rainbow Bridge: Animals in Transition," touched anyone who lost a pet. Joan and HRH Maharani spent an hour privately communicating with each other and Joan shared her notes with us.

The oldest person ever to grace the TEDxWilmington stage was the irresistible Victoria Schmidt, who was over 90 years old when she shared "Victoria's Secrets to Control the Aging Process."

I will never forget Ria Story's gut wrenching TEDx talk on how she survived sexual abuse by her father by sharing her lessons on resilience.

One of the best examples of a PowerPoint presentation I have seen at any TEDxWilmington can be seen in the TEDx talk given by Dr. Daniel Lieberman.

I was sitting at my weekly Rotary meeting one day next to Joan DelFattore. She told me about what she was working on in her retirement, and I immediately invited her to apply to give a TEDx talk. Her TEDx talk, entitled, "Sick While Single? Don't Die of Discrimination," got coverage in the *Washington Post*.

The TEDx talks of four speakers from this event have each attracted over 400,000 views and are among the most viewed TEDx talks from TEDxWilmington. They are Kalliope Barlis, Dr. Sheryl Ziegler, Rita Wilkins and Annie White. If you want to learn more about how their ideas worth spreading attracted so many views, please watch them.

Without any risk of contradiction, I can state that one of my favorite TEDxWilmington speakers is Diana Simone, the founder of the Amber Alert that has saved so many children who were abducted. Diana is one of the most low key people you will ever meet. I am thrilled to share her inspiring story with the world on the TEDx platform.

I would be remiss if I didn't highlight Dr. Sarah E. Brown's second TEDx talk, which is entitled, "What My Job Taught Me about Finding a Romantic Relationship." Even though our last names are different and many people don't realize we are a couple, we have been married since 1995. Even though my name or picture never shows up in her talk, you now know who she is taking about.

There were 36 speakers at this event. Below are the speakers' names and TEDx talk titles.

Rita Chang
Title: *Redesigning Our Future*

Anna Gatmon
Title: *You Can Eat Your Cake and Have Enlightenment Too*

Annie White
Title: *Why Ms. Independent Can't find Mr. Right*

Joy McBrien
Title: *How Women Rise*

Darnyelle Jervey-Harmon
Title: *Burn the Box; Shift Your Life*

Gabriela Pereira
Title: *Creativity is a Craft and it Belongs to Everyone*

Andrea Tinianow
Title: *The Power of Making Connections*

Brenda K. Reynolds
Title: *Navigating Transition Fog*

Victoria Schmidt
Title: *Take Control of the Aging Process with Victoria's Secrets*

Ellen Moyer
Title: *Nine Reasons for Hope in a World Out of Whack*

Mitchell Walker
Title: *Money, The Magic Multiplier*

Tonya Fitzpatrick
Title: *Finding Truth in an Uncertain World*

Madi Still
Title: *Using Pain as a Bridge to Discovering Your Purpose*

Alexia Vernon
Title: *A New Paradigm for Feminism*

Rita Wilkins
Title: *Downsize Your Life: Why Less is More*

Sarah E. Brown
Title: *What my Job Taught Me about Finding a Romantic Relationship*

KK Hart
Title: *F-IT: Life Hacks to Get Your FIT Together*

Margaret Joyce Tannian
Title: *Singing Water out of the Ground in Kenya*

Dana Dobson
Title: *Delusional Self-Promotion: The Bridge from Ego to Empathy*

Cindy Bo
Title: *Business Lessons Learned by Age Five, From My Immigrant Parents*

Erik Younger
Title: *Operation PTSD: Veterans Healing Themselves Through Meditation*

Tanya Barnett
Title: *I Found Myself When I Lost My Hair*

Ria Story
Title: *Bridges out of the Past: A Survivor's Lessons on Resilience*

Yolanda Schlabach
Title: *Life After Trafficking: The Bridge from Trauma to Triumph*

Dr. Rose G. Maina
Title: *Could There be a Pedophile Hiding in Your Family Tree?*

Kalliope Barlis
Title: *Phobia Relief: From Fear to Freedom*

Jennifer Myers
Title: *Don't Tell Me What You Did Wrong, Tell Me What You Do Right*

Dr. Daniel Lieberman
Title: *DOPAMINE: Driving Your Brain into the Future*

Diana Simone
Title: *Amber Alert: The Power of Response-Ability*

Maureen Bridget Rabotin
Title: *The Culture of Fear: Facing it with Courage and Curiosity*

Joan Ranquet
Title: *The Rainbow Bridge, Animals in Transition*

Christy Whitman
Title: *You and Your Life are Unlimited*

Joan DelFattore
Title: *Sick While Single? Don't Die of Discrimination*

Allison Ford
Title: *Why Strong People Finish Last*

Tamsen Webster
Title: *How to Bridge a Mental Gap*

Dr. Sheryl Ziegler
Title: *Why Moms are Miserable*

All attendees at each event get a survey from TED via email after the event. Each event gets a score based on the Net Promoter Score. This event received a score of 78 — 67 passives, 10 promoters and four detractors.

Below are some of the comments from audience members from this event and the score they gave.

6: There were far too many presentations and they lost impact by the afternoon. Very few talks stood out by that point; they were mostly sounding similar. I think a half-day would be great without being tiresome. More time needs to be planned for overages in speech times. There was also very little information on the front end of the event, like where to park, was lunch and refreshments included (what the $100 registration fee includes), no signage downstairs in the venue to direct you.

10: Some of the talks were so personal, I related so well with many of them. My circle of friends could benefit from the information the TEDx talks provided. The event was a great experience.

10: Life changing, inspiring, uplifting, motivating.

0: Ajit was much more attentive to the three men who participated. This should not have happened at an event for women. I know he will feel defensive about this comment.

10: It forces you to up your game with speaking, including speaking from memory, communicating something very important to you in just several minutes, and using body language effectively. Plus, you get to hear some amazing talks and meet great people!

10: Touching, real, inspirational and well organized.

10: The TEDxWilmingtonWomen experience was extraordinary. I would absolutely recommend it to others. I came from NJ with a group of nine other attendees. We were overly excited on the two-hour ride home. The speakers shared substantive content. The talks were inspiring, uplifting, motivating, educational, humorous and fun. I will do this again. I will invite others to participate.

TEDxWilmington Event #25

TEDxWilmingtonSalon
Theme: Technology and Innovation
November 28, 2017
The Mill Auditorium, Nemours Building
NPS: 80

When I first met Todd DeCapua, his business card stated that he was chief technology evangelist at Hewlett-Packard Enterprise and was commuting every week from Wilmington, Delaware to California. He was the source of inspiration for my organizing this TEDxWilmingtonSalon with the theme, "Technology and Innovation." Todd hosted this Salon, which featured a diverse collection of topics and speakers, including one from the United Kingdom and one from Israel.

I found Taha Abassi's TEDx talk on "Saving Lives with Blockchain" enlightening. It was fascinating to listen to Patrick Callahan's talk on chasing big data. Nissan Yaron, who is based in Israel, gave us a glimpse on what the future might hold regarding who should be the driver in the car.

There were 14 speakers at this event. Below are the speakers' names and TEDx talk titles.

Carlson Bull
Title: *How Holographic Training Can Help You Master Your Game*

Patrick Callahan
Title: *Chasing Big Data: My 6,000 Mile Journey to Find It*

Erica Nemser
Title: *Advanced Materials…
The New Innovation Area?*

Froilan Miranda
Title: *Are We the Robots?*

Alison Satkowski Vernamonti
Title: *How Potty Training is Like
Software Deployment*

Nissan Yaron
Title: *Iron Man or J.A.R.V.I.S, Who
Should be the Driver in the Car?*

Taha Abassi
Title: *Saving Lives with Blockchain*

Bill Jensen
Title: *Our Disruptive Tech Legacy:
Facing Difficult Truths*

Kjell Hegstad
Title: **The $100 POC & Prototype Innovation Lab**

John Jeremiah
Title: **Leading Digital**

Dion Kenney
Title: **Sociocultural Development and the Information Revolution**

Jonathon Wright
Title: **Cognitive Learning- 'Digital Evolution, Over Revolution'**

Dr. Setrag Khoshafian
Title: **How Culture Always Trumps Technology**

John Moore
Title: **Funding Our Schools: Turning Ivory Towers into Community Power**

All attendees at each event get a survey from TED via email after the event. Each event gets a score based on the Net Promoter Score. This event received a score of 80 — 48 passives, five promoters and three detractors.

Below are some of the comments from audience members from this event and the score they gave.

10: Great content, ability to connect with the speakers and other attendees.
10: The networking and the information were priceless.

3: I found the majority of speakers did not articulate "ideas worth sharing."

10: It's an opportunity to hear about new ideas worth understanding.

9: I enjoyed the experience and was engaged with the speakers. My only issue is that each speaker has such limited time to explore his or her respective topics.

10: The environment and energy in the room whether it is during the talk or intermission is very warm, however vibrant with opportunities to talk with phenomenal people who are experts and game changers in their respective industries.

TEDxWilmington Event #26

TEDxWilmingtonSalon
Theme: The Meaning of Leadership
December 5, 2017
The Soda House, Hagley Museum
NPS: 100

The three speakers chosen for this TEDxWilmington event truly embodied the theme, "The Meaning of Leadership." None of the speakers needed to give a TEDx talk, but they each choose to be vulnerable while adding humor as appropriate.

Below are the speakers' names and TEDx talk titles.

Chris F. Buccini and Dana Dobson
Title: *Title: How to Lead a Team When Everyone Thinks You're Crazy*

Michelle D. Freeman
Title: *Finding Healing and Purpose Through Service*

Michael D. Hankin
Title: *Speak Up. Where It Counts. Loudly.*

All attendees at each event get a survey from TED via email after the event. Each event gets a score based on the Net Promoter Score. This event received a score of 100 — zero passives, six promoters and 0 detractors.

Below are some of the comments from audience members from this event and the score they gave.

> **9:** It was the first TEDx talk I've attended, and it was spectacular. All of the talks were inspirational, and the speakers come across as passionate, sincere and emotional about their topics that they choose to speak about. I can't wait to attend the next TEDx event.

TEDxWilmington Event #27

TEDxWilmingtonSalon
Theme: Bridging Communities
Through Innovation
December 14, 2017
Route 9 Library and Innovation Center
NPS: 88

The Route 9 Library and Innovation Center is a beautiful new building that is located within an economically depressed area. Jessica Gibson, who gave a TEDx talk at the 1st Annual TEDxWilmingtonWomen Conference in 2016, wanted to organize an event in this new building, in part to demonstrate that TEDxWilmington events can be held anywhere and be open to anyone. The theme that was chosen for this event was, "Bridging Communities Through Innovation." It was the basis on which I selected the diverse group of 12 speakers to give TEDx talks at this sold out event.

Below are the speakers' names and TEDx talk titles.

Jason Aviles
Title: *Am I a Social Entrepreneur?*

Trevor Brown
Title: *Sustainable Medication Disposal*

Srinidhi Krishnaumurthy
Title: *Empowering Others Through Machine Learning*

Sean Douglas
Title: *Hack Your Brain for Success*

Nia Naylor
Title: *Finding a Different World*

Will Latif Little
Title: *How to Become the Very BEST Version of Yourself*

Trishtan Sapphire
Title: *Remove Those Negative Mental Blocks!*

Carolyn Bennett-Sullivan
Title: *Driving Innovation Through Curiosity*

Rob Bentley
Title: *Recoding the Community Through 140 Lives*

Jacqueline Means
Title: *STEM: Today's girls, Tomorrow's scientists*

Kalvin J. Evans
Title: *Social Media Becoming Second Best for Our Youth*

Dr. Jalaal A. Hayes
Title: *The Chemistry of Community Building*

All attendees at each event get a survey from TED via email after the event. Each event gets a score based on the Net Promoter Score. This event received a score of 88 — 45 passives, two promoters and two detractors.

Below are some of the comments from audience members from this event and the score they gave.

10: There were a few talks that gave me goose bumps. Talks that inspired me to make changes within myself. Talks that made me challenge the way I'd been looking at the world around me. I think these are valuable and precious moments that I will treasure for as long as I have the ability to remember them. Thank you TEDxWilmington for providing this access to experience these ideas and stories.

3: Staff was a bit tough. Room dynamics (video guy in the back kept talking). After clicking 3, I'd really say 5. I know it's a ton of work to do these things, and I'm grateful for the organizers and volunteers. There's just lots of room for improvement in many areas.

10: I found the speakers to be informative and delightful. Even the short films were good. The topics were very interesting, and the evening flowed. I would definitely come again and recommend the salon to my friends and colleagues. I did tell them how good the event was I attended.

TEDxWilmington Event #28

TEDxWilmingtonSalon
Theme: Fireside
December 21, 2017
The Delaware Historical Society
NPS: 82

Over the years, I have gotten to know Geoffrey Berwind well and I respect him as a great speaker coach. He is first and foremost a fabulous storyteller, which is why he and I discussed the idea of co-producing a TEDxWilmingtonSalon on Winter Solstice with the theme of Fireside. Stories used to be told by the fireside, and we invited 11 speakers who were considered great storytellers. The TEDx talk given by Steve Harrison, who is truly a gifted storyteller, attracted over 400,000 views, making it one of the most viewed TEDx talks given at TEDxWilmington. I give Geoffrey all the credit for the success of this sold out event, which was held in a new venue.

When this event ended, I could not believe that I had in fact organized 12 separate events in 2017, with three events in December. The pace of events and the number of speakers were simply hard to imagine in retrospect. I had no reason to repeat this level of insanity in 2018, which I considered would likely be my final year as an organizer in the TEDx community.

Below are the speakers' names and TEDx talk titles.

James Barnes
Title: *Missing Conversations*

Carolyn Coal
Title: *The Seeds of Creativity*

Doug Lipman
Title: *What Can Storytelling Teach Us About Creating Connection?*

Cari Feiler Bender
Title: *How to Make Your Story THE BIG STORY*

Carol Spacht
Title: *Being Betsy: Why Living History Matters*

Eric Okdeh
Title: *Art By All*

Noa Baum
Title: *Beyond Labels: Bridging Differences Through Storytelling*

Steve Harrison
Title: *How to Sell Without Selling Your Soul*

Charlotte Blake Alston
Title: *EHSOTI: Standing On Tradition*

Peter Hillard and Nicholas Hillard
Title: *Music: A Gift Best Given In Person*

A Journey Through All 32 TEDxWilmington Events

All attendees at each event get a survey from TED via email after the event. Each event gets a score based on the Net Promoter Score. This event received a score of 82 — 31 passives, seven promoters and zero detractors.

Below are some of the comments from audience members from this event and the score they gave.

10: The speakers were excellent. I appreciated the diverse panel and the knowledge they imparted. Each person's presentation was well-executed and kept my complete attention.

10: Wow! What an awesome experience! I was moved to tears. I also wanted to stand on top of a table and cheer on speakers. Loved all the emotions! I'll be back!

10: I think of TEDx talks as being the art of storytelling. It was great to hear so many great storytellers give TEDx talks.

TEDxWilmington Event #29

TEDxWilmingtonED
Theme: Education Possible
February 9, 2018
Gold Ballroom, Hotel DuPont
NPS: 77

I got to know Atnre Alleyne when he gave a TEDx talk at a TEDxWilmingtonSalon on December 6, 2016. Atnre is the founder and executive director of the Delaware Campaign for Achievement Now (DelawareCAN). In this role, he works to improve the quality of education in the state through the enactment of student-centered policies. At Atnre's urging, I applied for a new license from TED. Atnre served as the chairman of the speaker selection committee and worked very closely with me to organize TEDxWilmingtonED with 28 diverse speakers, all of whom talked about some aspect of education.

Michael Phillips gave a very engaging TEDx talk entitled, "When Kids Learn on Broken Chairs," which has attracted about 250,000 views, making it one of the top 20 TEDx talks given on the TEDxWilmington red carpet.

Below are the speakers' names and TEDx talk titles.

Ashley Berner
Title: *No One Way to School: Education Pluralism and Why it Matters*

Tatiana Poladko
Title: *Education's Well-Intentioned People Problem*

Vincent Cobb
Title: Black Male Educators Matter

Melissa Benbow
Title: The Princeton You Won't See in the Brochure

Melissa Corto
Title: Compliance is NOT Enough

Jordan Estock
Title: Authenticity Matters

Stephanie Diggins
Title: *#BeATeacher: Inside the Teacher Academy Initiative*

Lindsay Hill
Title: *Rebuilding the Inequitable Foundation of America*

Robyn Howton
Title: *The Key to Improving Schools is Already in the Classroom*

Ernest Hudson
Title: *Food and Education: A "Soup"er Connection*

Ross Kasun
Title: *Old School Does Not Work, So Let's Change What We Do Today*

Jason Lange
Title: *Is College Still Worth it*

Kendall Massett
Title: *How a Hospitality Mindset Can Set the Table for Learning*

Lisa Mims
Title: *The Power of a Caring Educator*

Lindsay Page
Title: *Proactively Supporting Students To and Through College*

Jessica Phillippe and Freire's Inferno Performance Team
Title: *Finesse the System*

Michael Phillips
Title: *When Kids Learn on Broken Chairs*

Jessica Santana
Title: *Tech Geniuses Can Come from Anywhere*

Benjamin Riley
Title: *The (Emerging) Science of Learning Organizations*

Ron Russo
Title: *Education is a Business*

Elaine Wells
Title: *Why The Fight is Never Over*

Marilyn Rhames
Title: *Why Faith Will Fix Education*

Sheila Sarem
Title: *The Social Capital Gap*

All attendees at each event get a survey from TED via email after the event. Each event gets a score based on the Net Promoter Score. This event received a score of 77 — 99 passives, 18 promoters and five detractors.

Below are some of the comments from audience members from this event and the score they gave.

10: It was an opportunity to hear from amazing education leaders about what's working and what's not working and how to move forward. I was truly inspired, and it encouraged me to find my voice in the conversation of education reform.

10: The speakers, content, and venue were amazing! Each speaker directly related to education in some form or another. What a diverse group, each an expert in their own right. And let's not forget about networking.

10: The hotel accommodations were outstanding. The participants and the subject of education stirred our hearts. The warmth of the MC/founder was caring and compassionate.

6: I don't think the day was structured well — there was no time to process throughout the day. I am also thinking about, "now what?" Additionally, I wish there were more Delaware speakers. Overall, good day!

8: This was a great event. I think the 8-5 format is a bit long for most people. Hard to take time from work and also hard to focus at the same level for so long.

TEDxWilmington Event #30

TEDxWilmingtonLive
Theme: Age of Amazement
April 28, 2018
Friends School
NPS: 97

For the first time since 2012 when we hosted our first event, TED invited its organizers to apply to organize an event in conjunction with TED's 2018 Annual Conference in Vancouver. In consideration of getting this license, we were required to live stream one session from TED's main stage. We had over 300 applications from around the world from people who wanted to give a TEDx talk at TEDxWilmington. Using the theme, "Age of Amazement," we were able to select a great group of speakers.

I will mention the following speakers, whose TEDx talks I will encourage you to watch if you need some recommendations:

1. Theresa Bodnar's talk on the "Gift of Gratitude in Foresight" resonated with me.
2. I loved how Sarah Greenfield was able to use humor to get our attention in her TEDx talk entitled "Does Your Poop Hold the Secret to Your Health?" I wanted to give poop sample kits as take home gifts, but my team persuaded me that this was in poor taste.
3. I first met Amy Ogden when she came from New York to attend as a paying guest at TEDxWilmingtonSalon in 2017. She and I became friends and had dinner in New York. She shared with me her story, which prompted me to invite her to apply. Her TEDx talk, entitled, "Sufficiency is Sexy. The Rest is Just

House Money," is worth watching. Amy is smart and engaging.

4. Having trained and mentored over 40,000 business leaders in multiple organizations, Jeff Patnaude has been described as the "Leonard Bernstein of leadership development," and gained an international reputation for his ability to orchestrate environments for transformation.

5. If you lived or live in the Delaware Valley and have followed the Philadelphia Phillies, you will be familiar with their mascot called the Philly Phanatic. David Raymond was the original Philly Phanatic and his TEDx talk required us to get approval from Major League Baseball, which owns all the rights of videos of most, if not all, Major League games.

6. John Livesay's talk, entitled, "Be the Lifeguard of Your Own Life," quickly hit over 100,000 views and is now our fourth most watched video in TEDxWilmington history, with over 1,120,000 views.

7. If you have only time to watch one TEDx talk from this event, I would like to persuade you to watch Alessandra Nicole's heartfelt talk entitled, "The Power of Paper Letter Exchange," and I cannot imagine your not being motivated to write a handwritten letter to someone.

There were 35 speakers at this event. Below are the speakers' names and TEDx talk titles.

Chase Reid
Title: *Can A.I. Save Humanity's Soul?*

Christophe Jelinski
Title: *The Cost of Paying Attention*

Sunil Robert
Title: *The Comeback: Rebound When Adversity Knocks You Down*

Terri Levine
Title: *How To Create Happiness and Success At Work*

Amy Ogden
Title: *Sufficiency is sexy. The rest is just house money.*

John Livesay
Title: *Be The Lifeguard of Your Own Life!*

Jody Wood
Title: *Improv-ing Lives Through Improv*

Bonnie St. John
Title: *Be More Resilient with a FIRST AID KIT FOR YOUR ATTITUDE*

Alessandra Nicole
Title: *The Power of Paper Letter Exchange*

Zachary Jones
Title: *Unlocking the Hidden Potential of High School Students*

Laura Wellington
Title: *What's She Got That I Don't?*

Tiffany Stallings
Title: *Unleash the Mom Guilt*

Jeff Patnaude
Title: *From Great to the Greater Good: When Great is Not Good Enough*

Sarah Greenfield
Title: *Does Your Poop Hold the Secret to Your Health?*

Millicent St. Clair
Title: *The Liberation of Human Genius*

Robin Burk
Title: *Countering Collapse of Our Interconnected, Interdependent World*

Aaron Shepard
Title: *Make America Space Again*

Massoma Alam
Title: *Go Spaghetti: Overcoming Anxiety*

Theresa Bodnar
Title: *The GIFT of Gratitude in Foresight*

Katherine Von Duyke
Title: *Why Do Urban Schools Rely on Discipline Rather Than on Democracy?*

LeslieBeth Wish
Title: *You Can't Always Trust Your Gut When it Comes to Dating and Mating*

Taria Pritchett
Title: *The Magic in Empowering Black Girls*

David Raymond
Title: *Be The Phanatic and Be Happier Now!*

Paul Dixon
Title: *Adults Let's Have Fun Playing with Your Favorite Childhood Toy*

Marie White
Title: *My Child was Abducted: How Branding Made My Family Heal*

Patsie McCandless
Title: *Saving the Magic of Childhood*

Allan Ting
Title: *How to Bounce Back from Burnout in 3 Simple Steps*

Dr. Felicia Clark
Title: *Pink Tax and the BS in Beauty Standards*

Renée Jones
Title: *Lose Weight AND Keep it Off: Emotional Eating*

Robert J. Ward, Jr.
Title: *The Importance of Effective Economic Sanctions*

Kate Kirkwood
Title: *Why You Should Worry About Lead Poisoning in NEW Homes*

Clarence E. Davis, PhD, L.C.P.C.
Title: *Preventing Suicide: Three Things Never to Do!*

Dan Casey
Title: *The Retirement Remedy: The Plan to Make Your Nest Egg Last*

Christine Upchurch
Title: *Feeling Like an Outsider: Embracing the Hidden Gifts*

Olivia O'Donnell
Title: *Changing the Narrative: Why Racism Continues to Plague the U.S.*

All attendees at each event get a survey from TED via email after the event. Each event gets a score based on the Net Promoter Score. This event received a score of 97 — 57 passives, two promoters and zero detractors.

Below are some of the comments from audience members from this event and the scores they gave.

10: Every TEDxWilmington event I attend has helpful and friendly staff, good food, and great talks. It's nearly impossible to verbally describe the energy of our local TEDx community. The word I use most is "exhilarating!"

10: This is a great way to get ideas across to a captivated global audience. The support along the journey was incredible as was the camaraderie during rehearsal, the rehearsal dinner, and of course the day of the TEDx event. To be exposed to so many wonderful people with wonderful ideas and stories to tell that were truly inspirational was a gift. This was absolutely a life changing experience for me!

10: It is evident how hard the TEDx tribe works to create a diverse, educational event that impacts the audience as well as makes its speakers feel supported.

TEDxWilmington Event #31
7th Annual TEDxWilmington Conference
Theme: NOW WHAT?
September 27, 2018
Bellevue State Park, Figure 8 Barn
NPS: 88

I wanted to make this event extra special, as it was most likely going to be my last TEDxWilmington Conference. My good friend, Mindy Tatz Chernoff, wanted to give a second TEDx talk with her favorite horse. None of the previous venues we had used would allow a horse on stage. I remembered attending an event at the Figure 8 Barn at Bellevue State Park, which was previously a beautiful Du Pont family estate. Mindy was thrilled to have the Figure 8 Barn, which was originally a horse barn.

To do a live stream from the Figure 8 Barn was very tricky, as there was no internet available. We were very blessed to have someone, who shall remain anonymous, donate everything we needed to do a Facebook Live broadcast of all the TEDx talks given from the Barn.

Barns were not designed to have speakers whose talks were being videotaped with three cameras. Getting the proper staging, lighting and sound required a lot of planning. Serving lunch and refreshments, taking into account all the dietary requirements, was very important. In the end, the venue was truly very special.

We had over 250 applications to choose from, and overall, the quality of the potential speakers and topics were great.

In addition to Mindy and her horse, who almost stole the entire show as the "Opening Act," there were several other TEDx speakers that require a special mention:

1. Akeem Lennard Jr. and Dr. Michael A. Turnbull came from the British Virgin Islands to give impassioned TEDx talks.
2. Dr. Monique Rainford's revealing talk on America's Maternal Nightmare.
3. Dr. Michelle Yep Martin's talk on, "Moving from Porn to Meaningful Connections."
4. Dr. Paul Rosen's TEDx talk on, "What I Learned from 100,000 Doctors."
5. Markevis Gideon's talk, "Finding Your China."
6. Richard Lackey's "Zero Hunger Formula."
7. Cassandra Pavolic's dramatic start of her talk as she shows what an aerialist can do by artfully climbing a piece of fabric from the floor to the ceiling, and then talking about lessons from a circus aerialist. Just breathtaking.
8. Sean Kennedy's talk on "Happy Accidents: Drumming up Serendipity."
9. Linda Tucker, who came from South Africa to talk about "Ignite Your Lionheart — I Speak for the Lion!" was greeted by a standing ovation at the end of her TEDx talk, with no dry eyes in the audience.

I can honestly say that I didn't want to see the event end, but the good news is that the British Virgin Islands Tourist Board hosted a reception at the end and served delicious painkillers to all the guests.

There were 32 speakers at this event. Below are the speakers' names and TEDx talk titles.

Sara Blanchard
Title: *How to be Happier: Ask Better Questions*

Richard Lackey
Title: *Zero Hunger Formula*

George Pagano
Title: *Rowing the Atlantic to Face Life's Challenges*

Colleen Cowles
Title: *The War on Drugs & Myths About Addiction Are Killing Our Kids*

Jodi Aman
Title: *Suck it up! Calm Anxious Kids with Simple Chores*

Errol Ebanks
Title: *A Cloud Full Of Memories*

Jennifer Behm-Lazzarini
Title: *Even Beauty Queens Get Dumped*

Gerald Leonard
Title: *What if Performance is the Performance: Falling In Love with Practice*

Cassandra Pavolic
Title: *Courage To Let Go: Life Lessons from a Circus Aerialist*

Susanne Birgersdotter
Title: *Pivotal Moments*

Dr. Wendy Leonard
Title: *Zebrafish: Practically People — How to Save the Human Species*

Phillip J. Roundtree
Title: *Black Mental Health Matters*

Dr. Monique Rainford
Title: *America's Maternal Nightmare*

Dr. Michael A. Turnbull
Title: *Live With the End in Mind*

Andrew Gabelic
Title: *Want Your Dream Job? A 21st Century Formula*

Akeem Lennard Jr.
Title: *Surviving Your Personal Hurricane*

Brandon Blackburn-Dwyer
Title: *Embrace Your Inner Millennial*

Sean J. Kennedy
Title: *Happy Accidents: Drumming up Serendipity*

Markevis Gideon
Title: *Find Your China*

Seth Rainess
Title: *Want to be a Real Man? Express Yourself!*

Dr. Michelle Yep Martin
Title: *Moving from porn to meaningful connections*

Adebisi Adebowale
Title: *Education for All*

Linda Tucker
Title: *Ignite YOUR LionHeart — I speak for the Lion!*

Mindy Tatz Chernoff
Title: *Love, Connection, and a Horse*

Glen Dunzweiler
Title: Small Business Homeless

Rod Wallace
Title: Meaningful Profit: When Business Solves Society's Big Problems

George Chanos
Title: Think & Thrive: A 21st Century Mindset

Carlyn Montes De Oca
Title: Life-Changing Powers of the Animal-Human Health Connection

Lisa Cuesta
Title: The Capital You Don't Find on the Balance Sheet

Johnny Gillespie
Title: Move out of Pain, Defining Functional Movement

Dr. Paul Rosen
Title: What I learned from 100,000 doctors

Paul B. Redman
Title: Seeing Beauty to Save Our Global Garden

All attendees at each event get a survey from TED via email after the event. Each event gets a score based on the Net Promoter Score. This event received a score of 88 — 70 passives, five promoters and two detractors.

Below are some of the comments from audience members from this event and the scores they gave.

8: The topics were interesting. The seating was not comfortable for that long a period of time.

10: The presentations were fascinating, with a diversity of topics that really make you think. Higher education was treated from a realistic and yet motivational standpoint, not just the usual happy fluff everyone should go to college for free speech, other topics were handled from similar perspectives where we were imbued with a true interest and not just being spoken to. Thoroughly enjoyed and was enlightened by TEDx!

10: It is the most organized and the most well run TEDx operation happening!

10: Going to TEDxWilmington was an amazing experience, especially for me as a student. I believe that it is a good place to go and see public speakers to inspire students who need to speak publicly for a class or assessment. Also, the messages were extremely interesting, educational, and inspiring!

3: It was in a barn.

6: Expensive and time intensive.

10: This was an amazing experience, awesome venue and the most organized event I have attended.

10: This was an incredibly well run event. On time, great speakers, fun, engaging. It was unique, and I loved the horse!

10: I was exposed to so many fascinating ideas and concepts — and to see a horse, gymnastics, and musicians throughout the day was incredible!

TEDxWilmington Event #32

3rd Annual TEDxWilmingtonWomen
Theme: Showing Up
November 30, 2018
The Mill Auditorium, Nemours Building
NPS: 81

Even though I hadn't publicly announced my retirement as the founding organizer of TEDxWilmington, I knew this would be most likely my final TEDxWilmington event. I invited Jake Voorhees and Alessandra Nicole to help me introduce one or more speakers to begin an orderly transition without any formal notice.

With over 400 applications to choose from, I was blessed to have a lot of choices for speakers.

I have selected 12 speakers for special recognition for reasons that are truly personal to me. I encourage you to view all the other 15 TEDx talks and make your own favorite list :

Linda Arrey-Mbi Nkwenti
Renae Baker
Mandy Bass
Nicole Black
Tiffany Gwilliam
Dave Nassaney

Mike O'Krent
Gudrun Penselin
Karen Pilgrim
Cheryl Rice
Lauri Robbins Ericson
Cyrus Rosen

I have shared Cyrus Rosen's thank you note to me after this event earlier in this book as the perfect way for me commemorate my final event.

There were 27 speakers at this event. Below are the speakers' names and TEDx talk titles.

Michelle Nagel
Title: *The True Secret to Happiness is Learning to ROAR*

Linda Arrey-Mbi Nkwenti
Title: *The Mistake of Waiting to Live in Fulfillment*

Karen Pilgrim
Title: *Visionboard vs Actionboard: Vision of me, who do you see*

Dr. Patrick Wright
Title: *How our Parents Screw Us Up*

Gudrun Penselin
Title: *Flowers that Heal Us*

Jaya Jaya Myra Godfrey
Title: *Is Living Your Purpose the Key to Better Health and Wellbeing?*

Mandy Bass
Title: *How to Build Your Courage Muscle*

Dominick Quartuccio
Title: *The Bold Journey Women Want Men to Take*

Tiffany Gwilliam
Title: *Women with Grit vs. The Third Leading Cause of Death*

David Nassaney
Title: *Caregivers Must Be Selfish To Survive*

Susan O'Malley
Title: *How Beauty Secrets Turned into Secret Weapons*

Frankie Bonilla
Title: *From Consumer to Creator That is Where the Brilliance Lies*

Jen Kluczkowski
Title: *Can Mindfulness Save the Earth?*

Ellie Laks
Title: *My Gentle Barn: Learning to Listen to Animals*

Susan Bremer O'Neill
Title: *Self Appeal, not Sex Appeal to Embrace Your Sexual Body*

Dr. Kien Vuu
Title: *The Unconventional Prescription: YOU are your Best Medicine*

Nicole Black
Title: *Conscious Uncoupling: How to Have a Mindful Divorce*

Chris Johnson
Title: *Attacking Urban Gun Violence*

Cynthia Dougherty
Title: *Fake News: The Lies Our Brains Tell Us*

Lauri Robbins Ericson
Title: *Shifting Gender Paradigms: Speak Up, Stand Up, Rise Up*

Renae Baker
Title: *Can Caroling Lead to World Peace?*

Mike O'Krent
Title: *How conversations with loved ones alter the path of our future*

Cyrus Rosen
Title: *Connection is Part of the Cure*

Janesha Bull
Title: *How Asking For Help Can Help Depression*

Monica LeSage
Title: *Does Somatic Experiencing (SE) Work? SE practices for healing*

Cheryl Rice
Title: *You Matter: Changing the World with Two Words*

Shavon Lindley
Title: *Disrupting Exclusionary Behavior*

All attendees at each event get a survey from TED via email after the event. Each event gets a score based on the Net Promoter Score. This event received a score of 81 — 58 passives, five promoters and four detractors.

Below are some of the comments from audience members from this event and the scores they gave.

5: The speakers were terrific, but the venue was not. Poor acoustics, no place to network easily, and the food was awful. I watched a volunteer cut a giant sub with a pair of scissors without any gloves on. Boxed lunches, a place to sit outside the speaking area so you could decompress and talk to others would have made all the difference!

10: The experience was like no other. The vast depth of each speaker was phenomenal, and the love and passion expressed was unmatched to any speaking event that I have previously attended. Thank you for such a remarkable event. The speakers were both easily and readily accessible as well as kind and generous with their time.

10: Fantastic support team; Ajit's warm, friendly and joyful nature and his ability to create such comfortable, positive and encouraging environment; positive support team including coaches; inclusion of rehearsal day; making services of make-up artist available; it is rare to be in an environment that is filled with so much positivity and hope. Hats off to everyone involved!

0: You need a new organizer. Ajit playing favorites, not managing time, and making comments about Jake, women, and their shoes was completely unprofessional.

8: Organization is a bit challenging. Those at the front desk assumed everyone coming in knew where to go/what to do. Giving directions like "go in there" isn't helpful to the new person who still seemed confused. However, they were abrupt in my view and could be a little more accommodating as they are in some other locations.

CHAPTER 6

Speakers Impact from TEDxWilmington

Curated by Dana Dobson

The following are speakers' answers to a survey we sent them prior to the writing of this book, asking four questions:

1. In one paragraph not to exceed 150 words, please share your experience on your way to the red carpet at TEDxWilmington.

2. If you could give your TEDx talk again, is there anything you would do differently (not to exceed 150 words).

3. In one paragraph not to exceed 150 words, please share your experiences after you gave your TEDx talk and your video was approved and posted on YouTube. For example, did you get any more publicity or additional speaking engagements? Did your TEDx talk have an impact on making your idea into reality?

4. Last but not least, please share in one paragraph not to exceed 150 words, your words of wisdom, based on your personal experience, to someone who might be thinking of sharing their idea worth spreading through a TEDx talk.

If you have already given a TEDx talk, then reading these answers may make you smile and nod with appreciation. If you haven't yet taken the roller coaster ride that lands you on a stage in the center of a round, red carpet, eyes and ears from around the world ready to lap up every word you say, then read on.

As I sorted through the answers and placed the best ones in the most appropriate categories, I didn't see any that described my own experience on the TEDx stage. (TEDxWilmingtonWomen, November 2, 2017.) That's a good thing, I suppose. It isn't anything I like to brag about, but I share it with you here to show you that none of us, no matter how experienced and capable we are as speakers, is infallible on the TEDx stage or anywhere else. We simply do the very best we can, damn the torpedoes.

Let me preface this to say that as a public relations professional and journalist I've been speaking, training speakers and writing speech scripts for the better part of 25 years. You'd think that for someone with my experience, doing a TEDx talk would be a walk in the park, right? Ha! I stand corrected, and I hope my story reassures you that any one of us who are on the path to self-actualization is going to stumble along the way, sometimes spectacularly.

It took me a good six months to prepare my TEDx talk. The first hardest part was refining my idea worth spreading. The next hardest part was condensing a lifetime of professional knowledge into a nine-minute script, which I revised almost daily. The third hardest part was memorizing and reciting the content over and over again until my words flowed naturally. By rehearsal night, by golly, I was ready.

When it was my turn, I walked onstage from the left, all mic'd up and raring to go, and took my place dead center of the red carpet. Before me was a vast, empty theater and a bright light in my face. For the past six months, aside from the times I'd given my talk a number of times to invited audiences, my rehearsal space had been my dining room in front of a video camera, and my audience was a white wall.

Can you say, "Deer in the headlights?" The shock of being in the actual venue of giving what I felt would be the most important talk of my life struck me dumb. If someone had asked me weeks earlier, "Well, what's the worse that could happen?" this would have been my answer. The person who had memorized my talk had left the building. Have you ever seen the movie, "The Shining?" The little voice inside my head whispered, "Dana isn't here, Mrs. Torrance."

Three of my clients were sitting in the front row, watching me wide-eyed. I knew Ajit was out there, too. I had wanted to dazzle all of them with my brilliance, and felt self-pressured to do so. I took a deep breath, opened my mouth to produce sound — and nothing. What seemed like an eternity later, Ajit said, "Don't worry, we'll try again tomorrow morning." I mean, that's horrible, right? So awkward. Cripes

As it happens, my actual talk on the big day went without a hitch. I got laughs in all the right places, and except for a minor slide mishap, I remembered every word. Was I the only person who had blanked during rehearsal? No. Was I the only person who couldn't remember a single word of her talk? Yes. I won first prize in that department.

It taught me a big lesson, one which I now share with my speaking clients: Before the big day, make effort to practice your talk on an actual stage, whether it's at your kid's school auditorium, in a local community theater or at a Toastmaster's meeting. Your brain will be less overwhelmed by the strangeness of the TEDx venue and prevent sensory overload.

In the following pages, you'll hear similar advice from other speakers who made it a point to rehearse their talks in places other than their dining rooms. It makes a big difference.

That said, please enjoy all of the insights and advice shared by the TEDxWilmington speakers whose talks you can now watch on YouTube.

We have reached out to a select few of our past TEDxWilmington speakers to fill out a four-part questionnaire to include their insights in this book. We would need a second book if we were to add all 490 speakers' responses.

On the Way to the Red Carpet

Question 1: In one paragraph not to exceed 150 words, please share your experience on your way to the red carpet at TEDxWilmington.

Susan Heitler, who gave a talk at the 5th Annual TEDxWilmington Conference (Event #12) on August 24, 2016 said, "Mostly, I was excited. At the same time, I had not anticipated that the shorter the talk the more preparation it seems to take. I've given all day workshops for years. Preparing for a TEDx talk turned out to feel far more challenging."

Terri Levine, who gave a talk at TEDxWilmingtonLive (Event #30) on April 28, 2018 said, "As I prepared my talk for TEDxWilmington, I learned how to keep a talk to under 10 minutes of time, yet bring together key points, create a powerful opening, tell engaging stories and leave the audience with a powerful message. This was an interesting opportunity to refine my way of speaking, since I have been speaking on stages since I was five years of age. I never had such a short time limit, and at the same time, never had such a desire to share a message that I truly wanted to share with as many people as possible."

TED talks set a new standard for how we present information and ideas in a clear and compelling manner.

Dr. Martin Rayala, who gave a talk at the 4th Annual TEDxWilmington Conference (Event #8) on October 28, 2015 said, "When I gave my TEDx talk, I had just created an innovative new high school and received a $10 million grant for educational innovation, so I felt I had something worth sharing. TED talks set a new standard for how we present information and ideas in a clear and compelling manner. I had 30 years of experience doing the typical 45-minute conference presentation, but doing a tight 15-minute talk presented new challenges. TED talks fall into the category of scripted and memorized presentation rather than speaking extemporaneously from a list of talking points. Fortunately, there are a number of books about how to prepare for TED talks and I recommend anyone planning to do such a talk read one or more of these books and look at related articles and videos."

Sharon Livingston, who gave a talk at the 1st Annual TEDxWilmingtonWomen Conference (Event #14) on October 27, 2016 said, "It was a wonderful surprise and great opportunity to grow beyond my other speaking experiences which were tailored to specific business audiences. I got to tell a highly personal story with a lesson on life to a general audience for the first time. Practice makes perfect. I worked with three different coaches to tell the story, refine the content and fine-tune my delivery. I actually gave my talk 40-plus times before the actual event. It was a challenge to bring it down to the short but potent set of messages I wanted the audience to hear and take away. At first it was 35 minutes and I needed to reduce it to 10 without losing the emotions or key points. It felt magical to be on stage and connect with the audience. All of my apprehensions dissolved as I related to the audience. What a rush!"

Gudrun Penselin, who gave a talk at the 3rd Annual TEDxWilmingtonWomen Conference (Event #32) on November 30, 2018 said, "The journey to the red carpet has been an amazing experience, providing great opportunities for personal growth, accompanied by many emotions and occasional challenges. Solidifying my idea into a short, 10-minute talk was probably one of the biggest tasks; every word and every transition count. I was surprised that developing the script was completely different from writing a book; it felt more like writing a script for a play. There were times when memorizing and rehearsing the script felt like a daunting task. I experienced myself as an observer of my brain as I rehearsed: staying totally focused in the present, while simultaneously being aware of the next sentence and in case of "losing" the script, making a quick judgment call if information was missing, needed to be added and if yes, where? All the efforts to get to the red carpet were well worth it!"

Maureen Bridget Rabotin, who gave a talk at the 2nd Annual TEDxWilmingtonWomen Conference (Event #24) on November 2, 2017 said, "The joy exploded within when I learned that my application had been accepted. As an author, keynote speaker, facilitator and university instructor, I know how to speak to big or small crowds. And that's when I recognized my overzealous self-assurance was trying to squelch the fear building up inside. Who am I to give a TEDx talk? How can I make my subject funny and still worth sharing? Since writing is my favorite pastime, I got out a fresh notebook and started putting ideas to paper. That's when the well-known difficulty hit me. How do you get 25 years' experience into a 10-minute talk? Not possible! My self-assurance quickly dissolved into serious self-doubt. I sprawled in front of my new Smart TV and started watching TED talks. This time, not for the pure pleasure, but more with a critical eye: "What makes her talk so impactful? Where's the hook? Why should I care? Still, self-doubt has this pernicious ability to crawl up and grab you when you least expect it. After scrapping several drafts which could have been books instead of a talk, I chose my idea worth sharing: "The Culture of Fear: Facing it with Courage and Curiosity.""

> **I actually gave my talk 40-plus times before the actual event. It was a challenge to bring it down to the short but potent set of messages I wanted the audience to hear and take away.**

Joseph B. Geraci, who gave a talk at the 2nd Annual TEDxWilmington Conference (Event #3) on August 7, 2013 said, "My experience was an exciting one that began the moment I was asked to speak. It was also a challenging one, given the amount of time to make my presentation. As a professor and one who has given many talks on the subject, I am more accustomed to being rather verbose. Compressing my knowledge on the subject in just a few minutes reminded me of writing my doctoral dissertation; clear, concise and to the point."

David C. Woessner, who gave a talk at a TEDxWilmingtonSalon (Event #23) on October 17, 2017 said, "Preparing for the red carpet was both humbling and insightful. I believed myself to be an accomplished public speaker, but the requirements and expectations of TEDxWilmington grounded my state of ability and forced further study and practice to rise to the occasion."

Therese Jornlin, who gave a talk at the 4th Annual TEDxWilmington Conference (Event #8) on October 28, 2015 said, "My experience on my way to the TEDx red carpet was highly creative, quite intense, exhausting and energizing at the same time! As a teacher and public speaker for nearly 40 years, I'm comfortable speaking in front of all kinds of people and in a wide variety of settings. So, I didn't anticipate the unique creative challenges I met preparing the TEDx talk. The parameters were new for me — time limits, and memorizing a lecture (versus teaching). In addition, I chose to use the TEDx platform to speak publicly on a topic that's taboo: the power of female biology, specifically, the urgent need for women to reclaim menstruation. Despite having taught these materials for 20 years in a transformative course called "Women Awake," I was facing my nerves over bringing them out of my own proverbial closet. But the need to do so was greater than my fear of staying silent."

George Chanos, who gave a talk at the 7th Annual TEDxWilmington Conference (Event #31) on September 27, 2018 said, "I was surprised to discover how challenging and rewarding it was for me to do my talk at TEDxWilmington. To begin with, although I had spoken my entire life, I had not done a fully memorized 12-minute speech before. That was a challenge and a wonderful learning experience. I was also covering a very broad topic, "A Mindset for the 21st Century," so the 12-minute time frame forced me to focus on only the most important information. Watching the preparation that went into the rehearsal, the day before speaking, was also enlightening. The moment before I went on stage, I told myself to be mindful of the entire experience. I enjoyed every moment."

Renée Jones, who gave a talk at TEDxWilmingtonLive (Event #30) on April 28, 2018 said, "The road to the red carpet for me was the most testing, terrifying, stretching, petrifying, exhilarating, and "comfort-zone-challenging" journeys of discovery I've ever traveled. A year prior to giving this talk, my husband suggested I think about speaking, and I said, "Love, I'm never going to be a speaker." Only three months later I was in a speaker training course and soon did my first public talk. I was shaking the whole time, but I did it. Then the opportunity for TEDxWilmington came along, and it was a mad six weeks of preparation. I had help from the TEDxWilmington group, my original coach, and then I added a new coach who truly upped my game. The diversity of styles, ideas, and skills improved my talk and helped me face my fears."

> **To begin with, although I had spoken my entire life, I had not done a fully memorized 12-minute speech before.**

Glory Crampton, who gave a talk at the 6th Annual TEDxWilmington Conference (Event #20) on August 16, 2017 said, "It was such an adventure! I had plenty of experience performing onstage, but none in public speaking. I worked on my speech, refining it over and over. My breakthrough happened when I realized I had to share my "vulnerability" with others. That is what connects human beings. Ajit pushed me to "show up" more in my talk. There were moments that became challenging. I pushed myself to continue sharing my journey as an actress, and tools that had helped me "own" the stage of my life! The TEDx family became a true gift and inspiration."

Nicole Black, who gave a talk at the 3rd Annual TEDxWilmingtonWomen Conference (Event #32) on November 30, 2018 said, "Truth? I had no idea I even wanted to give a TEDx talk until the day I met Ajit. For me, the road to the red circle was less of a straight line and more of curvy back road filled with plot twists and turns and an excitement deep down in my soul I hadn't felt for a very long time. From formulating my concept to actually constructing the talk, I treated it like it was my second full time job; and I loved every minute of it. I think the most challenging aspect is that there are things that you want to say that are funny or make sense to you, but you have to leave them out because they don't fit in the throughline. Honestly, the TEDx experience has made me a better speaker and even a better listener."

Paul Dixon, who gave a talk at TEDxWilmingtonLive (Event #30) on April 28, 2018 said, "I had an amazing experience preparing and giving my TEDxWilmington talk. I have worked in the business world for 32 years and this was one of the most difficult tasks I've ever had. The numerous hours of preparation and making many adjustments to my talk was exhausting. However, it was all worth it! My talk was approximately seven minutes and I was extremely nervous the entire morning prior to giving the talk. The time went by extremely fast and I was pleased with the end result!"

Seth Rainess, who gave a talk at the 7th Annual TEDxWilmington Conference (Event #31) on September 27, 2018 said, "After being rejected twice, it sunk in that I was on my way to the red carpet! No one was around when I let out a scream. I was finally going to get my turn. There was a list of what was required in two months and a talk that had no structure, no outline and no beginning. Of all my presentations, this was the hardest. There could be no fluff words; they were handpicked. I got to deliver a talk that no one else could give. Pacing the house, recording video and audio and transcribing was the way I crafted the talk. How many hours did they say it would take? 100? How about over 300 or more. Practicing happened everywhere at the drop of a hat. Realizing that no matter how many times it was recited, each time was new! Nerves? You bet, but I finally delivered my masterpiece."

> **For me, the road to the red circle was less of a straight line and more of curvy back road filled with plot twists and turns and an excitement deep down in my soul I hadn't felt for a very long time.**

Jaya Jaya Myra Godfrey, who gave a talk at the 3rd Annual TEDxWilmington Women Conference (Event #32) on November 30, 2018 said, "Preparation meant daily practice of my talk for over a month, plus lots of work to get to the point where I felt my talk was ready to even begin practicing. Constant repetition and getting comfortable with the content was important for me to feel prepared and for the talk to go smoothly. I wanted to have my talk memorized nearly verbatim so that I would not get flustered or distracted if something didn't go as expected."

Sean J. Kennedy, who gave a talk at the 7th Annual TEDxWilmington Conference (Event #31) on September 27, 2018 said, "After doing a short lecture on the history of jazz brushes in the middle of a jazz concert, the piano player, and TEDx alum, suggested that I submit my lecture to the TEDxWilmington folks. I thought that I had NO chance of even being considered, but I submitted anyway. Amazingly, the committee saw something of value in my presentation and offered me a spot! The weeks/months leading up to the red carpet were more intense than I could have imagined, but the personal growth that I experienced was all worth it."

Dr. Daniel Lieberman, who gave a talk at the 2nd Annual TEDxWilmingtonWomen Conference (Event #24) on November 2, 2017 said, "The trip to the red carpet was practice, practice, practice. I practiced every day, first thing in the morning when I got to work, for a month. Going through the talk so many times was a big help, but during the dress rehearsal, I suddenly drew a blank because I was so used to being in my office. I had forgotten that memory was state-dependent, i.e., where you learn is where you remember. Fortunately, I got past that, and everything went smoothly on the big day."

Anne Jolles, who gave a talk at the 1st Annual TEDxWilmingtonWomen Conference (Event #14) on October 27, 2016 said, "I practiced my TEDx talk by giving it to strangers in a café, my neighbors on a backyard porch, at a local high school where I was mic'd and also showed my slides to staff and students, on a stage at a private educational institution for millennial, for friends and family, and even in the bathtub! I slowly flexed my courage muscles and was vulnerable. I stumbled through it and took risks, and it evolved, improved and took on a life of its own. The feedback was priceless, and the practice was painfully worthwhile."

Stephen T. Lawless, MD, MBA, who gave a talk at a TEDxWilmingtonSalon (Event #13) on October 18, 2016 said, "After over 35 years of presenting in academic settings, this experience changed my entire outlook in regard to how to relate with authenticity to an audience. I realized that the power of presentation is not in the facts or figures, but in the audience connection to me as an authentic speaker."

Dinette Rivera, who gave a talk at the 6th Annual TEDxWilmington Conference (Event #20) on August 16, 2017 said, "My experience on the way to the TEDxWilmington red carpet was a mixed bag of emotions. Trying to put my 20 years of research into a one-minute video was quite the challenge. Once done, I realized how much we tend to ramble on with the backstory. After submitting my application and getting back what felt like the Dear John letter, I was disappointed. That feeling was followed by the determination to reapply soon. After a month or so, I received a letter congratulating me to speak at the TEDxWilmington Annual Conference in August of 2018. I was so excited. After the excitement, I realized the work ahead. This was an invitation to commit to months of deadlines, reading, perfecting and practicing for the red carpet. It was grueling. I am so grateful for it. It made me a better speaker."

> **The trip to the red carpet was practice, practice, practice. I practiced every day, first thing in the morning when I got to work, for a month.**

Carolyn Bennett-Sullivan, who gave a talk at a TEDxWilmingtonSalon (Event #27) on December 14, 2017 said, "Preparing for my TEDxWilmington talk was one intense experience. I had three weeks from the time I was accepted as a speaker until the TEDx event, at which I was sharing the red carpet with fellow presenters. Typically, I feel confident on the stage, yet I'd never had to know my talk cold; as a speaker, I'd previously had room for improvisation. Speaking on the TEDx stage required me to raise the bar and step into intense focus and disciplined practice like I'd never done before in order to be prepared and able to deliver when I stepped on the red carpet."

Arthuretta Homes-Martin, who gave a talk at a TEDxWilmingtonSalon (Event #11) on July 30, 2016 said, "I had the honor of participating in a TEDxWilmingtonSalon on Whistleblowing. My experience was different in that not only did I need to meet the criteria for a TEDx talk, I needed to first pass the criteria for being a whistleblower with a story to tell. The time frame for preparation was short. I was stretched — a good stretch. I had to perfect the talk (not a speech) and perfect the message to fit within the TEDx criteria without a coach. It was challenging but rewarding."

Christy Whitman, who gave a talk at the 2nd Annual TEDxWilmingtonWomen Conference on November 2, 2017 said, "As a professional speaker for over 10 years, I have presented to thousand-person live audiences and been interviewed numerous times on national television. However, the TEDxWilmington event was heads above my previous experience. I was chosen as the first speaker to kick off the event, and while normally I would thrive when given such an opportunity, I was initially nervous because I really wanted to do my best. I am truly grateful for this experience, as it focused me into a greater desire to practice what I preach, and place all of my attention and intention on the long-term outcome that I wanted to achieve, rather than on the momentary fears that were coming up."

Lindsay Page, who gave a talk at TEDxWilmingtonED on February 9, 2018 said, "Preparing for my talk was way more work than I could have imagined. I had plenty of experience with giving academic-style talks, which are typically heavily dependent on PowerPoint slides. This was something different entirely. I struggled to keep up with the preparation milestones and requirements, but in hindsight, I see how valuable they were for pushing me to refine the ideas that I wanted to share and the style that I wanted to take in my talk."

Galit Goldfarb, who gave a talk at the 5th Annual TEDxWilmington Conference (Event # 12) on August 24, 2016 said, "The day before I gave my talk, I slipped in the hotel breakfast room and twisted my ankle so much that I could barely walk. But it didn't matter to me. I was getting on that stage no matter what. Instead of wearing the pretty high heel shoes I had planned, I wore Crocs. Because I'm passionate about my work, nothing else mattered to me. It didn't even matter that as I got on stage, I spilled all the food that was supposed to be my prop! I just kept on going. Nothing was going to stop me from getting my message across."

Vincent James, who gave a talk at a TEDxWilmingtonSalon (Event #15) on November 17, 2016 said, "The one word that quickly comes to mind when thinking about my TEDx experience is growth. The process of applying for and preparing to give a talk was a period of incredible growth for me personally. It forced me further out of my shell so that I was able to deliver my message in a much more impactful way. The funny thing I remember about the preparation was Ajit's phone call after viewing my practice video. He had three words to say: "Where's the music?" Once again, Ajit coached me into uncomfortable territory and had me prepare playing and singing live music along with creating and memorizing my talk. I didn't know which part to be more nervous about — trying to perform perfectly for the live cameras and future YouTube audience, or my speaking parts. Just an amazing experience from beginning to end and I can't thank Ajit and TEDxWilmington enough for the opportunity."

Tonya Fitzpatrick, who gave a talk at the 2nd Annual TEDxWilmingtonWomen Conference (Event #24) on November 2, 2017 said, "I believe in the power of the Power Pose. After rehearsing behind the curtain one last time I shook my arms and legs to get rid of nervousness. Then I stood planted with feet slightly apart and hands on my hips while I spent time visualizing the delivery of my opening lines. As I was being introduced, I straightened my blouse, squared my shoulders and made sure my fingers were placed correctly on my clicker (this was the first time I incorporated slides in my presentation). When I walked out to the red carpet, I spotted my husband and a cousin who had traveled to see me on the stage. I stood on the red carpet and paused for a deep breath. I whispered 'Thank you, Jesus' as I exhaled and began my talk. When those first laughs came in the first minute, I knew that I 'had' this talk and I relaxed and relished the experience."

John Livesay, who gave a talk at TEDxWilmingtonLive (Event #30) on April 28, 2018 said, "The way to the red carpet at TEDxWilmington was one where I had to walk my talk of not taking previous rejections personally. When I was turned down by other TEDx organizers, I kept on refining my message and focused on finding an event that had a theme that fit my talk. Getting the "yes" was all the sweeter because I had to work for it."

Sara Blanchard, who gave a talk at the 7th Annual TEDxWilmington Conference (Event #30) on September 27, 2018 said, "The process of creating this talk forced me to put aside my ego and listen to my soul. In the past, though I often knew what I wanted to say, my messages would get muddled in the voices of those I admired — I'd compare myself to some made-up ideal, and the tone didn't feel compelling. But thanks to the keen insights of a supportive community, I broke down the "telling" and stepped into "showing," in a way that was authentic to me, why the questions we ask shape the answers we get. Even though I'd felt silenced in the past, becoming the person who delivers a powerful, meaningful, simple idea made me realize there is no point in hiding anymore. I can never go back to who I was before TEDxWilmington helped me to let my voice shine."

> **The process of creating this talk forced me to put aside my ego and listen to my soul.**

Dr. Annie Norman, who gave a talk at the 4th Annual TEDxWilmington Conference (Event #8) on October 28, 2015 said, "The TEDx talk was a chance of a lifetime, and a life altering experience. As an introvert, it was a leap and a risk for me to apply and subject myself to the spotlight. I had recently completed my doctorate and had a message to share that I thought everyone should know about, but not many people are willing to read a doctoral dissertation!"

Shane Coen, who gave a talk at the 6th Annual TEDxWilmington Conference (Event #20) on August 16, 2017 said, "Preparing for and giving a TEDx talk was a journey into my own life history in finding where my passion for contextual and minimalist design originated. It was not only the origin, which began at a very young age, but also how the passion followed me through periods of darkness and addiction and light and growth. It was in the preparation process that I realized my ever-racing mind calms when I design. Over the years, I saw how our landscapes affected people and I hope that in creating spaces with the approach of contextual based design that I can bring calm to thousands of people for hundreds of years. Both the preparation and the actual event were central to reigniting my love of design, and served as a turning point in moving forward to the next phase in my life's work."

Tiffany Gwilliam, who gave a talk at the 3rd Annual TEDxWilmingtonWomen Conference (Event #32) on November 30, 2018 said, "An email appeared in my inbox with my official invitation to give a TEDxWilmington talk. A door has opened with the opportunity of a lifetime to hopefully help many. Petrified, I have a responsibility to proceed. Preparing a TEDx talk is monumental, intense, and requires a village — family, friends, a speaking coach, and a professional writer to provide constructive feedback. Hours are spent writing, memorizing, and learning how to effectively deliver my talk. The day has arrived! Nervous, I hit the gym. I practice suggestions from the TEDx tribe. The speakers gather, supporting one another with encouraging words, hugs, and laughter. Connections have formed. We share a forever bond as the speakers of the 3rd Annual TEDxWilmingtonWomen Conference: Showing up and embracing my fears, I stand on the red carpet. I deliver my talk from my heart, offering the audience my greatest gift. Upon completion, an immediate sense of relief, gratitude, and peace washes over me."

Teresa Rodriguez, who gave a talk at the 2nd Annual TEDxWilmington Conference (Event #3) on August 7, 2013 said, "For many people, the opportunity to give a TEDx talk is a dream come true. And, for me, that was a distant aspiration I never thought would come to fruition. Although I didn't think much about my life experience, Mr. Ajit George believed that my life story and books about solo travel for women would be of great interest to the rest of the world. He found something in me that I didn't know I possessed — an inspiring tale of overcoming divorce, suicide attempts, mental institutions, and failure through traveling the world alone. I was honored to be given the opportunity to speak, albeit I was scared about becoming so vulnerable and speaking for 15 minutes straight in front of a live theater audience of hundreds of people. I had to do some intense soul searching to find the right words to share. Now, a few years later, I am honored to know that 767,246 people have been moved by my words."

> **Preparing a TEDx talk is monumental, intense, and requires a village — family, friends, a speaking coach, and a professional writer to provide constructive feedback.**

Rod Wallace, who gave a talk at the 7th Annual TEDxWilmington Conference (Event #31) on September 27, 2018 said, "My TEDx helped me understand and define who I was. I had a hazy idea who I wanted to be based on two years writing my book on the impact of digital technology on American culture, government, and economy (*Drowning in Potential: How American Society Can Survive Digital Technology*). However, I needed the concise story — and the TEDx 12 minutes for *my story* forced that. I spent hours agonizing alone with coaches, and gathering input from family. At one point I was told, "You're on track for the worst TEDx speech ever." I began again but looked deeper. By the time I reached the red carpet, I felt passionate about my content, I embraced my message, and I *cared* about the characters in my story."

Knowing what you know now, what would you do differently?

Question 2: If you could give your TEDx talk again, is there anything you would do differently (not to exceed 150 words).

Cindy Bo, who gave a talk at the 2nd Annual TEDxWilmingtonWomen Conference (Event #24) on November 2, 2017 said, "If I could redo my TEDx talk again, I would practice more! I think many TEDx speakers feel like they will never be 100 percent prepared and wished they had practiced more. I am no different. The only difference I would point out is that I would try to practice more with different audiences to evoke different emotions from the audience. I learned this after my TEDx Talk with my son who said that he appreciated the history of his family's past and how he is shaped by my own experiences from my parents. I presented this during one of my practice sessions to a colleague who was fourth generation here in the United States, and she could not relate to immigrants and their struggle. She told me that it sparked no emotion or call to action. She thought it was boring. Recognizing the range of feedback is key in preparation."

Kate Kirkwood, who gave a talk at TEDxWilmingtonLive (Event #30) on April 28, 2018 said, "I would practice more, in front of diverse groups. I would watch more talks before completing my script to get more of a feeling of the TEDx stage and process. Then, I would relax and just talk to the audience."

Dave Nassaney, who gave a talk at the 3rd Annual TEDxWilmingtonWomen Conference (Event #30) on November 30, 2018 said, "I really can't say that I would do anything differently, except prepare and rehearse even more than I did, so that I could focus more on my delivery and not on just remembering the next word. That would mean rehearsing another 1,000 times."

Alisa Morkides, who gave a talk at the 1st Annual TEDxWilmingtonWomen Conference (Event #14) on October 27, 2016 said, "Although I practiced my TEDx talk hundreds of times, the one thing I would have done more of was to watch more TEDx talks online before giving my own talk. I was so focused on my own talk I didn't take the opportunity to watch others — how they crafted their stories, their body language, use of humor, etc. — as much as I could have. I believe my talk would have been stronger had I done so. I'm now a regular watcher of TEDx talks on a wide variety of topics, and it's made me a better speaker and a less nervous one."

> **I really can't say that I would do anything differently, except prepare and rehearse even more than I did, so that I could focus more on my delivery and not on just remembering the next word.**

Cassandra Pavolic, who gave a talk at the 7th Annual TEDxWilmington Conference (Event #31) on September 27, 2018 said, "I would speak louder. I have a soft voice and noticed in viewing my TEDx talk I could have added a bit more volume during parts of my talk. I also wish I rehearsed more in front of people rather than just two of my friends. Getting feedback from people you trust is good, but I feel I should have done more of it as often as I could have for comfort and confidence."

Tony Selimi, who gave a talk at the 6th Annual TEDxWilmington Conference (Event #20) on August 16, 2017 said, "I've been giving talks and helping others create talks for long enough to know that a good speech takes work and a great speech takes a LOT of work, but to give an extraordinary TEDx talk is beyond anything any speaker can imagine. If I were to give another TEDx talk, the one thing I would do differently is to create a detailed plan of action on the day I get officially accepted. Take it very seriously. Make sure you email on time all the deliverables required by the organizers and complete your final speech early in the process to give you plenty of time to rehearse. So, daily practice your speech in front of a mirror, your family and friends, in nature and most importantly in front of an experienced speaker and vocal coach who can push you at times when your mind tells you to quit."

> **I would speak louder. I have a soft voice and noticed in viewing my TEDx talk I could have added a bit more volume during parts of my talk.**

Rob Bentley, who gave a talk at a TEDxWilmingtonSalon (Event #27) on December 14, 2017 said, "I would ensure I had the time to dedicate and better prepare for the talk. I would also begin researching what makes an excellent TED talk and practicing at least six months before making a submission by reaching out to learn from others that conducted talks before me, especially since I came into the process completely blind. When you only have one shot, you should always strive to make it your best, whether you have time or not."

Dune Thorne, who gave a talk at a TEDxWilmingtonSalon (Event #16) on December 6, 2016 said, "There is always more you can do to improve! I think I would focus more on the key points and not the exact words. I had my script almost memorized to the word and think it is probably better when you are less scripted. I think I also would have kept it shorter, and really aimed for 13 minutes. I also think bolder is better. In some places I was worried about pushing a message too hard and looking back pushing an issue and being bolder would have been better."

John Jeremiah, who gave a talk at TEDxWilmingtonSalon (Event #25) on November 28, 2017 said, "There are two things I would do differently. First, I would have further refined my content to pull in more real-world stories, examples, and statistics. Second, I would want to ditch my slides and go with a whiteboard or flipchart. Slides can be such a crutch for a speaker, and I think my talk would be even more compelling sans slides."

Carlyn Montes De Oca, who gave a talk at the 7th Annual TEDxWilmington Conference (Event #31) on September 27, 2018 said, "Better wardrobe and images. Before the TEDx event I had a wardrobe misfire. As I was rushing around the morning of my talk, I spilled my protein shake on my blouse. I tried to get the stain out but when I got to the venue, the stain was visible. Ugh. Luckily, I had brought an extra dress, but it wasn't my best look. I would have preferred to have gone on stage more stylish and with a more empowering color. Also, I was advised to stay away from using images during my talk because tech malfunctions are so common. And yes, this has happened to me a lot at other presentations. But I think that if I had a slide or two, I didn't have to rely on if something went wrong, but that still adds an emotional appeal if things went as planned — this would have been beneficial.

> **I would have further refined my content to pull in more real-world stories, examples, and statistics.**

Dr. Patrick Wright, who gave a talk at the 3rd Annual TEDxWilmingtonWomen Conference (Event #32) on November 30, 2018 said, "There are some tricks public speakers use to keep the audience focused that aren't as effective for a TEDx talk. I would coordinate the slides more precisely with the TEDx format to flow better."

Stephanie Diggins, who gave a talk at the TEDxWilmingtonED Conference (Event #29) on February 9, 2018 said, "I would try to remember every moment of the experience! After my talk, quite a few people asked me how it went and my response to every person was, 'I have no idea, I don't remember a thing!' My brain was so overwhelmed with the entire experience that I somehow managed to blackout my talk. I can't even remember my talk anymore. It was like as soon as I gave my talk, my brain was done!"

Errol Ebanks, who gave a talk at the 7th Annual TEDxWilmington Conference (Event #31) on September 27, 2018 said, "If I could give my TEDx talk again I would not over think it and enjoy the process. My biggest thing was trying to be perfect. I rehearsed it over and over, which only brought more nerves as I tried to be perfect, when in reality no one is perfect, but I can work to achieve my best. Looking back, I was stressed and worked really hard, wanting to strive for the best, but I should have just taken it all in and relaxed. One thing about being a perfectionist is you have a hard time trying to relax, and you miss some of the moments to enjoy the achievement itself."

Rachel Hutchisson, who gave a talk at the 5th Annual TEDxWilmington Conference (Event #12) on August 24, 2016 said, "Having now done a talk, when I look back at the result, I think two specific things. First, I needed to slow down a bit. I think that was a function of nerves, trying to remember word-for-word what I wanted to say, especially because it would live via a video. The second is that I would be much more specific in my recommendations at the end of the talk. It's way easier to see that now versus when I was crafting the talk!"

Michael Morgan, who gave a talk at the 5th Annual TEDxWilmington Conference (Event #12) on August 24, 2016 said, "I am not sure, except to say breathe and trust even more. Dig even deeper, and trust that the universe will provide. Part of the adventure is not knowing exactly what challenges will arise."

Michelle Nagel, who gave a talk at the 3rd Annual TEDxWilmingtonWomen Conference (Event #32) on November 30, 2018 said, "If I could do it again, I would not be so hung up on having to have my talk memorized. That one small word kept me so overwhelmed as to nearly incapacitate me. My brain interpreted that as "every single word must be spoken exactly." When a change was made to my talk the night before I was supposed to give it, I thought I was going to faint. The next morning, I caught my reflection in the mirror and said, "Michelle, stop it! You know your talk. You know your subject, you are an expert, and you teach this stuff all the time, so just relax!" When I did that, I was able to relax into my message. I believe it would have gone even better had I not been so uptight about it for such a long time."

> **Looking back, I was stressed and worked really hard, wanting to strive for the best, but I should have just taken it all in and relaxed.**

Peter Atwater, who gave a talk at the 2nd Annual TEDxWilmington Conference (Event #3) on August 7, 2013 said, "I would tell more stories and narrow the scope of my talk. I was so excited to share everything I had found that I put too much content into my presentation."

Sara Crawford Jones, who gave a talk at the 6th Annual TEDxWilmington Conference (Event #20) on August 16, 2017 said, "I would have dug even deeper in to my idea, my takeaways — there was so much more I should have included — so much more to share. Additionally, I would have drank a bit more water prior. My mouth was a bit dry and although there was water on stage, I just couldn't leave the red carpet."

Mary Morrissey, who gave a talk at the 1st Annual TEDxWilmingtonWomen Conference (Event #14) on October 27, 2016 said, "I decided that I wanted to share that there's an invisible side of success — a pattern by which success occurs. I decided to demonstrate the difference between someone who *wants* to change and someone who actually *does* change. I also decided to weave in my own personal story for the purpose of showing how it's possible to transform your life. Looking back, I would cut out about a quarter of what I shared, so I could *slow down* and deliver the message with more power and emotion, in the manner I normally speak."

> **I would tell more stories and narrow the scope of my talk. I was so excited to share everything I had found that I put too much content into my presentation.**

Sean Douglas, who gave a talk at a TEDxWilmingtonSalon (Event #27) on December 14, 2017 said, "Watching my talk on YouTube, I felt it was a little dry and not energetic. If I had to do it over, I would put more energy and more humor into the talk."

Bill Haley, who gave a talk at the 6th Annual TEDxWilmington Conference (Event #20) on August 16, 2017 said, "I was very focused on getting the content right — making sure my talk hit on all the points that mattered and was cohesive and understandable. If I were to do it again, I think I'd bring more of myself into it, maybe a little bit of humor and personal insights."

Vicky Kelly, who gave a talk at the 3rd Annual TEDxWilmington Conference (Event #4) on August 6, 2014 said, "Yes, I would be even more brave and direct. I was still in a very public job at the time, so felt a bit constrained by that. I also wish that I had chosen a catchier, broader title. I thought I had a good title, but I should have tried it out on more people to get their feedback."

> **If I had to do it over, I would put more energy and more humor into the talk.**

Amy Ogden, who gave a talk at TEDxWilmingtonLive (Event #30) on April 28, 2018 said, "I would invite my friends and family to attend. I was so scared to have them there and be distracted by them that I asked them all to not attend. I would share that experience with the ones I love the most."

Claudia Six, who gave a talk at the 5th Annual TEDxWilmington Conference (Event #12) on August 24, 2016 said, "If I were to give my TEDx talk again, I would stand closer to the front of my little red round TEDx carpet. In watching the video afterwards, I noticed that despite all my rehearsing, travelling, preparing, dress and make-up, there was still a part of me that did not present to the audience the way I would have preferred. My being at the back of my carpet belied my stage fright. That's now the advice I give anyone considering a TED talk: stand at the front of your carpet — own it!"

Jen Kluczkowski, who gave a talk at the 3rd Annual TEDxWilmingtonWomen Conference (Event #32) on November 30, 2018 said, "I'd take in less outside opinion about my direction and stick to working solely with my coach. My talk got a little crowded with outside voices chirping away (all with great intentions!) and I think I could have trusted more in my own ability to speak from my heart."

> I also wish that I had chosen a catchier, broader title. I thought I had a good title, but I should have tried it out on more people to get their feedback.

Debra Laino, who gave a talk at the 2nd Annual TEDxWilmington Conference (Event #3) on August 7, 2013 and a TEDxWilmingtonSalon (Event #17) on February 16, 2017 said, "Sleep better the night before! I can't stress this enough. During both of my TEDx talks, I was lacking sleep. I really liked the material I put together for both talks and thought they were both fun and educational."

Dr. Kien Vuu, who gave a talk at the 3rd Annual TEDxWilmingtonWomen Conference (Event #32) on November 30, 2018 said, "If I could give my talk again, I would spend more time getting to know the people in the audience. Because the thrill of being on stage wasn't the best part of my TEDx experience, it was actually the people. Seeing the audience respond to my idea felt incredible. The questions and insights other speakers who came to me after my talk surprised me and rooted me in the understanding that we are in the middle of a medical paradigm shift. Modern medicine is a miracle. But so is the new knowledge coming into the world about just how powerful we are and how we can use that power to live our most healthy, happy lives. I feel like this experience has allowed me to fulfill my purpose of sharing this big idea — *you are your best medicine* — so that it finds the people who need to hear it, and if I could do it again, I'd connect more with the people who were there."

Robyn Howton, who gave a talk at the TEDxWilmingtonED Conference (Event #29) on February 9, 2018 said, "I would change my topic. My son called me after watching my TEDx Talk live streamed. He told me I had done a wonderful job, but asked why I didn't talk about my students. He made me realize I passed up the opportunity to speak about my truest passion — my students, and the responsibility we have as a society to provide each of them with a high-quality education."

Lauri Robbins Ericson, who gave a talk at the 3rd Annual TEDxWilmingtonWomen Conference (Event #32) on November 30, 2018 said, "If I were to give my TEDx talk again, I would have more fun and play with it. I will also try to be less data driven and connect more with the audience. I'm still reflecting on this, as I feel like the message is so important and wondering the most impactful way to continue to make this an idea we're spreading."

Tom Devine, who gave a talk at a TEDxWilmingtonSalon (Event #11) on July 30, 2016 said, "The main thing would be training myself not to say "um." I also wonder if I should have outlined more of a call to action instead of only praising whistleblowers and explaining their role in society."

> **If I were to give my TEDx talk again, I would have more fun and play with it. I will also try to be less data driven and connect more with the audience.**

Shavon Lindley, who gave a talk at the 3rd Annual TEDxWilmingtonWomen Conference (Event #32) on November 30, 2018 said, "In preparation, I hired an expert TED speaker coach, read all recommended books and articles, watched tons of talks, practiced daily meditation, and hired spiritual coaches to help reprogram my unconscious mind of any self-limiting beliefs that were holding me back from speaking my truth. Was I perfect? Absolutely not, but I am 100 percent confident that I did everything in my power to do my absolute best for where I was in my life at that moment. I wouldn't have done anything differently."

Rani St. Pucci, who gave a talk at the 6th Annual TEDxWilmington Conference (Event #20) on August 16, 2017 said, "Here are some things I would be more mindful about:

1. Let go of the thought of having to be perfect.
2. Be sure to get plenty of sleep and rest prior to the speech.
3. Avoid too many caffeinated drinks the day of.
4. Test the clicker for my PowerPoint presentation (it got stuck a few times).
5. Have some water close by in case my throat feels dry, or to take a sip when I need to pause and collect my thoughts.
6. Remember to smile!"

> **Let go of the thought of having to be perfect.**
> **What Impact Did Your TEDx Talk Have?**

Question 3: In one paragraph not to exceed 150 words, please share your experiences after you gave your TEDx talk and your video was approved and posted on YouTube. For example, did you get any more publicity or additional speaking engagements? Did your TEDx talk have an impact on making your idea into reality?

Gustavo Grodnitzky, who gave a talk at the 6th Annual TEDxWilmington Conference (Event #20) on August 16, 2017 said, "Particularly if you speak for a living, a TEDx talk has become like a website was 20 years ago. It simply adds a level of credibility that is unequaled. It is common for people to do a Google search of you when you are going to speak to an audience. When that Google search brings up your TEDx talk and people watch it, you begin to hear things like, 'I watched your TEDx talk,' and, 'I loved your TEDx talk.' 'I think your TEDx talk is right on the money.' It is rewarding to feel like you are making an impact."

Adebisi Adebowale, who gave a talk at the 7th Annual TEDxWilmington Conference (Event #31) on September 27, 2018 said, "After my TEDx talk I have received more attention to my business. I received one of my first large coaching clients, and I do believe that my TEDx talk helped my new client come to a decision to trust my expertise. I'm also looking forward to booking many more engagements and conferences and believe event planners use my talk as a reference point of my potential to engage their audience and provide authentic and trustworthy information."

> **A TEDx talk has become like a website was 20 years ago.
> It simply adds a level of credibility that is unequaled.**

Cornelius "Nippy" Betz, who gave a talk at the 5th Annual TEDxWilmington Conference (Event #12) on August 24, 2016 said, "We have gained exposure in ways I never imagined. Corporate America now takes Scholarship Leadership Institute (SLI) more seriously, as I won an idol contest for minority owned business. It led to me pitching Dell Technologies last year in hopes of eventually serving as a human resource benefit for 145,000-plus employees. SLI has been selected for a $17 thousand award to help 4,000 students prepare for and get into college. Although San Antonio wasn't eventually selected by the Department of Education for the contract, SLI's selection, along with companies like Princeton Review, Texas A&M, etc. was big! Our company's credibility grew exponentially because of my TEDx talk exposure. We have been hired by people who attended or watched the talk, which led to ongoing financial rewards and travel. We made $11,000 last month directly related to me standing on that stage. I now get paid to help more students because of TEDx!"

Kevin Carr, who gave a talk at a TEDxWilmingtonSalon (Event #17) on February 16, 2017 said, "My talk is still growing. Well, the idea I should say. Since the talk I landed a literary agent who is now shopping my manuscript, which shares the same title and theme of the talk. I would say all and all the talk has given more credibility to my work."

> **We have been hired by people who attended or watched the talk, which led to ongoing financial rewards and travel.**

Dr. Michelle Yep Martin, who gave a talk at the 7th Annual TEDxWilmington Conference (Event #31) on September 27, 2018 said, "My talk hit over 26,000 views in a short amount of time, so it was quite a high to say the least. I did get a lot more attention, publicity and additional speaking engagements. My TEDx talk did have an impact on turning my idea into reality.

It has helped me fine-tune my online courses, my book, and how I introduce myself to others. Additionally, I have obtained at least four speaking engagements since it was published. And there are smaller things that are easier now, too, because the TEDx talk gave me additional credibility, so people argue less with me when I'm on the stand in court as an expert witness — which is an awesome bonus."

Melissa Root, who gave a talk at the 6th Annual TEDxWilmington Conference (Event # 20) on August 16, 2017 said, "Giving my TEDx talk added a level of credibility to my ideas that even my Ph.D. didn't. I was once asked to meet with two people for a discussion about a business idea, but then eight high-level professionals filed into the meeting. The first and second told me they would be grilling me. I was the outsider with a new idea, and they wanted to be sure I was legitimate. Then someone mentioned they watched my TEDx talk and the tenor of the room changed. It became a genuine discussion of ideas, the kind you always relish when you're in a room full of brilliant minds from different backgrounds. That simple statement, 'I watched your TEDx talk,' seemed to give me credibility in their minds. That meeting was the basis for a successful and innovative project we completed together that will impact important people across the globe."

Allan Ting, who gave a talk at TEDxWilmingtonLive (Event #30) on April 28, 2018 said, "I did get more publicity and speaking engagements. One in particular, I have been invited to lead meditation sessions at WorkHuman (a 4,000 people seminar for Human Resource Officers, Directors and Managers) that comes together on talking about how to make work more human. Some of the past speakers at the conference included Michelle Obama, George Clooney, Viola Davis, Kat Cole and many more."

> **It has helped me fine-tune my online courses, my book, and how I introduce myself to others.**

Robert J. Ward Jr., who gave a talk at TEDxWilmingtonLive (Event #30) on April 28, 2018 said, "After my TEDx talk, I did manage to obtain additional speaking engagements (one in Las Vegas and three in my native town of Houston). Recently, I learned my new job as director of trade compliance at Wesco International, Inc. all started because someone in their legal team happened to listen to my YouTube TEDx talk. In short, one could say I owe my current job to my TEDx talk exposure! In addition, I received an invite to participate as a speaker at Wesco International, Inc.'s management leadership team meeting in Costa Rica. My speaking style definitely reflected the TEDx way. I pointed out how our personnel in China, for instance, might think it is okay to send U.S. content products to North Korea and Iran, because both ZTE and Huawei have done so. Similarly, I pointed out how our personnel in Dubai might think it is perfectly okay to divert U.S. content product to Iran, as Dubai is the biggest transshipment point for Iran. Of course, as a U.S. owned company distributing principally U.S. content product, my advice was a big 'No!' To date, I still have our personnel in both China and Dubai approaching me with caution to ensure our business is compliant with U.S. Sanctions law."

Tamsen Webster, who gave a talk at the 2nd Annual TEDxWilmingtonWomen Conference (Event #24) on November 2, 2017 said, "My TEDxWilmingtonWomen talk continues to be an important proof point for those looking to work with me, especially when it's a fellow speaker or someone aspiring to speak on a TEDx stage. That 'speaker's eye' perspective has been so valuable."

> **I learned my new job all started because someone in their legal team happened to listen to my YouTube TEDx talk.**

Karen Mayo, who gave a talk at the 4th Annual TEDxWilmington Conference (Event #8) on October 28, 2015 said, "Yes, yes and yes! The TEDx talk did impact my publicity and speaking engagements. It made a huge difference in booking health and wellness events. It gave me more credibility. I'm very grateful to Ajit and the whole TEDx Team in Wilmington, Delaware."

Marie White, who gave a talk at TEDxWilmingtonLive (Event #30) on April 28, 2018 said, "After appearing on the TEDx stage, I gained an incredible amount of credibility. Hosts that hadn't given me much thought invited me onto their shows. Once the talk was uploaded to YouTube, people began to share it with family and friends. And most importantly, our abducted child looked my name up on YouTube and was able to watch the talk several weeks before being returned to us."

Marianne Ryan, who gave a talk at a TEDxWilmingtonSalon (Event #15) on November 17, 2016 said, "After my TEDx talk, 'What Your Momma Never Told You About Childbirth,' was published, it helped open doors to several speaking engagements. I was invited to China to teach workshops in Guangzhou and Beijing in 2018. I also spoke at several different workshops and seminars in the US and have created a professional four-day workshop to train physical therapists and personal trainers in the Baby Bod Method. My new goal is to no longer just make the general public aware that new moms need better medical care. I am now determined to train as many professionals in the evidenced based program I developed to help women reclaim their bodies after childbirth."

> **Our abducted child looked my name up on YouTube and was able to watch the talk several weeks before being returned to us.**

Diane Capaldi, who gave a talk at the 1st Annual TEDxWilmingtonWomen Conference (Event #14) on October 27, 2016 said, "Once the video was released, it helped me to engage in conversations with my community about cultural and societal norms. Being a TEDx speaker gave my resume a boost, and I am sure has contributed to my many sponsors and press related interviews."

Dion Kenney, who gave a talk at a TEDxWilmingtonSalon (Event #25) on November 28, 2017 said, "Primarily, the notoriety that resulted was from my personal relationships within my industry. It is not an ordinary thing to have a TEDx talk and people definitely pay attention when they hear you've done one. Within a few months, I was offered a new position with a great company. They did not hire me because of the TEDx Talk, but they mentioned that it distinguished me from the rest of the pack. And it's true. You will be a member of a unique group of people — those that have a great idea and are willing (and able) to share it with the world."

Susan Bremer O'Neill, who gave a talk at the 3rd Annual TEDxWilmingtonWomen Conference (Event #32) on November 30, 2018 said, "To be accepted to give a TEDx talk indicated to me that my 20 years of work and passion were not only accepted, but also valued. It has been a long journey to become comfortable with my history and subject matter and the fact that I stood on the stage, shared my story and 'Self Appeal' philosophy was a huge confidence boost for me. Today, using the TEDx logo on my marketing materials lends credibility and shows I have expertise. While introducing myself, I'm proud to say 'TEDx speaker,' and this has elicited conversation with others. Through being elevated in this public way, I more easily reach and empower other women. I intend to use this talk for years to come to open doors, influence others toward empowerment and to shape the work that I do."

> **Being a TEDx speaker gave my resume a boost, and I am sure has contributed to my many sponsors and press related interviews.**

Arthur Brodsky, who gave a talk at a TEDxWilmingtonSalon (Event #13) on October 18, 2016 said, "My TEDx talk paid incredible dividends for me. Since that talk, which has now been viewed over 20,000 times, I have had many people, from patients interested in learning more, to scientists seeking to improve their own communication skills, reach out to me after watching my talk. I've also received several professional opportunities, including a documentary on immunotherapy for which I was interviewed last week."

Dr. Felicia Clark, who gave a talk at TEDxWilmingtonLive (Event #30) on April 28, 2018 said, "Immediately after doing my TEDx talk, I was invited to speak in Paris, and people who do not focus on my topic of body image requested me to speak where we found a way to make our different platforms blend. I booked multiple interviews and with media outlets with large audiences. My network grew, I got appointed to a board, and it has been much easier to do collaborative projects with supporters who back my Ms. American Goddess Pageant. When I call to book talks, people call back quickly. I also received lots of testimonials, which had been a logistical challenge prior to doing my TEDx talk. I believe doing a TEDx talk makes it easy to sell myself as a serious speaker and clients expect to pay the honorarium that I request."

Peter Hillard, who gave a talk at a TEDxWilmingtonSalon (Event #28) on December 21, 2017 said, "The experience of having given a TEDx talk that is widely available online has been delightful. I was approached by a voiceover agency about doing voiceover work, a family friend was inspired on a college audition trip by seeing my video unexpectedly on the hotel television, and a few colleagues use my talk to start discussions with their classes. I have also been asked to speak at various functions, and the talk has raised my profile considerably on the national level."

> **I've also received several professional opportunities, including a documentary on immunotherapy for which I was interviewed last week.**

Joan DelFattore, who gave a talk at the 2nd Annual TEDxWilmingtonWomen Conference (Event #24) on November 2, 2017 said, "Even before giving the TEDx talk, I'd published several articles about prejudice against unmarried patients in American health care, notably one in the *Washington Post* that I mentioned in the TEDx talk. After the talk, I wrote another article for the *Washington Post* specifically focused on what I'd said in the TEDx presentation. Since then, I've had several other pieces published, and a research article submitted to a medical journal is out for peer review. Although it's hard to separate the TEDx talk from the publications and from my activity on relevant social media sites, I believe that being able to attach the talk to publication queries is helpful. It shows that the topic has public interest and met the high standards for TEDx, and the format is much more personal than articles."

Diana Simone, who gave a talk at the 2nd Annual TEDxWilmingtonWomen Conference (Event #24) on November 2, 2017 said, "My talk itself has been very well received by all those I am aware of that have watched it. My son G. Russell Reynolds (aka Mr. Make it Happen) has arranged for me to do a radio and video blog interview next month. I will be interviewed on Life Masters TV. For me, one of the most exciting things is that I was contacted by a young high school student in Texas whose history class is doing a project for National History Day, and she has chosen the Amber Alert as her topic. She has taken a great deal of information from the TEDxWilmington talk, and so far, she has made it all the way to the National competition. Young people getting the message that everyone can make a difference in this world makes my heart smile."

Bill Walshe, who gave a talk at a TEDxWilmingtonSalon (Event #19) on June 7, 2017 said, "The reaction to my TEDx Talk, 'Prideology' was simply phenomenal. I received numerous speaking invitations as a result, and as CEO of Viceroy, this generated significant publicity for our brand. I also got to speak to audiences outside of hospitality, which strengthened my belief that my idea had application possibilities across multiple

sectors. My talk even became a powerful recruitment tool for my company. People would email saying, 'I have watched your TEDx talk and I want to work in that culture.' I now have a link to my TEDx talk in my email signature — not out of arrogance, but out of pride. Speaking at TEDxWilmington took my public profile to the next level."

Laura Wellington, who gave a talk at TEDxWilmingtonLive (Event #30) on April 28, 2018 said, "I received an enormous number of opportunities, speaking and otherwise. I signed a deal to adapt my upcoming children's book series, 'Jasper's Giant Imagination,' to television and already have an interested U.S. broadcaster. I received the opportunity to write a parenting book from a prestigious publisher, which I am also doing. I have been asked to consider branding my own wine tours out of Napa. Those are just some of the results that arrived from giving my TEDx. I've also met so many interesting people who have reached out."

> **I have met over a thousand people who have watched my TEDx talk and said it changed their lives.**

Robert (Dusty) Staub, who gave a talk at the 5th Annual TEDxWilmington Conference (Event #12) on August 24, 2016 said, "I already had a robust consulting business and have achieved best-selling status in having sold 50,000 copies of my books, 'The 7 Acts of Courage,' and 'The Heart of Leadership.' What I did get after the posting of the YouTube video were invitations for more speaking engagements, as well as a "calling card" that my current clients really liked, which led to more engagement with them as well as new client interest. My insights and book on breaking C.O.U.R.A.G.E. into discrete *acts* had already inspired thousands of people and given them a more powerful process of creating personal mastery. The TEDx talk expanded the number of people being reached and inspired by the simple idea that, 'small, daily acts of courage can change your world.'"

Arianne Missimer, who gave a talk at the 1st Annual TEDxWilmingtonWomen Conference (Event #14) on October 27, 2016 said, "Speaking at TEDx Wilmington was nothing short of an absolutely amazing experience. When people have asked me how it was, I've said it was one of the most rewarding experiences, both personally and professionally, that I've done so far. I was in complete awe of the incredible speakers and I feel so very blessed that I was among them. It was such a powerful day with women who are truly changing the world! I was so impressed by Ajit and the entire TEDx tribe who were so professional and compassionate and made the event so special. After reading books, memorizing, practicing, listening to TED talks, working with media and speaking professionals, it has been an incredible learning experience, one that I will carry with me for a lifetime. When it was posted on YouTube and shared, it was life-changing!"

Anisha Abraham, who gave a talk at the 4th Annual TEDxWilmington Conference (Event #8) on October 28, 2015 said, 'In a world that is increasingly reliant on short, visual messaging to get a concept across, the TEDx platform is an excellent medium to bring a specific topic or concern to a larger audience, particularly for those of us in more traditional professional career pathways. After my TEDx, I was approached by a publisher about writing a book on parenting teens. As a result, I am now in the process of completing a book entitled, "Raising the Global Teen" to be published in 2020! I have also been speaking to groups around the world on teen health, including recently a lightning talk (which is six minutes and only 20 slides that automatically advance) in Bangkok. Had it not been for my initial TEDx experience, I am not sure I would have had considered writing a book and speaking regularly on the global stage, in the same way."

Linda Arrey-Mbi Nkwenti, who gave a talk at the 3rd Annual TEDxWilmingtonWomen Conference (Event #32) on November 30, 2018 said, "I was excited to watch and share my TEDx talk with my community. It definitely elevated my platform as a professional speaker, and I have since received more speaking engagements for women's conferences, corporations and schools. Many women continue to reach out to me expressing how my talk motivated them to live their best life each day."

Ellie Laks, who gave a talk at the 3rd Annual TEDxWilmingtonWomen Conference (Event #32) on November 30, 2018 said, "I am getting more speaking opportunities and more recognition as a speaker, but the most important and fulfilling difference after the video aired is that I hear over and over again that people are actually adopting a vegan diet after hearing my talk. There are even more people visiting the Gentle Barn to meet the animals that I talked about in my speech. And so many have said that they never knew that animals had so much personality and intelligence, their lives are different forever more. That was my goal and I am very happy!"

Donna Duffy, who gave a talk at the 1st Annual TEDxWilmingtonWomen Conference (Event #14) on October 27, 2016 said, "My TEDx talk did not have an impact in that way. Rather, it was the opportunity to share a dream that had already become a reality years before. I was sharing that story and the lessons I learned living in an Arabic neighborhood. That experience profoundly impacted my life, and it was my joy to share those lessons learned with others through my TEDx talk."

> **After my TEDx, I was approached by a publisher about writing a book on parenting teens.**

James Lee, who gave a talk at the 2nd Annual TEDxWilmington Conference (Event #3) on August 7, 2013 said, "So, a deeply personal story here: my dad was sick with leukemia and it was getting clear that he wasn't going to last much longer. He couldn't make it to the TEDx event, and I was nervous because this was my first "big" talk as a futurist. My dad said, 'Jim,

I saw your video and I was impressed.' It was one of our last conversations. He was a brilliant man of few words, and this was an unexpected gift; I had made my father proud."

Greg Plum, who gave a talk at the 4th Annual TEDxWilmington Conference (Event #8) on October 28, 2015 said, "This has been the best part. Even though it has been over two years since I delivered my talk, people that I meet usually say: 'Oh, you did a TEDx talk,' which is usually followed by a fun discussion around technology, fear of public speaking, or how to earn a spot on the red circle. It is almost like being branded with a scarlet letter, only these letters are a different red and carry a very different meaning. I would not have traded that gut-wrenching, all-consuming experience for anything. In fact, I may be just sick enough to try again!"

Dr. Clint Rogers, who gave a talk at the 6th Annual TEDxWilmington Conference (Event #20) on August 16, 2017 said, "As one of the most satisfying experiences of my life, I have met over a thousand people who have watched my TEDx talk and said it changed their lives. I remember the first person I met as a result of them watching my TEDx talk and then coming to one of our clinics. He walked up to me and gave me a big hug. I was struck by the look of awe in his eyes, and the feeling of gratitude in my heart. Now, having this same experience over a thousand times with people from all over the world, it doesn't get old. If anything, it gets sweeter each time. I'm in Italy and just minutes ago met in the hall a woman who brought her mother, and both hugged me. I'm grateful that the message about the ancient healing secrets which helped my father are spreading, but also that there are so many golden-hearted people from around the world that I now consider friends."

Jody Wood, who gave a talk at TEDxWilmingtonLive (Event #30) on April 28, 2018 said, "I was absolutely blown away by the response. I was introduced to two very prominent doctors in the field and met with both, one in Cherry Hill, N.J. and one in Beverly Hills, Calif. Dr. Dan Gottlieb and Dr. Mark Goulston. They both have agreed to be on our Advisory Board.

I never would have met them had I not been given the honor of being chosen to give the TEDx talk. I also had a few investors as well as gained a godsend of a partner who is handling more of the business details so I can focus more on the creative end of things. Not a chance of that happening if not for the talk. I have been asked to speak at Bristol-Myers Squib in Princeton, N.J. as well as the NJ/PA chapters of Neurosurgeons in Philadelphia, Pa."

> **I got an overwhelming response from individuals expressing their gratitude to me for sharing my story and tools that helped me overcome my anxiety.**

Massoma Alam, who gave a talk at TEDxWilmington Live (Event #30) on April 28, 2018 said, "After my TEDx talk was posted on YouTube, my life changed for the better! I got an overwhelming response from individuals expressing their gratitude to me for sharing my story and tools that helped me overcome my anxiety. Many articulated that they found me to be an inspiration and they discovered the strategies I shared in my talk to be extremely helpful. This really made me quite tearful, because initially I was reluctant to be so open and vulnerable in my talk, but these positive responses made it all worth it. I did get offers to do speaking engagements including doing a webinar with University at Buffalo Alumni Speaker series. It also led me to start writing my own book which is about anxiety in the workplace combining my interests of Industrial & Organizational psychology and my own personal and others experience with anxiety."

Words of Wisdom

Question 4: Last but not least, please share in one paragraph not to exceed 150 words, your words of wisdom, based on your personal experience, to someone who might be thinking of sharing their idea worth spreading through a TEDx talk:

•

Mindy Tatz Chernoff, who gave a talk at the 4th Annual TEDxWilmington Conference (Event #8) on October 28, 2015 and at the 7th Annual TEDxWilmington Conference (Event #31) on September 27, 2018 said, "You must have something burning within you which needs to be told. But, not so that you can just tell it. It goes far beyond that. You have a fire within you that needs to get out, which is much larger and grander than you. It is an idea that others must hear. And then, you must be prepared to work hard, very hard. Incredibly hard. Take the advice and suggestions offered by the coaches. Read the suggested books. Watch a lot of TED and TEDx Talks. And then, practice, practice, practice. And practice some more. So, when you get up on that stage, you can be *FREE.*"

Joe del Tufo, who gave a talk at a TEDxWilmingtonSalon (Event #7) on July 31, 2015 said, "The preparation is harder than you think. If you try to wing it, you will regret it even if your talk is a success. But once you are prepared, assuming you are not already a professional speaker, it will elevate what you are capable of and make lesser challenges simpler to overcome."

> **You have a fire within you that needs to get out, which is much larger and grander than you. It is an idea that others must hear.**

Dr. Jalaal Hayes, who gave a talk at a TEDxWilmingtonSalon (Event #27) on December 14, 2017 said, "To someone who might be thinking about their idea worth spreading through a TEDx talk, I would say the following: practice, practice, and practice. Your talk will be posted online and many platforms for the world to see. Therefore, make sure that you look presentable, talk clearly, and nevertheless have fun. If you have fun and express the passion of your idea, I guarantee that people will connect with you and the idea that you are spreading."

Jill Sherer Murray, who gave a talk at the 1st Annual TEDxWilmingtonWomen Conference (Event #14) on October 27, 2016 said, "First, prepare. Rehearse your talk *hundreds* of times. Practice in front of real people, with the television blaring so distractions don't get you, and on the treadmill to learn to steady your breath. Second, be real, vulnerable, and inspiring. People want connection, so give them something they can connect to. Let them know your triumph can be theirs, too. Third, put your audience first — you're in service. Even as you appeal to organizers: What are the stakes for them? It will be tempting, wherever you are in the process, to make that talk all about you. Resist. When you find yourself worried about how you'll look on stage or what people will think of you, reframe immediately. Lastly, work with a coach. You need someone objective to weigh in. To catch the 'potholes' in your talk you will miss, simply by being too close to it and too invested in the experience."

Mark LoGiudice, who gave a talk at a TEDxWilmingtonSalon (Event #21) on September 12, 2017 said, "Do it; it's rewarding and gives a sense of accomplishment. All that attention given to your thought, your idea, your passion. Practice, practice and practice. Also go without slides and have a conversation with the audience."

Harold Lathon, who gave a talk at a TEDxWilmingtonSalon (Event #10) on July 21, 2016 said, "You must have a unique idea, and you must prepare and perform in your delivery and presentation. Rest before the event, and if you practice, practice, practice, you will be perfect."

> **If you have fun and express the passion of your idea, I guarantee that people will connect with you and the idea that you are spreading.**

Kalvin J. Evans, who gave a talk at a TEDxWilmingtonSalon (Event #27) on December 14, 2017 said, "My advice and wisdom regarding anyone who might be thinking of sharing their idea through a TEDx talk is this: There are some times that those who started with you won't be there in the end when you decide to move forward with the calling on your life. Don't ever give up even when the stakes are high. Use it to strengthen your resolve to see it through and inspire someone else who will need encouragement and comfort to carry on!"

Linda Farquhar, who gave a talk at the 4th Annual TEDxWilmington Conference (Event #8) on October 28, 2015 said, "Accepting the opportunity to do a TEDx talk can have significant benefits to you, the speaker, in addition to the audience you seek to enlighten. Obviously, your primary goal is to share your amazing idea, but if you post the YouTube link to your email signature, LinkedIn profile, resume, and other platforms, you will notice that some readers will immediately hold you in higher regard, without ever watching your video or seeing you speak. If your topic is timely and relevant, and you capture it well, you will now be deemed an expert in your field and may become an in-demand speaker on the topic. These are all wonderful opportunities of which to take advantage. Face it — you have an idea worth spreading. Try not to stress out. Enjoy the ride."

Joia Jefferson Nuri, who gave a talk at the 6th Annual TEDxWilmington Conference (Event #20) on August 16, 2017 said, "When I first realized that my TEDx talk was on YouTube, I couldn't open it. I could only remember the mistakes, the second-guessing of my outfit and all the things that filled me with doubt. Then one night, all alone at home, I leaped. I was so impressed. I was so happy about my topic and the presentation. I proudly posted it on my social media sites and on my web page. Since then I've been speaking on panels about the media, and have gained new clients who want me to teach them how to speak in front of large audiences. TEDx is not a place to show off. It truly is a place to present your ideas worth sharing. So many people approach me and say, 'I want to do a TEDx Talk.' When asked about which topic and what is so special about their topic, generally they fumble around with the answer. It's not a place of prestige. Even though it's very prestigious to have been selected. But it is a place of education and enlightenment. People depend on TEDx speakers to bring a new light to their everyday lives. So, before you decide that you want to be on a TEDx stage, make sure what you want to talk about is an idea worth sharing to the entire world."

Dr. Setrag Khoshafian, who gave a talk at a TEDxWilmingtonSalon (Event #25) on November 28, 2017 said, "Giving a TEDx talk is an incredible experience. It is one of the best tools to get you additional recognition and help you promote your ideas, views, solutions, or research. Now here is a word of caution. When I applied and was accepted to do the talk, I did not realize the amount of work it would involve. Be prepared to spend a good 50 hours in preparation. You might be frustrated sometimes and wonder why there are so many deliverables and so much practice. At the end you will appreciate the finished product — your presentation on YouTube under the banner of TEDx!"

> **Don't ever give up even when the stakes are high. Use it to strengthen your resolve to see it through and inspire someone else who will need encouragement and comfort to carry on!**

Liane Hansen, who gave a talk at the 2nd Annual TEDxWilmington Conference (Event #3) on August 7, 2013 said, "The best talks are those designed to spark the audience's imagination, inspire them to consider new ways to solve problems, overcome adversity and contribute to society. It is neither a soapbox nor a vanity project."

Bill Jensen, who gave a talk at a TEDxWilmingtonSalon (Event #25) on November 28, 2017 said,

"1.) Don't go for going viral. Go for a more powerful you! Even if your video doesn't get viewed a gazillion times, define success by how much more powerful, clear, succinct, and valuable your one big idea has become.

2.) No matter how much rehearsal time you think you need, multiply that number by 10. And make sure to rehearse in front of others, too, and listen carefully to their feedback.

3.) Simple, bold, powerful, clear visuals with as few words as possible. (If you use slides at all).

4.) Stories and feelings have far more impact than logic and structure. Touch people's souls with your storytelling.

5.) Cut yourself some slack! This is not easy! Even for those who made it look easy!"

Eric Okdeh, who gave a talk at a TEDxWilmingtonSalon (Event #28) on December 21, 2017 said, "I would encourage other prospective speakers, as I was encouraged in the original questionnaire, to consider TED talks, or other lectures that resonate with them and why. Really pick apart the qualities in each talk that speak to you and apply these qualities in your own talk. This was how I structured the ultimate goals of my talk. I believe that if you were to watch it with the talks that inspired me, you could see the throughline. The talk differs from traditional lectures in the sense that audience reaction is largely absent from the final video. People must consider this when constructing a talk so that it doesn't rely so heavily on the audible cues of the audiences' engagement. The silence in the video can be deafening, and a sharp contrast to my talk where I felt as engaged and in the moment as everyone in the room."

Mikki Williams, who gave a talk at the 4th Annual TEDxWilmington Conference on (Event #8) October 28, 2015 said, "As I coach many speakers and aspiring speakers who want to do a TEDx talk, I have shared a great deal of advice. They must have a new idea or put a spin on an existing one. They must know how to use stories to deliver their points.

They must understand and respect the red circle, how to use PowerPoint if appropriate, how to use humor no matter the topic and how to make an impact in the short time allotted. You cannot just take an existing speech and cut it to the TEDx time length. It takes practice in this new model of presenting and preparation and coaching is key."

Dr. Paul Rosen, who gave a talk at the 3rd Annual TEDxWilmington Conference (Event #4) on August 6, 2014, a TEDxWilmingtonSalon (Event #13) on October 18, 2016, and the 7th Annual TEDxWilmington Conference (Event #31) on September 27, 2018 said, "I would say that although the prospect of giving a TEDx talk is anxiety-provoking, it is an opportunity you do not want to pass up. Trust in the preparation process and everything will go fine. I have chosen to give TEDx talks devoid of any slides or other technology to minimize the chance of a problem. For experienced speakers, like my colleagues at the university, I would say that despite delivering hundreds of lectures, a TEDx talk is a unique experience that requires the investment in time to be successful. I would also recommend a speaker's coach regardless of previous speaking experience."

> **The best talks are those designed to spark the audience's imagination... It is neither a soapbox nor a vanity project.**

Taria Pritchett, who gave a talk at TEDxWilmingtonLive (Event #30) on April 28, 2018 said, "Since I am also a high school English teacher, I have created a TEDx talk unit as an alternative to the traditional senior research paper. In addition, I had the pleasure of mentoring a high school student through his TEDxYouth talk. As a result, I have developed a wealth of knowledge about giving an effective talk. I loved getting to know and understand what makes a great TEDx talk in comparison to a regular speech. I am already a speaker, but TEDx talks certainly have their own characteristics, which fascinates me. The biggest piece of wisdom I would give is to ensure that you select a topic you are very passionate about and embed as much as your personal narrative as possible. Facts tell, but stories sell. It makes it more engaging and vivid to use descriptive language, real world examples, and personal anecdotes to your audience. You want there to be memorable sound bites from your talk that make you stand out in your field. Prior to gracing the stage, many of my students, family, and friends texted with excitement and encouragement. Afterwards, many shared that they were moved to tears by my talk, and this is what made it such a worthwhile experience. My favorite part was the teacher in the audience who was able to make a paradigm shift about her approach to black girls in the classroom moving forward. This solidified for me that it was time for me to spread this idea, and I am thankful that TEDxWilmington gave me this amazing opportunity."

David Raymond, who gave a talk at TEDxWilmingtonLive (Event #30) on April 28, 2018 said, "Your ability to speak effectively from the red circle has almost nothing to do with your previous experience on the stage. Don't think just because you have not ever been a 'public speaker' it disqualifies you from being on a TED or TEDx stage. In some cases, it actually makes you more effective. In my TEDxWilmington speaker group there were at least two presenters that had little or no experience speaking, and I believe they stole the show. Focus on your message that is worth sharing. That message is the most important. Then share it by telling stories. Yes, the same stories you have been telling for years will captivate your TEDx audience and make your 'message worth sharing' be memorable. Good luck!"

Phil Spampinato, who gave a talk at the 2nd Annual TEDxWilmington Conference (Event #3) on August 7, 2013 said, "All the ubiquitous words of advice apply. Do your homework. Practice. Be yourself. Take time to enjoy the experience. Most speakers have a passion for their subject. Focus on getting that passion across to the audience. Use a diverse set of reviewers during the preparation period. Tell them to focus on how well you got the audience to feel your passion. People remember talks to which they make a connection, especially an emotional connection. Make them remember!"

Otto Borsich, who gave a talk at the 3rd Annual TEDxWilmington Conference (Event #4) on August 6, 2014 said, "Don't give a TEDx. Be the TEDx. Why is this topic important to you? How will it touch the listeners? The TEDx is about the audience and the message you want them to think about, feel, and call them to action. Keep it simple: less is more. Do not use PowerPoint. If there is technical difficulty, you are now powerless during the most significant speech of your life. The majority of the world's greatest speeches were delivered without PowerPoint or props. The Gettysburg Address has 270 words, mostly one and two syllables. Keep it simple — everyone loves a story, so tell your story. Be honest and factual. Remain authentic, embrace yourself, sell your uniqueness. Display absolute integrity. Interject humor, because being an expert in your field spewing data grows old quickly, and everyone loves to laugh. Lastly, love what you do, love the audience, and in return, they will love you."

Pina Anna-Grace De Rosa, who gave a talk at the 5th Annual TEDxWilmington Conference (Event #12) on August 24, 2016 said, "If you've been thinking about doing a TEDx for some time, listen to your heart, and speak from your heart. Then, share your story. Focus on your audience and the contribution that your message can be for them. In focusing on that, you will see any nervousness, anxiousness, or doubt dissipate. Your 'idea worth spreading' will give your audience wings!"

> **Keep it simple — everyone loves a story, so tell your story. Be honest and factual. Remain authentic, embrace yourself, sell your uniqueness.**

Markevis Gideon, who gave a talk at the 7th Annual TEDxWilmington Conference (Event #31) on September 27, 2018 said, "After giving my talk, I was instantly asked to speak at several other conferences. This was such an amazing feeling and opportunity, as my dream is to share my idea to the world. But something beyond that had a greater impression on me. I was the second to last person to speak during my session, and when the break came, I was approached by several individuals. There was one in particular that I will never forget. A woman approached me with tears in her eyes, and as she spoke, I could hear the pain in her voice. She told me that like me, she too had at one time lost everything. But it wasn't over for her. She had a dream that she wanted to pursue, and she could not think of any better time to find her China!"

Sunil Robert, who gave a talk at TEDxWilmingtonLive (Event #30) on April 28, 2018 said, "Enjoy the process — I was a bit begrudging about the tight deadlines I had to meet with the organizers, but I did not realize at that time that they were enforcing a discipline that worked for hundreds of other speakers, and I was being offered that best practice. So, enjoy the preparation. Secondly, enjoy the big day. I had to wait until post lunch for my turn, but I enjoyed myself to the hilt. I made new connections and cheered other speakers without being totally consumed my own forthcoming speech. Forget about yourself. Just be passionate about the idea, the story, the impact you'd like to have, and that enthusiasm will carry you to the finish line. I was totally switched off up until my turn came. My wife, who is also my fiercest critic, looked at me after I came back to my seat and said 'Wow! I have never seen you so animated and excited about any speech.' I truly enjoyed giving that speech. If you don't believe me, hear me out. I jokingly told a few friends that now I can die happy."

John Quinlan, who gave a talk at the 6th Annual TEDxWilmington Conference (Event #20) on August 16, 2017 said, "When my first TEDx talk application was rejected, along with about a hundred query letters to publishers about my book, despondency came a-knockin' in my soul. Why care enough to persist and to share? The writer Joseph Campbell reminds me: 'Bringing the boon back can be even more difficult than going down into your own depths in the first place.' I was emboldened to keep letting go of both self-rejection and self-grandiosity and winnowing out myself to obtain wisdom. Between dejection and faith, I found that my vulnerability, humility and integrity continued to develop. The TEDx stage provides a sacred space where, as mutual occupants of this shared planet, we connect through stories and ideas. We are pushed out of comfort zones and invited to be truly engaged with each other. It is fearful yet elating."

Kevin Rose, who gave a talk at the 5th Annual TEDxWilmington Conference (Event #12) on August 24, 2016 said, "You're going to freak out at some point, probably several points, but if you remember that you are there to be of service, grounding and peace will prevail. Be yourself, breathe, have fun, and most importantly, know that everyone is pulling for you. There is no road map for the perfect talk because there is no such thing. Your authenticity got you to this place and, if you allow, it will lead you successfully to the finish line. And whatever you do, remember to smile!"

Lisa Mims, who gave a talk at TEDxWilmingtonED (Event #29) on February 9, 2018 said, "One thing that I was asked over and over again was, 'What is the idea you want to share?' That's what I kept in my mind the entire time I was writing my speech. Remember, it isn't about you, it is about an idea worth sharing! Meet every deadline. At first, I was overwhelmed by the constant deadlines. But it truly helped break what I had to do into bite-size pieces. Listen to the advice you are given. I am so glad that I did, because it helped my speech evolve into its final product. Create a support system. I have to admit; my hubby wasn't into listening to my speech over and over. But my girlfriends, sister, and RODEL team were always willing. Most of all, believe in yourself and be confident that you have something to say that others will want to hear."

> **You're going to freak out at some point, probably several points, but if you remember that you are there to be of service, grounding and peace will prevail.**

Ria Story, who gave a talk at the 2nd Annual TEDxWilmingtonWomen Conference (Event #24) on November 2, 2017 said, "Less is more. As a speaker who is passionate about your subject, it's very tempting to pack multiple concepts or ideas and as many words as possible into a few short minutes. But, as Chris Anderson, curator of TED, said, 'Overstuffed is under explained.' Focus on *one* central idea and then support it with stories, facts, and figures. And, plan for dramatic pauses, laughter, or even applause in order to shift the emotional energy in the room. Channel your passion for your idea and the audience will feel it, too. Prepare, prepare, and, prepare some more. Practice until you are so comfortable with your presentation you could give it while rushing out of a burning building! You don't have to script every word if that's not your style, but you *must* know your outline, bullet points, and supporting material."

Rita Wilkins, who gave a talk at the 2nd Annual TEDxWilmingtonWomen Conference (Event #24) on November 2, 2017 said, "TEDx will make a difference in your life, not just for yourself, but for millions of people in your audience. Crafting your TEDx talk will help you more clearly articulate ideas both in writing and in your speaking. I had no idea that my words could impact so many, but one year and three months after my TEDx talk was put on YouTube, there are over half a million viewers. This was something I would have never realized, how much my story could impact the lives of so many."

Kristofer Younger, who gave a talk at the 4th Annual TEDxWilmington Conference (Event #8) on October 28, 2015 said, "Do it. If you can, several times on a couple of different topics, if possible. But do it. It's very empowering."

> **Practice until you are so comfortable with your presentation you could give it while rushing out of a burning building!**

Cyndi O'Meara, who gave a talk at the 6th Annual TEDxWilmington Conference (Event #20) on August 16, 2017 said, "Be prepared, know your topic and learn from the coaches. Being a TEDx speaker is a wonderful platform to spread your message."

Tiffany Stallings, who gave a talk at TEDxWilmingtonLive (Event #30) on April 28, 2018 said, "Five years ago, I went through one of the worst times in my life. I lost everything that I had held dear. Normally, I am a resilient person. I had overcome many odds and had also experienced great success. However, there was a period of time where I thought the only solution to all of my problems was death. I know we all go through difficult times. Perseverance is not a novel idea. I just knew that someone would benefit from hearing my story of overcoming insurmountable odds. I knew that there was a mother somewhere that needed to know that she was not alone. This is why I was so determined to deliver a TEDx talk on the topic of mom guilt. Therefore, I highly suggest to someone who feels that they have a message worth sharing that they do so. We all need words of encouragement and messages of hope. The world is always hungry for innovative ideas. If it is your spirit to share your ideas with the world, then I encourage you to do so."

Allington Creque, who gave a talk at the 5th Annual TEDxWilmington Conference (Event #12) on August 24, 2016 said, "We all have a story. Whether we tell it privately, publicly or not at all, we all have a story. Just sometimes a story is worth telling. It makes you feel great as well as the people who are listening. One out of five people need to hear your story mainly because they will know they're not the only ones who feel the same way or are experiencing the same thing. Sometimes holding back, a story can affect someone who needs to hear it. People are online looking for a story, perhaps looking for your story, so share it with the world. After all, I'm sure your story is an idea that's worth telling."

Seth Rainess, who gave a talk at the 7th Annual TEDxWilmington Conference (Event #31) on September 27, 2018 said, "To anyone who believes that they have an idea that could cause someone to sit up and think about something differently, I say go for it. Accept the big undertaking and responsibility to do your part to deliver the most important talk of your life. Know that the time involvement behind the scenes is way more structured and for good reason, so that the world will get to see the best you as you deliver your idea worth spreading."

Areeba Khan, who gave a talk at TEDxYouth@Wilmington (Event #18) on April 2, 2017 said, "Have a meaning and a mission for giving your talk. Don't do it for publicity. I know so many people that are interested in giving a talk for the mere purpose of getting "fame," and it's perfectly okay to want attention and feel honorable. However, don't forget that the purpose of your talk should be seen as a service to others. Your lessons and your story are to benefit those around you. Be confident and don't let others put words in your mouth."

> **One out of five people need to hear your story mainly because they will know they're not the only ones who feel the same way or are experiencing the same thing.**

Jennifer Myers, who gave a talk at the 2nd Annual TEDxWilmingtonWomen Conference (Event #24) on November 2, 2017 said, "It is an honor to be invited to speak on a TEDx stage. Above all else, remembering this, and always having humility, will provide such a strong base for success when delivering a TEDx talk. Secondly, I believe it's crucial to remember why you want to deliver the talk and follow the threads of your passion, understand where you want them to lead you, and why, and how you'd like your talk to change not only one person, but also the world. When a TEDx talk is delivered with a giving attitude, it becomes more than just information. It becomes an inspiring gift — in my opinion, the main purpose to give a TED talk at all!"

CHAPTER 7
Through the TEDx-Wilmington Process
Curated by Alessandra Nicole

I think one of the best things we told people who were interested in volunteering with us was to sign up to help with something that they were not already doing in their day job. If you are volunteering your skills that you ordinarily are paid for, you will eventually become demotivated to help, if not also slightly resentful for giving it away for free. Volunteering for TEDxWilmington gave people the opportunity to use a skill set that they wouldn't normally use and even learn about and grow a completely new skill set that they wouldn't have had a chance to otherwise.

In early 2017, as I decided to find roles to take on to help in TEDxWilmington, I noticed one area that could use some consistent attention was the blog section on our website. I am a photographer, and for me this meant I could take a break from working on images and was able to use my skills in words, copyediting, programming and a little bit of design. Our blog existed, but almost as an afterthought as our then-tiny core team was already running around wearing many hats. I could see our blog becoming an important tool to bring new traffic to our website. We built it into our speaker agreement that they would have to submit three short (around 300 words) blogs on a schedule to give us special insight into their journey.

Curating these blogs had many benefits. First, they caused the speakers to periodically pause and internalize what they were going through. The weeks and short months leading up to their event would pass by in a flurry of revisions and memorization marathons otherwise. Second, I wanted to create a constant way to feed fresh content to the site that wouldn't cause our team a lot of extra work and time, as we were already very busy. My idea was the more unique organic traffic flowing to the site to read blogs potentially meant more viewership of our TEDxWilmington talks on YouTube, and hopefully, the end result would strengthen ticket sales.

The speakers were given unique links for their blogs to use on their own social media and promoting the event to their individual spheres of influence, which gave us far broader reach (and hopefully translated to ticket sales). The speakers would have something to take pride in, as not only their static biographies were on a website with official TEDx branding, but blogs in their own words, too, were living on there that would carve out their hero's journey to the red circle carpet (and hopefully drive ticket sales). Curious speakers could learn about with whom they would be sharing the stage and even share their blogs, too, cross promoting themselves and their talks. We had constant waves of new content to use to promote the speakers and the event. Meanwhile, speakers' friends, families and peers had a story, a journey they could hook into, creating buzz and hopefully compelling them to, well, purchase tickets to attend the big day!

We did this using three general topics: "Meet the Speaker," "The TEDx Process," and "Reflecting," and each complete set would be designed to also reflect the individual thematic design of the particular event, creating units or something like little graduating classes of speakers. In each blog I had headings that repeated the speakers' names, talk titles, dates, venues, and had multiple links and buttons that would easily link back to their full biographies and, of course, to where tickets could be purchased. The final blog evolved to feature a photo of them speaking on stage and multiple ways to link to their talk for view on YouTube. The more linking to other parts of our website and to TEDx on YouTube, the better for our SEO and the SEO for the speakers, too, repeating their names and talk titles.

In their first blog, "Meet the Speaker," the speaker-to-be would get to talk about how thrilled they were to receive the invitation to come speak (and the inevitable fear that would immediately follow), as well as authenticate themselves by giving an overview of their expertise and what they hoped to accomplish with their topic and time on the red circle carpet. "The TEDx Process" was about a month or so into the preparation and generally sounded like, "Whew, in all my decades of professional keynote speaking around the world, nothing has been remotely as challenging as preparing to give a TEDx talk," "These constant deadlines are a nuisance, who are these people to demand videos and outlines and blogs out of me on their strict timetable?", to "I have practiced my talk so many times my spouse/child/dog has heard me reciting it in my sleep," and of course their thrill and enthusiasm about what's to come. But the speakers were still on their private island at this point, proverbially speaking, having been working on their talks for a couple of months at home with their families and speaker coaches, and not having met any of us or any other speakers in person yet.

The final blog, "Reflecting," was my favorite. It was actually due a week or two *after* they delivered their TEDx talks (and we told the speakers that their talks wouldn't get uploaded to YouTube unless they submitted this key 300-word post-mortem, which absolutely ensured they didn't forget about it!) I loved these. These were generally the glowy love letters to the TEDxWilmington team and everyone they finally got to meet in person, and they sounded like, "That was hardest thing I've ever done and I am so proud of myself for accomplishing that!" "I met the most amazing people from all around the world and we bonded. My life is changed."

What I didn't expect in early 2017 was that by the end of 2018 I would have curated more than 550 blogs and that there would be 647 in total since 2014. I didn't expect to have many of the blogs bring tears to my eyes for how heartfelt or surprising or humorous they were. If we didn't have our speakers write these blogs, we never would've known that a speaker at one of our events felt so down on herself after rehearsal the night before her event that she seriously considered flying home and not even showing up the next day! We wouldn't have been able to take this hero's journey with them, to internalize their trials and triumphs, and so when we met that person, we were even more personally invested in their success than anyone dreamed possible.

Mandy Bass

Event #31: 3rd Annual TEDxWilmington
Women Conference
November 30, 2018
TEDx Title:
How to Build Your Courage Muscle

Meet the Speakers: Mandy Bass for TEDxWilmingtonWomen

Since my acceptance to be a speaker at TEDxWilmingtonWomen two short weeks ago, I've been on a rollercoaster. Last week I rode effortlessly to the top of the hill, enormously grateful to be selected from over 200 applicants, breathing in the thrilling opportunity to positively impact the world, excited about the possibilities around the bend.

"What a rush that will be!" I said, as I crafted my outline, imagining myself looking out at the TEDxWilmington audience. My chest expanded thinking about what will surely be a peak experience.

Then I look down to see what comes next. My stomach clenches and I feel myself dropping precipitously into a heart-stopping dive. Adrenalin pumping, I am screaming inside, "What? I only have 10 short minutes? But you can't do anything in 10 minutes."

Panic creeps into my awareness. *Get me off this ride!*

"Breathe!" I tell myself. Then I google: "What can you do in 10 minutes?"

In my research I discover that every 10 minutes people generate 25,000 tons of garbage and three million tons of ice melts in Antarctica. A lot can happen in 10 minutes.

Instantaneously, I am back in my seat, enjoying the ride, relaxed and smiling as confidence rushes into my veins. I know that my message about fear and forgiveness will change lives.

Suddenly, a corkscrew bend appears from nowhere: My first blog post due in an hour. How did that get here so fast? I stare at the blank page. What was I thinking when I decided to get on this ride?

I sit down at my computer and start typing. Three hundred and fifty words later, I take a deep breath and look out the window as the sun peeks out from behind a cloud, and my worries melt like fog in sunlight. I have 14 minutes to spare.

I step off the rollercoaster — but only for a while — itching for another ride.

The TEDx Process: Mandy Bass for TEDxWilmingtonWomen

10 Things I've Learned About Preparing a 10-Minute TEDx talk

- Is your opening attention grabbing?
- You are not your audience. Get feedback. Lots of it.
- If you are a little thin skinned, this strategy could help: Imagine you have a Plexiglas shield surrounding you, and when people offer feedback, see whatever they say as necessary information, signals on the road in front of you, guiding you to change direction, slow down, speed up or make a detour. Allow whatever you perceive as criticism to splatter on the glass like bird poop on a windshield. Just wash it away and let it go.
- Accept that a 10-minute talk will likely take more than 10 times longer to write than a 20-minute one. The good news is that you will have half as much to memorize.
- Accept the fact that no matter how good you think your first draft is, there is a lot of room for improvement. Ditto for the second draft and the third. The more rewriting you do, the better it will be. Try to see each version as one step closer to your best.
- Implement Chris Anderson's valuable advice on naming your drafts: Each time you create a new version of your talk, save it as a new document with an easily identifiable name such as v1 TEDx talk; then v2 TEDx talk, etc. By placing the number at the beginning of the document's name, you can more easily locate the "right" version when you need it.
- Saving old drafts will give you peace of mind that you won't lose any good bits you may want to reconsider later, and you can edit without fear.
- It is true: you have no words to waste — but put that fact out of your mind when you are starting out, or you will stymie your creative process. Start off by pretending there is no time limit and record or write everything you want to say about your idea. Often the best ideas are afterthoughts.
- After you have written your first draft, take out the best 15 minutes and save that as v2. Ask yourself: Is the "big idea" clear? Have I introduced the throughline early enough? Does the theme weave through the entire talk? Are there any segments that may be good but don't really forward the one idea I want to share? Delete them.

- Read the script aloud and talk it out as you go. Are you using words, sentences and phrases that are natural to the way you typically speak? If not, rewrite.

Is your opening attention grabbing? Can you improve your close and call to action? Can you be more concise? Edit. Rewrite. Is there a shorter way to get this part across? Edit again. You are now ready for your first round of feedback.

Reflecting: Mandy Bass for TEDxWilmingtonWomen

I am so happy, humbled and grateful to have had the experience of speaking at TEDxWilmingtonWomen last week. The day of the event was almost surreal, like a symphony in slow motion, a peak experience, worth every second of sacrifice, every moment spent.

Though I traveled the 1,000-mile journey from Florida alone, I felt incredibly supported by the dedicated, generous and talented organizing team, led by Ajit Mathew George, and fellow speakers, all of whom did a beautiful job crafting and delivering their words of wisdom. It is truly an honor to be a part of this tribe.

As I reflect on the whole experience, three things stand out as being most important for aspiring TEDx speakers, and/or those preparing for their big day:

1. Humility
2. Flexibility
3. Focus

When I first began preparing my TEDx talk, "How to Build Your Courage Muscle," the presentation was light years away from the final version. Now I realize that quite unconsciously my past speaking experience and personal agendas influenced my judgment in the beginning. Without candid feedback from people I respected, I don't think I would have been able to have that awareness.

In some ways I think that the less experience you have as a speaker, in this environment, the easier the preparation may be. That is because experienced speakers (myself included) understandably tend to lack humility when it comes to creating their talks. As a result, they tend to be less flexible and responsive to feedback.

A TEDx talk is very different than what most speakers are used to. It is about the idea, not about you or your expertise. And it is short — very short. Without a lot of feedback and the help of my professional coaches, there is no way I could have created as much impact in 10 minutes. Of course, accepting and integrating advice from others requires one to be flexible and open. That is why I put flexibility at the top of the list.

As the process unfolded, the overarching theme for me became one of discernment and focus. Before working on my talk each day, I brought to mind a symbol from Vedic Mythology, the Kala Hamsa Swan that symbolizes wisdom. The interesting thing about this mythical bird is that it drinks milk, ingesting *only* the cream. It leaves the water behind. It is that kind of discrimination that produces a great TEDx talk. It is a constant culling, a continual evolution and pruning of non-essentials to produce a small valuable gift to share with the world. Once the gift is wrapped, it takes practice to deliver it. A lot of it.

A week later, this sacred journey continues to nourish my soul. Now I pray that my message of courage, compassion and forgiveness will touch the hearts of people around the globe, and in some small way, make a difference in the world.

Dr. Michelle Yep Martin

Event #31: 7th Annual TEDxWimington Conference
September 27, 2018
TEDx Title: *Moving from Porn to Meaningful Connections*

Meet the Speakers: Dr. Michelle Yep Martin for TEDxWilmington

For 13 years, I've talked about people who have sexually offended. I am cautious with people who ask, "What do you do for a living?" "I'm a psychologist," I reply. "What population do you work with?" "People who have sexually offended." Instantly conversations stop, someone makes "that" face, where your nose and forehead get scrunched as if you smelled something terrible.

I now tell people I work with sexual victimization, which garners less criticism, judgment, and comments about how a woman could choose to work with such a dangerous/

disgusting/horrible population. What people believe is I side with offenders by offering treatment; I work with them because I like hearing their stories or have no problem with their choices.

The opposite is true. I choose to provide treatment to people who made terrible decisions, and who wish to not reoffend. I work with people who want to change the trajectory of their lives, even if they can't change what they've done they can ensure there will be no more victims. I choose to work to ensure there will be no more victims. No more victims. While not everyone has the constitution to listen to what I hear, I believe by taking on these stories and reframing them I am helping to create a safer place for our children.

When I applied to TEDxWilmington, I was met not with disgust, but intrigue. They supported me and my idea. I am working hard to create a talk leading others to think, "What now?" What now, indeed? How do we can change something with which we've seen so ingrained in our lives? I know I can change it in my own small corner of the world, but that's not enough. We can see through the media and our own lives that's not enough. So, what now?

The TEDx Process: Dr. Michelle Yep Martin for TEDxWilmington

I knew this TEDxWilmington talk would be a lot of work; I didn't realize how much I'd have to balance to accomplish everything and create an idea worth spreading. Three weeks ago, I had neurosurgery. Surgery isn't fun, but this kind of surgery, the kind that puts you flat on your back for weeks, leaving you feeling weak, is not a surgery that someone who helps others for a living can tolerate.

I've been told the do's and don'ts by the neurosurgeon; some directions I've followed, and some I haven't. Not because I don't want to heal, but it's hard as the healer not to be healing — having to force myself to slow down, to really look at what's important in life, and ensure things that need to get done are accomplished when I have energy. I see this as a new challenge.

My TEDxWilmington talk is centered around caring for others. It's meant to spread hope for a worldwide problem. I want it to resonate with people. I want people to walk away with hope: that they can change their lives, their decisions, and their relationships. But to do that, I must take care of myself first, and that's hard.

I'm lucky to be working with an amazing coach and have the blessing of feedback that is useful from the curating team. One day, I mentioned to someone that I wanted to just quit. Not the TEDxWilmington talk, but everything I was dealing with — pain, healing, itching, and boredom. She asked me, "Criticism makes you want to quit?" My answer? "No, criticism and feedback help me grow. It's what moves me forward." If anything, criticism and feedback are what make me want to do better. I want to get up on that TEDxWilmington stage and knock it out of the park.

Reflecting: Michelle Yep Martin for TEDxWilmington

There's no way I can put into words what this experience is like, and I'm afraid by trying that I'll minimize.

Before the talk, there were times I thought to myself, "Who am I? Just some girl from Alaska who wants to talk to people about uncomfortable things. What makes me an expert? Why in the world would they pick me of all people?" Fear held me back a lot; I see that now. On rehearsal day, I saw people on stage, running their talks, and everyone's was powerful, and I'm thinking, "What am I doing here?" Then I stepped on stage for rehearsal, and it felt better. I knew I'd prepared; I knew I had an idea worth spreading, something important that no one wants to talk about, but that we *must* talk about. I went back to the hotel, ran it once, and then let myself go to sleep. I was anxious, again, until I stepped up on stage. And then — blink! — it was over, and I was stepping off stage to hugs and congratulations, and perhaps more important, people approaching me from the audience with genuine questions about how to help their sons, husbands, partners, and families.

All I wanted was someone to connect with what I said. Of course, with the bravado that comes with stepping off stage and being done, came the idea of, "When can I do this again?" I didn't share with my husband right away though, because I think, at that point, he had had his fill of TEDx for a couple of days. I'll broach the topic with him gently in a month or so, after he's had a great dinner and maybe just falling asleep, so I can casually mention it and he won't even notice. I think by starting with TEDxWilmington, I've been spoiled, because they were so organized, kind, generous, and incredibly supportive, and I'm sure it's not like this anywhere else. So, to Ajit and his whole team — you are all amazing, wonderful, smart and incredible. Thank you so much for the opportunity to push myself in this way.

Markevis Gideon

Event #31: 7th Annual TEDxWilmington Conference
September 27, 2018
TEDx Title: *Find Your China!*

Meet the Speakers: Markevis Gideon for TEDxWilmington

Who would have ever guessed? Surely not me! Within the next few weeks, I will be afforded the opportunity to fulfill something that I once thought would be a dream that most would agree is too good to be true. Browsing through countless TED/TEDx talks, I must admit that I am extremely nervous as I prepare to get ready!

I recall sitting on the beach in Thailand, speaking with my wife during our honeymoon, when I told her that I wanted this year to be different. I wanted to be able to share some information with as many people who would listen who could possibly give them a new perspective when it comes to following their dreams and accomplishing their goals. When we returned mid-January, windows and doors of opportunities just began to open. Having two speaking engagements in Wilmington to parents and students within the low-income community, as well as being accepted as a TEDxWilmington speaker, is further confirmation that my goals are coming into fruition.

But now that I have the platform to project my ideas to the world, am I ready? I have been constantly bouncing back and forth with this question, and then it all becomes clear when I think of my topic, "Find Your China." Now if you see me, I am a skinny black guy who grew up in Wilmington, Del., and you would never guess that I have spent most of my adult life in Asia. Hence the title: "Find Your China." I have been asked what that means, and as I search for my throughline, I find myself at times wondering the same thing.

Preparing for the 7th Annual TEDxWilmington Conference means a great deal to me, and I pray that I am able to reach those who are currently looking for their next steps in life. You see, finding your China doesn't necessarily mean leaving anything and everything that you know to travel abroad, but it does mean to go above and beyond to find *you*! Far too often, we find ourselves stuck with nowhere to turn. So, as I am preparing over the next few weeks, I am molding this conversation to show how one can go beyond limitations imposed upon us by others to climb extravagant heights to find our China!

The TEDx Process: Markevis Gideon for TEDxWilmington

The 7th Annual TEDxWilmington Conference is less than 30 days away, and the anticipation has given me an abundant feeling of excitement. As the days progress, I'm beginning to feel the pressure of relating a message to my peers that they will not only find to be relatable, but informative as well. My goal is to help others like myself "Find Your China." Day after day I have been practicing my talk in front of various audiences, and for the most part, I have been getting a great amount of feedback. Being that this is the first TEDx talk that I have ever done, I quickly realized that doing a TEDx talk is completely different from any speech that I have ever done in the past. This presented a slight challenge for me that I have never encountered before, and I knew that I had to completely alter the way I approached this. Some things I noticed about myself are that I had a less structured style of doing things, and by adding a more organized thought process to my talk would be beneficial. Although this may have started out as a challenge for me with all of the support I have around me, I believe this will truly be a success.

I have been working closely with two individuals who are helping to mold me into a better TEDx presenter. Not only has their constructive criticism and great advice helped change my style to be more structured and detailed, their advice stresses the importance of having takeaways that are relatable to most, but also making sure I don't jump around too much where my audience can no longer keep up. I am sure that at the end of the day other speakers and I all share the common goal to have a positive impact in the TEDx community, but we also want to reach those who may not be a part of TEDx.

Reflecting: Markevis Gideon for TEDxWilmington

It is now 2:30 p.m., and my time is almost near. Sitting backstage, I see that I am just as nervous as the other speakers. As my nerves begin to kick into high gear, the angelic speaker angel comes my way and informs me that my time is coming. I'm equipped with the microphone, and within a few minutes, I hear my name being called. My heart begins to beat fast as I watch Ajit walk down the stairs, and I knew it was now my turn to walk up. There it was — the infamous red circle in the middle of the stage. I step into the middle of the circle and before I begin speaking, I first scan the room to find my wife. Good! I find her, then look down and see that the timer has started. It's go time!

It seems like in no time the timer gets to 10 minutes and 28 seconds, and I am done. My first thought is, "Let's get off of this stage," but I remember Ajit's comment that we should allow the audience to clap. It gets quiet for a second, and then I hear a clap, followed by another clap, then more claps. Next thing you know a few people even began standing. It was a success! All of the preparation, all of the deadlines, all of the rehearsals, it was all worth it.

Prior to standing on that red circle, I was unsure of what to expect, but once I stepped off, I grew a large appreciation for the TEDxWilmington tribe. Actually, going through the whole process from the application to giving my talk, I would say it was one of the most strenuous processes I have ever encountered, and again I say it was worth it. Thanks to the tribe, I was fully prepared to give the best talk that I could, which made it easy for the audience to receive it. As I stepped off the stage, I was encountered by two individuals with very similar stories to mine, both stating that they, too, are going to "Find their China!" That moment was so exciting. I felt honored to be afforded this opportunity. I just know that this opportunity will have a huge impact on my life in so many ways. So much so that I now want to help others in the future who are presented with the same opportunity that I was. I couldn't think of anything better but to join the TEDxWilmington tribe as a volunteer. I salute the tribe, and I salute all of my fellow speakers from that day and past events!

David Raymond
Event #30: TEDxWilmingtonLive
April 28, 2018
TEDx Title:
Be the Phanatic, Be Happier Now!

Meet the Speakers: David Raymond for TEDxWilmington

Squish a 40-year career of brilliant stupidity into a brief 18-minute presentation? Whoa! What did I get myself into? Well, I didn't really get myself into it. Technically, TEDxWilmington and their Age of Amazement did, with some wonderful news. The power of fun will be an idea worth spreading!

For most of my career, I have had to deal with my fear and anxiety of people assuming I had no appreciable skills and was getting paid just to have fun. Such is the life of a professional idiot, or for those of you who don't know, the "OG" Phillie Phanatic. My speaking career has been fraught with similar concerns of inferiority. It has been hard work trying to understand the dynamics of giving audiences messages that are for and about them. My experiences inhabiting the big green guy has uniquely prepared me for this moment, except for the fact that I can't hide behind the fur anymore and I have to speak. Okay, wait. That was supposed to make me feel better!

I am sure almost every speaker who has been honored by an invitation to give a TED or TEDx talk must feel similar anxiety and insecurity. At least I am familiar with it. So, now I find myself spending an inordinate amount of time in my bathroom, staring at myself in the mirror, practicing my opening and then looking down at my iPhone stopwatch exclaiming, "Oh my god, that took me two-and-a-half minutes!" Hopefully, I will make it to the finish line with brilliant stupidity in under 18. Stay tuned.

The TEDx Process: David Raymond for TEDxWilmington

I sent the first video draft of my TEDx talk to what they described to me as the curating committee for their review. My anxiety meter was on high alert. Who are these nameless and faceless people? Are they going to enjoy my talk? How critical are they going to be? Well, a few short days after delivery, I received my answer in an e-mail. It was filled with suggestions, input, critique and concerns. In big bold print was the saying, "Trust the Process."

Immediately, I knew they were not Sixers fans because "Trust the Process" is, at the very least, a polarizing label. I have to tell you my first response was, "Wait — they don't know, they don't understand, and can I quit now?" My ego was firmly in play and it prevented me from seeing the wisdom of their input until I called my coach, Geoffrey Berwind (yes, there really are TEDx speaker coaches) who, at his count, has mentored and coached over 50 TEDx speakers and counting. I was tired and a little frustrated when I reached Geoffrey. After listening, he told me I was going on a bird walk. What? "What is a bird walk?" I asked. Seems like I was looking outside of myself and more focused on everything else except how I could be better. My ego was distracting me from recognizing that it was up to me to make this talk better, and the curating committee was doing exactly what they are supposed to do. Develop a process that is set up for us, as TEDx speakers, to create the best presentation possible so it truly will become an idea worth spreading. All I have to do is trust it, Philadelphia 76ers aside.

Well, now I have hope and the power of fun to get me across the finish line. I know with Geoffrey's help I have a chance, as long as my ego stops taking me out for a bird walk!

Reflecting: David Raymond for TEDxWilmington

My TEDx fear!

I remember when I was 10 years old, I was asked to be an acolyte at my Methodist church in Newark, Del. This was quite the honor for a young boy, and a proud moment for my mom. Unfortunately, I was petrified with fear of the prospect of coming out in front of the entire congregation every Sunday to light and then extinguish the alter candles. I would get to wear what I thought were some pretty cool robes, but I knew I would become known as the only Methodist acolyte to burn down his congregation's church! I apologized to Mom and told her I could not agree to do this because I was just too scared. She smiled and said "David, if fear is the only reason you would not try something new, then you will miss so much joy in life." This simple advice, given with Mom's love, has been a powerful guiding principle in my life ever since, and came into play with my TEDx experience.

The journey — from the moment I celebrated my selection as a TEDx speaker until I left the TEDxWilmington red circle Saturday afternoon — was trying because it was complicated by fear. It was my TEDx fear, however, that made this experience so powerful and one I will forever be grateful for. TEDx fear is good! It isn't any less scary than fear in general, and it can make you feel like abandoning the opportunity altogether, but it helped me focus on the joy. My TEDx fear allowed me to bond better with my 22 fellow speakers. I focused on their efforts to deliver ideas worth sharing. I watched them more closely and listened more intently throughout our two days together. Their goals became mine, and we got to know each other with conversations that were fueled by nervous energy and excitement. Their messages resonated with me, and we experienced the joy of bringing them to the TEDxWilmington stage together.

I now have 22 powerful tools to help me in life. I have gained 22 friends, followers and supporters. I have the joy of overcoming my TEDx fear, and maybe most important, I didn't burn the church down!

Elaine Wells

Event #29: TEDxWilmingtonED
February 9, 2018
TEDx Title: *Why the Fight is Never Over*

Reflecting: Elaine Wells for TEDxWilmingtonED

First and foremost, let me state that this whole experience was all at once the most terrifying, yet the most rewarding thing I have ever done personally; losing out only to the birth of my three beautiful sons, to whom much of my talk was dedicated.

I don't think I fully realized what the impact of giving a TEDx talk would be when I initially applied to be a speaker. It was only until people started congratulating me in really big ways, and saying how impressed they were, and how epic I must be to have been chosen to give a talk, and how what I have to say must be groundbreaking for it to have made it onto a TEDx platform, and on and on, the compliments came, until I said to myself, "What am I doing?" Obviously, this platform wasn't meant for someone like me; a single mom, struggling to get a good education for my sons and fighting this constant battle to make sure that great opportunities for kids who looked like mine, and lived like we lived, were inclusive of them. Surely, I had overstepped my boundaries. I mean, this wasn't a school district meeting, or a place where I'm rallying alongside hundreds of other moms and dads for access to quality schools. This was TEDx. Was my message really an idea worth spreading? I think it's fair to share how I got roped into applying. The administrator of one of the programs that I had researched and applied to as a supplement to the less than satisfactory education my sons were receiving at the time, who was also privy to many of the struggles and frustrations I had been going through, asked me if I had thought about applying for an upcoming TEDx talk, highlighting "Education Possible." My immediate (and what I thought was my final) answer was "No."

I offered that it felt kind of hypocritical for *me*, a parent still presently struggling to make sure that kids like mine are let into spaces where they would flourish if given the opportunity, even though, through no fault of their own, they may not be able to gain access because the failing school systems they were seemingly locked into hadn't prepared them to, it just didn't seem like I had anything to offer as far as making education possible. A parent, who was still fighting with her own sons to take advantage of programs and opportunities outside of school, where no one else looked like them, because for so many years they've been conditioned to believe that they didn't belong in those spaces; what could *I* possibly have to offer people that would be inspirational enough to be a TEDx talk? Nothing that I had been through in the last 19 years of fighting was pretty, glorious, or inspirational in my mind.

That began the onslaught of reasons from the administrator of why people needed to hear what I've been through; how the parent experience always needs to be heard; and that there aren't a lot of places where parents' perspectives, no matter how raw and un-pretty, were voiced. He said it would do parents who are in the same situations some good to know that there are other parents out here experiencing the same thing. He wore me down, and by the next day (right before the deadline to apply ended) I submitted my application.

To my complete surprise, I received an email congratulating me on being selected, which contained a boatload of attachments, directions, deadlines, confirmations, contractual material, rules, regulations, and a multitude of "do's and don'ts." The one thing that stuck out for me was, "You must deliver your talk from memory" — without prompts, cards, cheat sheets, or even a podium. *Whaaaat?* Surely that was a mistake, because even though I had been actively speaking on the same subjects for years, it had never been without some type of note, or written reminder, or even a prompt in the back of the room, and yes, the blessed podium that offered at least a little support and something to lean on when you were nervous.

Saying that the next couple of weeks were filled with anxiety, stress, and having to be talked off a ledge more than twice (meaning I was going to withdraw) was an understatement. According to the feedback I was receiving from the TEDx tribe (the people who kept you and your talk in check), what I thought was a pretty good talk was too long, too fast, not pertinent enough in the first three quarters of the talk — and some of that was received a few days before the actual talk! I recorded myself saying the talk, and then listened to it every chance I had, until I was overly annoyed at the sound of my own voice. I did the whole speech on index cards and tried to memorize it by chunking the parts of the speech. (That doesn't work, by the way.) It also didn't help to get the constant reminders of the event being almost sold out, and then officially sold out, and then finally *because* it was officially sold out, it would be live streamed *internationally*. No pressure, right?

In retrospect, and being completely transparent, although I heavily promoted the event on social media, I didn't invite any of my family or friends to come see me speak because I was so sure that my worst nightmare was going to come true: that I would freeze, or totally black out, when it came to reciting my talk. If the international community saw me fail on the live stream, then fine. At least they didn't know me personally. Even though I shared the updates, I may not have emphasized the live stream, for fear of choking with the added pressure. I'm glad to report though, that a lot of my friends who are great readers (and supporters) had found the live stream link information, and a few even made it to the event. Although I was a little mad that they were unknowingly adding to my fainting quota, I found myself looking for them as I was on stage giving my talk, and I walked straight into their congratulatory hugs once I was done.

One other thing that I think is really important to mention is the group of individuals with whom I had the honor of co-talking, I have never bonded with a group as diverse and supportive as those 23 people during our dress rehearsal and at our first time ever meeting. Of course, I choked — a "nightmare come true" kind of choked, at the dress rehearsal, not once but three times, to the point where I was close to tears and praying Mr. Ajit just finally said, "Okay, you can go; you're done here." He didn't of course, but what was said was, "Take as many times as you need to get it. You'll get it." These words, among many other encouraging words from fellow presenters who had every right to be just as nervous and stressed as me, but still found the time to offer comfort, hugs, words of support, and more hugs — those were the best. I got to spend a little more time with them at the gorgeous home of one of the sponsors for dinner and networking, and that too was amazing! I figured afterwards I would still have a couple of hours at home to get those parts I kept forgetting down, but the night lasted a lot longer than anyone planned.

The night I got home after the rehearsal I asked myself, "Why are you doing this to yourself?" Which meant not eating, not sleeping, writing and re-writing, and *still* trying to memorize my talk and *still* not being able to get all the way through it, and then silently cursing the program administrator for being so persuasive. Finally, I resigned myself to the fact that I was just not going to show up the next day. What were they going to do, fire me? They couldn't, because I wasn't getting paid!

I shared with my younger sons that I decided not to do it, and they both asked in unison, *"Why not?"* I explained about my choking multiple times at the rehearsal, how exhausted I was, how I had lost seven pounds since signing up to do this, and before I could finish, my younger son said (repeating to me some of the lines I had used on him and his brother, "Well, it sounds like you need to push yourself a little, *Mother*. No matter how hard it 'feels,' if you don't' stretch your boundaries, you'll never grow, and you'll regret not knowing how far you can go!" He was mimicking me! He said it with a sarcastic grin full of challenge, like he dared me to say I wasn't doing it. The one thing I try never to choke on is the chance to teach my sons a lesson that would be a great benefit to them, and myself as well, so I decided, without any further practice, that I was going to show up for my TEDx talk in the morning, and prayed about it that night.

The day was here, and I was a hyperventilating mess. I couldn't eat and could barely hold a conversation with anyone prior to going on. I was number five in the first cohort of speakers, and the closer my time got, the more "out-of-body" this experience felt. There was standing room only in the venue, there were three cameras filming from every angle, and to top it off, THE Dr. Howard Fuller (my education reform idol, who I'd been following for many years), sat down right at our table, just one seat away from me! It was all too much; I was waiting for the darkness of my fainting spell that I was sure was coming to overtake me, but it didn't. I was called, prepped, mic'd up, encouraged, and hugged some more by the TEDx comfort angel (yes, that's a thing!), and then they called me.

I really don't remember much about my time on stage delivering my talk. I remembered there were some rounds of applause several times during my speech where people thought I had made a good point. I remembered that the brightness of the spotlight allowed me to have the illusion of anonymity because I couldn't see the standing room only crowd in its entirety, even if it was just in my head. I remembered seeing my babies' pictures on the slide monitor in front of me on the floor, and thought, "This is for them, I can do this," and I did.

When it registered in my brain that I had delivered the ending phrase: "Until there is no longer a need to fight for one single child, the fight is never over," and I realized my talk was done, everything around me faded to a blur except the steps to exit off of the stage, so it was where I focused all of my energy, and attempted to exit stage left. I had done it! I was free! I was exiting to the beat of the applause, when a figure stopped me, and directed me back onto the stage. Mr. Ajit was blocking my escape! I had almost made it off! I returned with him to a standing ovation and some very kind and touching remarks from him as he recounted to the audience about my choking episodes the day before, and how he knew my talk would be one of the best there that day. Overwhelmed with relief and emotion, I let that response sink in. I guess the administrator was right. People did indeed want to hear my story, and judging from the comments of the many strangers and attendees, and fellow struggling parents, and even a few students in the audience, sharing my journey in this fight was indeed an idea worth spreading.

Bashar Wali

Event #19: TEDxWilmingtonSalon
June 7, 2017
TEDx Title: *A Hotel is Just a Building*

Meet the Speakers: Bashar Wali for TEDxWilmingtonSalon

"My name is Bashar Wali, I am a human being, and this is what I like." — or — A Guaranteed Methodology for Managing the Chaos of Preparing for a TEDx Talk

The scribbled notes sprawled across the desk, the balled-up notes mounting in the trash. The setting aside of time that, mathematically, you know full well you'll never have. The bookmarking, the compiling, the collating, the sudden questioning of the very things that have made you successful enough to even be in this situation. The generating of potential titles, the scrubbing of said titles, the starting again.

The writing, the re-writing, the reading, the re-reading, the re-reading aloud, the panic that ensues when your assistant tells you it's nine-and-a-half minutes over. The scrapping of whole sections, the killing of your babies (your ideas, not actual babies — though it feels like it). The mid-chaos blogging, wherein you attempt to convey to your hosts that, "everything is moving along precisely as planned." The sense of relief when they fall for your subterfuge so that you may resume this madness. The realization that you will also need slides for this talk. Self-doubt now bordering on self-loathing. The wide-awake hours in bed at night agonizing about whether your ideas will be worth spreading — or forgetting. The filmed run-throughs. "Why do I do that thing with my glasses?" "Do I have time to get a personal trainer?" "I wonder what their speaker cancellation policy is?"

Then, late one anxious evening in your study, a single, angelic thought slips into your head and changes everything: This is not brain surgery. Of course, this talk deserves all the rigorous preparation I've put into it. But, at the nub of everything, what I'm really communicating is this: "Hello, my name is Bashar Wali, I'm a human being, and this is what I like." Surely any calm, collected, curious, and passionate person can do that.

Right?

Jane Lyons
Event #18: TEDxYouth@Wilmington
April 2, 2017
TEDx Title: *Second Chances to Save Our Community*

Reflecting: Jane Lyons for TEDxYouth@Wilmington

Giving a TEDx talk has to have been the most empowering moment of my life. Standing in front of a room filled with 300 people (as well as a live stream audience from all across the globe) was exciting, yet challenging. As a 16-year-old girl, I stood up on that stage and forced myself to put my nerves aside. I reminded myself that my TEDx talk was not about me, but about the lives I will change by sharing this important message. I told myself that if teens living in the crime-ridden city of Wilmington can overcome the obstacles that they face in life, then I can stand up on stage to tell their stories, to unify our community in acknowledging the need in our society for second chances, and most importantly, to recognize an injustice in our world today that we can do something about — an injustice that exists in a very real way just a couple of miles down the road.

Although I admit that the TEDx journey was an arduous one, I would not have changed a thing. Looking back on this whirlwind experience, I am so grateful for the friendships I have made through many hours of speech prep and weeks of organizational duties leading up to an event that has changed my life forever. The hard work and dedication of our TEDxWilmington youth tribe really shined through on April 2nd. I am confident that I speak for the entire tribe when I say that the event truly exceeded our expectations, and I am so thankful to have been a part of such an inspiring day. If I could give any advice to someone who is considering embarking on this journey, I would say do not hesitate — just do it!

Jessica Falasco
Event #18: TEDxYouth@Wilmington
April 2, 2018
TEDx Title: *Solve the Cube, Solve Your Life*

Reflecting: Jessica Falasco for TEDxYouth@Wilmington

Giving a TEDx talk was the most incredible journey of my life so far. It taught me so many valuable lessons that I will never forget. I can now express my ideas clearly in front of large audiences without stage fright, give and receive feedback, and be confident in everything I do.

I made so many new friends throughout the journey as well. I met people I would probably never have met if I didn't give a talk. My mind is widened due to all the inspiring ideas my peers shared during their talks. Although I gained so many things from this experience, it was the most challenging thing I have done up to this point.

Some nights, I couldn't sleep because I was thinking about what to add to my talk, trying to memorize it, and hoping that I wouldn't mess up when I got on stage. Up until the actual date of the TEDxYouth@Wilmington conference, it never really set in that I was actually giving a talk! As I stood backstage listening to my introduction and waiting to go out onstage is when the nerves set in. But, as soon as I made it onto the red circle, heard everyone clapping, and felt the bright lights on my face, I felt exhilarated! As I spoke, I felt empowered because I realized everyone was listening to the ideas I had to share.

I am so glad I had the opportunity to give a TEDx talk at such a young age! This was such a unique moment in my life that I will never forget.

Diana Simone

Event #24: 2nd Annual TEDxWilmington
Women Conference
November 2, 2017
TEDx Title: *Amber Alert:
The Power of Response-Ability*

Meet the Speakers: Diana Simone for TEDxWilmingtonWomen

There is an old Zen proverb that states: "Before enlightenment, chop wood, carry water; after enlightenment, chop wood, carry water." And that pretty much sums up my world before and after the creation of the Amber Alert, that is, until a long-awaited dream came true and I received the invitation to give a TEDxWilmington talk.

Honestly, my initial reaction was a tidal wave of self-doubt and a bit of panic. After all, who was I to think that I could take my place among some of the most powerful and impressive speakers in the world? But then I recognized those feelings; they were the same demons of doubt that tried to prevent me from making the call that resulted in the birth of one of the most successful grass-roots movements in the history of this country and the recovery of 881 abducted children to date. Doubt didn't win then, and I'm not about to let it win now.

So I accepted with honor, gratitude and humility, and have begun to prepare the talk that will inspire the next life changing, life saving movement, and the next, and the next by proving beyond doubt that one person, one ordinary person, can in fact make a difference in this world.

The support and excitement this opportunity has generated has been overwhelming. I have been astounded by the number of people who have offered me an opportunity to practice my talk at their church groups, at a Toastmasters group, and in private gatherings, and now a dear friend with extensive public speaking experience and expertise has offered his help as well. I am so thankful for all of them.

Every day I become a little more confident and excited about giving my talk and about 2nd Annual TedxWilmingtonWomen. I know I won't let you down.

The TEDx Process: Diana Simone for TEDxWilmingtonWomen

Look Mom, I'm blogging! For those who don't know me, the likelihood of me blogging, climbing Mt. Everest and giving a TEDx talk were all about equal, and now, well, Everest is still out but as the old song said, two out of three ain't bad.

My world is expanding at such a rapid pace. Part of the preparation for giving a TEDxWilmington talk is being "encouraged strongly" to actually attend a TEDxWilmington event prior to your own. Wanting to comply, as well as understanding how incredibly helpful that could be, I purchased my tickets, packed my bags and headed for Wilmington, thinking that seeing an event live, meeting some of the people involved, becoming familiar with the airport, hotel etc. would make my experience in November less stressful. Little did I know my world would never be the same.

I'm honestly not sure what I expected; however I am sure it wasn't what I found. My expectation may have been along the lines of a "production company" with various gifted speakers "performing" their own brand of magic in their talks. That couldn't be further from the truth.

What I found was a family, a global family of people dedicated to making this world a better place for everyone, coming from their hearts and honestly and sincerely sharing their observations, experiences, ideas and dreams, led by a team devoted to bringing out the best in everyone and in humanity in general. I met amazing people of all ages, from all walks of life, races, and countries. Their camaraderie, mutual respect and support not only of each other, but of me, a guest, touched my heart and lifted me up in so many ways. I made so many new friends and shared so many common experiences, fears, hopes and dreams. Not only do I feel more confident about giving my talk now that I have a greater understanding of the TEDxWilmington sincere intent of "giving," I feel more confident about a positive future for this world in general. In my talk, I emphasize that one person can make a difference, and now I feel part of that global family of thousands of individuals that really do. All is well.

Dr. Kien Vuu

Event #32: 3rd Annual TEDxWilmington Women Conference
November 30, 2018
TEDx Title: *The Unconventional Prescription: YOU are Your Best Medicine*

Meet the Speakers: Dr. Kien Vuu for TEDxWilmingtonWomen

"Don't be boring… don't be boring… don't be boring…"

That's been my non-stop inner dialogue since I got the incredible news that I'd been accepted to share my idea at TEDxWilmingtonWomen this November. I mean, Simon Sinek, Dr. Mark Hyman, Dr. Rangan Chatterjee… they make it look so easy!

Don't get me wrong. I love to joke around. I chat up strangers, and I find ways to get my patients laughing every day.

But there's something about presenting an idea that's really close to your heart and close to your soul that's just *difficult*. It's not easy taking something important to you that's also large in scope, and making it succinct, funny, and actionable.

Thankfully, I've got a handy list of *deadlines* to keep me from overthinking this too much. It's been an incredible experience working through my big idea and hammering it down into something more simple, more powerful, and more helpful to others as I prepare to share it on stage.

I've seen firsthand how *we are our own best medicine* — I'm an interventional oncologist and radiologist. I work with cutting edge technology every day to diagnose and treat patients as they navigate the different stages of life with cancer and chronic disease. But the most powerful, inspirational, miraculous healing that I've seen (and personally experienced) hasn't been because of cutting edge technology. It's come about because of something deceptively simple and surprisingly profound: tapping into our own unique passion, purpose, and power.

Organizing these experiences in a way that's captivating and not boring is no small task. But I'm focusing on the audience and that's helping me craft my message. Because, ultimately, I believe in this idea. And I believe that the more people understand their own power, the better our health, our quality of life, and our futures will be. Because *you* are your best medicine.

The TEDx Process: Dr. Kien Vuu for TEDxWilmingtonWomen

When I was a kid, I thought I was a pretty good basketball player. I was smaller than the other guys in the neighborhood, but I could run between other players, dish assists, and sink basket after basket. But when I made my high school basketball team, I realized that no matter how many times you've done something, you can still learn a way to do it better.

And that's how I feel about my TEDxWilmington experience so far. I've spoken internationally about medicine, purpose, and the healing powers inside each of us. But the TEDx format has pushed me to rethink how I'm sharing my story.

Where I'd focus on covering a lot of statistics and qualifying my claims, I'm trying to focus on how the audience will relate to my idea. Why they will care about the unconventional prescription I've discovered? Why they might want to begin using it in their lives and how to want to take action?

I'm a goofball by nature and love getting people laughing. While my first approach is often to develop a knee-slapping talk, the TEDx process is helping me dig deeper into the *connection* between my idea, my experience, and the audience. There may be a few laughs, but I'm focusing on the most impactful way to connect with the audience.

And perhaps the most universal part of my TEDxWilmington experience so far is the drafts or drafts of drafts piling up in the Google Drive. As of today, I believe I'm up to around 23 versions of outlines and script drafts. But each edit brings my idea closer to a new level of clarity, and that clarity will help others relate to and apply my big idea in their lives.

Reflecting: Dr. Kien Vuu for TEDxWilmingtonWomen

Who doesn't love a surprise?

When I was accepted to speak at TEDxWilmington last November, I had to pinch myself. I couldn't wait to share my big idea with the TEDx world. I thought that being on the stage, laughing, and hamming it up would be the highlight for me. Growing up, I dreamed of being a comedian or motivational speaker, not a doctor.

But I was in for a surprise. Because the thrill of being on stage wasn't the best part of my TEDx experience. The best part was actually the people.

Seeing the audience respond to my idea felt incredible. The questions and insights other speakers came to me with after my talk surprised me and rooted me in the understanding that we are in the middle of a medical paradigm shift. Modern medicine is a miracle. But so is the new knowledge coming into the world about just how powerful we are and how we can use that power to live our most healthy, happy lives.

When I reflect on my experience, I remember the countless drafts, revisions, the painful process of applying the pressure of deadlines that transformed my idea into something clear and powerful.

But more than anything, I see faces. I see my coach, my friends, my coworkers who let me practice reading them draft after draft. I see the faces of the other speakers, my new friends, laughing around a table as we share a meal and we share our souls. I see the faces of the audience members laughing and nodding in understanding.

More than fulfilling my personal desire to be a TEDx speaker, I feel like this experience has allowed me to fulfill my purpose of sharing this big idea — *you are your best medicine* — so that it finds the people who need to hear it.

Thank you, TEDxWilmington, for this opportunity. And thank you to everyone who was a part of sharing this big idea, from the first draft to the end of my talk. Thank you.

Janine Driver

Event #20: 6th Annual TEDxWilmington
Conference
August 16, 2017
TEDx Title: *The Cooperation Paradigm:
How to Get People to Listen & Cooperate*

Meet the Speakers: Janine Driver for TEDxWilmington

"As Maya Angelou would say, *'When you know better, you do better.'* This time last year, at the start of preparing for my first TEDx talk, I was in what my Dad would call 'The Nut House.' Even my face launched a full force open rebellion, exploding electric red rosacea everywhere, for a little more than six-and-a-half days each week.

Here's the deal: A year ago, I made a huge mistake by having two different TEDx coaches, and as a result I was pulled in different directions. It was like driving a racecar without wearing a seatbelt. How many people are going to bet on you winning the race? Not many, right? Yeah, it wasn't just stupid, it was reckless. And at the end of the day, I changed my idea worth spreading numerous times — as you might imagine, not to the approval of the TEDxWilmington organizer Ajit George, mind you.

This year, things are different (thanks for another time up at bat, Ajit). After interviewing a couple different TEDx coaches, I found the perfect person for me: Fia Fastbinder (hit Google and check out her unrelenting awesomeness). Yesterday, we had our first one-hour session together to create an outline for my talk, and Fia rocked my world. She helped me get very clear on what my idea worth spreading truly is: Talk to the people in your life like a hostage negotiator, because if you don't start talking to each other this way, those people may be feeling full of shame and isolation and ultimately lack of belonging in society.

Next Fia asked me, *'How will the world be changed in some small way if people implement my idea?'* And *'What's at stake if we don't do this?'* When putting together my outline, Fia chunked my points/thoughts/data into 'buckets.' Had you been on our online chat, you would've heard me share story after story and how I thought they linked to my idea worth spreading. Then Fia helped me figure out what may belong in each bucket and what is irrelevant.

Yup, this time my seatbelt is buckled as I start this amazing race. I'm *soooo happy* to have a plan and a system to do this right this time.

The TEDx Process: Janine Driver for TEDxWilmington

"Operation Editing Completed and a Potential Disaster Hopefully Averted"

As I prepare to give my upcoming TEDx talk in Wilmington, DE, on August 16th, I finally finished editing and editing and editing some more, and now I'm in memorization mode. Phew!

My biggest challenge with editing was with regard to my opening story, which involves a super controversial raid conducted by the federal law-enforcement agency I used to work for, the Bureau of Alcohol, Tobacco, Firearms & Explosives (ATF), back in 1993. In my talk, I'm *not* discussing the pros and cons of who was right or who was wrong, because frankly, both sides has innocent people killed because of their delusional leader's deadly decisions.

However, what I am talking about is how the hostage negotiator, during that 51-day siege, saved 18 children's lives by using a technique we use in law-enforcement to get people to cooperate. This technique has made me a better mother, better investigator, better interviewer, better leader, and overall a better human being.

As you might imagine, my biggest concern has been that when I begin talking about the raid, I may accidentally polarize people in the audience. With that being said, my hope is that through my well-thought-out wording, a whole bunch of heart, and the perfect visual picture that says both sides were wrong in several ways, I just might keep people focused on the actual idea worth spreading: Talk like a hostage negotiator and get people to cooperate — even in the toughest situations.

Fingers' crossed! Wish me luck…. pleaseeeee!

Before I sign off and say, "I hope I see you in Delaware, on August 16th, where you can judge for yourself, if I pull it off or polarized the audience," I'd like to end with an epic expression that my mother always used to share with me. I'm sure you've heard it yourself many times.

"If you can't say something nice, then don't say anything at all!" Except, I want to tweak that expression just a little bit and end with, "If you can't say something nice, then rally your inner hostage negotiator, and assign the person you're in conflict with a trait you want them to have!"

By finding the strength of talking like a hostage negotiator, you will not only get that person to cooperate, it will literally change their brain. And here's the thing, when you assign a positive trait to someone else, it changes your brain, too!

Wouldn't you agree that it's time to look at our world in a different way?

Okay, now here's my official call to action... I hope I see you in Delaware, on August 16th, where you can judge for yourself whether I pull it off or polarize the audience!"

Chris Johnson

Event #32: 3rd Annual TEDxWilmington Women Conference
November 30, 2018
TEDx Title: *Attacking Urban Gun Violence*

Meet the Speakers: Chris Johnson for TEDxWilmingtonWomen

As a first-time TEDxWilmington speaker, I was unsure what to expect. In preparing my presentation for the Women's Conference on November 30, I have been incredibly impressed with TEDxWilmington's organization and support. The producers have been professional and cordial and have worked around my extremely hectic schedule as a lawyer in solo practice in Philadelphia.

The detailed timeline and links to other TEDxWilmington speakers have greatly assisted me in executing my deliverables. The instructions are clear and concise, and the timeframe specified for different submissions in advance of the Women's Conference, are very reasonable. I have also been extremely grateful for the flexibility of the producers, Alessandra and Elissa. I have been fortunate enough to have spoken all over Delaware to all kinds of audiences, including serving as a speaker at the 2017 Millennial Summit. I have never had as positive an experience in preparing to speak. The producers serve as careful and considerate curators. This is all the more impressive, since the producers work with numerous speakers for each TEDxWilmington event.

In my work with Governor John Carney, and while running for the position of Delaware's Attorney General, I learned about TEDxWilmington and its reputation for attracting amazing speakers and engaged audiences. I fully understand now what has inspired so many people to participate in TEDxWilmington, as speakers, audience members and volunteers. I am delighted that I was chosen as a speaker and am honored to have been invited to speak at the 3rd Annual TEDxWilmingtonWomen.

The TEDx Process: Chris Johnson for TEDxWilmingtonWomen

You never know how much you don't know until you try something new. During my preparation for the upcoming 3rd Annual TEDxWilmingtonWomen on November 30th, I realized how much there is to learn about public speaking. Fortunately, TEDx has provided me with excellent resources, coaches, and mentors to get the job done!

As an attorney who has appeared in front of countless judges and juries, I approached TEDxWilmingtonWomen feeling hopeful that preparing for a TEDx talk would not be a steep learning curve. However, upon receiving the critique of my first video submission, I learned that the storytelling elements of a TEDx talk are vastly different than how a legal argument is constructed. In the legal world, there are certain key pieces of evidence, legal standards, and other legal placeholders you must make during an oral argument. On the other hand, with in a TEDx talk, the emphasis is on the story being told and not necessarily every iota and detail of your subject. Learning how to craft a better story and condense many facts, and in an entertaining way, is one of the true lessons that I have learned preparing for my first TEDx talk.

Now that I am in the final stretch in preparation for my TEDx talk, I am honestly still very nervous, but thrilled for the opportunity to be able to tell my "story." So far during this process, I have only watched videos of TEDx talks from across the nation, so I am looking forward to rehearsals in a few weeks when I get to practice with my fellow TEDxWilmingtonWomen speakers. I look forward to rock and rolling on November 30th!

Reflecting: Chris Johnson for TEDxWilmingtonWomen

Wow! What an experience! I am extremely honored to have been part of the exhilarating experience at TEDxWilmingtonWomen 2018: "Showing Up." Looking back on the transformational aspect of my participation, honestly, I am already interested in participating in another TEDxWilmington event!

Upon reflection, November 30th was actually the easiest part of the entire experience. After over 50 hours of preparation over the past few months, I felt fully prepared for the main event under the bright lights of the TEDxWilmington stage. The great resources of TED and TEDx videos, practices and a full rehearsal, allowed me to work through the pre-talk jitters that come with giving a presentation. Further, it was great to engage and bond with my fellow TEDxWilmington speakers during the dress rehearsal and our speakers' dinner. It was comforting to see the other TEDx speakers make mistakes, forget lines, or experience technical glitches, because it proved that we are all learning together. It was rewarding to see my fellow speakers improve right before my eyes. I commend Ajit George, TEDxWilmington organizer and the rest of the TEDxWilmington tribe for creating such a sense of community and empowering us to improve and learn from each other.

In closing, I am truly grateful for having the opportunity of a lifetime and to perform in front of a *worldwide* (Yes, it was!) audience. The guts, tenacity, organization, and toughness it took for each of us to prepare for our talks, while balancing careers and families, are truly amazing. Hats off to TEDxWilmington for organizing such a life-changing event and I look forward to supporting future ideas worth spreading!

Valerie Biden Owens

Event #20: TEDxWilmingtonSalon
August 16, 2017
TEDx Title: *The Contribution Code: Three B's That Make All the Difference*

Meet the Speakers: Valerie Biden Owens for TEDxWilmington

Okay — I've asked myself a hundred times — how did this happen? Three weeks ago, I was content. My work at the Biden Institute was very satisfying, the plans for my daughter's wedding were coming together, and I was preparing to do a leadership training seminar and a commencement address. I was busy, productive, and feeling pretty good about myself and my summer visits to the beach.

Then… TEDx knocked on my door in the person of Janine Driver. "I've nominated you for a TEDx talk in Wilmington. Come on and join the fun — you'll love it, and you'll be great," she exclaimed with enthusiasm.

My responses ranged from — "Sounds neat," "Don't have time," "That's a lot to memorize," "It's in the middle of August," to — "Okay, let me see."

Well, I'm three weeks into it. Fun — are you kidding me? This process is grueling, and daunting, and somewhat intimidating. It is demanding of excellence and does not accept personal limitations. It is a call to action, or more simply put — a challenge.

Intimidation sets up so may roadblocks, especially when it is self-imposed. It could be debilitating, or you could choose to go through it, over it or around it. So, I choose the latter. I choose to reframe my thinking, to strike *intimidation* and insert *possibility* as the operative word in my TEDx experience.

TEDx requires that I live up to one of the principles of my Mom's code — *Be bold, not brash*. It requires that I do as I say, so that's what I'll do on August 16th — Be bold, not brash. I'm stepping up to the plate.

I hope you'll join me.

The TEDx Process: Valerie Biden Owens for TEDxWilmington

TEDx is demanding, it wants the best, the brightest, the most polished version of your idea worth spreading. It is unrelenting — awakens you in the night, pesters you in the day. You might say 'go away' but it won't. It has a mission — converting knowledge into wisdom — conversational wisdom, not so much institutional wisdom. It is overreaching, overarching and overachieving. In a word, it is awesome.

This year's topic, "Limitless: Ideas Beyond Borders" is so broad you could get lost in its depth. The challenge is to interpret it in a way that you can make a game plan to be better — better at whatever it is you want to do. People are less than they can be if they put limits on themselves or allow limits to be put upon them. "The Contribution Code" will show them how to break down those limits and sweep away the barriers.

The TEDxWilmington team is encouraging, capable and experienced. The team stands ready to help, and members are called upon to do so. I don't know how they keep us all straight while working full time on their own individual careers. They are not only keepers of the faith — they spread the faith.

So, it is with eager trepidation that I approach August 16th to join my fellow presenters at the Queen Theater in Wilmington, Delaware. There is history there and more history to make, and I hope my *Contribution Code* will do just that. It will show in simple language, and through storytelling, how we can become better. All stories carry some magic in them for either the storyteller or the listener. I hope "The Contribution Code" will carry some magic for the TEDx audiences. It is a way of thinking and acting that I have found reassuring and secure.

Doug Lipman

Event #28: TEDxWilmingtonSalon
December 21, 2017
TEDx Title: *What Storytelling Can Teach Us About Creating Connection*

Meet the Speakers: Doug Lipman for TEDxWilmingtonSalon

When I was asked about giving a talk at TEDxWilmington, my first problem was what *not* to talk about. I have been a performing storyteller and storytelling coach for several decades. Along the way, I have taught storytelling in many contexts. I have taught how to coach storytellers, how to use storytelling in marketing, and much more. Which broad topic should I focus on?

My first idea was based on a 20-lesson course I offer, "How to Grow a Story." After several unsuccessful drafts, though, one of my coaching buddies (people who coach me in return for my coaching them), gave me the bad news. "Doug," she said, "You've trimmed your 20 lessons of content, but you're still outlining a six-week course!"

"Okay," I thought. "I need to stop trying to *teach* storytelling and focus more on conveying a single idea about storytelling." I chose "Is there an Organic Way to Grow Stories?" When I talked through this topic with another coaching buddy, she offered me a suggestion: "It seems to me that your topic is not actually storytelling. You're really talking about how to *connect* to people."

That was the turning point. With help from several other coaching buddies, I shifted my focus to, "What Storytelling Can Teach Us About Connection." After another two weeks of work, I had created a new draft that, as of this writing, actually seems like a TEDx talk.

So far, my experience with TEDxWilmington has taught me a new strategy for coping with "the problem of too much knowledge," i.e., how to pull out a single thread from the fabric of a subject. I expect that this strategy will help me in future projects, too!

The TEDx Process: Doug Lipman for TEDxWilmingtonSalon

Tell, Listen, or Reflect?

With only a few months (already filled with other work) to develop this TEDxWilmington talk, I have needed to be more deliberate than ever about which "practice modality" to use at any given moment.

Modality #1: Being Listened To

I believe that it's not generally possible to practice communicating without actually communicating.

As a result, I do the work of *developing* the talk — of knowing what to say and how to say it — by talking to helping listeners (who are listening for my sake, as a favor to me). As I speak to them, I seldom focus on the words I'm saying. Rather, I focus on what I'm trying to communicate, in a way that builds on the responses of my listener. The words vary at first, but a "best way to say it" emerges over time.

Modality #2: Being My Own Listener

I record all my practices, then often listen to the most recent — as a way of reminding myself of what I said and in what sequence. This experience of listening to myself frequently spurs new ideas about what I mean to say, how to say it, or what to include or omit.

Modality #3: Working Offline

There are also times that I work on my talks alone, to:

1) Get an overview of the order of my ideas and examples;
2) Check on what might be missing or what should be omitted, and
3) Make sure I know what comes next at each point.

I sometimes talk aloud about the above to a listening helper. But much of this work goes best for me when I do it off-line.

For me, therefore, the key to a productive, efficient process is to:

1) Use actual communication as my primary way to develop a talk;
2) Listen to recordings of myself as a way to gain the perspective of a listener;
3) Work alone only on those things that talking and listening don't allow me to do efficiently.

The compressed schedule for developing this talk has forced me to be more aware of these three modalities — and more discerning about when to use each one.

Reflecting: Doug Lipman for TEDxWilmingtonSalon

I was accepted for "TEDxWilmingtonSalon: Fireside" only three months before the event. By the time I had a solid draft of the talk, only four weeks remained. From that point, I wanted to give the talk to live listeners at least 30 times, to be sure of it, and that meant averaging one listener a day! Sure, I could tell it over Skype or the telephone to individual listeners, but where would I find 30 helpers who could fit into my hectic schedule?

Who Should I Ask? How?

I felt shy about asking for this help. Sure, I was used to trading listening time with other storytellers, but with this short time frame, I needed one-way help. Who did I dare to ask? In the end, I asked everybody. All my previous students from online courses. All my previous and current coaching clients. Even all the members of two storytelling email lists. I created a Doodle poll with my available times, then emailed the link to it to all those folks. But would anyone sign up? If not, how would I get the practice I needed?

Success!

The first day, over 10 people signed up. Soon, my biggest problem was handling the logistics. At one point, I sent another email asking for folks to fill in certain dates that weren't covered. Within a day or two, I had filled up all the spaces. I ended up booking helping listeners for nearly every day until the talk!

But I Still Needed More!

As the talk began to solidify, I realized that I had two needs that still weren't met:

1) I needed to tell it to some in-person groups, so I could block out where to stand for each part of the talk;
2) On the home stretch, I would need to tell it more than once a day.

More emails. More willing helpers. I was able to schedule five in-person sessions at my home in Western Massachusetts and three-to-five distant listeners a day during the last week. All in all, I told the completed talk 54 times before the event to folks on four continents!

They Thanked *Me*

When I first thought of this plan, I thought I would have to beg unwilling helpers to listen. Instead, listener after listener responded to my thanks by saying that they were honored to help and grateful to be included.

Noa Baum
Event #28: TEDxWilmingtonSalon
December 21, 2017
TEDx Title: *Beyond Labels: Bridging Differences Through Storytelling*

Meet the Speakers: Noa Baum for TEDxWilmingtonSalon

I was so enthusiastic to be invited to TEDxWilmington and honored to be part of such a distinguished line of speakers on the topic I'm so passionate about — storytelling. But I am very nervous.

I've always been a worrier. It could be something in my Israeli Jewish genes. My family loves making fun of it; my friends suffer gallantly and miraculously still love me. It is ridiculous, but I can't control it. Writing about it may help, so bear with me.

As a professional storyteller, I've been a public speaker for more than three decades. Talking in front of people is what I do. I've learned to live with some "stage fright" as part of the creative process. So public speaking cannot possibly be making me so nervous.

In his book *TED Talks*, Chris Anderson says: "The only thing that truly matters in public speaking is not confidence, stage presence or smooth talking. It's having something worth saying." I worry that my talk will not be worthy of this platform and I won't communicate a coherent message in 15 minutes.

My idea is something that matters deeply to me: the power of storytelling to build bridges for peace, to connect across differences. I've been performing a one-woman show and written an award-winning book about it: "A Land Twice Promised: An Israeli Woman's Quest for Peace."

I passionately believe in the power of story to open a path for dialogue and peace. But in Israel, where I was born and raised, despair and cynicism rule, peace is almost a dirty word, and people like me are considered naive at best. In the U.S., where I've lived since 1990, the divisiveness, hate crimes and general discourse against "the other" are on the rise.

I can just imagine the scorn on people's faces as I speak: "Storytelling for peace? Really? Be realistic and look at the world around you!" I've struggled with these demons before. I didn't imagine I would meet them again in preparing for this talk, but here they are.

But Chris Anderson also wrote: "Your goal is not to be Winston Churchill or Nelson Mandela. It is to be you." I'll try to stay true to who I am and look forward to getting support in this process from the TEDxWilmington team.

The TEDx Process: Noa Baum for TEDxWilmingtonSalon

As we approach the darkest time of the year, it seems that 2017 has been darker than most, with natural and man-made calamities and the ongoing unreality show of U.S. politics, not to mention the Middle East…

Personally, we've been through difficult times with my beloved husband reacting badly to a new MS treatment and spending an entire month mostly paralyzed in hospital. He returned home a few days ago and continues to inch his way out of the valley of shadows.

I'm embarrassed to report that a Hanukkah childhood song has invaded my mind this week. It is accompanied by vivid images of my long-ago preschool days in Jerusalem: A gleeful march in line with my fellow three-year-old warriors, enthusiastically waving hands carrying imaginary torches and stomping in rhythm with the words: *Banu Choshech Le'garesh* ...

Here's a hopelessly crude translation of the Hebrew:

We have come to drive away the darkness!
In our hands fire and light.
Each alone is a tiny light but together we are a mighty light.
(stomp...stomp...) Move away Darkness,
(stomp...stomp...) Off with you Pitch Blackness.
(stomp...stomp...) Move away here comes the light!

Going back to nursery rhymes seems simplistic, but these words have acquired new meaning for me.

During this difficult time, I have been overwhelmed by the mighty light showered upon us by so many: my amazing adult kids, Maya and Ittai, our friends and neighbors, my beloved Adat Shalom congregation and the devoted caregivers and helpers that surround us. With countless acts of kindness and generosity and love, they have pushed away the darkness!

Once again, I'm affirmed in my belief that we have the power to do this for each other. My late father reminded me often: "The good in this world far outweighs the evil. But because it is so common, we forget and focus on the out of the ordinary, the less common evil."

So, in spite of ongoing dire and disturbing news, my heart is brimming with gratitude. Grateful and feeling so blessed that only the words of this childhood song can match the delight: *Move away darkness, here comes the light!*

On the upcoming winter's darkest day next Thursday, I have the honor to be included in "TEDxWilmingtonSalon: Fireside," devoted to storytelling and promising to illuminate and warm hearts.

Reflecting: Noa Baum for TEDxWilmingtonSalon

The shortest day of 2017 has come and gone, and with it our "TEDxWilmingtonSalon: Fireside" event. By all accounts, the sold-out event was indeed illuminating and exceeded my expectations.

It was a delight to discover the connections *and* the inter-connectedness of one speaker's work to another's, and their use of story to make an impact and effect change. It was inspiring to witness and thrilling to be part of this collective reminder, that in spite of the advancements in communications that technology offers, a human's basic and central need is still for a person-to-person connection. Each talk, in a different and unique form, showed the vast power of story in its many applications, to answer that need.

From the first idea and draft to the final moment before audience and cameras, The TEDx Process was very demanding. It became daunting when life got in the way: my husband was hospitalized for an entire month and I had no time or ability to focus on preparing. I wasn't sure I'd make it at all.

I didn't want to give up, but knew I would miss several deadlines, so I gathered my courage and asked the producers for help. The answer was, "family comes first," and they supported and worked with my unpredictable schedule. The TEDx experience taught me the importance of persevering, seeking and receiving help and trusting in the process.

With my preparation time dramatically reduced, I was so grateful for the support of producer Geoffrey Berwind with the initial draft. But for refining and revising my talk, I did as I do when crafting a new story — work with my storytelling peers. I was particularly grateful to the valuable insight and suggestions of colleagues and mentors Doug Lipman and Charlotte Blake Alston.

Stepping onto that red circle on stage, I was very nervous. In spite of years of professional speaking before diverse and large audiences, it was stressful to stand before three cameras knowing this talk may reach countless viewers around the globe.

But producer Ajit George's pep talk at rehearsal, reminding us that those global viewers are people like me, for whom English is a second language, somehow helped. I breathed, ignored the cameras and focused on the living, breathing people before me as at any storytelling performance. Their rapt attention affirmed they were with me, the enthusiastic applause that my talk had resonated.

There are many paths on the journey into TEDx world. If you'd like to embark on this journey, know that you will be supported, but it is up to you to choose the path that works best for you. Seek help from fellow travelers and allow the support of others to carry you to the finish line when life poses challenges along the way. After all, it is our human connections that make a difference.

Ellie Laks

Event #32: 3rd Annual TEDxWilmington
Women Conference
November 30, 2018
TEDx Title: *My Gentle Barn:
Learning to Listen!*

Meet the Speakers: Ellie Laks for TEDxWilmingtonWomen

I have wanted to do a TEDx talk for years, and now I am finally preparing for it; it is a dream come true! Getting the invitation was pure elation as my head filled with ideas for my talk. It was as if each animal that I have ever known was asking for his or her story to be shared and asking me to pick them. I imagined to myself what I would say about each animal and how I would describe their tale, and then one animal rose to the surface, took center stage in my mind, and almost demanded that I share her story. "Karma" is the matriarch of our bovine family, and has a story that people can really relate to, so it seemed fitting that her story would be the one worth sharing.

As I go over and over the talk in my mind, in the shower, in the car, before I fall asleep at night, I get more and more excited. Ideas come to me as to how to begin or end the talk, and it's almost like Karma and me are in partnership as I feel her silently guiding me and inspiring me. As I stroke her soft fur and gaze into her deep, soulful eyes, I pray that I do her justice, tell her story for the most impact, and change the way people see animals forever after. The truth is that it's really Karma giving this talk, and I am her translator. It is her message and her life that I will be talking about, and I feel both elated and a deep sense of responsibility. May the weeks ahead bring clarity and focus, and may I deliver justice to Karma, her life, her family, and all animals that are counting on me to be their voice!

The TEDx Process: Ellie Laks for TEDxWilmingtonWomen

Being invited to speak at TEDxWilmingtonWomen is a dream come true and the process has been almost as delicious as giving the actual talk. From writing the very first outline, practicing that first talk, receiving notes, and then redoing it for the finished product, it's been nerve wracking at times, but rewarding nonetheless. To me, the process is like molding a big chunk of clay. At first it has no form or shape.

But then the chiseling begins, and from nothing, something starts to take shape. Little by little more and more of it emerges until what the message is, is clear and bright. And once the main shape of it is clear, the fine sculpting and small details become the focus. In the last few weeks while the main vision of my talk is now clear, tweaking small sentences and refining timing has been my focus. And getting feedback from the TEDxWilmington team has been very helpful. It is easy to have a story or vision in our heads, but to make it clear, in focus, and meaningful to others is the hard part. The hardest part of this process is making my talk crystal-clear to others so they can see what I see in my mind. And I guess that is this last part of the fine-tuning, even down to the last detail.

When I watch inspiring TED talks now, I'm reminded of the effort behind the scenes that goes into that one great moment. And it is evident that in all masterpieces, in all inspiring, life altering acts, tremendous refinements and practice comes first. I am grateful to partake in this experience, not just the finished product, but each baby step towards it!

Lauren Smith

Event #23: TEDxWilmingtonSalon
October 17, 2017
TEDx Title: *What's Driving the Connected Car? Data, It Turns Out*

Meet the Speakers: Lauren Smith for TEDxWilmington

The prospect of a TEDx talk was thrilling, but to be honest, also daunting. I had only started public speaking a year earlier. I completed nearly 20 talks in that time, and they had gone well, but TEDxWilmington was going to be different from all of those. I know the topic on which I speak inside and out, and have shared it with academics, policymakers, and conferences, but for a TEDx talk I was going to have to change the framing completely. It would be the talk I had long wanted to give, a talk that would pull the uninitiated into this little world that I find so fascinating. Give them a succinct, engaging pitch, hook them on how this topic was going to transform their world, and they — everyone — should care. That was not the way of policy conferences.

But I hesitated. The idea of submitting a one-minute audition video seemed suddenly paralyzing. How would I reframe the topic? What was the clever anecdote and five-word slide that could encapsulate my work? What would I wear? How would I talk? The deadline of August 16 would not come for a month. I did not want to submit last minute, but for weeks, I nervously put off recording, while versions of how to deliver the talk played constantly in the back of my brain.

Then the unexpected struck. On Friday August 11, five days before the application deadline, I started feeling very sleepy. I slept most of the weekend. I stopped by a doctor's office on the way to work on Tuesday, and they sent me instead straight to the ER. When they told me I likely had viral meningitis and should do nothing for at least a week, I went home to the couch and hardly moved for, it turned out, a whole month.

The only problem was, the TEDxWilmington application was due the day after I came home from the ER. I had put it off too long, but I had become so enthralled by the idea of giving this talk that I couldn't, even in my sickness, let it go. In the fog of meningitis, I scraped together a script. I peeled myself off of the couch to manage a shower, and endeavored to, it felt, put lipstick on a pig — to see if the right outfit, and makeup, and lighting could transform me for 60 seconds from someone who could barely place one foot in front of the other into someone who could persuade a TEDxWilmington selection committee that I could wow a crowd.

To my surprise, it worked. And while I remain anxious with anticipation for October 17, if that muted version of myself was able to make a compelling case in August, I hope that means the now-healed version will truly reel you in this October.

The TEDx Process: Lauren Smith for TEDxWilmington

It's hard to believe that TEDxWilmington is only one week away. I have learned that the organizers were serious when saying this process would involve hours and hours of work. Now I think I understand a bit of what makes TEDx talks so engaging — even the busiest speakers have to take the time to pour themselves into their talks.

More than just the deadlines and resources to review, this talk and its content have been omnipresent in my mind since I first applied to speak. The process to turn a wonky policy subject into a relatable and engaging story requires a creativity that I don't get to use often enough in my daily work on law and policy. Content and anecdotes have been swirling in the back of my mind for weeks, but piecing them together proved challenging, and the upcoming outline deadline loomed constantly in my mind. Then, one rainy day, I was sitting in a café mourning my ruined outdoor plans when suddenly I reached for my notebook. Out of nowhere, I began writing, and each piece fell in place. In an hour in that café I wrote my talk's entire script. Creativity, it seems, strikes unexpectedly.

Life events can strike unexpectedly, too. At the end of September, I braced for what I knew would be a very hectic October — a number of talks, big regulatory developments for connected cars, and several out-of-town weddings. Things were on pace, but it was going to be a lot. Never could I have imagined that these worries would soon be minimalized when our house caught fire just two weeks before the TEDx talk. As the house was deemed uninhabitable, I spent the week I intended to be TEDx memorization-focused bouncing between Airbnbs, indexing belongings for cleaning or disposal, consoling a traumatized dog, and searching for a new place to live. It was overwhelming and exhausting.

I write this post from a rental couch in my new temporary apartment. I now have a bed and a few items of clothing that I picked out for emergency cleaning. I won't move back home before the TEDx talk, and to be honest, I'll have just started putting things back together. My hope is that, as before, everything will come together at an unexpected moment. Maybe adversity forges the strongest TED talks, but I guess you'll have to tune in October 17 to find out.

Dr. Wendy Leonard

Event #31: 7th Annual TEDxWilmington Conference
September 27, 2018
TEDx Title: *Zebra Fish: Practically People — How to Save the Human Species*

Meet the Speakers: Dr. Wendy Leonard for TEDxWilmington

I'm still stunned, thrilled, and scared to death thinking about doing a TEDx talk. I imagine standing on that stage, as so many others have done before me. People whose talks have inspired me, engaged me, given me goose bumps; people whose talks have so profoundly embraced spreading that one idea worth sharing. They all amaze me. Their courage, their poise, and their authenticity.

I can feel the excitement coursing through my veins; but then, the doubts and fears creep in. I wrote a quick note to the organizer/executive producer of TEDxWilmington expressing my humble gratitude when I learned I'd been chosen to participate. In that note to him, I also confided, "I'm scared to death." His reply? "If you weren't, you would not be normal."

I cannot begin to express how powerful and soothing those words were to me. I am so lucky to have some of the best friends and family in the universe. They are all so supportive of this intense adventure I'm taking. They say such kind, loving, and supportive things like, "You got this!" and "Enjoy every moment!" and "We can hardly wait!"

Here's the thing: If it were just about me, that's one thing. But it's not. It's about the whole team of dedicated folks who made our scientific documentary short film what it is: A powerful, compelling, important, award-winning film that could change how we conduct scientific research — impacting the rate with which we identify treatments, and even cures, for some of the most horrible diseases, such as pancreatic and breast cancer, Parkinson's disease, addiction, Alzheimer's, depression — not to mention a game-changer for rare diseases that usually don't get the funding they need. We, of "team zebra fish," truly want to help spread the word; our team chose me. So, I'm all in! Goooo Team Zebra Fish!

The TEDx Process: Dr. Wendy Leonard for TEDxWilmington

The TEDx process so far? It's as daunting as it is exhilarating. Seriously. The self-inflicted mental barriers, juxtaposed to the streams of consciousness that veritably glow with Divine inspiration, are stunning. And you know what else? It's super self-revealing, which is something I neither considered nor expected on this journey.

You know that famous Eleanor Roosevelt quote, "A woman is like a tea bag — you can't tell how strong she is until you put her in hot water?" I really get that. Thing is, generally speaking, I like hot water. Case in point, a few months back, I took one of those silly online "tests" to see what my "last five words" would be before I die. The result? "I can make that jump!"

Here's the thing: By nature, I'm curious. Heck, I'm a researcher: I delight in mining deep down into what others write, suggest, feel, and propose. Doing so greatly informs my writing. I'm also an active listener, by nature. I've said many times over the years that

I've never really learned anything from talking, myself. But now, because of TEDx, I believe I may have to reconsider that last self-assertion.

TEDxWilmington has forced me to listen to myself in a way I've never done before. Their process is rigorously iterative, for sure — but that's my style, too, so it's not that. What's different is the passionate support and the wise, actionable critiques the TEDxWilmington team provides. And the kindness with which they do this is off the charts!

Oh my, I just figured it out: TEDx is like an honest-to-goodness mentor! I've never had a mentor before! They unabashedly want us to grow — challenging us to dig deep and self-reflect, whilst guiding us down a path of contemplation, inspiration, and self-realization. It's scary. It's wonderful. Gratitude abounds.

Reflecting: Dr. Wendy Leonard for TEDxWilmington

At the reception following everyone's TEDx talk, a lovely woman, with the warmest, biggest, smile on her face (whom I hadn't met prior) walked right up to me, gave me a big hug, and said "Wendy, I have two words for you: Mind blown!" She then shared how she'd known nothing about zebra fish (my TEDx topic) and thanked me for giving her hope for future treatments and cures! Another person came up to me and said that he "was sure" he wasn't going to find my topic "of interest" to him, and how "boy, was I wrong!" Then, there was the woman who asked how she could get this information sent to her husband, as he was a scientist, and how working with zebra fish would change everything for him at his lab!

When I sat down to write this blog, I'd planned on sharing how "mind blown" was the perfect phrase to illuminate my reflections on the entire TEDxWimington process — from submitting a cellphone video, through actually standing up on that stage and giving a talk. And that's still true; but, there's so much more!

For anyone considering going on this incredible journey: The process is far bigger than I had even imagined, and I'd imagined it was going to be one of the toughest challenges, ever! But I didn't do this alone; far from it. My friends and family were amazing; TEDx coach Dana Dobson was lifesaving; and, the entire TEDxWilmington tribe was extraordinary, inspiring, kind, supportive, and exquisitely candid! And know this — particularly if you're apprehensive about going on stage: I had been told by the awesome Ajit George (aka: Executive Producer & Magic Dust maker) that the TEDxWilmington audiences are the best: Warm, highly engaged, and incredibly supportive — and they sure are! They veritably beam love up onto the stage, with a palpable energy that can only be described as electric! From beginning to end, for me, this journey was life changing, gratitude-filled, exhilarating, humbling, and truly magical.

Robyn Howton
Event #29: TEDxWilmingtonED
February 9, 2018
TEDx Title: *The Key to Improving Schools is Already in the Classroom*

Reflecting: Robyn Howton TEDxWilmingtonED

Just moments before I went on the red carpet at TEDxWilmingtonED, I glanced at my phone to see the time. I had a message from my son: "Mom, I've got the live stream up and am waiting to see your beautiful face. You're going to do great. I have no doubt. I am so proud of you." Suddenly my nerves calmed, and once I wiped a tear from my eye, I was ready to take the stage.

Preparing for my moment on the TEDx stage allowed me the opportunity to reflect on core beliefs as an educator. Using the chance to share a learner's journey with my students began as I explained to them my process for writing the talk and how it related to their writing process. I let them see me stumble; I shared the feedback that caused me to rewrite parts of the talk; I felt the pressure to be a success so they would see a triumph ending to the journey. They sent me a message early in the day saying, "Good luck, Ms. Howton. You got this!" They welcomed me back to school with notes on my board saying they were proud of me.

While choosing which of my personal stories of "why" to support my belief in the power of teachers to be leaders in improving education, I found myself posting a closed family Facebook group asking for some information and pictures. The ensuing conversation reminded me how much of my story is a family story of believing in the power of education to change lives. It also let me peek back into family history and see pictures of the one room schoolhouse where my dad and his brothers and sisters started out their schooling. My aunt is sharing a book of memories about the school. A cousin shared a picture of the book her mom used to teach arithmetic when she was the teacher there. And we counted the number of us who are educators and came up with at least 20. It made all of us proud.

Once I took the stage, it was my moment. I have been frustrated by the lack of teacher voice in education policy and reform my entire career. I had carefully crafted my message and practiced my delivery so I would engage my audience in considering the benefits of my idea for all students. The energy in the room throughout the day had been positive and hopeful, despite some bleak pictures that had to be painted about the state of American public education today. I wanted my message to end the day with an example of where we can find a source of hope that we can truly create an educational system that works for all kids in all zip codes. As I ended the speech, I could see people nodding yes and giving me positive acknowledgement. I was proud of myself in a way I haven't experienced in a long time. I had achieved a goal that was truly a challenge for me.

Giving a TEDx talk has changed me. It has reminded me what it means to push myself not only to work hard, but to learn something completely new. Stepping on the stage and speaking not as a teacher to a class or a presenter to fellow educators, but as Robyn Howton, my passion and my beliefs, was empowering. It reminded me how much satisfaction it brings to succeed when you are afraid you will fail. After taking off my microphone and doing my post-talk interview, I looked at my phone. I had a message from my dad that said, "You are up there with the Eagles." If you saw my talk, you know that is the highest praise I could receive from my dad. I hope my talk will inspire those who are seeking to improve education to include more teacher-leaders in fundamental conversations. However, I will treasure the experience because of the opportunity for personal growth, and to share that growth with the people in my life who matter the most to me.

Areeba Khan

Event #18: TEDxYouth@Wilmington
April 2, 2018
TEDx Title: *Muslim, American, Female: America's Future*

Meet the Speakers: Areeba Khan for TEDxYouth@Wilmington

This TEDx process has been enlightening and exhausting. I have never been more mentally stimulated and challenged in my life. My personal topic is emotionally hard to discuss, as it is very real, and I am essentially opening every single thing about myself to others.

I'm discussing controversial issues that are real and powerful. I'm coming out as who I am and my journey throughout my life. This is going to be the speech of my life and everything I've accomplished, but most importantly, these are lessons I have learned. These are lessons I have experienced throughout my life and I want others to learn these values. I want others to know that they are not alone in their struggles. I'm just a normal 17-year-old Muslim teenager who has been challenged to fight for what she believes in. This is my country, and I'm not going anywhere.

I plan on making a difference with my speech, but also continuing that mission in serving those around me. I'm thankful for all the support I have received from friends and family members. Giving a TEDx talk is going to be challenging, but I know that I will work as hard as I can to get through this and become successful.

The TEDx Process: Areeba Khan for TEDxYouth@Wilmington

The process of giving a TEDx talk has been stressful, yet enlightening. It was not until this past Monday night that I finally found exactly what I want to say in my talk. My title has been changed a minimum of five times, covering about five different topics, but I am thankful for all the support and love I have received from everyone.

The talk is finally going to be titled, "Muslim, American, Female: America's Future." Everyone has something important and powerful to share with others; my whole life has been filled with different puzzles that now, as a [high school] senior, have been put together to form this story. Every major experience and every school I have attended have shaped my identity into the confident Muslim American female I am. This talk is personal, it's real, and I know it will benefit every single person regardless of your race, religion, culture, or gender. I am so excited for this talk and can't wait for #TEDxYouth@Wilmington!!

Reflecting: Areeba Khan for TEDxYouth@Wilmington

The process of giving a TEDx talk has been life changing. I remember how nervous and excited I was the days leading up to the event. I didn't actually think I would have been able to give this talk because of how difficult it can be to memorize, rehearse, and perfect the experience.

Once I arrived on the red carpet, all my fears went away, and I was left with passion. Passion that came from my heart that let me enjoy being up there (it helped that I couldn't exactly see the audience because of how dark it was). If it wasn't for all the loving people, especially the speaker angel, Mrs. Kampert, my best friends who drove more than two hours, yes two hours, to watch my talk, and of course Mr. George, I don't think I could have done what I have done but I kept remembering the reason for my talk. Its message was for everyone out there who was struggling, everyone out there who was different, everyone out there who was afraid like I was four years ago.

Now that I am a senior at Ursuline, I can say that the process of giving a TEDx talk has fulfilled my Ursuline experience in preparing me to take on the world. This experience has helped me to find my story and accept who I am. I am incredibly honored and blessed to have been a TEDxYouthWilmington speaker. The friendships and memories made will last me a lifetime. I look forward to becoming a mentor and easing the process of a future TEDx star!

Molly Clark

Event #18: TEDxYouth@Wilmington
April 2, 2018
TEDx Title: *Stand by Your Sisters*

Reflecting: Molly Clark for TEDxYouth@Wilmington

I cannot believe it has been a month since the first TEDxYouth@Wilmington! It seems like just yesterday we were meeting at the kickoff event for the first time. This sure has been an experience that I will never forget! I feel more confident in myself because if I can get in front of 300 people as well as the live stream audience, what can't I do? I was amazed at how many people my talk inspired. Although I was often stressed, all of my hard work paid off.

    I made a lot of new friends that, without TEDx, I probably would have never had the chance to meet. As one of the youngest speakers at the event, I really enjoyed getting to see what kids a few years older than me had experienced. I really think that TEDx has given me a way to build my web and connect with people. I will be honest; the process wasn't always pretty. There were a lot of late nights and a few tears. The day of the event I was more nervous than I had ever been. However, when I stepped on stage, I took a deep breath and did just what I had practiced so often. It was the best feeling in the world to have the applause from the audience. I am so grateful for this experience, but there is no way I could have ever pulled this off without the support from my friends, family, teachers, and the TEDx Tribe. Thank you all!

Bonnie St. John

Event #30: TEDxWilmingtonLive
April 28, 2018
TEDx *Title: Be More Resilient with a First Aid Kit for Your Attitude!*

Meet the Speakers: Bonnie St. John for TEDxWilmington

Preparing to talk for around ten minutes at TEDxWilmingtonLive in April looms ahead of me as a rather daunting task. Not because I fear speaking more than death, like 75 percent of the general population. In fact, I have been a professional speaker for more than two decades. I had no problem speaking before a crowd of over 30,000 at the opening ceremonies for the 2002 Paralympics in Salt Lake City, or emceeing an event in India that included the Dalai Lama, or being simultaneously translated into seven languages and beamed around the world for a global leadership conference in Las Vegas. But it is exactly *because* I do this a lot that I know how hard it is to pack 10 minutes with valuable insight, focus on one actionable morsel, and get it right. There's an old saying attributed to Abraham Lincoln about speaking:

> "If you want me to speak for ten minutes, it takes me two weeks to prepare it; if it is a half-hour speech, it takes me a week; if I can talk as long as I want, I am ready now."

Given this amazing opportunity to communicate with the vast TEDx audience, my mind floods with nuggets of wisdom from my broad set of life experiences: as an amputee, a survivor of abuse, a mother, a black woman in America, a graduate of Harvard and Oxford, a Paralympic ski medalist, Rhodes Scholar, White House official, CEO of my own business, author of seven books… You can see why ten minutes seems challenging. It's like asking a parent, "Which of your children do you like best?"

Come on, Abe. Gimme a little help here. Four score and seven years ago? That was a good one. Maybe I can do something with that…

The TEDx Process: Bonnie St. John for TEDxWilmington

The real art of a TEDx talk is conveying that *one* idea worth spreading; but, to me, ideas are like Lays Potato Chips: it's really hard to have just one.

I sent in my practice video, and part of the feedback was that there were too many takeaways for people to remember. But I was so sure I had focused on *one* thing! My talk is all about micro-resilience, the term we coined to spotlight small, evidence-based steps you can take to be more resilient every day, all day long. I began with how personal resilience is for me; my "why," as Simon Sinek would say. My life is all about resilience: my leg was amputated when I was 5 years old, my father left before I was born, and my step father sexually abused my sister and me for years. Despite growing up in San Diego with no snow — and no money either — I became the first African-American to win medals in Winter Olympic competition. I couldn't possibly be who I am today without a healthy dose of resilience.

Next, to illustrate how to put micro-resilience into action, I shared the idea of a "First Aid Kit for your Attitude." In the same way that you need a kit with Band-Aids or burn cream in case of emergency, you can be prepared for injuries to your attitude! An angry client, a shift in deadlines, or even a technology crash can put you in a bad mood that affects everything else you do. So, we recommend using a box, bag, or drawer in your desk to gather up pictures, mementos, thank you notes, or anything that can help turn your attitude back to the positive when you need that boost. You can stay in the driver's seat. It is a powerful idea to share with coworkers so that you can help each other — you can give them a small gift and say, "This is for your first-aid kit; it looks like you could use a lift today!" Even kids can learn this powerful lesson: we are always in control of our own attitude.

I guess I should have stopped there, but I went on to explain the umbrella idea of micro-resilience as a whole and the research behind the central idea: that mini-recoveries along the way actually make you more competitive. And I closed with an inspirational thought from my mentor and ski coach, Warren Witherell, about his views on resilience.

I did pack it all into 11 minutes and 34 seconds, but I can see in hindsight that there was too much information. I deluded myself into thinking it was all one idea — micro-resilience. I now need to channel my inner Oliver Wendell Holmes and seek that elusive "simplicity on the other side of complexity." Wish me luck!

Reflecting: Bonnie St. John for TEDxWilmington

Wow — We did it!

When I accepted my invitation to give my TEDx talk, I was so focused on the time limit, meeting the requirements for practice videos, blogs, outlines, slides, etc. that I didn't realize there would be so much more to participating in the TEDxWilmington experience. The people I met were amazing — the organizers, the many volunteers in the 'tribe,' and of course, the other speakers. I gained new ideas, new friends, and became part of an incredible community with smarts and heart.

Over the course of the two days in Wilmington, one question seemed to come up several times: "This experience is so rewarding. How can I do this more often and get paid for it?" Since I have been a professional speaker for over 20 years and it is the primary way I make my living, I thought I would share a few tips.

Look up the National Speakers Association (https://www.nsaspeaker.org) — it's the best group for learning about the *business* of speaking. NSA helps you understand how to market your material, how to organize your office (contracts, calendar, logistics, etc.). I was given this advice, I did it, and it helped me avoid many mistakes!

You don't have to be exotic or famous to be a professional speaker. I didn't automatically get hired to speak just because of my achievements. Meeting planners are risk averse; they write big checks to speakers who are proven to be good at conferences. Doing the *business* of speaking — setting up systems, building a track record of performance, and serving your clients well is the best way to build a reputation. Word of mouth and people seeing you speak are the best ways to sell yourself.

If you work your speaking as a business, it will grow, but it does take time to develop. The more you speak, the more referrals you will receive. Yes, writing a book helps, but it can also derail you with the amount of promotion you do for the book vs. your speaking.

My best advice, though, is to keep re-inventing yourself. Stay aware of trends in the areas of your expertise, and constantly adjust your presentations to remain relevant to your clients.

Finally, if you are wondering whether you can really add anything different from all the other speakers out there, the answer is yes! No one can share the ideas, experiences, and insights that you have… except you.

Good luck!

Jeff Patnaude

Event #30: TEDxWilmingtonLive
April 28, 2018
TEDx Title: *From Great to the Greater Good: When Great is Not Good Enough*

Meet the Speakers: Jeff Patnaude for TEDxWilmingtonLive

So far, preparing for a TEDx talk is proving to be an uncomfortable surprise after having been considered a public voice for half a century. Giving my first recitation at the age of six and a sermon at the age of 11, I have honored the privilege of speaking before groups thousands of times. Because our ancestors most likely made auditory sounds to communicate long before inscription, public speaking might be considered the first form of connecting and the sharing of an idea in the art of communicating. I have always felt humbled when invited to stand, speak and participate in this ancient and esteemed tradition.

The reason for the surprise has been the difficulty of trying to hone the idea worth sharing. Always attempting to think in unique ways for applying ideas for positive change, I have enjoyed that opportunity by publishing multiple books in the areas of leadership, mentoring and personal growth. But for some reason, this idea of, "From Great to the Greater Good" has not yet gelled. Although I started work on this title several years ago and wrote 40 pages of what I thought might be credible material, I am finding it challenging to determine the desired outcome. This process of distilling a complex concept into a clear, concise and relevant talk is disruptive — and yet delicious.

I have heard that the people of Appalachia have a question for a traveler when meeting another along their way and that is this: "What's workin' ya?" This process is working me! Although I have discovered in the writing of a book that the book will take on a life of its own and eventually begin to write itself, I am hoping that this talk will follow the same generous template and begin to speak to me with clarity and form.

To achieve this outcome, I am doing what I always do: Rise very early, follow my practices, read, journal, reflect and most importantly, listen for the wisdom that may be hidden in the obvious and obscured by the evident.

The TEDx Process: Jeff Patnaude for TEDxWilmingtonLive

It took just one phrase that I have listened to hundreds of times, but on this occasion, I heard it with new ears. And there it was — the breakthrough idea I was looking for — hidden in the obvious, obscured by the evident. This thought now serves as a basis for my talk: "From Great to the Greater Good — When Great is Not Good Enough," and I am grateful to TEDxWilmington for insuring a process where they ask of you great questions and as a result, "what's workin' ya" finally works its way out.

Perhaps most questions remain the same throughout our lives like: Who are you, why are you here on the planet, and what difference will you make? We can struggle with those three great inquiries most of our lives, as they will remain forever constant. It's just the answers that change.

Albert Einstein was once asked by his teaching assistant: *"Dr. Einstein, were the questions on the final exam the same questions as on last year's exam?"* Einstein replied, *"Yes they were." "Why would you ask the very same questions year after year?"* asked the assistant. *"Because the answers always change,"* said the professor.

I have many questions as I continue this process of honing a talk, feeling confident in the premise and subjecting others to my ruminations. I like "what if" questions the best. For instance, what if wild flower seeds were put into dog food? What if we captured the solar energy from just one day that would power all the needs of the world for seven years? What if we had a Conscription Congress where every qualified citizen served four years and had no constituents and no party affiliation? What if our garbage was our fuel and we no longer had trash?

Living the questions can be a creative way to live as it provides options not often recognizable at first. Having all the answers can be presumptuous and dangerous by creating a closed mind to the options that await discovery. I celebrate the questions and look forward to sharing some new ones by the time April 28 arrives.

Reflecting: Jeff Patnaude for TEDxWilmingtonLive

The definition of the word postpartum is: "that which follows birth." That seems apt, as participating in TEDxWilmington was a birth experience. As I indicated at the dinner evening, I am not sure if the review committee noticed that each of my three videos was a different topic. Unable to narrow the options or get clarity, I continued to forge a path forward (or backward) as I waited for "the message to arrive." It didn't — until Thursday morning, one day before rehearsal day. And that was due to the gathering of six friends on Wednesday evening to preview my talk and give their feedback. They did, and it wasn't good.

They said it wasn't me — that I was trying to be a TEDx speaker instead of being Jeff on a TEDx stage. They had heard me speak many times, so it was my opportunity to hear them. I got the message, scrapped all the slides and subject matter that I had worked on for the past two weeks, and went to bed. In every Myers-Briggs typology indicator, I am a strong *perceiving* type — we can handle living on the edge, waiting until the last minute, and in fact get energized from such a delay. This time was no different. Early Thursday morning I began again.

Ideation and strategic thinking are most successful when one is not attached to an outcome. Being flexible about the process, open to iterations about the content and willing to say, "I don't know," are key contributors to breakthrough thinking.

For my experience with TEDxWilmington, I am most grateful for the opportunity to be stretched, to be received, to have had fun and to have learned from this remarkable process. When can I come back for another shot?

Cyrus Rosen

Event #32: 3rd Annual TEDxWilmington
Women Conference
November 30, 2018
TEDx Title: *Connection is Part of the Cure*

Meet the Speakers: Cyrus Rosen for TEDxWilmingtonWomen

Recently, I watched my father give a TEDx talk at the 7th Annual TEDxWilmington Conference. Now it's my turn to deliver my TEDx talk at the 3rd Annual TEDxWilmingtonWomen. I spent the last three months watching him prepare for his talk. I watched how his talk evolved over the iterations with feedback from a network of supporters. I helped him film practicing his talk. From watching him, I've learned how to prepare for a TEDx talk. I am currently writing my first draft and will send it to friends and family for feedback. I think the hardest part about writing a TEDx talk is the first draft. It's the time when everything is from scratch. You need to find your content, resources, style, format, and solidify your message. You are laying the groundwork for the final draft.

My idea worth spreading is we can overcome the isolation patients feel when they are first diagnosed. In my TEDx talk, I will share what I learned from interviews with patients. Later today I am meeting with one of those patients to more deeply understand her story and the challenges she faced. The preparation for TEDxWilmingtonWomen will be a grueling process, but I know it will be worth it in the end.

The TEDx Process: Cyrus Rosen for TEDxWilmingtonWomen

I spent the past five weeks writing my TEDx talk. I started by writing down everything I know about my topic. Next, I whittled the information into a structured outline. I focused the structure of my talk on a timeline of epiphanies that lead to my idea. The epiphanies include discovering the problem, discovering the problem is widespread, discovering the current solution, and discovering that technology can be used to improve the solution. My talk tells the stories of two young women and their experiences with medical conditions. These stories unveiled problems patients face when they are diagnosed with a medical condition. Those problems are overwhelming isolation and a lack of patient centered information.

After writing the basic outline and finding the structure of my talk, I worked every day to refine my ideas and shape them to the outline. I wrote a new draft every day for a week until I found a flow that worked. Next, I sent my talk to a network of editors that include family members, friends, and teachers. It took another week of continuous edits while the stream of feedback trickled in, feeding my progress.

I now have just weeks until November 30, the day of TEDxWilmingtonWomen. I am a few edits away from finalizing my talk. The next three weeks will be devoted to practicing and memorizing my talk. I am also working with a speaking coach to ensure I deliver my message clearly and powerfully.

Reflecting: Cyrus Rosen for TEDxWilmingtonWomen

I feel great relief now that my TEDx talk is done. The final week before the 3rd Annual TEDxWilmingtonWomen was hectic. I practiced my talk five times a day to anyone and everyone who would listen, including my dogs! I was scheduled to speak close to last. On the big day, I tried to focus on the other speakers' talks, but found it increasingly hard to focus as my time slowly drew nearer. The anticipation fueled my nerves until my relative calm of the morning seemed like a distant memory. As the final session of the day began, I started to shiver and sweat. All of my pent-up energy from sitting still for seven hours reached its peak and my hands shook. The final talk before I had to go backstage and get mic'd up seemed to last for hours. Once backstage, I paced nervously behind the curtain. I could feel my body sweating, but I was ice cold. Then, I tried some power poses another speaker named Tiffany had shown me. I reached both hands up to the ceiling and expanded my chest, then brought my hands to my hips as I inhaled. I almost fainted as my time to walk on stage approached. But, support from Jake and an incredibly warm welcome from Ajit and the audience gave me the confidence to walk on stage with a smile and a wave.

I would like to express my gratitude to Ajit for taking me under his wing during the entire process, as well as the TEDxWilmington tribe for their support and feedback. I also wish to acknowledge my speaker coach Geoffrey for his countless hours of collaboration. He helped me mold my talk into one big story and gave me the tools needed to express that story. Thank you to the 3rd Annual TEDxWilmingtonWomen speakers, for the constant support and encouragement. Finally, thanks to all of my friends and family who watched the event in person or over the live stream. I truly couldn't have done my talk without the help and support of all of you.

Sarah Brown

Event #24: 2nd Annual TEDxWilmington Women Conference
November 2, 2017
TEDx Title: *What My Job Taught Me About Finding a Romantic Partner*

Meet the Speakers: Sarah Brown for TEDxWilmingtonWomen

This is where my journey begins — making sure I have a crisp idea worth spreading. I want this to be something useful and memorable, and something I can explain in just 10 minutes. My idea right now is: If we use the three standard job interview questions as a guide, we can learn a lot about what we *should* be looking for when we are searching for a romantic partner.

I am sure that I have sufficient content to address this. I have a degree in PsychoEducational Processes (group psychology and adult learning). I have 20-plus years of organizational development experience studying and working with how individuals and teams "click" or "conflict." I have 15-plus years' talent management experience. I have lots of lessons from the workplace that can be applied to the topic of finding a compatible mate. But can I explain it simply?

I have read Chris Anderson's book "TED Talks" several times. There are many helpful ideas and, more importantly, examples in the book. But every time I go to look for an example that applies to my specific topic, I do not find what I am looking for. So I am going to have to be creative.

Next week (August 16, 2017) I will go to the TEDxWilmington Annual Conference. These speakers are approaching the end of their TEDx talk journey. They are spending every spare minute rehearsing and trying to tame or at least orchestrate the butterflies in their tummies. My talk time is almost three months away, but I bet not one of the speakers next week is any more nervous than I am right now. I am worried about embarrassing myself, but I am more worried about ensuring that I have something worthwhile enough for people to spend time listening to.

The TEDx Process: Sarah Brown for TEDxWilmingtonWomen

My dog, Maharani, knows every word of my TEDx talk by heart, even if I don't. I rehearse when I am walking her. She seems a bit bored and has suggested that she be given extra treats for having to listen to this over and over. But I had a rehearsal with my speaker coach today and he said all the rehearsals had made a difference. My coach said I was on track. That was certainly more feedback than I had gotten from Maharani.

There are less than four weeks to go, and my second video is due this coming Monday. I am hoping that I will get even more feedback then.

I am in that stage where almost every waking moment is occupied with thinking about this talk. I think about it and practice first thing when I wake up, when in the shower, every time I walk the dog, while driving the car, most of the time I am not in direct conversation with someone else, and when I am lying in bed trying to go to sleep. At this last time, my thinking is coupled with worry. Do I have the right focus? Are my examples clear? Do I have a good call to action? Is there anything I can take out so that there is nothing said that is not needed? On this last point, I am reminded of the saying on the T-shirt of the TEDxWilmington volunteers: "Talk less. Say more."

I believe I have a message that can help a lot of people improve their relationships with others, so I am happy to spend the time preparing, rehearsing, and worrying to make sure it is digestible and enjoyable. And I am grateful for TEDxWilmington as a platform to share these ideas.

Dr. Sheryl Ziegler
Event #24: 2nd Annual TEDxWilmington Women Conference
November 2, 2017
TEDx Title: *Why Moms are Miserable*

Meet the Speakers: Sheryl Ziegler for TEDxWilmingtonWomen

On July 19, 2017, I received an email with the subject line, "Your Formal Invitation To Give A TEDxWilmingtonWomen Talk on November 2." I loved it already. They cut right to the chase in the subject line and I was thrilled! I called my husband first, but could not get him, so I called a friend next who had helped me prepare and she shared in my excitement. After about the first hour of pure joy, I got into action mode. I thought about all I had to do, deadlines, coaches, slides and ultimately the talk. A sense of accomplishment mixed with fear kept swirling about as I realized that now I have to actually do it.

I signed the agreement form and returned it by that evening. I went on Amazon and promptly ordered Chris Anderson's "TED Talks" book. The next day, after staying up quite late the night before, I contacted a total of five TEDx talk coaches across the country and over the course of a few days spoke to four out of five of them. I found that their styles, fees and arrangements were different from one another, and ultimately, I chose someone local who I felt the best connection with. Yesterday, my coach Erin and I worked a total of over four hours on what she called the "deep dive." I left with an outline in hand, feeling like I was actually going to be able to pull this off!

I have a lot more to do but so far, so good. Right now, what I am most struck by is my support system and how I truly would not be doing this without them and for that I am deeply grateful.

The TEDx Process: Sheryl Ziegler for TEDxWilmingtonWomen

Preparing for TEDxWilmingtonWomen has been more intense than I could have ever imagined. Where I started and what I thought I would talk about has evolved from observations around me to more about me and my experience of being a woman today. The way in which I have become more connected to the message has truly been a transformation.

I also realized that the support that I need right now is essential to this process. I started off with one coach and have switched to another. This was not easy for me, as I am a loyal person, but I knew I could not bring my message about motherhood and the lack of satisfaction in our lives in the coaching relationship that I was in. It was an incredible relief that when I asked for help in finding someone new, people really showed up. I received great leads and lots of words of encouragement. I am now working with two people, one to help me write the speech and the other to help me deliver it.

One of the things I have heard along the way is to not over think things. I find that to be a tough piece of advice to follow. I am much less concerned about me and how I do, and more concerned with doing the topic justice. Representing mothers of all ages and backgrounds and sharing universal truths that will help women feel validated and inspired is what I care most about. I want to start this conversation in a way that women feel understood and inspired for action.

So, as the window of within a month is here, I am excited, nervous and curious. I look forward to embarking into the world of sharing my idea worth spreading.

Mike O'Krent

Event #32: 3rd Annual TEDxWilmington
Women Conference
November 30, 2018
TEDx Title: *How Conversations with Loved Ones Alter the Path of our Future*

Meet the Speakers: Mike O'Krent for TEDxWilmingtonWomen

It would probably seem odd to most folks that a guy whose expertise for over a decade has been to produce living stories for families and helping them share their private "ideas worth spreading," has yet to find a place to share his own idea worth spreading. Well, I am that guy.

I became a fan of TED talks soon after I started my business in 2006. In the speeches I give to groups in and around central Texas, I reference a few of my favorite TED speakers. With admiration, I've told myself for years, "Boy, I'd love to be on one of those stages someday."

You can't imagine how thrilled I was when I received an email that read, "…the TEDxWilmington tribe is delighted to inform you that you have been officially selected from a large pool of applicants to give a TEDx talk at our 3rd Annual Women Conference on Friday, November 30, 2018!" I was doing the "happy dance" for days.

Soon after the first happy dance was over, I then thought, "Oh, no! Now I have to prepare a talk that is worthy of the TEDx stage!" Fortunately for me, TEDxWilmington's organizer, Ajit George, and the team at TEDxWilmington, have proven (as we say in Texas) "this isn't their first rodeo." Their processes, instructions, and requirements for preparation before the event immediately put my mind at ease. They know what they are doing, and will be sure my TEDx talk is worthy of the big red carpeted circle.

As I go through each step of the process, I am gaining more and more confidence my talk will be one that I will be proud of. I can't wait to share my idea worth spreading with the world. If you've ever dreamt of being on a meaningful stage feeling confidence, apply immediately to be a speaker at TEDxWilmington. You'll be glad you did.

The TEDx Process: Mike O'Krent for TEDxWilmingtonWomen

With every speech I have ever given in the past, I've had with me either the speech in print or a written outline of notes to fall back on in case I ran into trouble. This TEDx format is a whole new ballgame! No notes. No outline. Nothing but a smile, perhaps a few slides on a screen, and a well-rehearsed speech. Oops. What did I get myself into?

What I got myself into was a lesson in professional speaking. As mentioned in my last blog, the people at TEDxWilmington have a process that is both proven and successful. Never before would I have dreamt of giving a full 10-minute talk without notes and with full confidence. But I now feel great about getting in front of a crowd and a camera to deliver my idea worth spreading.

I must confess at this point that I had an additional tool in my toolbox to accomplish this feat. As suggested by the TEDxWilmington team, I hired a speech coach. In my case, I am fortunate to be working with two pros who work together, specializing in helping people make their TEDx talks successful: Taylor Conroy and Tucker Stine.

The Idea Collective is Taylor and a team of specialists helping people become thought leaders in their industry, using the best tool in the world, the TEDx stage. I feel fortunate to have the two organizations, TEDxWilmington and The Idea Collective, working together to make my TEDx talk a success.

I invite all of you to see the fruits of their labors by attending TEDxWilmingtonWomen on November 30, 2018. I look forward to giving them their due credit when my talk is finished. And if it bombs, it's all their (oops) all my fault!

Reflecting: Mike O'Krent for TEDxWilmingtonWomen

After painstakingly crafting your "idea worth spreading," after months of tireless rehearsal, after a full day of rehearsal on the TEDx stage the day before, you now find yourself backstage, the lights are on, the cameras are rolling, the live audience of 100-plus people are waiting… and then they introduce you, "Please welcome to the TEDxWilmingtonWomen red carpet, Mike O'Krent!" Deep breath, big smile, *action*!

What an incredibly satisfying experience it was to be honored to deliver a TEDx talk on the TEDxWilmingtonWomen red carpet. The past few months have been filled with thoughts of what that moment would feel like. Now that it's over, I can confidently sit back and smile. Mission accomplished. Because of the hard work and professionalism of Producer/Director Ajit Matthew George and his "tribe" of volunteers, the experience was a joy.

A few years ago, I attended (not as a speaker, but as an audience member) my first TEDx event in Austin, Texas. Comparing that event to 2018's TEDxWilmingtonWomen event is like comparing a local Little League baseball game to game seven of the Major League Baseball World Series! Ajit and his tribe put on a production that they proudly inscribe with their personal signatures. And that kind of dedication is palpable from stage.

If you have an "idea worth spreading," apply to TEDxWilmington. You owe it to yourself, the idea, and the world that needs to hear it!

Glen A. Dunzweiler

Event #31: 7th Annual TEDxWilmington Conference
September 27, 2018
TEDx Title: *Small Business Homeless*

Meet the Speakers: Glen A. Dunzweiler for TEDxWilmington

Creating a talk is sculpting the story in front of me. For this TEDxWilmington talk, I have all of these great homeless experiences to pull from that I get to use in formulating a (hopefully) potent 10 minutes "thought pill."

My father's challenge, "What's your point?" constantly rings in my head as I play at replacing and moving parts to my talk around like a mental Erector Set.

"What if this part goes here? Does that make sense?" These are the questions I ask myself and my coach (who always seems to find a point or reflection that I had not recognized). Preparing for a talk is play time. I am slinging thoughts on to a sculpting wheel and feeling my way through the creation process. Once I am happy with the shape, then the craft of refinement can start. The challenging part for me has been fitting my process in to the rules of TEDx.

I never have been big on rules. I understand guidelines and I respect other people's "houses," but I am ultimately just trying to live my life. So, rules are sometimes hard for me to accept. That being said, I love learning how TEDxWilmington does things. I am seeing why they do the things they do, and they have been really open about explaining their rules to me. For example, TEDxWilmington asked me to friend them on Facebook for marketing purposes — but Facebook is a sacred repository of connection to me. I friend friends, and not potential followers. TEDx was very kind to me and assured me that they would not be spamming my friends, which I greatly appreciated.

I appreciate the integrity of TEDx, and I am finding that their rules are only there to maintain that integrity.

The TEDx Process: Glen Dunzweiler for TEDxWilmington

I enjoy writing these blog posts, because I can work on them around my bizarre schedule. Even though I am a filmmaker and producer, I have found the video post requirements for TEDxWilmington to be much more difficult to fulfill.

Being a presenter and a producer on the same project comes with its own special set of demands. Not only do I need to make sure the environment, lighting, and sound are as good as they can be, but I also have to make sure I am personally as good as I can be.

My first video requirement was to make a pitch video for my talk. I ended up making two of them, after getting feedback on the first. The first was done in my documentary style of video making, and a person who coaches TEDx speakers told me I needed to look directly into the camera and use a pitch formula he found to be successful for TEDx talks. I got accepted, so I guess he was right.

My second video requirement was to create a promotional video for my talk. Right when I applied for TEDxWilmington, my mother went into the hospital with a diagnosis of cancer, so I have been flying home to visit and care for her (which takes me away from my production tools and also makes me stressed and tired — something presenters don't usually wish to convey). In order to make the second video deadline, I had to shoot the video at my parents' house on my smart phone with a broken blood vessel in my left eye. It was after a long day of caring for my mom and, on camera, I came off as crazed and damaged. I looked and sounded like I had just come from a fight and was trying to make myself excited and happy. Fortunately, I was allowed to resubmit it after my life had calmed down a bit.

The third video I had to submit was an early version of my talk. Fortunately, I shot it before flying up to visit my mom, but I didn't have time to edit and upload it. My father doesn't know how the process works to allow me to join his WiFi network, so I spent the five days before the video was due trying to figure that out. I was unsuccessful, and on the morning the video was due (at 3:30 a.m. after caring for my mother), I transferred the edited video to my smart phone in an attempt to upload it. I was unfortunately unsuccessful, so at 4:15 a.m. I sent a request to TEDxWilmington for a 36-hour extension and went to bed for a couple of hours before needing to check on my mom again. TEDxWilmington was again gracious and allowed me to upload the video when I got home, but I hate missing deadlines.

The third and final video will be a completed version of my talk, and I hope I can get that ready before I head home again. In the meantime, I can work on this blog post while I'm tired, stressed, ugly, and without my equipment and no one will be the wiser.

Reflecting: Glen Dunzweiler for TEDxWilmington

Now that TEDxWilmington is over, I have learned the following from this experience:

> It gets warm in a barn.
> A horse makes photographs more interesting.
> Never trust Uber to find your location in a state park and always wait for your fellow speakers until the ride gets there.
> Meeting thoughtful people is an absolute inspiration.
> If you don't like rules, you will have a hard time keeping your inspiration.

TEDx was a rough experience for me. I had a hard time wrapping the needs of TED into my message. I also found out that apparently, I am a difficult speaker in the TEDx world. For that, I apologize. That was never my intention.

The tribe (as the TEDxWilmington organizers call themselves) was great. Everyone tried their best to support my journey through their world and I think that in the end, I was able to deliver my idea in a way that TED guidelines could accept. It was, however, a bumpy ride, and I think both sides came away from the experience with a fair bit of frustration.

When I had arrived for rehearsal, I had memorized and thrown away nine previous drafts of my talk. The notes I was getting from the tribe, my coaches, and test audiences were starting to eat away at my confidence in being able to communicate my message without losing my audience in some detail. The notes became an analog for every homeless naysayer I had ever talked to. I couldn't get to my idea because the listener would get hung up on the validity of a certain anecdote or proposal. I started to hate to give the talk. Every word came with the fear that I'd lose my audience. Finally, I knew I had to heal my psyche and let things fly. I *had* to listen to *me*.

At rehearsal, the producer introduced me as his most complicated speaker to date. He then told us (or maybe reminded us) that we could not greet the audience when we started our talk. This devastated my emotional standing. How could I make that initial connection with my audience if I had no way to form a relationship with them. It can't be complicated. I'm not complicated. How can I be complicated? I hang with homeless people. That's basic human connection. Any emotional headway I had made before rehearsal was lost.

When I rehearsed my speech on stage, I had been sweating in a barn for about 10 hours. I entered that stage and I hated myself. I could tell that I felt no love for the audience, and I hated *me* for it. I spit through the talk with no humor and I was sorry people had to see it. People were kind, but my talk was trash, because my head was in the wrong place. I personally scored my talk at a " minus one." I was being complicated. I had also held out to keep a reference to a certain group in my talk that had gotten some bad press in 2014. The producer said that the reference had to go. The scarlet letter that we put on homeless people had now been transferred to a homeless service provider, and society was sending them out into the woods to die. I was pissed.

The tribe did their best to console me, but I knew my only chance for success was to get to my "happy place" on my own. I rewrote my talk for the 11th time and tried to figure out how to connect with my audience, within the rules. In the morning, I was working towards my joy when Philly Phil gave a devastatingly touching talk that sent me into tears. His pain was now mine, and I was reduced to emotional mush. I'm The Inspirational Homeless Guy damn it! I can't cry!

But, Phil made me feel again and it was what I needed to rebuild myself. I had a few hours to figure out how *not* to go to the crying place and I got strong. The great thing about having a theatre and music background is that I know "showtime" means you just let it all go and do it! I rocked that damn stage.

At the end of the night, the producer of the event thanked me for finding my humor while on stage, and I thanked him for the opportunity, shook his hand, and said, "Good fight!"

My advice to people preparing to give a TEDx talk is to thoroughly understand all of the TED guidelines. Many of them can intimately affect your performance. Let the organizers run their event and expect to roll with the punches. Ultimately, it is futile to challenge the almighty TED, for they built the house and while in it, you follow their rules. I can absolutely respect that.

TEDxWilmington is no joke. They have built a respectable platform to curate ideas worth spreading, and I am grateful my idea was given an opportunity. Not many people want to tackle the subject of homelessness, but TEDxWilmington invited me to their party and I whole-heartedly thank them, and so do the homeless.

Gerald J. Leonard

Event #31: 7th Annual TEDxWilmington Conference
September 27, 2018
TEDx Title: *What if Practice is the Performance: Falling In Love with Practices*

Meet the Speakers: Gerald J. Leonard for TEDxWilmington

My TEDx talk is entitled, "What if Practice is the Performance?" And as I practice for my talk after reading some scholarly research articles on the benefit of practicing, I'm more excited about practicing and working on my talk. I've discovered benefits about practicing that I hadn't realized, such as how the brain rewires itself while you practice even if you've had a brain injury, and how our brains reduce stimuli that would normally distract us under normal circumstances. In other words, our brain becomes very selective when we've made a decision to perform deliberate practice.

In the past few years, I've worked with the National Speakers Association in Washington, D.C., and created a talk using my upright bass and although I liked the talk and wasn't in love with the talk and I didn't feel that it was a message word spreading. After mulling over what I'm passionate about, the title of my talk came to me. You see, I realized that if I'm only onstage performing five percent of the time and, the rest was spent in practicing or rehearsing, then I needed to love the journey more than I loved simply performing.

I'm excited about the future because this principle of deliberate practice can be applied to any topic, field or musical genre. Our performance really is the totality of our practice on display.

The TEDx Process: Gerald J. Leonard for TEDxWilmington

In preparing for my TEDx talk, TEDxWilmington has provided a detailed checklist of everything that I need to think about to get ready for my talk. The TEDx Process is very interactive and milestone driven, and having a detailed checklist makes the process much easier to stay on top of the activities required to get prepared for my talk.

For example, one of the first things I had to do was provide a detailed outline of my talk, in which they provided feedback on the outline structure and content. The next thing required was a 60-second promotional video with the challenge to keep it within the 60-second time limit. Going through this process, you learn quickly that you have to honor the time constraints because of the number of other people who are delivering talks that the TEDxWilmington team have to coach through the process.

All of the speakers had to provide a 300-word blog post reflecting on our experience and share what we were learning as we were going through the process. For me, the greatest benefit of going through this process is learning how to present an idea clearly and succinctly, while including research and stories to bring my talk to life. And again, the goal is to keep our talks within the allotted time provided while making it an idea worth spreading.

Finally, I had to provide a video of my talk to show the team how far my talk has come along, and they provided feedback and suggestions on things to do to make the talk better, more engaging and universally appealing. I'm finding that this process that I'm going through can be adapted to my other presentations and talks in the future.

Reflecting: Gerald J. Leonard for TEDxWilmington

In delivering my TEDx Talk, I had an amazing experience working with the TEDxWilmington tribe, as I came up with the idea for the title "What If Practice Is Performance?" Then, my initial outline and script were updated, edited, and I created my first video and modified it and started working with Geoffrey Berwind, my coach. Honestly, it was an amazing process of watching the talk mature, transform, become more consistent and authentic.

Then in the middle of the whole process, I got vertigo, which at the time, I'm thinking, "Oh my God, how am I going to get past this one?" It actually worked out that what I had based my talk on and the neuroscience I had researched was the answer to accelerating my brain's ability to balance and recover from vertigo. I'm still recovering. I have to go to physical therapy twice a week, but I know that I'm on this lifelong journey and that

I've been given a gift of practicing and learning. Even seeing that vertigo, in some ways, has been a gift, because it gave me a platform to share my message and made it so much more personal in a way that I'm not sure if that didn't happen, it would've come across, especially after I wrote the song "Vertigo" at the end of the talk.

The whole experience was an amazing time working with the TEDxWilmington team. They have a rigorous process, but they are an amazing group of people. They are passionate about what they do. They love, love, love helping speakers share their message and do it in the best way possible. I am forever indebted in my heart, mind, and soul to the TEDxWilmington tribe, and Ajit for his vision for turning the East Coast upside down with messages worth spreading through the TEDxWilmington tribe. Thank you, thank you, thank you so much for selecting me, I am deeply honored.

Alex Cabañas

Event #19: TEDxWilmingtonSalon
June 7, 2017
TEDx Title: *The Bar is So Low: The Realities of Memorable Service*

Meet the Speakers: Alex Cabañas for TEDxWilmingtonSalon

Over the years, I've admired TED and TEDx talks in general. I like speaking about passionate topics and I find that too few times in life do people get to speak publicly. When the opportunity came up, I jumped at the chance.

And then, the weight of preparation and rigor began. The preparation "magna carta" I received after signing up was enough to make you second guess the decision! I've never prepared to so much for a speech!

After missing a few deadlines, I was passively-aggressively scolded by Ajit George, the TEDxWilmington organizer. I felt like I was back in school and missed turning in my homework. But, the process does produce results. I have outlined and thought through my points in much more succinct fashion, and I believe it will pay off in the end.

Looking forward to finally standing on that infamous red TEDx carpet and hoping that others think my ideas are worthy of spreading.

Mindy Tatz Chernoff

Event #31: 7th Annual TEDxWilmington Conference
September 27, 2018
TEDx Title: *Love, Connection, and a Horse*

Meet the Speakers: Mindy Tatz Chernoff for TEDxWilmington

WELCOME! I have been wanting to tell you what is going on here for weeks! I can now tell you what the buzz around here is all about! The Resonant Horse is about to make history (I think!) Yep, little ole' us! Wanna know how? I will not keep you in suspense any longer…

We are going to be offering our *second* TEDx talk on September 27, 2018! That makes Viton, I think, the only horse in the world that is not only featured in one TEDx talk, but two! And, drum roll please… This talk will actually end with Viton coming out and sitting on a beanbag chair! Yep! Real live and in the flesh! If you are local to the Wilmington/Philadelphia area, heck, if you live up and down the east coast… You need to be at the Figure 8 Barn, Bellevue State Park, on September 27th!

The TEDx Process: Mindy Tatz Chernoff for TEDxWilmington

The speakers for TEDxWilmington's 7th Annual Conference are now all chosen. As I scrolled through the bios (and blogs) of every speaker, I am brought to my knees. It's so humbling to read a portion of their stories, what has brought them to this place, this moment of "Now What?" Such a stellar group of people. I am so excited just knowing we are all on this journey together! I echoed so many of their thoughts and sentiments, the excitement, the gratitude, the terror. Some may think that, since this is my second time offering a TEDx talk, it would be "in the bag" as they say. No way!

My previous talk was a whittled down version of the workshops I offered. I had no notes. It was all in my brain, and just needed to be spoken in a format which fit the time. It still had to be rehearsed again and again, over and over.

Well, things have changed. I am finding this experience is totally new and unfamiliar. I have my thoughts, which are fine, but I also have comments from others. And, I also have research I am quoting. It is so hard to memorize what are not my thoughts! Of course, I already know the answer to that — memorize until they *are my thoughts*!

All I know is that by connecting with the speakers, and by diligently applying myself to this task, love and connection will be the result! That is what I trust will happen! Not just for me, but for 29 amazing speakers!

Reflecting: Mindy Tatz Chernoff for TEDxWilmington

Memorizing my text was a herculean task, but I also had to focus on my precious horse, Viton. I was asking a lot from him. Now that it is behind me, gratitude and satisfaction are my greatest feelings — that, and awe. I had so much at stake in my final presentation. Viton had not "sat" that morning on the beanbag chair when I practiced with him. I went on the TEDx stage not knowing if he was going to sit. Such pressure! All I could do was trust, let go, and believe. Sure enough, at first, he said "no" and did not "sit." I regrouped, asked him again, and he did. Phew! What an answer to prayer! A colleague, watching on Livestream, had this insight:

> "Mindy's presentation contained abundant wisdom, but her silent response to Viton's "no" contained a lesson as powerful as her words. Partnering with horses (or with humans), we must be willing to give freedom, flexibility, and options and to be prepared for a response we don't like. If Mindy had gotten upset and had let herself go down the very human path of anxiety and fear, Viton would not have sat down because he would deem it as unsafe. Instead, Mindy stayed fully present and grounded. She did not pressure Viton, she respected his decision, gave him some time and gently asked again. She honored his wishes and embodied everything she had said in her talk about love being a state of being, not doing. Since Mindy accepted the no gracefully, Viton felt safe and loved and trusted Mindy enough to change his answer to yes."

I am thankful that even though I was not aware, the essence of my TEDx talk shined in the moment a horse sat on a beanbag chair.

Phillip J. Roundtree

Event #31: 7th Annual TEDxWilmington Conference
September 27, 2018
TEDx Title: *Black Mental Health Matters*

Meet the Speakers: Phillip J. Roundtree for TEDxWilmington

The date was July 12, 2018 at approximately 3:00 p.m. Eastern Standard Time. I'm sitting with a young, autistic black male providing therapeutic services. During our break, I checked my email, and immediately saw that I received an email from TEDxWilmington. I was apprehensive to open it, unsure as to whether it was a rejection of my request to present a TEDx talk at TEDxWilmington's 7th annual conference.

The email was quite the contrary. It was a congratulatory email informing me of my selection as a TEDx presenter. I immediately shed a few tears; not necessarily because of this achievement, which is amazing, but because it affords me an opportunity to take another step in my purpose, which is to emphasize the importance of mental and emotional wellness, especially to black and brown communities.

For the past two years, I've embarked on this journey of providing mental health awareness to anyone that'll listen. My passion has taken me to colleges and universities, professional conferences, high schools, elementary schools, and now the TEDx stage. I don't take this opportunity lightly, especially since I'll be discussing a topic that will impact everyone at some point in their life. My talk will outline why I hold this topic near and dear to my heart; hence, why I'm preparing myself mentally, emotionally, physically, and spiritually daily. My desire is for this talk to resonate for myself, those in attendance, and those who view online.

Since being notified three weeks ago, I've worked diligently in meeting deadline requirements, often sending in required content at exactly noon on the due date. I've recorded videos numerous times, rewritten outlines several times, trying to recreate the energy necessary for that day. As I write, I've had to remind myself to be gentle with myself. I recognize that I will not be able to recreate that same energy that I give when I speak. When I speak, it's the spirits of my ancestors, suicide successes, and others coping with mental wellness issues that give me life. So, forgive me in advance if my blogs seem dry, or videos lackluster, those previously mentioned are allowing me to reserve energy stores, preparing for September 27th.

The TEDx Process: Phillip J. Roundtree for TEDxWilmington

Peace, peace, peace. It has been four weeks since my last blog entry. To say my life has been a whirlwind would be an understatement. I studied for, and eventually took, the GRE with hopes of getting into a fully funded doctoral program in 2019. In addition, I resigned from my job as a child therapist to be a full-time entrepreneur, all the while continuing to prepare for the TEDx talk. A theme that's prevalent in my TEDx talk is the idea of resilience, which has been an important concept for me to remember as I continue to embark upon this journey of enlightenment.

Despite the ebb and flows of life, I've been able to fulfill my commitments to TEDxWilmington, including writing and recording the first video of the talk. As a speaker, I usually have an idea of what I'm going to say, but I allow the spirits of the ancestors to give me energy and information to convey. No two talks I've given have been the same. This process was rather different for me, as I was forced to sit and write, and rewrite, and write some more, until I had a product that I felt secure in sharing.

Prior to recording, I knew that I wouldn't be able to replicate the energy and confidence that'll be present on September 27th, but I persevered. At its conclusion, a dope young woman who assisted me with recording showered me with accolades. I live with depression and anxiety, and receiving compliments is something that I'm learning to become comfortable in accepting. Her sentiments would be echoed by the select few who I allowed to view the video, which further encouraged me. The feedback from TEDx reviewers solidified that I'm headed in the right direction, which also was encouraging. All the feedback received reinforced the importance of this topic and why I am the one who should be presenting it.

Reflecting: Phillip J. Roundtree for TEDxWilmington

It's now a few days since the 7th Annual TEDxWilmington, one of the most memorable experiences that I've had. The experience was amazing for many different reasons. The first was being afforded the opportunity to meet new people, who all had amazing "ideas worth spreading" Being able to forge connections with people who were passionate about their respective topics is something that I'll take with me as I embark on this journey of self-actualization through passion sharing.

The next reason this was an amazing experience was my performance, both the rehearsal and show day. I had general anxiety; however, I was able to transfer that energy into the performance, which received rave reviews from my fellow speakers. I was relieved that rehearsal was over, but became even more anxious due to concerns that I wouldn't be able to replicate the same emotional energy for show day.

Later that evening, as I entered the speaker's dinner, those feelings persisted. I was put at ease by some of my fellow speakers, who'd offer verbal encouragement throughout the wonderful dinner. The hospitality of Ajit, and the TEDxWilmington tribe was top notch throughout the dinner and this entire experience.

It's show day! As I watched speaker after speaker present, I became more anxious, yet excited. I'd utilize positive self-talk and other strategies to improve my mindset. It was my turn, and as Ajit began to read my "thank yous," which was a salute to those who've died by suicide, I began to cry. This lasted even as I walked on stage. The audience was gracious, allowing me time to regain my composure. Then I began, "When you look at me…", and that was it. I poured everything into this performance, with the result being a standing ovation from the crowd. As I exited the stage, the kudos and support continued, from people of all ages and ethnicities. I felt accomplished and grateful.

This TEDx experience was one I'll remember forever, as I'll be immortalized, along with my TEDxWilmington class, as individuals who believed in something bigger than them and gave their all.

Marla Blunt-Carter

Event #20: TEDxWilmingtonSalon
August 16, 2017
TEDx Title: *The Importance of Being Color-Full: A Journey in Black & White*

Meet the Speakers: Marla Blunt-Carter for TEDxWilmington

It's been a few weeks since I learned that I would be giving a TEDx talk, and I've had vivid dreams of standing on the red carpet with TEDxWilmington in the background. My family and close friends know how much this means to me and are also excited about what I will be sharing with the world.

I feel humbled to be included in such a wonderful group of speakers. As the other presenters are announced, I am blown away by their talk topics and what they've accomplished. I have often pondered what idea I would share if given the opportunity. As an educator, I use TED talks to introduce topics and to inspire my students. Many students have asked why I haven't given one. My answer was simple, 'When I believe that I have something to share, then I will apply.'

It was an "a-ha" moment, as I taught a course on diversity and oppression last fall, when I realized that my TEDx talk resided in me. I decided that now was the time and I was the one to give it. I have to admit that I am a little anxious because the topic of race is a difficult one. However, a few hours after Mr. George, TEDxWilmington organizer, shared my bio and TEDx talk topic, I received an email from a high school student. She, and other students of color, experience racism every day in school and she wanted to know how to deal with the pain, mistreatment, and discrimination.

My hope is that my TEDx talk will begin a revolution against racism. I also hope that it provides answers, comfort, and hope to that high school student and others desiring to becoming colorful instead of remaining colorblind.

The TEDx Process: Marla Blunt-Carter for TEDxWilmington

Eight minutes. On August 16, 2017, I will have eight minutes to reveal my idea to the world, share my journey, and inspire others to move beyond borders.

Initially, it seemed like a lot of time to be by myself, on stage, with only my thoughts, a few slides and a lot of apprehension. However, as I continue to prepare to stand on the red carpet, eight minutes now seems like a blink of an eye. The words, the images, the message must all come together to help convey an idea truly worth spreading. I now wish that I had 80 minutes instead of eight.

My preparation for my talk has been a daily project that requires both research and self-reflection. The most challenging part of my preparation happened the other day when I visited my parents' home to find a picture of my younger self. My mother was happy to reminisce, relive my childhood and share stories. I, on the other hand, was not as nostalgic. I was flooded with feelings of sadness and a sense of loss. For 40 years, my skin had been a rich caramel brown, and the old photos captured a happy brown girl, not the beige woman that I am today.

As the day draws near to the moment that I become transparent with the world about my battle with vitiligo and my experience as a racially ambiguous woman, I hope that my talk will encourage people to see their challenges as opportunities to do good. I also want others to embrace difference and fight ignorance with love and knowledge. My desire is that through compassion, competence, and courage we will be able to break down the barriers that separate us and see each other as colorful and beautiful, as we all are.

Erik Younger

Event #24: 2nd Annual TEDxWilmington Women Conference
November 2, 2017
TEDx Title: *Operation PTSD; Veterans Using Meditation to Heal Their Bodies and Minds*

The TEDx Process: Erik Younger for TEDxWilmingtonWomen

In the days leading up to the invitation, I was only just beginning to figure out exactly what a TEDx talk was. I honestly had never even watched one and had no idea about the global reach or scope of the TED program. Please do not think less of me, I just did not have a Facebook, Twitter or Instagram account, nor did I spend much time on-line watching videos of this nature. Now, before you say it, yes, I do believe I have lived under a rock. In fact, my wife and children have already pointed out which rock in the back yard I called home.

The rock I have lived under for many years has been PTSD. Not only have I missed out on TED talks, I have missed the majority of my adult life, punishing myself for things I have done and unable to move forward.

It is fitting that this year's theme is "Bridges: We build them, we cross them, and sometimes we even burn them, for better or worse."

I am excited to share with you my story of that dark place I lived, only because I will also share with you how I was able find a bridge that helped me find my way forward to actually living with peace in my life. I won't lie to you, having PTSD, I am very nervous about being silhouetted up on a stage, in front of a large group. Nor am I a public speaker or famous author with years of experience on being inspirational. I am simply a vet, and that is strong enough, to tell the world what it is like to suffer from PTSD with a newly found passion about helping other veterans overcome the crippling effects of war.

Alessandra Nicole

Event #30: TEDxWilmingtonLive
April 28, 2018
TEDx Title: *The Power of Paper Letter Exchange*

Meet the Speakers: Alessandra Nicole for TEDxWilmington

I am a wide-eyed introvert quite content to spend my life hiding on the other side of the camera (or behind a large potted ficus, whichever is readily available), very happily documenting everyone else's milestones and moments in the sun. I have been a primary photographer for our TEDxWilmington events since mid-2016 and the curator / editor of these very blogs, so a big blessed part of my life the past 500 or so days has been to support all of our courageous and heart-centric TEDx speakers that have come through this great little city. I never once entertained the idea of talking in front of one of our audiences like I am about to, and definitely not for lack of extraordinary life experiences to speak on (that is another talk or two, preferably over a brilliant bottle of red.) Rather, I am a writer by nature and all things I will ever say I felt would naturally come out in essay, novel, and short film form as has been my world since I could hold a pencil.

The invitation to speak came organically in the dining room of founder Ajit M. George one night at the end of February, when I came by for a completely regular reason, to pick up some paperwork or something. My beloved grandmother had just died a week and a half before, and my health was just returning after my first round of two of the flu this winter. I was visibly exhausted through and through.

In very casual conversation, I was giving the background story that inspired a heart project of sorts with him and one of our assistant producers, Kelsey. By the end of it, Ajit surprised all three of us, even himself, and said, "That is a TEDx talk and you are giving it at our event in April." My initial reaction was actually *not* resistance! I was pie-eyed and suddenly silent, but not resistant.

Now, here I am being subjected to the preparation and the deadlines of our stringent process for speakers and their various talks, seeing it all from a brand-new perspective with respect, gravity, and unexpected hyperawareness. Typing my own blog into our website tonight is surreal, seeing my photo of "seriousitude" up there on the left (chuckling). This is an extraordinary opportunity and our tribe is world class, so I have full trust that all of us TEDxWilmingtonLive speakers are in the best hands! I am leaning into my grief and nervousness (oh yes, a bit of fear has recently remembered my address) to see, to just see, if I can stand fully visible and verbally tell this quite simple and beautiful little story in the way it deserves to be told and allow myself to become transformed in the process.

The TEDx Process: Alessandra Nicole for TEDxWilmington

I don't even know where to begin on my TEDx process. I have stared at this blinking cursor for the past 20 minutes and each sentence is taking that long to create. So much has transpired that I could never have foreseen. My journey and process have been tough to keep up with given the short amount of time I have to nail each deadline. Even having worked on the other side as a core tribe member through 13 events and knowing about our low and no tolerance policy for turning in videos, outlines and slide decks late it has been a steep climb. Getting a strongly worded email from my own associate producer in the name of our founding organizer was stressful!

Last week I was given the profound gift to travel to NYC for six days for TEDFest2018 where I interacted and bonded with more than 600 TEDx organizers from 58 countries as we enjoyed direct live streaming from TED2018 in Vancouver. Recalling the deep dive conversations I have had and the new meaningful friendships I have made is making my gratitude overflow from my eyes and stream down my cheeks. I returned to Wilmington, Delaware on Sunday evening a changed human feeling supported by this phenomenal global community and even the universe itself.

When some organizers last week heard I would be giving my first TEDx talk at the end of the month, they drew it out of me for constructive criticism and powerful feedback. I got coaching from Canada to Brazil, France to Dubai, in the backs of shared Ubers from event to dinners, in the corners of bars at after parties and after-after parties. With so much travel and my attention divided this month keeping one speaker coach on has been impossible. My global tribe though filled in the spaces and with great care and amazing interest helped me to break down my talk and rebuild it to be more effective. I have some work cut out for me in a short amount of time! But I have confidence now that was missing a week ago. I have come out of my neurotic little shell and evolved into someone much more sturdy on her own two legs within her unique passions. I can't ever thank my new friends enough for it.

Our TEDxWilmingtonLive event carries the same theme and branding that I have been steeped in all week with TED2018; to step onto our local stage feeling like a micro-extension of the brand new TED talks from Vancouver as we explore the same theme at a local level — I am so honored, thrilled, excited, and overall grateful. The way certain things have aligned for me since my grandmother's passing in the middle of February has been miraculous. Making it full circle from TEDFest2018 to our red circle at TEDxWilmingtonLive on April 28th will be very powerful for me as I step into the light of my own "Age of Amazement."

Reflecting: Alessandra Nicole for TEDxWilmington

Whew, lengthy. I have a lot to say here before I go back to the silent work of copyediting these blogs for everyone else for the rest of our 2018 season.

First — a well-deserved love note to my tribe: Seeing how TEDxWilmington works from the point of view of a speaker has given me a newfound respect for what we do as a tribe to support and produce our events. I already held my tribe mates in high regard, but now I am absolutely astounded. We have it down to a well-oiled machine, operating at a higher volume than most TEDx organizations, and our tireless and hard-working assistant producers Kelsey and Evan are phenomenal at on-the-fly problem solving, logistics, and patience with our humanness. With so many moving parts to these things it is incredible how well it goes and how smoothly it *feels* it goes. Kelsey, Evan, Bob, 'Speaker Angel' Denise, Megan, Jake, Ajit, and our day-of volunteers... They set the tone for these events and the speakers are set up for success in an environment of calm, ease, and *fun*. As core tribe members for TEDxWilmington, we come from a depth of mutual admiration and adoration that lifts everyone up together, we are people inspiring each other to be greater together than could we be alone.

With every blown deadline (yep, that happened — and my self flagellation game is strong!) and firm email in response, I respect the process we have put in place, what a major commitment it is and how it behooves you to prioritize it as a speaker because it readies you to perform at your best and with a message that is really worth others' time. I am proud of myself for getting through it all in less than 60 days, and despite a relentless travel schedule, for the graciousness of a *very* busy couple of assistant producers. If you could all witness the behind-the-scenes like I am privy to, you might feel like you were pretty lazy in comparison. It's truly a lot.

Secondly — The two months from being told February 27th that I would be speaking on April 28th provided sheer terror that I had to lean into with all of my might. I have never spoken on stage like this in front of a live audience like that and with so many people tuning in on the live stream from around the world and the thing being recorded for public record and posterity (*no pressure!*). I am the camera girl! I take pictures of *everyone else's* moments in the sun; *I* don't have moments in the sun!

I went through a lot of ups and downs in 60 days and was carrying a lot of grief and heartache. Initially, I put a lot of pressure on myself to do everyone involved with my story justice and handle the subject with a great deal of respect and honor. I wanted to draw my connections and make my case with great tenderness and care. I had to really show up in a way I have never before been called, and there is *no hiding* on the TEDxWilmington stage. None! Although, creating an aesthetically appealing slide show presentation on the largest screen we have ever used helped at least divert some attention away from me (muahaha). But my voice was crystal clear and filled the auditorium through the sound system. For a soft-spoken woman, it was both scary and thrilling.

Seeing other speakers' kind, attentive faces in the audience during rehearsal the day before was oddly calming. I thought giving this talk in front of them and my own

TEDxWilmington tribe on home territory would be the toughest crowd, but I could not have been more wrong. I finished my closing sentence and although I had lost my place twice and froze, fellow TEDx speaker Amy Ogden immediately responded with, "Tears. Your talk is going to impact people." My jaw dropped. Others echoed the sentiment and gave *very* constructive feedback. It gave me comfort to know that the essence of what I was saying made my mistakes forgivable. I couldn't fail.

All month long the constant mantra from my friends and colleagues on phone calls and on social media was, "You got this!" Realizing that I had so many friends and strangers pulling for me to be successful has given me something I really needed in my life. I was surprised by the turnout of my own coterie the next day; friends that bought tickets to be in the auditorium, friends that woke up at all time zones around the world on a Saturday to make sure they were tuned into the live stream, fellow tribe members and speakers back stage and in the audience… I realized that even if I froze again and left out lines I still couldn't really fail and that this would be one of the greatest experiences of my life to date. It is the most positive environment on earth to step out into. I still felt my stomach in my throat, but I knew I was doing this in front of the best kind of people possible, an instant family.

Holy cow! Never in a million years did I expect a standing ovation. Wow. Stunned and fully appreciative, I just wanted to cry at the sight and sound. My heart has been overflowing with the amazing special moments and memories people came up to me and shared during breaks throughout the rest of the day and in email and in the mail I've received since. It's been a happy problem having so many handwritten letters to write now in return. I thought at best I would be one of the flowery but forgettable talks of the long day. Yes, please let me hide somewhere in the middle. But something bigger happened — through my wavering voice my raw open heart was absolutely seen and heard. *There is so much love for this subject.* The response has been just beautiful. It has affirmed in me a deeply meaningful new purpose. It is an unexpected inheritance from my grandmother that is worth more than all of the gold in the world.

Thirdly — Thank you to our founding organizer Ajit George for seeing something that I did not and for the subsequent, "no negotiating, you're doing this" kick out of the proverbial nest. I am grateful beyond measure for the TEDx platform, the TEDxWilmington community, and for each and every one connected to it, as an organizer in our community and others globally (TEDFest!), a tribe member, fan and audience member, as a fellow speaker, as a speaker coach… I have been truly enriched by our conversations that helped me clarify and strengthen my delivery (as best as could be done for a wildly inexperienced speaker), those that held space for me and helped talk me down from ledges and back into my power again, that took time to take me aside and advise me in quiet hallways, greenrooms, and for profound amounts of moral support as I took the biggest breath of my life and went out there and declared courage.

And finally: For those on the path to giving a TEDx talk, really *embrace* it. Relish every moment of it and allow it to move your life around a little bit and to move you around inside too. Let it be absolutely vivid in your life, this burning coal in the pit of your stomach, this bright star shine in your heart. It is a special, special time and everyone wants to see you win. We all work very hard to position you to win and to help you hone your message through a thoughtful process so that it adds great value to the universal collective conversation. If you let it, it will be an incredibly vibrant journey.

The prep process is a bit isolating and disorienting where you shadowbox yourself a bit, but then there is the rehearsal where you finally meet everyone and form great lasting bonds, and sometimes a dinner to further foster this, one more sleep and then it is *game on, baby*. Relish the special conversations you will have back stage with your fellow speakers, the conversations you'll have during breaks when you mingle with those who came from far and wide to see you in person, treasure your own nervousness and the relief after you have walked off the stage and notice how your applause for everyone before and after you is with more gusto than you've ever applauded before. We're all on your team and it's all gonna be *Magnificent*. The people you will meet along the way, embrace them, and the people who fall away along the way, let them go. Focus on your talk and how your message will serve others. Declare courage and own that little red carpet and trust that whatever comes out, however it comes out, is how it was meant… let perfection go. *And remember to send me all of your blogs on time!*

I look forward to better serving our future speakers in 2018 and pay forward some of the great stuff I was given as a way-too-long winter finally gave way to spring.

Jane Krukiel

Event #18: TEDxYouth@Wilmington
April 2, 2017
TEDx Title: *The Power of Depression in Shaping Our Lives*

Meet the Speakers: Jane Krukiel for TEDxWilmington

Preparing for and creating a TEDx talk has been a challenging, yet exciting process to undergo. It has presented me with countless opportunities to explore my inner self, question human nature, and craft a TEDx talk that works toward conveying the true powers of depression in my life. By looking into my own past and collecting memories have allowed me to truly question how depression affected me emotionally and physically, and it has opened my eyes to the progress that must be made in regard to complete acceptance of mental illnesses.

Adding to the challenge of creating a personal talk has been the time limit. Crafting a complete TEDx talk in less than a month has certainly presented its challenges, along with meeting frequent deadlines and submitting my information and findings in an accurate and well-written manner. Reflecting on this overall experience has provided me with careful insight on how my own work ethic meets rigorous challenges, how determination and strength to create an exceptional TEDx talk has reacted, and how my inner vulnerability to expose a personal topic of my life has faced the expectations of sharing it with a large group of people. I am excited, yet nervous, to present my findings to the TEDx community in a timely and prepared manner. I believe that my first TEDx talk will be successful and will inspire others to consider depression and other mental illnesses with a different view and allow them to connect their own lives with factors that cause depression.

The TEDx Process: Jane Krukiel for TEDxWilmington

My journey in creating and preparing for a TEDx talk has been a life changing experience. It has allowed for me to effectively manage my time in order to meet rigorous deadlines, to reach into the depths of myself to find stories and memories that I can share with the TEDx community and prepare a speech that works to convey my personal message about depression. Even while juggling the challenges of academics and sports, this challenge has forced me to manage my priorities in order to create an exceptional TEDx talk. Throughout this experience, my confidence has grown tremendously with continued practice and preparation. I have felt my self-esteem rise as I share my personal story with the TEDx community, for which I am grateful and appreciative. I am excited, but nervous, to give my final performance on April 2.

I hope that this offers further opportunities in the future where I can progress myself, embrace opportunities, and act as a leader for myself and others. My favorite memory throughout this experience were the bonds I was able to create between my classmates as we work to craft a TEDx talk together, while using and trusting one another with our ideas and personal stories. I will be forever grateful for the leadership opportunity this experience has given me; giving a TEDx talk can open up countless doors for me in the future.

Reflecting: Jane Krukiel for TEDxWilmington

I truly appreciated the opportunity that TEDxWilmington presented me in creating and performing a TEDxYouth talk. Being able to fully present myself in a poised and eloquent manner to the community on a topic that I was passionate about was a dream that I was able to fulfill. Looking back, I have gained so many life and leadership skills, including the ability to speak in public, prepare speeches, and do so with confidence. This was a life-changing experience for me; all of the memories and relationships I have forged are everlasting. I hope that others are able to acquire the same opportunities that I have through Ursuline Academy and TEDx, in addition to having the positive experience that I have had.

As I reflect on this experience and my story, I could never have foreseen the growth of myself throughout these past months. I have come so far since my days in middle school, where I was feeling hopeless and without an escape. So many opportunities, including this one, have shown me the light out of my darkness and introduced me into a loving community, where I am able to fully express myself without judgment. I couldn't have asked for a better platform to share my story than TEDxWilmington; I've truly been given the tools to inspire and influence others from my story.

Abby Larmore

Event #18: TEDxYouth@Wilmington
April 2, 2017
TEDx Title: *The Shirtless Man*

Reflecting: Abby Larmore for TEDxYouth@Wilmington

Not only has the experience of giving a TEDx talk helped me create new friendships, it helped me mature as a young woman and find parts of myself involving self-confidence and self-worth. These are qualities I did not think I had. I learned and gained characteristics of self-discipline and motivation that have helped me transform to be a better student and better worker through all aspects of life. All should have the ability to be nurtured to feel welcomed and wanted as I did during my experience of giving a TEDx talk at TEDxWilmington. The ability to share a message that I am so passionate about and to hopefully help others through difficulties in life is one of the most rewarding and humbling experiences one can ask for.

Madi Still

Event #24: 2nd Annual TEDxWilmington
Women Conference
November 2, 2017
TEDx Title: *Using Pain as a Bridge to Discovering Your Purpose*

Reflecting: Madi Still for TEDxWilmingtonWomen

In the movie Cinderella, the clock chimes midnight. Her chariot returns to a pumpkin. Her clothes become a disheveled mess, a stark contrast from the glorious ball gown she wore while dancing with the prince. All she has left are memories of the best night of her life.

I do not live in a pumpkin. I do not own disheveled clothes. I am still living my "happily ever after" (with my prince); however, the morning after my TEDxWilmingtonWomen talk, I could relate to Cinderella. The magic of the night was gone, leaving a melancholy feeling in my spirit for at least one brief moment. A single glass slipper tucked away in my pocket the memory of the magic tucked inside my heart. Then I began to reflect, and I smiled.

I knew that I was chosen to share the most powerful story of my life. What I did not know was how that story would creep back into my heart and peek inside my soul from deep crevices I thought were hidden. I forgot the pain of losing my first-born son. I forgot the darkness. I forgot the intense grieving. Reliving those intimate scenes reconnected me to my story (and my son) in a very powerful way that I'm truly grateful for.

It feels now as though my son has been reborn with renewed purpose. I expected to feel fulfilled in sharing his story, but I did not expect to feel such immense pride. I'm proud that I was chosen to be his mother. He died 10 years ago, and yet, he continues to live on through his story. His purpose touches the lives of countless people grappling with their own pain. How did I get so lucky to be chosen as the communicator of his life?

Weeks leading up to the talk, I felt very much "over it." I was just about one week out from presenting and sleep evaded me. 3:00 a.m. became my wake-up call, and I would lie in bed repeating and reviewing my talk no less than three times every single night. I would make minor changes, obsess over minutiae, and remind myself that I was chosen for a reason.

On Halloween, I took my son trick or treating with a knot in my stomach. I was honestly more nervous about rehearsals the next day than I was about the event itself. I was extremely anxious to present in front of the other speakers. If they heard my story in rehearsals, how would the story continue to impact them the day of when it *had* to count? I honestly resisted the idea, until rehearsals actually came.

Once I entered the auditorium, I saw the stage and oh, what a stage it was. It was not like the stages I'm familiar with, however. It was a *global* stage, and my excitement began to rise. The feelings of anticipation and even relief escalated when a few of the speakers "choked." I thought, "Wow. As established as these heartfelt leaders are in the world, they are just like me: nervous." I also truly appreciated the amazing coaching I heard for each speaker. I found it incredibly valuable and as each speaker presented, our group grew closer. We bonded through our stories, our nerves, and our need to be connected. Hugs were exchanged, along with tears, and heartfelt praise. Honestly, rehearsal day solidified my love for the TEDx journey and crew.

Many of the speakers in our group mentioned that they got no sleep the night before the main event; I, on the other hand, slept soundly. Perhaps it was the eight-hour rehearsal day. Or maybe it was the very personal hour I spent sitting inside the window frame in my hotel room in prayer. Either way, I felt as though I was truly ready.

The day was, for lack of a better word, magical. From the emotional highs and lows of each speaker, to the praise I received from the audience in a resounding standing ovation, I felt as though this "bucket list day" was everything I had hoped for and so much more.

All 36 speakers are now connected by our stories, our desire to succeed, and our experience of sharing the honor and privilege of standing on that red carpet. I can truly say I will never forget the way the rug felt under my multi-colored flats, nor the way I felt wiping away tears as I sat in the audience, listening to powerful talks. I will never forget the kindness of the TEDxWilmington tribe, nor will I forget feeling a part of something far bigger than myself.

If I can impart any wisdom to someone wanting to share their own story on the TEDxWilmington platform, it would be to embrace their vulnerability. Something happened to *me* as I allowed my own story to touch me once again to my very core, and I allowed those emotions to reverberate off the walls of an auditorium and into the souls of the audience. What I would say to future TEDxWilmington speakers is, "let go." Let go and be free.

Maureen Bridget Rabotin

Event #24: 2nd Annual TEDxWilmington
Women Conference
November 2, 2017
TEDx Title: *The Culture of Fear: Facing it with Courage and Curiosity*

Reflecting: Maureen Bridget Rabotin for TEDxWilmingtonWomen

November 3rd, 6:39 a.m. I do what I have been doing every morning for the last 30 days: I roll over and start to recite my TEDxWilmington talk. I mentally edit a word here, a word there with that incessant hope of trying to get the most impactful message of an idea worth spreading come to life with pace, presence and pause.

But today, the words don't come to my mind. A feeling of panic grips me. I can't remember my talk, then finally words do pierce my foggy yet focused mind: "It is Nov 3rd. It's over. You delivered your talk yesterday. Relax". So, as relief rolls over me, my mind drifts back to a sleepy state, allowing me to revisit yesterday as I entertain my new morning ritual. Start to follow some of the advice from Victoria, the 96-year young woman who spoke of the aging process, then a leisurely breakfast at 9:30 with some fellow TEDxWilmingtonWomen speakers. A warm sense of belonging to some kind of speaker tribe envelops me in my dreamy state. Isn't that what we, as humans, all seek: to belong?

November 4th, 5: 12 a.m. Now you have probably guessed it. I'm not much of a sleeper. The adage of the "early riser catches the worm" was ground into my routine at a very young age. This morning, as I rolled over, the lines of this third blog came to mind, now replacing the thoughts where my TEDxWilmington talk once lived.

The incessant cycle of self-assurance boosting me to levels unknown — of high energy and back to doubt — where low-energy consumed me, was a learning cycle of growth that I could not have imagined when I accepted the invitation to talk at this TEDxWilmingtonWomen event. What goes into a successful TEDx talk? The secret sauce is made up of a variety of ingredients: morale boosting from family and friends, Ajit George, the organizer's clearly outlined process, then the discreet way Ajit has of warmly accompanying his TEDx speakers with his right hand man, Evan Bartle, at his side. Evan's role among many was to kindly send us individually addressed emails about an overlook or readjustment as if each speaker was the only one.

The day of the event, the amazing TEDx tribe, all those volunteers, coming out from behind the scenes, gave me that feeling again: one of belonging. For an organizer, getting that balance right between disciplined processes and a delicious desire to be part of something bigger than your craziest imagination is at the foundation of a successful event. I have always wanted to give a talk that, up until Nov 2, 2017, was unimaginable. Yet, the desire to do so was never about me. It was and always will be for the very essence of what TED and TEDx means to me: Hope. Bringing people together across cultural, linguistic, generational and gender divides to share what it means to be human: a sense of belonging to a better world. Thank you for letting me be part of this adventure. Now, I know, it's only a 300-word blog, so I'll stop here even though going over a minute doesn't matter anymore. Thank you.

Dr. Paul Rosen

Event #31: 7th Annual TEDxWilmington Conference
September 27, 2018
TEDx Title: *What I learned from 100,000 Doctors*

Meet the Speakers: Paul Rosen for TEDxWilmington

Two months ago, I lost a dear friend and mentor to cancer. Susan not only endured the suffering of battling cancer, but she also struggled to navigate the complexity of the healthcare system. I am delivering this TEDx talk in her honor.

I am encouraged about the future of medicine because of a project I am working on. The project focuses on transforming how medicine is currently being practiced. In the future, we will have a system based on patient health outcomes and patient-centeredness.

I plan to share the lessons I have been learning from all of the doctors, nurses, social workers, physician assistants, and other clinicians working on the project. In fact, we have more than 100,000 signed up thus far.

Right now, I have about a dozen friends and family reviewing the talk and giving me feedback. Some of my tribe are professional writers and others just give very pointed feedback:

> My wife: "…You need to do a better job linking the different ideas. And your description of the government work is boring: either do an extreme makeover or delete it."

> My teenage son: "You need to stay focused and avoid going off on tangents. TEDx is about one idea worth spreading. Make sure all the material ties back to the main idea."

Writing and delivering a TEDx talk is not easy. However, I am grateful for the opportunity to share my passion about large-scale healthcare quality improvement.

I am not there yet, but my family is working on getting me ready for the TEDx stage. I hope the final product honors the memory of my friend, Susan.

The TEDx Process: Paul Rosen for TEDxWilmington

With the event only a month away, I am re-working my talk with the help of friends and family. They are coaching me to keep the idea worth spreading front and center, and to tighten the transitions between stories. The main message I want to express is that, despite healthcare being riddled with problems for both patients and doctors, change is happening now that will transform the system.

I was reminded of the struggle last week when I saw a teenage patient and his mother in my office. We were simultaneously trying to make the correct diagnosis, get him the right treatment, and navigate the expenses based on his insurance plan. Healthcare quality will improve in the future as we focus on patient-centered care, medical teams, population health, and data analytics. TEDxWilmington has advised me to let my passion for healthcare improvement come out during the talk. I hope I can adequately express the hope and passion I feel at TEDxWilmington's 7th Annual Conference on September 27.

Reflecting: Paul Rosen for TEDxWilmington

Wow! What an experience this has been. From first hearing that my talk was accepted to delivering the talk has been a crescendo building over the past three months. The process included 23 revisions, suggestions from 10 friends and family, and rehearsals in the car, in the ice rink, and at the dog park. The best part is the connection made with the TEDxWilmington tribe and with the other speakers. The tribe offers not only technical support, but also moral support to speakers. Although we were together for just one practice day and one performance day, the speakers have a bond.

Since the TEDxWilmington event, I have already met one speaker for coffee and connected online with several others. I have found myself reflecting on all the great talks I heard and mulling over their lessons: surviving a hurricane, finding your China, overcoming rejection, the power of animal-human interactions, defeating hunger and homelessness, overcoming fear, and many more amazing ideas worth spreading. I plan to share them broadly once they are published online.

Right now, I am a bit exhausted, but exhilarated at the same time, with a strong feeling of accomplishment. There is not much time to rest. TEDxWilmingtonWomen is in two months and I am helping two speakers with their talks. In medical school the saying goes, see one, do one, teach one. I am looking forward to now being a coach instead of a speaker. I will take my seat in the audience for the next TEDxWilmington event. I am looking forward to further connecting with the Wilmington community and the global community.

Monica LeSage

Event #32: 3rd Annual TEDxWilmington
Women Conference
November 30, 2018
TEDx Title: *Showing up to Face Trauma:
A Survivor's Story of Using Somatic Experiencing
to Gain Freedom for Mind, Body, and Soul*

Meet the Speakers: Monica LeSage for TEDxWilmingtonWomen

I've been dreaming of my round, red carpet moment since I saw Simon Sinek explain the Golden Circle in 2010. I didn't know *what* my idea worth spreading was then, but I did know my *why*: to help the world, deeply and powerfully; and I knew my *how*: the TEDx platform.

Knowing my *why* and my *how*, I geeked out on the ideas that other TED and TEDx speakers have spread, looking for my *what*. I promoted the surprising truth about motivation, as explained by TED speaker Daniel Pink; and power posed in bathrooms when nervous, as TED alum Amy Cuddy suggested; and joined Brené Brown's famous crusade to embrace the power of vulnerability by being my "perfectly imperfect" self and inviting others to do the same.

Despite the staggering number of people affected by physical or emotional trauma, no one has spoken about Somatic Experiencing on any TED or TEDx stage, *ever*. Identifying this gap revealed my *what*, since I have been practicing this healing modality for over 600 hours across the last five years, and now help others to use it. It has helped me lower chronic pain, control neurologic irregularities, and regain a sense of self-mastery I lost in the years since the accident.

When I learned that I was invited to speak at TEDxWilmingtonWomen, I screamed, "What? Really?" I'm overwhelmed again, remembering the moment when I learned I was "in" — that my *why*, *how*, and *what* had finally aligned for my round, red carpet moment. I remain in awe, comparing my emergency room experience two weeks ago, to the one a decade ago, because *this* time I used Somatic Experiencing.

I'm so excited to share more about this process at TEDxWilmingtonWomen in Wilmington, DE, on November 30th, where I have the honor of spreading an idea that can potentially bring relief to millions of people affected by trauma.

The TEDx Process: Monica LeSage for TEDxWilmingtonWomen

I've heard that it's common for people to rework their talks in the weeks, and even days, leading up to their event. However, I didn't think it would happen to me. After all, I've been telling my story to different audiences for a few years. That being said, you can imagine my surprise and dismay as I watched the recording of my first full-length talk and thought to myself, "Oh no. I can't use this. It's too sad, too heavy. And it's all about me. Not enough about the powerfully transformative process I'm trying to share."

This was where the structure and support of the TEDxWilimington team came into play. Thankfully, they have a precise assignment list set up that helped make sure I had recorded my first version of the talk early enough that once I realized it had to be scrapped, I had enough time to rework it. So that left me wondering how. I knew the content needed to remain the same, since that core of my message is still the core, "Practice Somatic Experiencing to recover from trauma," but the story aspect needed to be different, and so did the timeline I shared it in.

As a trainer in communication, I have seen over and over that what we have in our heads can be difficult to convey to a group. So, I sought input from my "tribe." They are a group of people that have been a part of my healing and professional journey, especially during these last five years, and they have borne witness to how I have transformed from a person that physically couldn't make my bed or vacuum, let alone get through a day without tears, to become a person they can count on when the stuff of their own lives piles up and they need an anchor or a listening ear, who is back to rock climbing and Acroyoga in my spare time. ("Spare time" is this cute phrase I use to talk about the time that I am not working, preparing for TEDxWilmingtonWomen, or continuing my healing journey. It seems to be missing lately, except for my jaunt into the Shawangunk mountains for a day of climbing.)

Feedback from my tribe confirmed my belief that the first version was informational and professional, but heavy. Some suggested a joke to lighten things up, but I was hesitant, due to my topic. But that person planted a seed. Another person reminded me that the process had elements that I use on a daily basis but hadn't made it into the 10-minute time slot. She made me ask myself what *had* to be in, and what might have to go, to make it possible to add it in.

In the week I submitted the video, life presented me with an opportunity to see my full transformation when I needed to visit an ER for an unrelated issue. I was seriously triggered by the visit, since it looked, smelled, and felt like the place that had held so much pain and fear for me from years ago. But this time, as soon as I realized my brain was going into "collapse," a symptom of trauma that causes the brain to freeze, often resulting in vision changes, difficulty breathing, withdrawal from human connection, and in severe situations even losing the ability to speak, I knew what to do. I used the process to transform the experience, and within a few minutes I was breathing calmly and actually giggled, which is a good sign the process is working.

The final piece of help I needed to rework my talk came from a TED talk by Nancy Duarte titled, "The Secret Structure of Great Talks." My final version of the talk will follow the algorithm she identified that was used by Dr. Martin Luther King, Jr., and even President Abraham Lincoln in the Gettysburg Address. She broke it down, explained what it looks like, and now I have put in the other elements I am sharing.

And I even found the joke that I can use to set the tone of the talk! So, my tribe's input helped me, as did the structure provided by TEDxWilmington, and TED fellows like Nancy Duarte.

Can't wait to see you in Wilmington DE on November 30th. There is so much to be thankful for in the meantime.

Reflecting: Monica LeSage for TEDxWilmingtonWomen

It. Is. Finished. Those ancient words have a very significant meaning to me. And now that I have accomplished a dream of mine, and it is firmly fixed in the past, I feel I own them as part of my own story and journey. TEDxWilmingtonWomen 2018 is finished.

Completing my TEDx "Round, Red Carpet Moment" is a huge accomplishment, and I am equally thrilled I had the opportunity as I am thrilled it is finished. As one of the speakers, I got to meet so many wonderful people who I never would have met if I hadn't done this. And I got to hear from many people in person, as well as those who saw the live stream of the event that they were inspired and experienced thought-provoking ideas. I got to challenge myself to step up my own trauma recovery to an all new high, to be able to manage the challenges, deadlines, and standing up in front of three cameras to talk about something with very deep meaning for me. I received a lot from the experience, and I am grateful.

Regarding the event, I was so impressed with members of the volunteer tribe that helped make this a reality. I was struck by how composed Elissa Ben-Eli remained, despite the pressures of being a first-time producer of a TEDxWilmington event, and making an event a reality with only two weeks' notice that TED had given the green light. She kept a smile on her face and kept the best interests of the speakers top of mind throughout the two-day event. She demonstrated this even when I needed to add a slide the day of the event, and instead of concerning herself with the stress that might bring her into the midst of the live stream, she was concerned it might throw me off as speaker. And she trusted me when I let her know that the slide was mission critical, and she worked with Evan, who has more experience as a producer, to get it in. She and Evan were very impactful in so many ways!

The tribe's photographer, Alessandra Nicole, is a person with a tremendous background in living bravely and facing adversity with grace, as well as a person with huge heart, who happens to also be a great photographer and visual storyteller. She also demonstrated her helpfulness throughout the days I was there, even helping me get from the speaker dinner to my hotel, since I didn't have a car.

Jake Voorhees also played a huge role in making the event what it was for me and others. He offered balanced, constructive feedback to the speakers during our dress rehearsal. And he managed to do that with a smile on his face and new responsibilities out on stage. He gave my introduction, and demonstrated that he clearly understood the effort I had put into my talk preparation, as well as my journey as a person recovering from trauma who wants to help the world do the same, incorporating Somatic Experiencing into their journey to recover from or prepare for traumatic situations. Jake saw my vision and helped me get it the point that it was on November 30th. I cannot give enough credit to the impact Jake has had on the trajectory of my life through who he is, and how he employs that on behalf of this tribe of volunteers.

And don't let their titles fool you; every tribe member does so much more than their titles imply — Alessandra, Elissa, Evan, and Jake — they were called on to give speaker feedback during our dress rehearsal, right alongside the folks who make their living coaching speakers. These folks played a significant role in making the event all it was.

As for the speakers, I cannot say enough good things about them. I drove to the event sitting on a red bath mat that reminded me of the vision of success I was embarking on, and heard a speaker talk about how vision boards change lives. I'm living proof that Karen's message was spot on (pun intended). I saw men like Dominick and Frankie, who were willing to show their feelings so deeply in ways that men often do not, and call men and women alike to live powerful lives full of feeling and bravery and art. I saw women overcoming debilitating illness to find healing and health in alternative ways and suggesting how we can advocate for ourselves with our doctors. Women with a vision for the future of our young ladies, wanting to impact them as leaders from a young age. Women who want to provide structure for how we can stand up and say so when we have been spoken to in an exclusionary way, or if we have been the one to speak out of turn. We heard wisdom on how to divorce "happily ever after" through mindfulness. How to turn your passion into your health and wellness.

Every single speaker and speaker coach (like Angela Jo Manieri, Geoffrey Berwind, Laura Harrison, and Tucker Stine) imparted their knowledge, passion, feedback and ideas to me. And an idea is a gift as much as feedback is. Getting to hear all the speakers and feedback given to them on dress rehearsal day, and then many talks on the day of the event, I had the blessing of hearing many twice. Because of them, I learned about the ways to tell stories of family members before they are gone, to consider giving up eating meat for the benefit of the planet *and* the animals. To tell everyone I meet that *you matter*.

Like many things, the hardest things are often the most rewarding, despite the bumps and hurdles. And that is how I sum up my TEDxWilmingtonWomen 2018 experience. It was one of the hardest things I have done, and it was so rewarding. And though the event itself is done, the relationships that were forged through the heat of pressure and deep desire to make an impact will continue to make an impact on me. And once the talks are live on YouTube, they will continue to make an impact on many, *hopefully countless others*. And ideas will spread, which is the point of all of this.

Allington "Gumption" Creque

Event12 #: 5th Annual TEDxWilmington Conference
August 24, 2016
TEDx Title: *9 No's and 1 Yes: How Not Quitting My Dreams Changed My Life*

Meet the Speakers: for TEDxWilmington

My experience of being a TEDx speaker is like a dream come to life. Knowing my background of education, where I came from, and where I am today, is nothing short of amazing.

I've heard of TEDx and seen many tapes and pictured myself on TEDx, but it seems like it was so far away. From the first email on April 23, 2016 about being a part of TEDx, to submitting and being qualified for TEDx, is beyond a dream come true. It was made more real after I spent over an hour talking to a professional speech coach named Dr. Robyn Odegaard, who took me under her wing. She has guided many people and helped them deliver the best TEDx talks ever. To have that kind of focus on me makes me feel very fortunate.

I was thinking it was going to be easy. It's hard, yet fun, and because I'm having fun while preparing for TEDx — it's becoming easier for me. The journey so far on the road to TEDx has been amazing, and if I'm dreaming, I don't want to wake up until it's over, and if I do wake up and realize it's a dream, that will suck, but I'll admit it's the best dream ever. My journey so far on the road to TEDxWilmington has been a fantastic one.

The TEDx Process: for TEDxWilmington

My recent experience in terms of getting ready for TEDxWilmington 2016 has been a very exciting and learning adventure. I've was very lucky to have given a talk in front of BVIslanders and get truly amazing feedback from them all, which I took to heart and was grateful.

The very next day, I was lucky enough to meet and give a live practice in front of Mr. Ajit George himself, who's the founder of TEDxWilmington, during the amazing evening when we chose to take my talk public and do it over dinner.

However, my zest built even more when I was lucky enough to give a real live practice talk in front of Sir Richard Branson, his family and special friend for over seven years — the one and only beautiful Kate Winslet — on July 19th 2016. I wasn't nervous at all, as I was around friends who felt like family.

At this point, just under 24 days away from my TEDx 2016, I'm feeling amazingly awesome about myself and my confidence has grown since. I'm ready for my TEDx talk on August 24th, 2016.

Reflecting: for TEDxWilmington

My experience in being a part of TEDx 2016 Wilmington was indeed a very historical one — historic for country, my family last name and myself, even the state of Delaware, as they brought the very first speaker from the Virgin Islands. Being a part of something I've seen on YouTube many times and a few times on Necker Island and to actually be on a stage with a massive TEDx logo behind me was truly beyond a dream come to life. I've watched many amazing TEDx talks via YouTube and felt very inspired, but it can't compare to actually seeing one take place live in front of your eyes with a chance of meeting and shaking the speakers' hands one by one.

I now know what they mean by 15 minutes of fame as I stepped out on the red carpet. I only had 15 minutes to tell my story and inspire 360 people who were in the room, but also millions around the world. I call it fame for a cause, as I was a bit known before TEDx for the charitable work I've been doing, and what TEDx did is make me a bit more known, meaning I have to work extra hard. Getting ready for TEDx wasn't as easy as I thought it would be — the long bio, the short bio, the short video the long video etc., yet despite it all, with the right support I managed to get it right and was allowed to share the stage with 37 amazing speakers who all had very interesting topics, which were ideas worth spreading. Being on TEDx Wilmington will give the little boys and girls in my little village of a population of about 500 people a sign of hope that anything can happen if we only believe and work hard.

This hope reached many villages around the world, and all who see our talks will be inspired. TEDx Wilmington opened up a world of possibilities and after doing my TEDx I pinched myself to make sure it was real. My experience on TEDx Wilmington 2016 will go down in my history and in my county as a day a BVIslander made us all proud. I'll urge each speaker to keep true to their passion and keep inspiring others. To the founder of TEDx Wilmington, who worked hard with me and figured out what I typed (being dyslexic isn't easy), but we did it. To my TEDx speech coach, Robyn, who helped me to give the best talk ever, really worked hard to see me give the best talk I could have ever given at an important, peak time of my life.

I'm very happy after this last write up that I have no more to write, no more short or long bio, no short or long videos, but I can now sit on a beach, watch the waves and smile, because Allington Creque, known as "Gumption," did it. My experience at TEDxWilmington 2016 was a magical and historic one.

CHAPTER 8
It Takes a Village to Produce a TEDxWilmington Event

What is a tribe? Sebastian Junger, the author of *Tribe* said, "we have a strong instinct to belong to small groups defined by clear purpose and understanding — "tribes." Anyone who has volunteered for any one of the 32 TEDxWilmington events is considered part of the TEDxWilmington tribe. We may come from different backgrounds, professions, live in different areas, and be a range of ages, but we all come together for the common goal of spreading ideas on a TEDx stage. When someone volunteers for TEDxWilmington, they truly feel like they are part of something bigger than themselves, connected to people who have similar interests as their own, and are more like family members to one another.

The Tribe

Fun, fellowship, family. These are just a few of the words TEDxWilmington volunteers ("the tribe") use to describe their experience of working back stage in a variety of capacities to make our sold-out events seamless and unforgettable. We offered a few members of our core team the opportunity to share their thoughts on what it was like to collaborate with dozens of others to create the TEDxWilmington experience, and how their lives were affected.

Question 1: In one paragraph not to exceed 150 words, please share your experiences as a member of the TEDxWilmington Tribe.

Ken Grant: Being a member of the TEDxWilmington tribe is life enhancing. The people who are attracted to anything related to TED are clearly interested in exploring ideas, but all of us come from a wide variety of backgrounds and interests. I've met artists, entrepreneurs, students, and retirees with a zest for life and an appreciation for ideas that challenge, encourage, and inspire.

Jake Voorhees: Being a TEDxWilmington Assistant Producer and a part of Ajit's core team has been a life changing experience, in one word, intoxicating. All of the most interesting people and fulfilling activities I'm involved with today came to me through TEDxWilmington. I owe all of this to Ajit George. Ajit's concept of tribe is one like I have never been a part of before. Everyone involved is intellectual, pursuing their passion, flexible, friendly and open minded to the next tribe member. Leaving this energy behind after an event was troublesome. The day after was always depressing. I have been able to help with 12 events, video interview 171 speakers as they exited the TEDx stage, and help coach dozens as they prepare for their talk. After bonding with speakers, I've had the opportunity to collaborate with many, including travelling to six countries on two continents.

George Waterman: I was looking for a volunteer opportunity that allowed me to meet new and interesting people and gain exposure to perspectives and subjects outside my realm of personal experience. The members of the TEDxWilmington tribe are an extremely interesting, intelligent and diverse group with a wide range of skills and expertise. I have thoroughly enjoyed the time I have been a participant in this group. The presenters and presentations at the various events I have been able to volunteer for have provided me an insight into a wide range of topics and perspectives that have been at once entertaining, thought provoking and humbling. I am extremely grateful that I have been fortunate to have those experiences. Without a doubt, my involvement in TEDxWilmington has exceeded my personal goals and expectations.

Laura Harrison: Being a member of this particular tribe was an amazing experience — and one that I feel is totally unique based on the limited knowledge I have about other TEDx organizations. Across the board, the tribe members seem really more like a family instead of a group of volunteers thrown together. Everyone knows their responsibilities and follows through exceptionally well — but there is also an incredible willingness to jump in and help where it might be needed. The attention to detail makes all the difference, from the all-day rehearsal the day before to a dinner that evening where all the speakers and key tribe members can mingle and network. The loyalty of this tribe — not only to Ajit but also to the TED organization — is unparalleled. I feel very lucky and blessed to have been able to participate in some wonderful TEDx events, with super speakers. The connections and friends I have made will last a lifetime!

Dana Dobson: When Ajit George put out a call for volunteers for TEDxWilmington in 2015, I nearly tripped over myself to get onboard. Having been a TED junkie for years, I had an idea of the kinds of people I would get to meet: authors, thought leaders, innovators in science and technology, artists — a virtual smorgasbord of experts who wanted to share their ideas with the world, and for many, an opportunity to overcome feelings of fear and grab the experience of standing on the red carpet by the horns. Such a treat! Most important, though, were my fellow volunteers and tribe members. The bonds we formed don't grow on trees, and I savored every moment we were together.

Bob Turner: Having been the volunteer coordinator for TEDxWilmington since December 2016, I have had the pleasure of meeting people — fellow tribe members, volunteers, speakers, and audience members — that I would never have met if it wasn't for

TEDxWilmington. I've had access to people and places in our city that I never thought I'd meet or visit. The speakers I have met and their "ideas worth spreading" have helped me both personally and professionally. I've also made new friends. And that, to me, is priceless.

Angela Jo Manieri: It was an honor to be a part of this amazing group of individuals, from all sorts of backgrounds. The energy and synergy that we share is beyond measure. Our passion and like-mindedness as a group fueled one another and created an atmosphere for people to flourish. As one of the coaches, it was an honor to help people in offering feedback and confidence during their rehearsals. My passion is to support those in this arena during the process, so they can discover their voice, stand in their power and share their story with ease, eloquence and excellence.

Julie Vernot: I've been involved with TEDxWilmington almost since its beginning, having been working on Ajit's MidAtlantic Wine + Food Festival at the time he got his first TEDxWilmington license. Along the way, I've made great friends and have been exposed to people who think and live their lives completely differently than I do. This has left me with confidence, new skills, perspective, and personal connections and inspiration to act on ideas. It has also left me with some memorable late nights, the fulfilling feeling of helping some evolve their idea and TEDx Talk, and the satisfaction of recruiting new tribe members and watching them find their place. And a lot of gratitude. One of my favorite emotions is the thrill that comes from finally meeting all of the people from around the world who have been preparing for the day of the event. As the event plays out over two days of rehearsal, pre-event dinner and event, it feels like a bit of a homecoming as everyone descends on Wilmington and come together as a group. There's a shared joy and enthusiasm for the work we've done and what's to come that is made, perhaps, from everyone's feelings melding together after having worked individually, but not in person, for so many months to prepare for the day.

Lynne Williams: As an attendee at my first TEDxWilmington event, I was so moved with emotion and brought to tears by a speaker. It was at that moment that I knew I needed to get involved on a regular basis and be at all events, so I asked if I could volunteer. When I met the other tribe members, I quickly felt I was part of a team, which encompassed individuals of all ages and was full of diversity. With everyone committed to the same goal of having a successful live event, we all dove in to work together to address the task at hand to get done what needed to get done before, during, or after the event. This was true teamwork, or should I say, "tribework!"

Jeet Patel: "One For All and All For One" — We are really blessed that we encountered Ajit the way we did. We had no intention to be part of the TEDxWilmington tribe in our wildest dreams. Everything has changed the day we met Ajit, at an event at the church. We were lucky to meet most of the tribe that night and instantly wanted to be part of it. We really like how everyone in the tribe is so welcoming and willing to help each other as a family.

Question 2: What is the one thing that stands out in your journey as a TEDx tribe member? (not to exceed 150 words)

Ken Grant: Through TEDxWilmington, I have met truly amazing people — from television stars to scientists to the woman who came up with the idea of "Amber Alerts" to government officials. The people — that is what stands out.

Jake Voorhees: Ajit would support us as a core tribe in more ways than providing events, community, and a rolodex of speakers from around the world. He would help us attend regional TEDx and TED events like TEDxMidAtlantic and TEDFest 2018. This allowed three tribe members, Rhianon Husmann, Alessandra Nicole, and myself, to travel to New York City, visit TED headquarters, and participate in a four-day conference called TEDFest 2018. Here we met 600 other TEDx organizers from 60 different countries. I was introduced to the concept of "Creating Impossible Encounters," which is exactly what TEDx produces. TEDx provides a platform for local leaders to present their ideas and be exposed to funding and partnerships that may otherwise be impossible. It allows for out-of-town speakers to present for their local community. And TEDx puts audience members in a room together who may otherwise never have met. TEDx makes the impossible, possible.

George Waterman: The one thing that stands out in my journey as a TEDxWilmington tribe member has been to see and experience the commitment the tribe has to "delivering ideas worth sharing." Understanding that it takes a diversity of skills to accomplish this objective, the team has demonstrated an openness to adopt new members into the tribe, the trust to allow each member to determine how they can best contribute to the team and camaraderie to work to accomplish their objective.

Laura Harrison: I would have to say the one thing that stands out for me as a tribe member is the recommitment to the importance of being flexible *and* teachable, while still being disciplined and dedicated to that throughline — and that the *one idea* worth sharing, plus the willingness of both the tribe members and the speakers to seek *that* out more than anything else has really changed and enhanced how I look at speaking in general. The idea that less is more, which I have always adhered to as a theater director, is always on full display at any great TEDx event. Talk less, say more.

Dana Dobson: I had the pleasure of coaching many TEDx speakers, from the writing of their scripts to the delivery of their talks on the red carpet. What struck me the most is that people are people, whether they are CEOs of top companies accustomed to giving speeches, to regular members of the community who had no speaking experience but were bursting to tell their stories for the benefit of others. Everyone felt unequal to the task, at first. Everyone wondered how they were going to squeeze a lifetime of knowledge into a 10-minute speech. Everyone trembled with fear before walking onto the stage, and everyone was deliriously happy when the deed was done. No matter how high a person's status, or what country they're from, we all have more similarities that we realize. It inspired me.

Bob Turner: The one thing that stands out in my journey as a TEDx tribe member is that "it takes a village." If you want to do great things (like put on a TEDx event), it means involving people that you'd never think could do what you need done. Maybe you've known those people forever, or you've just met them. It doesn't matter. There is desire, talent and potential in the world. You need to find it and give it the opportunity to shine! I love the quote, "You are what you give, not what you are given." I've found that to be true, being involved with TEDxWilmington.

Angela Jo Manieri: The greatest thing was working with individuals and watching their stories evolve. Getting to help fine-tune their talks, rehearse with them, give tips on body language and tone, was so rewarding. The greatest gift of all was watching them shine! Being there when they came off stage, to congratulate them, hug them and say, "You did it! Well done!"

Julie Vernot: I've played many roles in our tribe, but designing and publishing the newsletter was a unique pleasure because it allowed me to capture the *special somethings* that I was fortunate enough to witness and share it with others through words and visually. *Special somethings* are things that made my heart grow or peaked an interest. Things like relationships formed between speakers — lifting another one up or others teaming up to innovate. *Special somethings* like the Governor's office requesting a meeting with a passionate speaker because they had seen her on the TEDxWilmington stage, or my personal experience spending the evening at the rarely-open-to-the-public Nemours Mansion following the Innovation in Healthcare TEDxWilmington@Nemours event. Being able to tell these stories from a behind the scenes view has been a standout experience for me.

Lynne Williams: The one thing that stands out most for me is the involvement of multigenerational speakers as well as tribe members. It's such a wonderful experience to be entertained by the talents of teenagers to boomers. It's also a wonderful experience to work with others of all generations and realize we can all learn from each other by sharing our own gifts and talents.

Jeet Patel: We were really fascinated at how Ajit was able to hand pick and filter out speakers from diverse backgrounds with amazing ideas worth spreading. The best part of being a tribe member was that we got to meet them all personally and pick their brains.

Question 3: Last but not least, please share in one paragraph not to exceed 150 words, how you think TEDxWilmington has made an impact?

Ken Grant: Because of TEDxWilmington, human trafficking concerns are being addressed statewide. Because of TEDxWilmington, people coming out of our prison system are given new options. Because of TEDxWilmington, thousands of people are finding their voice. Because of TEDxWilmington, ideas are spreading.

Jake Voorhees: TEDxWilmington has created a local community and utilized the TEDx platform to amplify 486 speakers who have given 466 talks at 32 events over seven years. These talks have collectively have accounted for 18.2 million views at the time of me writing this (March 27, 2019). This is incredible, because Wilmington, Delaware only has

70,000 residents. Delaware itself has fewer than one million residents. Ajit has enabled the transmission of ideas far beyond what would normally be possible.

George Waterman: I believe that TEDxWilmington has made an impact through the power of the presentations it has hosted. By carefully selecting and nurturing them through the process, TEDxWilmington has enabled its presenters to deliver emotionally powerful messages that resonated with its audience. I believe the evidence of the power and authenticity of these messages is in the documented statistics of their online viewership and, in at least one instance, the resultant political policy and legal changes.

Laura Harrison: Where to begin? Firstly, this organization makes such a difference in the lives of all the volunteers, some of whom travel great distances to be a part of each live event, is astounding. They feel a community within this TEDx organization that gives them a sense of belonging to something far greater than themselves, all working together toward a single goal. They are learning *while* they are volunteering. They know that they make a difference with the part they play. Secondly, TEDxWilmington has made a huge difference in the surrounding community itself. Speakers from all over the U.S. and internationally have come to little Wilmington to share their ideas worth spreading. The sheer number of events, total talks and total views are astounding. One would be hard pressed to say that this particular organization has not made a difference worldwide, especially when you realize that most views are international, not U.S.

Dana Dobson: I think the number of views of TEDxWilmington's YouTube videos has now exceeded 20 million. We never thought worldwide exposure for our speakers would be so significant. I think, though, the biggest impact was on our speakers and how they felt about themselves. Following their talks, our speakers have a higher level of credibility and admiration from people than they'd ever imagined. Authors sold books. Coaches got clients. People got great jobs. Saying you've done a TEDx talk impresses people, makes them say, "Wow! I've always wanted to do that!" Moreover, having given a TEDx talk has increased the confidence and feelings of self-worthiness of hundreds of people around the world.

Bob Turner: When I reflect on all that has been accomplished by Ajit Mathew George and everyone involved with TEDxWilmington over the years, I believe the biggest impact TEDxWilmington has made is that it has brought the world to Wilmington, Delaware.

The city has a population of just over 70,000 people. Yet the "ideas worth spreading" have been shared worldwide. We'll never know the entire impact that has been made, but I know the impact it has had on me. And for that, I am most thankful.

Angela Jo Manieri: TEDx Wilmington has made a huge impact on providing people a platform to share their ideas. It is professional, supportive and life changing.

Julie Vernot: Connections — to ideas, different ways of thinking, concepts, people — TEDxWilmington has created at least six degrees of connections between the organizers, speakers, volunteers, event attendees, partners, and the one-million-plus online viewers of the TEDxWilmington talks. Attending events are moving and memorable. They are worth every bit of the investment of time and focus. You will be drawn in, yet have the flexibility to manage your day, take mental breaks, meet new people, whatever fits right for you. Interacting as an audience member and a speaker, and observing others do the same, is as interesting as the talks themselves. It's stimulating from many perspectives.

Lynne Williams: Because of technology, TEDxWilmington has made a local, regional, and global impact. There are sell-out live performances with people locally and regionally. Speakers have come from around the world to share their stories and the videos of the speakers are viewed from around the world. Stories, lessons, and important messages are able to be shared internationally to help make our world a better place where we can all learn from and respect each other. TEDxWilmington really rings true that, "It's a small world after all!"

Jeet Patel: We got exposure to unconditional kindness and positivity that reached many lives. TEDxWilmington gives diversity a chance to be heard and make an impact on the community. TEDxWilmington also brings awareness to social/cultural topics that would never be recognized or introduced on a daily basis. We personally made so many connections that it has been overwhelming.

A Tribute to Andy Halligan
May His Soul Rest In Peace

This Tribute was written by Julie Vernot, who introduced Andy to the TEDxWilmington Tribe

You've heard a lot about the TEDxWilmington tribe over the years, our special and welcoming group of diverse individuals who come together with a common goal of putting on world class TEDxWilmington events and who together create a community full of inspiration. I am saddened to share that we lost a great tribe member on Easter Sunday, 2019 — Andy Halligan.

Andy joined the tribe leadership team a couple of years ago. Andy was a friend and work colleague. We had worked together several times over our 20-plus year careers and stayed in touch over the years. Whether we were working together or not, we would get together and end up talking about visionary and big ideas. He had many ideas, but Andy also loved sharing other people's ideas and often times provided inspiration to help bring life to them.

Andy knew that I was involved with TEDxWilmington through our personal conversations, plus he couldn't miss all of the posts about it on Facebook. He had recently started on a new journey to be true to himself by exploring and acting on his deepest interests. His number one focus was always his three kids. Andy was the King of Dad Jokes and gushed with pride when he spoke of them, but he was on the path to becoming a renaissance man. He pursued his interest in art by getting in to metal work. He reconnected with old friends and went in search of new ones with common interests and mindsets.

I was thrilled to receive a text from Andy on a random day asking how to get involved with TEDxWilmington. That exchange concluded with his revelation that being a part of TEDx was on his bucket list. A couple weeks later, he joined me at TEDxWilmington's TEDx Global event. A few months later, Andy stood in front of our tribe at an end-of-year celebration and recap. He shared all of the interesting analysis he had done to learn about what people thought about our events and individual talks. He dove in and became an enthusiastic tribe member connecting with most everyone on the team. Next, Andy took on the role of speaker curator. His unique personality — a curious visionary with a heart of gold — made him the perfect coach for many of our speakers. In a relatively short time, Andy connected with and touched the lives of so many people through TEDxWilmington. He felt extreme fulfillment from his involvement with TEDxWilmington. I thank you all for welcoming him to our tribe and want you to know that each of you who knew him made a positive impact on his happiness.

Thank You TEDxWilmington Tribe

From 2012 to 2018, I have produced 32 events. This would not have happened without the help of our TEDxWilmington tribe. We have had over 140 volunteers who have helped with one or more events since 2012. They have helped with updating our website, speaker curation, stage design, creating program guides, designing name tags for the event, registration for the event, photographing or videotaping the events, and much more.

DaLynne Adderley	Leah Coles	Bryce Fender
Alice Aluoch	Malcolm Coley	David Fleming
Denise Angeli-Desiderio	Pam Cornforth	Bette Francis
Megan Anthony	Karyn Cortez	Meera Gandhi
Maggie Anton	Kate Cowperthwait	Markevis Gideon
Renae Baker	Rachel Dance	Rebecca Girten
Evan Bartle	Melinda Davis	LaDonna Graham
Brad Beebe	Todd DeCapua	Ken Grant
Elissa Ben-Eli	Joe del Tufo	Kelsey Guinnup
Geoffrey Berwind	Destiny Dennis	Jason Gulotta
Crystal Boddy	Val Denton	Maria Gunther
Steve Boyden	Aru Deshmukh	Elizabeth Habash
Todd Breitling	Samantha Diedrick	Andy Halligan
Ken Briscoe	Dana Dobson	Laura Harrison
Sarah Brown	Jim Donahue	Sue Hastings
Robin Burk	David Dooley	Sonja Hegman
Malaika Carpenter	Rashid Duggan	Michael Hendry
Moira Casey	Nathan Eckel	Karen Huller
Molly Clark	Kia Ervin	D. Layne Humphrey, MSEd
Carolyn Cole	PJ Facciolo	Gladys Hunt

Rhianon Husmann
Kathryn Jakabcin
Vincent James
Cory Johnson
Wendy Johnson
Sue Kampert
Ciara Kehoe
Gretchen Kennedy
Hughlett Kirby
Anne Kisielewski
Tapesh Kotwani
Annabelle Kressman
Jonathan David Lake
Kai Lassen
Brian Loy
Wendi Lucas Caple
Terry Luckey
Sierra Lundstrom
Angela Jo Manieri
Donna May
Trey May
Angeline May
Meredith McAloon
Ray Meyers
Tyler Meyers
Barb Miller
Melissa Miller
Will Minster

Dhruv Mohnot
Aisha Monroe
Anthony Muia
Alessandra Nicole
Lin Nordmeyer
Troy Nuss
Jeanette Nyarko
Margaret O'Dwyer
Julie Olley
Chaitali Patel
Jeet Patel
Richard Paverd
Yasser Payne
Joann Pierdomenico
Vincent Pistritto
Alex Platt
Greg Plum
Kisha Rivers
Pam Sapko
John Schelich
Riya Setty
Sapna Setty
Rev. Stephen Setzer
Nina Sherak
Wil Sherk
Kevin Smith
Mac Sommerlatte
Kristin (Davis) Sommers

Ann Exline Starr
Richard Stat
Laura Stimson
Matt Sullivan
Tatiana Swedek
Bob Turner
Tes Turner
Mariya Udud
Matt Urban
Summer Rain Ursomarso
Megan Varley
Julie Vernot
Jane Vincent
Jake Voorhees
Fawn Walker
Brad Wason
Angie Waterman
George Waterman
Lynne Williams
Davina Wilson
Mike Wilson
Aniyah Wright
Darren Wright
Kris Younger
Laurie Ann Zerumsky
Donglai Zhang

CHAPTER 9
Wisdom from Around the World

The TEDx Organizer's Experience

As I did with a number of our TEDx speakers, I reached out to 10 of my fellow TEDx organizers around the world to share their unique experiences so that anyone with the ambition to create a TEDx community of their own can have wise words to live by.

Viiveck Verma
TEDxHyderabad, India

Mark Sylvester
TEDxSantaBarbara, U.S.

Pablo Barrera
TEDxGuatamalaCity, Guatamala

Randy Bretz
TEDxLincoln, U.S.

Jimmy Tan
TEDxXiguan, China

Kat Haber
TEDxVail, U.S.

Abigail O'Neal
TEDxRoadTown,
British Virgin Islands

Sabry Ben Radhia
TEDxIHEParis, France

Mark Lovett
TEDxSanDiego, U.S.

Alysia Dahir
TEDxFountainHills, U.S.

Question 1: In one paragraph not to exceed 150 words, please share your experience with your TEDx organization.

Viiveck Verma, TEDxHyderabad, India: A wonderful four years with TEDxHyderabad are over, and I step into the fifth year. When I embarked on this journey as a volunteer, little did I know that I would love it so much. It has been an immensely satisfying and a hugely fulfilling experience. It has also been a platform that has helped me grow as an individual in very unique ways, adding undiscovered dimensions to my personality. Being part of TEDxHyderabad gave me the opportunity to interact with fabulous speakers and equally passionate audiences to discover meaningful ways to get the community involved in taking these ideas forward. It was my chance as an individual to create a sustainable impact, for which I am being recognized now.

Mark Sylvester, TEDxSantaBarbara, U.S.: Since 2010, I have led a team of committed volunteers to bring the very best of the TED platform to Santa Barbara in the form of TEDx. This yearly effort has become a nearly full-time pursuit and the search for new ideas seems endless. Thankfully, I am extremely curious and always on the lookout for a new point of view. Producing this event has allowed us to shine a light on the inventions and innovative thinking here in Santa Barbara. We've also been fortunate to bring outside speakers with big ideas to the community to share their thinking and how their mission might change the world. In the spirit of TED, we strive to provide a balanced day comprised of talks that address technology, performances that entertain, and examples of design-thinking that inspire the audience. We've also made hundreds of new friends and connections.

Pablo Barrera, TEDxGuatemalaCity, Guatemala: Being the first TEDx event in my country has been a life changing experience. It is amazing how life works when you want to make a change in your community. I have met new true friends in Guatemala and outside Guatemala. I met my tribe.

Randy Bretz, TEDxLincoln, U.S.: Acting on a suggestion from a friend, I applied for my first TEDxLincoln license in 2011. Since then, I served as licensee for seven main events, four youth events, three women's events, several salons and helped produce a TEDx event in one of Nebraska's correctional institutions. Through those events I've seen more than 200 people share their ideas, seen more than 5,000 in our live audiences and been amazed at more than three million views of our videos. I've attended two TEDActive events, the TEDxSummit in 2017 and TEDxFest in 2018. I've been in the audience for a number of TEDx events, including in Grand Rapids, Mich., Fargo, N.D., Omaha, Neb., and Boston, Mass. I've become known in Lincoln and across Nebraska as "the man who brought us TEDx." I've connected with dozens of TEDx curators around the world, and regularly interact with TEDx folks on the TEDxHub and Facebook. Being part of the TEDx world has positively impacted my life.

Jimmy Tan, TEDxXiguan, China: I first started organizing TEDx events in 2011. We started the TEDx event in our university. After leaving the school, I felt TEDx was still one of my passions, so I took out a license, TEDxXiguan, in 2014. The first event of TEDxXiguan was a TEDxLive event, a small one. Now it's one of the most active in China and I became a TEDx ambassador in 2019. I started TEDxXiguan, and TEDxXiguan shaped me in many ways — curation, management, and dedication. I think it's fair to say TEDxXiguan has given more to me than I did for it.

Kat Haber, TEDxVail, U.S.: Surprise, curiosity, wonder, epiphanous, practical, positive, generous, life-affirming, ever changing, painful in moments, peaceful in others, skill sharing, relationship polishing, business sharpening all describe aspects of TEDx-ness. In the course of the past decade of producing dozens of TEDx's, we've helped to save lives, launch new careers and companies, connect partners in business and life, produced new forms of artful Xpressions, clarified NGO missions, made real peoples' dreams, and learned powerful lessons about people in the process. Volunteers on our teams use their newly gained skills and recommendations to move to bigger responsibilities professionally. I am constantly impressed with the human capacity to fail fast and forward, succeeding beyond imagination, Xperiencing the vast range of human emotions, while delivering worthy ideas to hearts which might not have known they were eager to hear just that solution. We curate, generate, amplify, and ripple together frustrations turned to revelations.

Abigail O'Neal, TEDxRoadTown, British Virgin Islands: I have found that over the short four years, holding three events so far, that we are fast becoming a group that collaborates on varied professional projects and great real-life friends. It is a true tribe that not only comes together for TEDxRoadTown, but we are there to support each other in all areas of our lives.

Sabry Ben Radhia, TEDxIHEParis, France: I started my TEDx experience back in 2015 with a small event for 100 people that grew into 850 and three million views. After two years of running TEDxIHEParis, I left the school and decided to start TEDxBelleville that took place a week ago from the moment I am writing these lines.

Mark Lovett, TEDxSanDiego, U.S.: The one phrase that every organizer uses is "life changing," and I'm no different. Having an opportunity to highlight speakers with brilliant ideas and interesting perspectives across a wide range of topics is nothing short of miraculous. That said, it's also like having another full-time job, which can be rather challenging, but there's nothing quite like seeing the effect those talks have on the attendees. And since there's never a profit motive, 100 percent of the team's effort is spent with spreading ideas as the focus, from start to finish. Producing a successful event requires the work of an amazing team, and I've been blessed in that respect, as none of our events would be possible without my co-organizer and team leads taking on any task that comes their way. Beyond being a team, we're a family.

Alysia Dahir, TEDxFountainHills, U.S.: TED started with me in a Think Tank Academic Non-Profit Government Military Contractor team called ACGE. Look me up — I'm still listed on the website. I was the controller working as an analyst with intelligence Army and Navy projects focused on the Middle East and Africa. I actually got pretty good exposure of the project's scopes by drawing budgets with the executives, directors and military commanders. That being shared, we used TED talks in our curriculum work. A few years later, a community member posted an RFP to the community to found TEDxFountainHills, and my colleagues and I in the Nonprofit DQDinc agreed to this work. I have collectively six years into my TED work, but three years in the TEDxFountainHills program. We have straddled the views now with a grass roots approach with common folk voices topping 35,000 individually. Our referred speakers come from community groups, arts collectives, local school districts, and occasionally I move outside my boundaries for the sizzle ideas I really feel can make a difference and give me a good stretching.

Question 2: If you could do things differently, what would they be? (Not to exceed 150 words.)

Viiveck Verma, TEDxHyderabad, India: If I could do things differently, the one most important thing I would do would be to get into the social sector earlier in life. Having been successful in my corporate career, I never really got to explore the chance to become part of the social sector. I realized that the skills required were the same, but the satisfaction experienced by creating even small ripples of change was massive. It took too many years to realize my ability to enable connections and work on new ideas and concepts. My skills could have been put to better use earlier, allowing me more time and deeper understanding of a sector where I feel the most comfortable.

Mark Sylvester, TEDxSantaBarbara, U.S.: The biggest ongoing challenge is funding the operation. If possible, I'd like to have formed a non-profit organization that could fundraise independently, then allocate finances for the annual event.

Pablo Barrera, TEDxGuatemalaCity, Guatemala: I would make it more sustainable from the beginning, not just from personal efforts.

Randy Bretz, TEDxLincoln, U.S.: There's not much I'd change except in my administration related to the production of the events for which I have been licensee. While I established a Nebraska nonprofit corporation and obtained IRS tax exempt status (501c3), I'd do more related to how I managed the TEDxLincoln leadership team. While my way of accomplishing things is rather informal, upon reflection I'd be better organized in my administration of the team with such things as developing position descriptions and listing requirements for each position for a more efficient operation. I would seek to give more specific direction to each volunteer, whether in leadership or simply showing up to help on the day of an event.

Jimmy Tan, TEDxXiguan, China: If I could do things differently, I would organize TEDx events full time. The organization remains non-profit, but I would be able to provide salary for a small core team. Of course, I understand the reason TED doesn't allow TEDx's to do this (not now and not in a foreseeable future).

Kat Haber, TEDxVail, U.S.: I'd have another me as my partner to give myself more space and ease in creating these Xperiences so that I could share them more broadly and deeply. I'd wake each morning to say, "Hello, my other self!" Then, we'd go about the joys of making ideas matter. Growing deeper impact grows with the level of connectedness. I live in Vail Valley half of each year, so I miss the nuances of many of the connections and relationships that could advance these powerful proposals of change making. My other self could cover the summer crowd. Together we could have a year-round presence of adventures, Xperiences, and TED influencing.

Abigail O'Neal, TEDxRoadTown, British Virgin Islands: Honestly, I would have more male members of our team who contribute in the early stages. The guys are always there for us, but it would be nice to have their points of view and more input from them on things like recruitment of speakers. Perhaps we have recruited a few additions this year who will be there in the early stages.

Sabry Ben Radhia, TEDxIHEParis, France: I always believed that our ego is our greatest enemy, and sometimes it can push us to make the wrong decision, even if the intention was good. And this is why if there is something I could do differently, it is definitely not to choose speakers I chose or to choose speakers I didn't choose. Curating speakers is a big responsibility, and we as curators should respect and be aware of what kind of ideas we put on stage. We are all human, we can make mistakes, and we can choose speakers who shouldn't be on stage or the other way around. The most important thing is to learn from those mistakes and ask for help and advice when curating speakers.

Mark Lovett, TEDxSanDiego, U.S.: Creating a TEDx event is a lot like running a company, but with one significant difference — the entire team comprises volunteers, and that means there's a change in team structure every year as volunteers move on to other projects and new team members must be recruited. While I've been blessed with an amazing co-organizer, we share the bad' habit of putting too much on our plate, and that has highlighted one area that could have used more attention — the recruiting of new talent to fill spots which invariably open up throughout the year. Having a full-time resource dedicated to volunteer recruitment and training would be the one thing I would have done differently.

Alysia Dahir, TEDxFountainHills, U.S.: First, I would have speakers clearly understand it's their friends that sell out our shows. I would demonstrate with a few of my first-year speakers how invaluable having those people in the audience accelerated the way they gave the talk. Second, I would give orientations to speaker coaches. I'm a classroom teacher I like how I know my kids know I'm always in their life. They can come back to me any day. So, become the coaches to TEDx speakers — it's a lifetime influence and should be acknowledged as such.

Question 3: In one paragraph not to exceed 150 words, please share how being part of the TEDx community has shaped you.

Viiveck Verma, TEDxHyderabad, India: The journey for me has been an enlightening one. After a successful corporate stint, during the time I took a short sabbatical and I was exploring myself, TEDxHyderabad came along as a god sent opportunity. It gave me purpose, joy and contentment — a feeling I had not had in my corporate stint for over 28 years. Through the TEDx platform, I developed global and local perspectives on various topics and ideas. Among the many beautiful things about TEDx, I loved the fact that I could pursue my creative side unhindered and along the way I would find people whose thought process matched mine. TEDxHyderabad has given me friends for life. It is also responsible for getting me recognition as a change maker and enabler, a tag that I very proudly wear. Suddenly, the world that I was living in shrunk, making it so within reach.

Mark Sylvester, TEDxSantaBarbara, U.S.: For the past 25 years, I self-identify as a TEDster. I started going to TED when it was in Monterey and followed it to Long Beach, then on to Vancouver. My wife and I created an application called introNetworks for TED2003 that eventually was the basis for TEDConnect. That project launched a company that continues to this day, and the TED thinking and sensibility permeates our business. In 2009, when TEDx was announced, we saw that opportunity as one we'd been desperate for — to bring the TED experience we so looked forward to each year, to Santa Barbara. Since then, we've fully embraced the community through attendance at TEDSummit and TEDFest. Two years ago, I wanted to capture best practices for creating and organizing TEDx events and started a podcast, Hacking the Red Circle, to give me an excuse to talk to organizers around the world.

Pablo Barrera, TEDxGuatemalaCity, Guatemala: Being a TEDx organizer made me have a purpose and a tribe.

Randy Bretz, TEDxLincoln, U.S.: Perhaps the greatest impact on me has been my increased awareness of people and places in the world. As I've gotten to know TEDx curators around the world, it's opened my eyes to just how much we have in common. It's helped me appreciate that, for the most part, we have very similar hopes and desires in life. My international connections with TEDx curators have given me great hope in the future of things across the United States and in the most remote parts of the world. Most of all, I've been shaped by the friendships I've made with people throughout the world. In addition, being the TEDx licensee made me just a bit famous in my hometown of Lincoln, as witnessed by a feature story about me in "L Magazine" in 2013. https://journalstar.com/niche/l-magazine/profiles/randy-bretz-the-man-behind-tedx/article_7c505743-5ea3-5a3c-b486-e5376f311efe.html

Jimmy Tan, TEDxXiguan, China: I'd say I feel more connected and I identify with the global citizen identity even more. It's a powerful feeling knowing virtually in every corner of the world, there's a TEDx organizer doing really hard work purely for ideas worth spreading. I feel purpose, and responsibility. It's also great to know wherever you go in the world, you can look up a TEDx organizer and you will click like old friends!

Kat Haber, TEDxVail, U.S.: For the past decade I've been enrolled in the voluntary, free, full-time course called TEDx organizing, first in Homer, Alaska, then in both Vail, Colorado and Homer for four years, and currently only Vail, Colo. I've skill shared with young professionals and teens. I've generated community conversations about tricky subjects. Through TEDx I've saved lives, launched businesses and NGOs, given deep dives to talented creatives into what's next, and connected change makers for global impacts even they could not have imagined. Within all of that, I've received far more than what I've given to my communities. I've reached within to find fuller, fairer promises of my ever-braver heart. I've learned to speak up and stand up as I've coached over 200 speakers to do the same. I've been inspired to see the world through so many other organizers' cultures. I've kept pace with tech innovations. I am grateful for TEDx-ness.

Abigail O'Neal, TEDxRoadTown, British Virgin Islands: This community has taught me to value myself more and that I can make a contribution to my community in a different and selfless kind of way. I now understand how to truly collaborate with a group of extremely professional, intelligent and diverse individuals. It has reinforced that saying for me in day-to day-life, that when you are not sure, ask a question. There is always someone in the TEDx community willing to offer advice. TEDxers genuinely care and are excited for each other.

Sabry Ben Radhia, TEDxIHEParis, France: Being part of the TEDx community has definitely shaped me as a person. It's such a powerful community that is selfless and ambitious, willing to change other people's lives and to create a transformative experience. Whether through TED gatherings, TEDx events or virtual chats, the TEDx community is always committed to sharing the knowledge and expertise they have to help you get better at running your event, but also to help you be a better person. This community is magical, and I am grateful to be part of it.

Mark Lovett, TEDxSanDiego, U.S.: In a corporate setting there is some level of sharing and cooperation, but there's always the reality of competition and trade secrets. The amazing thing about being part of the TEDx community is that everyone shares everything. There is this unique sense of camaraderie in which every TEDx organizer is committed, without reservation, to the success of all other organizers. "How can I help?" is part of each conversation. It's also an environment in which gender, faith, age, and ethnicity are not factors. It's like the United Nations of spreading great ideas. Meeting organizers from every corner of the world who share a common goal radically alters one's view of what is possible when creating a TEDx event.

Alysia Dahir, TEDxFountainHills, U.S.: I have made the most fascinating friends who challenge me to discover my greatness every day. I have taken that influence and poured it into the speakers and our community. I have found faith in myself in ways I wasn't even sure were possible because I trusted my intuition. I told myself to grow the distance to reach my potential. I stand alongside genuine people committed to making a difference in our lives, in the communities and the world. In this community we do these things together sharing resources and provide each other support and acceptance.

Question 4: Last but not least, please share in one paragraph not to exceed 150 words, your words of wisdom, based on your personal experience, to someone who might be thinking of becoming a new TEDx organizer.

Viiveck Verma, TEDxHyderabad, India: If you are considering becoming a TEDx organizer — first of all, welcome to the tribe. TEDx is something you bring into your life because you are a passionate, deep thinking person with immense patience and drive. You will have some amazing experiences, each a lesson unto its own. You will learn to view the world in a very different way than all your friends do. Suddenly you will have global reach. Places and people will surprise you. You will suddenly become part of a huge movement, which has only a forward button. There will be some difficult times as well, but do know that you will have a compassionate community backing you. You will feel liberated and no goal will seem too small. The negatives will not matter, because the positives will outshine them.

Mark Sylvester, TEDxSantaBarbara, U.S.: Before you consider taking the leap to become an organizer, I'd encourage you to ask yourself three simple questions. Write down the answers and share them with your significant other or best friend. You'll need their support if you're going to be a success in this effort. The first question is, "What outcome are you seeking by producing a TEDx event?" You should also include this in the answer "Why you're doing it?," which ties into the expected outcome. The second question is, "How will you measure success?" It won't be finances, as you can't make money with a TEDx, so you'll need to understand the metrics at which you'll be looking. The third question is, "What is the value I expect from producing this event?" Be honest with yourself. The answers to these questions will inform every decision you make on your own road to the red circle.

Pablo Barrera, TEDxGuatemalaCity, Guatemala: Don't think about how big your event is or having huge names on your lineup, think about the little ones that are doing great things and deserve to be known.

Randy Bretz, TEDxLincoln, U.S.: Words of wisdom — From my perspective of involvement in the world of TEDx for more than eight years, I urge those new and experienced TEDx folks to connect with one another, to share with one another, to learn from one another. The TEDxHub, in my mind, is the best way to accomplish this connection. And, where possible, join the TEDx Community on Facebook. Make it a practice to drop in on the Hub at least twice a week, read what others are sharing, look at their photos, benefit from the files they share. And, on top of that, take the time to share your thoughts and concerns. The TEDxHub is home to an incredible community of like-minded people eager to connect. Next, I urge all TEDx folks to participate in TEDxFest, TEDxSummit, TEDActive and other events, not just to qualify for hosting a larger event, but to connect with this incredible family of dedicated people. Then, I suggest that you attend TEDx events nearby. If you can hop in a car and make a quick trip, do it. And, on top of that, schedule the time to watch the live web streams of events near and far. In short, get connected, reach out and share with the TEDx community.

Jimmy Tan, TEDxXiguan, China: When I started organizing TEDx events, I was timid in many ways. In particular, I had no idea how to train speakers. To be honest, I didn't even think you needed to prepare them for the event. So, the advice I would give to any new organizer is that don't lower your standard for what is an idea-based talk, or what is a good event. Learn from the existing events, but build on their experience. Don't try to become them! And last but not least, don't think the 100-attendee rule is unfair or limiting you in any way. It's actually harder to create a great feeling for 100 people than for a larger audience.

Kat Haber, TEDxVail, U.S.: Thinking of becoming a TEDx organizer? I admire your courage! This road is not for the timid, not for the content, not for the stingy. You are choosing to grow and give endlessly as called upon by your own intuition and your community. You will demand the highest of yourself and team and they of you. Constant communication will become your creative command of doing your best. You'll make the most of your opportunity to connect creatives with criminals, hard workers with dreamy visionaries, bridge builders with roofers, kids with elders, food growers with car drivers, plumbers with politicians, inventors with executors, travelers with stay-at-home-moms, suicide survivors with first-time speakers. You may uncover ugly parts of yourself that have yet to be polished. You may be surprised by the depth of your integrity, genius and compassion. Your experiences may inspire listeners, standing upon the foundation you've built and refined.

Abigail O'Neal, TEDxRoadTown, British Virgin Islands: Do it! You will find in your own ever growing and evolving tribe talent, boldness, professionalism, grit, dogged determination true friends and connections the universe has to offer that you may never find if you don't. You will learn a lot about yourself. The one piece of advice that I got from one of the TEDx Organizers that TEDx connected me with in my first year was to have lots of long breaks. Pure gold. I actually got to meet him and thank him in person.

Sabry Ben Radhia, TEDxIHEParis, France: First of all, if you are thinking of becoming a new TEDx organizer, I would say stop thinking and go for it. But you should find a purpose behind running a TEDx event, find a way to create a positive impact around your community. Find a way of making TEDx a platform and a safe place for the people of your community and let them get the chance to access ideas that can help them on a daily basis. A TEDx event is time and energy consuming, and you should be careful to not lose yourself in it. Do it as long as you have the passion for it. When you feel that you don't anymore, pass it on to someone else so you keep the spark going and the ideas spreading!

Mark Lovett, TEDxSanDiego, U.S.: The team is so important to your success, so build the best one you can, and also realize it will change every year, so be prepared for that eventuality. The second tip is to stay on top of your budget — it is the lifeblood of every event. Balancing revenues and expenses must be maintained, or you'll be writing a personal check to cover the difference. Crafting a compelling event program takes a lot of work. You need to find speakers who have something to say, something relevant to an audience in the theatre, but also to the global audience who will be watching the speaker videos on YouTube. Final tip, don't cut corners on audio/video/lighting. The quality of your videos is dependent on great people and the best equipment. And before you think about organizing a TEDx event, attend other events to see how they do it.

Alysia Dahir, TEDxFountainHills, U.S.: Consensus and consent mean that a decision is reached once there are no longer any (major) objections from the participants in the conversation. Be in consent with intentions and your support.

CHAPTER 10
Rehearsal Dinner: Where People Bond, Connect, and Relax Before the Big Day

Reception: Where Speakers Can Exhale After Giving Their TEDx Talk

By Elissa Ben-Eli

I joined TEDxWilmington as a Public Ally through AmeriCorps right before the 7th Annual TEDxWilmington Conference in September 2018. I have watched a plethora of TED and TEDx videos through school and for my own pleasure, but have not been to a TED or TEDx event before. I actually went to rehearsal and rehearsal dinner prior to even attending my first TEDx event.

I had a chance to watch the final video submissions from the speakers of the 7th Annual TEDxWilmington Conference, so I had a grasp of what their talks would be, but I didn't fully understand what went into creating a TEDx event until I helped with the next event.

I was lucky enough to sit during the rehearsal and just be the timer for each speaker's talk. This truly gave me a front row experience of what TEDx is all about. Right after rehearsal, the speakers, volunteers, and some of the speakers' spouses and guests met at a restaurant down the street in Wilmington to enjoy a rehearsal dinner. We had a private room designated for us.

Right when we walked in, waiters offered us wine as we settled down. Ajit made place cards with each person's name and arranged them in various seats around the table. He does this so no two people who know each other sit by one another, and for everyone to create connections. This gave everyone a chance to talk to someone they normally wouldn't. I, not being so brave, was grateful to have a familiar tribe member across from me amongst the TEDx speakers. Although he and I chatted a bit, I really did enjoy engaging with the speakers around me.

Once we were all seated and gave the staff our dinner choices out of many great options, Ajit stood in front of the room introducing himself and what TEDx is all about. After he spoke, we went around the room stating our name, what brought us to be part of TEDxWilmington, how we are connected to Ajit, where we are from, and little anecdotes about ourselves. The speakers were asked to explain their TEDx talk and the significance of their ideas worth spreading.

Rehearsal Dinner

 This being my first glimpse into TEDxWilmington, it was incredible to see the relationships and connections people have made to the organization from 2011 to 2018. Many of the tribe members were alongside Ajit since day one, while others have been with him for as little as a year. What was even more remarkable is that even though the speakers have been in communication with the tribe for months, this was the first time they met in person, and they seemed to fit right in.

I was nervous walking into my first event, well, rehearsal, without truly knowing anyone, but the rehearsal dinner is a place for everyone to bond, make connections, and relax. What was I even nervous about? It was not like I was giving a TEDx talk the following day!

After some of our events, we hosted a reception for speakers and in some cases we invited our audience to meet our speakers. Here are some pictures from some of the receptions we hosted where the speakers could breathe more easily after giving their TEDx talk.

One of the most memorable receptions that TEDxWilmington hosted was at Nemours, the 300-acre estate of the late Alfred I. du Pont. The mansion is an excellent example of modified Louis XVI French château. It was built between 1909 and 1910. The mansion has 102 rooms and is furnished with fine period antiques, rare oriental rugs, tapestries and paintings dating back as far as the 15th century. The design of their gardens, influenced by Mr. duPont's many trips to Europe, are beautifully landscaped and include a working carillon tower, natural woodlands and extensive formal French gardens. It served as a magical setting for a reception following the TEDxWilmingtonSalon held on October 18, 2016 held at the attached Nemours Alfred I. DuPont Hospital for Children.

Reception for TEDxWilmingtonSalon at Nemours Estate

Dana Dobson, Ciara Kehoe, Brian Loy, and Rhianon Husmann

The Gardens at Nemours Estate

Ajit being welcomed by John Rumm, Executive Director, Nemours Estate

Rehearsal Dinner

Reception after TEDxWilmingtonSalon: Fireside at The Delaware Historical Society's Old City Hall

Reception hosted by the British Virgin Islands Tourist Board featuring BVI's famous painkillers at the Figure 8 Barn, Bellevue State Park after the 7th Annual TEDxWilmington Conference

The Reception at The Mill in the Nemours Building after the TEDxWilmingtonSalon on Adulting 101: Your Path. Your Purpose.

CHAPTER 11

Life Lessons Learned Directing, Filming, and Live streaming TEDx events

By Matt Urban

I've had the distinct privilege of directing the filming of almost all of the TEDx Wilmington events over the past six years, many of them also live streamed across the world. To say that I've seen hundreds of hours of TEDx talks is not an exaggeration. The talks have been on far more subjects than I can count — some incredibly earth shattering and insightful talks, some hilarious, some deeply humbling and sad, and yes — even a small percentage that are dull, lifeless, and boring.

These past years have been an amazing adventure with a lot of learning — both because of the talks themselves and also because of the work involved and the lessons that work has taught me. Some of those lessons are reinforcements of things I already knew, and some were new to me.

My role, and my team's role, has been to set up and run the cameras that record the videos that end up in the TEDx library. Setting up and filming these events is quite involved. We load in multiple cameras, tripods, sliders and other camera supports, monitors, switcher, audio equipment, crew communication system, and more. We essentially set up a portable TV production studio each and every time. And it has to be done right, because each talk happens only once (except in some VERY rare instances).

We've done this in some incredibly diverse locations — concert halls, converted movie theaters, inside libraries, inside museums, in schools, even in a prison. Every situation is different and requires slightly different setups. It requires attention to detail, preparation, and thinking on your toes.

And as I was reflecting on my experiences and thinking about what to write for this chapter, I began to realize just like the best TEDx talks, the lessons learned seem to apply to many areas of life. Here are just a few of the many things I've learned over the years that I'd like to share.

Nothing ever goes exactly as planned. Cameras don't always behave, cables can break, power supplies go bad, things get forgotten, crewmembers get sick and have bad days. Be prepared for what you know is going to happen, and more importantly, be prepared for what you don't know is going to happen. If you expect that something is most likely going to go wrong at some point, then it'll be less stressful when it does. And then, above all else, don't sweat it when the worst happens. Solutions to problems that arise are generally found much easier if you can keep your attitude positive, or at least neutral. And if you're ready for whatever may happen, chances are everything will work out just fine. So, when the inevitable happens—stop, take a deep breath, give yourself a moment to figure out a work around, and get to it.

I'll never forget the first time we filmed in one particularly old school auditorium and showed up expecting to be able to get a good audio feed from the house sound system, only to find out that there was no house sound system we could plug into. Fortunately, I'd brought along a set of microphones and stands, and was able to set them up in time to pick up the sound from an amplified speaker. It was a MacGyver solution, but nevertheless, it worked!

Trust your team and be trustworthy yourself. One person simply cannot reasonably manage everything that goes into filming TEDx events, and therefore it's critical that you have a team you can trust. There's nothing more meaningful to me in a team setting than someone saying, "I got it," and knowing that they have things under control. On the flip side of that are those situations when a team member is not pulling their weight in some way or another and bringing the entire team down. And sometimes this means confronting a crewmember and having difficult conversations or letting someone go. That's what leadership is, though — get used to it.

I find that there are few things more rewarding to me than being reliable to others. Some of that comes over time, and consistency is important. Some of this relates back to being prepared for the worst. I have learned that the more I can consistently deliver, the more trust is solidified with event staff and other people around me. And then what might be a long conversation with an event organizer about how I will solve a problem, instead becomes a simple conversation letting them know quickly that I have things under control.

Ultimately, it comes down to team dynamics. The best teams trust each other unconditionally and know that everyone is in it together. Those relationships matter.

Real-time communication is critical, and often fun! In pretty much all of the TEDx events we film, our crew is connected via wireless headsets so that we can all communicate in real time. That's critical for my role, because I need to tell each camera person how to compose their shots, if any adjustments are needed, when I'll be cutting to one camera or another, and more. Camera operators can also let me know when they see something I don't, have suggestions, etc. The com system is an essential part of what we do.

We also use the com system to have fun. Some of the conversations we have are absolutely hysterical. We quietly poke fun at ourselves, speakers, attendees, the locations— just about anything can be fair game. Never in a mean-spirited way though—it's harmless and playful banter. Since these events can be long, being able to joke around with each other keeps us alert for the long haul. And there are many times I've wished we'd recorded our chats, maybe for a "director's cut"/alternate audio track version of a talk.

Full attention is required, and caffeine is your friend. TEDx days are a strange mix of both completely exhilarating and utterly exhausting. That's true for both the audience and those working it. But for my crew working the event, it's mostly exhausting. The degree of mental focus needed to pay attention to the speakers is hard enough. Camera operators are standing for full days at a time with few breaks. And for me or whoever is directing, the complexity of managing multiple cameras, calling shots for each camera person, and ensuring that everything is recorded and live streamed as best possible, can be mind-numbing. I always plan ahead and bring what I need to keep myself alert. There might be coffee on site, but I'm not a coffee drinker. I learned a few years ago to bring at least three caffeinated sodas with me, since often there aren't any at the event!

Technology is fickle. The list of what could go wrong because of technology is immense and there's no way I could capture everything that might happen. But here are a few of the most important things I've found out from experience:

a. Computers never have enough video outputs. Usually, there's a master computer that's used for showing each speaker's presentation, and that has to send a video signal to the projector/screen, plus a monitor that the presenter can see, plus to our video switching/recording system. That's a tall order for most laptop computers. That's a long-winded way of saying—bring EVERY video adapter cable and every splitter you can think of! And then double that. I've had times when I've needed to take one video output and turn it in to four separate outputs with splitters connected to splitters. It might not look pretty, but it worked.

b. In-house internet connections—particularly wireless networks—don't always play well with others. I got on site to one event location at a historic school and connected to the wireless network to set up a live streamed event, only to find out that any streaming services were blocked. I would have been completely DOA except for the fact that I had spoken to the building IT person a few days prior and he'd given me his cell phone number in case of issues. A quick call and they'd given me an administrator login, and voila! Back in business. But had I not thought to have that conversation in advance, we would not have been able to live stream that event.

c. Software doesn't always work how it's supposed to. I can't even tell you how many times I've been just about to start a live stream event and the software crashes or doesn't even launch correctly in the first place. See item number one above. We've even run into situations with live streaming where we needed to set up a completely different computer. Roll with it. Deep breath. Reboot. Reinstall. Or in worst case, swap out equipment.

Allow plenty of preparation time. Feeling rushed is the *worst*. I'd much rather be sitting for an hour with everything set up and ready and waiting for the event to start, than be rushing up until minutes beforehand. The more preparation time, the more chance to address any issues, and the more relaxed the event, consistently and without fail.

There are never enough of some absolutely essential items. In all my years doing TEDx events, I've found that there are some items that there are just never enough of, no matter what. Here are some of them:

o Tables—needed for video switcher, audio mixer, HD recorder, monitors, computer, etc. It's rare that a table is set up, and of the appropriate size.

- Outlets—they're always too scarce or too far away. Of course.

- Lights—most don't realize how essential proper light can be to film a good TEDx event. And many venues just don't have enough (or any) lights. We and our local TEDx team learned years ago to always be sure to set up professional stage lighting. It makes all the difference in creating a professional video.

The items above mostly pertain to what happens behind the scenes in the filming process. But having seen a large number of talks over the years, we've also learned a few things about speakers and their talks. If you're an aspiring TEDx speaker, here are a few points to consider.

Nothing is ever perfect. What's most important is authenticity. An audience seeing you stumble during a talk and need to pause, and restart actually creates a connection with them. Some of the best talks have been from speakers whose true humanity shows through. They *want* you to succeed. If you stumble, just pause, maybe briefly acknowledge the stumble, and move on.

There is no "good side." We've had speakers specifically ask for us to edit out one side of their face or another. I can tell you with confidence that no one but you believes you have a better side of your face than another. Be you, do your talk, be authentic, and your authenticity combined with the good sound, lights, and video will have you look fantastic.

Dangling jewelry is almost always a distraction, especially with microphones. Most microphones used for speakers are small tie clip mics. The few times we've ever had to re-record someone's talk are because jewelry rubbing against a microphone ruined the audio from a talk. And trust me, no one will think less of you because of what jewelry you wear. It's the words that come out of your mouth that count.

It's not about you. It's not about you being smarter than anyone else in the room in your subject area. It's about your passion for your subject shining through in your talk. If you're going up on stage to be in the spotlight or promote yourself, that's the wrong reason. If you're up there to share an idea with the world, then welcome to the red carpet.

Assume your microphone is always on. No side chatter backstage! There have been a number of occasions where a microphone is on and hot when it isn't supposed to be and a backstage conversation is heard, either in the recording, or worse—in the venue. There's probably nothing more embarrassing than being the person talking over the house sound system when another presenter is on stage. Don't be that person.

Practice the clicker during rehearsal. Clicker issues are one of the biggest issues for speakers. If slides don't advance correctly, then often speakers will stumble on their presentation. So be prepared and practice it in advance. And if all else fails and your slides don't work, just move on with your talk. People are there to hear your words and be with you, not to focus on your slides.

Above all else, we have your back. Chances are if something happens on stage, we can fix it in the final editing process. If you stumble and have to back up and restart, we can cut out the dead air. If a slide ends up in the wrong place in your talk, we can put it back in the correct place. Remember, our job is to make everyone look good, and give everyone's talk the highest likelihood of being chosen to be in the TEDx library online.

I can say with certainty having been involved with TEDx over the years that my life is richer for these experiences. I am better at my job, better at my relationships, and better equipped for life as a result. It's been a joy, a challenge, and incredibly fulfilling.

Who could really ask for anything more?

CHAPTER 12
My Journey with TED

By Sheryl Winarick

I first met Sheryl Winarick in December 2015 at TEDGlobal in Geneva, Switzerland. I then reconnected with her in June 2016 at TEDSummit in Banff, Canada. Sheryl's collection of friends is truly amazing—they are from all over the world. She is one of the most engaging people I have ever met in my life. I invited her to join me in the summer of 2016 for a few days of intellectually stimulating conversation at Sunset Watch Villa, our home away from home, in Virgin Gorda, British Virgin Islands.

We tried to solve all the problems of the world in these few days. Sheryl came to Wilmington, Del. to kickoff a nationwide tour on the Art of Migration, where I hosted a dinner at Christ Church Christiana Hundred. I also invited her to be the guest speaker at the Rotary Club of Wilmington, Del. while she was visiting us. I asked her to write this chapter on her TED and TEDx journey, because I know of no one else who has done all the following **TEDx talks:**

- Building Bridges of Understanding (TEDxDanubia, May 2017)
- Welcoming the Stranger Inspires Hope (TEDxVail, Jan 2017)
- Inspired People Inspire People—Ask an Immigrant! (TEDxBeaconStreet, Nov 2016)
- Talking to Each Other is the Only Way to Heal our Divided Nation (TEDxMidAtlantic, Oct 2016)
- Immigrants Keep America Great (TED Residency, July 2016)
- StoryCorps | Sheryl Winarick & Esther Fanord (TEDxAmericanUniversity, Apr 2015)

–Ajit Mathew George

In 2008, a friend sent me the video of Dave Eggers accepting the TED Prize. This was the first time I had ever heard of TED. Immediately, I was captivated, and the feeling grew stronger with time. Can you imagine my surprise, about three years later, when my friend, Bruce Campbell, called to tell me TED contacted him looking for an immigration lawyer, and he recommended me? After a phone interview, I took the train from Washington, D.C. to visit TED headquarters in New York City. Little did I know how much this engagement would alter the course of my life.

Living in DC, I was already surrounded by an incredibly diverse family of friends. From the international students at George Washington University Law School to my clients from across the globe, to the community I cultivated through the United Nations Association and friends who worked at the World Bank and countless international NGOs—my world looked and felt very different than my previous life in Texas. TED took things to another level completely.

I was called to help, because TED had partnered with the Gates Foundation to provide scholarships for TEDx organizers and TED translators to participate in the big TED conferences in the U.S. and the UK, and later in Canada, too, but the visa process was proving to be a major obstacle. Several scholarship recipients had already been denied visas several times. I was asked to help these individuals from India and Pakistan and various countries in Africa to navigate the visa process. In most cases, we were successful. Then, after visas were secured, we got to meet in person at the TED conferences. The dynamic, diverse collection of TEDx organizers and TED translators from all around the world quickly started to feel like a global, borderless family.

I went to TED and TEDGlobal in 2012, 2013, and 2014; to TEDGlobal in Geneva in 2015; and to TEDSummit in Banff, Canada in 2016. Every event, the bonds grow deeper and stronger among people I got to meet in person, as well as friends who keep in touch online via Facebook and through WhatsApp groups.

The first TED-related event I ever attended will always hold a special place in my heart: TEDxMidAtlantic in 2011, just a few weeks after my interview at TED HQ in NY. Lara Stein, who started the TEDx program, suggested I participate to get a better feel both for TED as an organization and for the local TEDx community. I remember meeting the organizers, Nate Mook and David Troy, who are now great friends. I've been to every TEDxMidAtlantic since then, and now I help to curate the events.

Over the years, in addition to the big TED conferences and TEDxMidAtlantic, I've visited many TEDx events around the world and spoken at several, too. Some of the TEDx organizers have even helped me organize community gatherings where they live.

This is the magic of TED. You surround yourself with hopeful, solutions-oriented people who are both dreamers and doers. Before you know it, you are pushing yourself to think of new, creative ways to make a positive impact in the world.

That's what happened to me. When the TED Residency was announced, I joined the first cohort in Spring 2016 to incubate a project to explore culture and identity the different ways people experience migration through intimate community conversations. As an immigration lawyer, I was interested in finding ways to bring people together to connect on a level deeper than the labels we wear, to challenge stereotypes about immigrants and refugees, and cultivate understanding. Since then, over the past few years, I have been traveling all around the U.S. and the world, connecting people where they live, usually over a home-cooked meal. My project, originally called Hope Dominos, has evolved into The Art of Migration, and TEDx organizers have played a significant role, inviting me into their communities and helping to bring people together.

I started my journey with The Art of Migration in McPherson, Kansas in the summer of 2016, after meeting Shannon Brake, a TED-Ed Innovative Educator, at TEDSummit in Banff. I then traveled to Atlanta, Ga. and Huntsville, Ala., where TEDx organizers Jacqui Chew and Everett Alexander invited me to engage their communities.

The following year, I drove across the United States, starting in Delaware, the first state, at the invitation of Ajit Mathew George, who organizes TEDxWilmington. I first met Ajit at TEDGlobal in Geneva. I remember vividly, he was sitting with Claire Kennedy, a former refugee lawyer in the U.K., who now organizes TEDxExeter. We connected quickly over deep conversation and laughter, and I knew we would all stay in touch. When I visited Ajit's community in Wilmington, I got to speak to the local Rotary Club and facilitate a dinner gathering at a local church. The experience was so beautiful.

Everywhere I go, local TEDx communities welcome me like family, and we go on a journey together, building and deepening relationships through the sharing of personal stories and experiences. In the summer of 2018, I drove across 20 countries in Eastern Europe and Central Asia. TEDx organizers are everywhere, and we are family.

If I could offer one piece of advice, one slice of wisdom, from everything I've had the privilege to experience, I would say "showing up" might be the most important thing you can do—showing up for other people; showing up for yourself; showing up with an open mind and an open heart, ready to receive and prepared to share.

I am immensely grateful for the TED/TEDx community—people all across the world who are committed to the sharing of ideas, with the hope of leaving this world a little better than we found it and enjoying the journey together while we're here.

CHAPTER 13
Speakers Resources

From 2011 through 2013, TEDxWilmington did not have a structured process on how applicants became speakers. There was no formal application, no video submission, and no structured feedback once speakers were chosen. There was not even a rehearsal to make sure everyone was ready for the day of event.

Since 2014, TEDxWilmington had a very thorough application process that I will discuss in further detail momentarily. Once an applicant is selected as a speaker, there are rigorous deadlines to meet; submitting bios, headshots, outlines, multiple video submissions along the way, blogs of their experience and TEDx process, image rights for any photos they plan to use during their TEDx talk, drafts of their PowerPoints, and much more.

The most important thing in this process is making sure that the speakers are fully prepared for the day of the event. The first thing all TEDxWilmington applicants are required to do is purchase Chris Anderson's "TED Talks: The Official TED Guide to Public Speaking." The main thing to focus on is, "Chapter 4: The Throughline." Without a throughline, the talk does not have a distinct direction. We also required applicants to submit a one- to two-minute video with their application that gives our speaker selection committee a better grasp of what their idea worth spreading is and how well they are prepared.

No matter how important someone is, we still read their application in the same way asevery other applicant. One of the biggest issues when going through the applications is having applicants not follow directions. This is a warning sign that this applicant will most likely not follow the requirements to give a talk. The video submissions need to be uploaded to YouTube, not set as "private," and the video has to be "unlisted." Many speakers do not give us permission to view the videos or give us a password to open. Their application is put to the side. The video submitted by an applicant is to be solely created for a TEDxWilmington application, which is stated clearly in the application. Many applicants submit a video that was used for a marketing video or try to sell their own business and not share an idea worth spreading. The best video submissions are taken in a well-lit room, where the applicant speaks with confidence and shares their idea worth spreading in a succinct manner.

    I have read thousands of applications and watched all of their video submissions. It is so hard to turn people down, but after reading this book, it will hopefully give people tips to improve their application prior to submitting to any TEDx organization. The first thing I look at is their video submission; do they seem confident, do they have a new idea, do they have an idea at all, etc. Then I move on and review the written part of their application. Why do they want to give a TEDx talk, what TED and TEDx talks have they watched and why did they like them? We get applicants from all over the world from so many backgrounds. We want to make sure our events are diverse and that everyone in the audience and around the world will be able to relate to the speakers and their ideas. We try our best to make sure we have a diverse group of speakers.

TEDxWilmington Speaker Application

Thank you for your interest in being a speaker at TEDxWilmington!

Before you apply, you MUST read the book "TED Talks: The Official TED Guide to Public Speaking" by Chris Anderson. This book is available on Amazon. Please pay close attention to Chapter 4: The Throughline. You will be required to answer what the throughline of your proposed TEDx talk will be in this application. Being clear on your throughline will make a difference in how you present your talk, how you convey your idea, and what the listeners takeaway from your talk.

The following APPLICATION CANNOT BE PARTIALLY SAVED. You will need to complete the application in its entirety at one time. Please review the entire form and make sure you have enough time to fill it out before you start.

There are a few things to know before starting:

- Always say TEDx; never TED when referring to your talk or TEDxWilmington.
- Your talk must be 12 minutes or less. While a TED or TEDx talk can be up to 18 minutes long, TEDxWilmington has decided to limit most talks to 12 minutes.
- Your "Idea Worth Spreading" must be your own and may not address political/religious agendas or directly promote a company, business, or product.
- You will be required to sign a release form prepared by TED.
- In this application, you will be required to submit a short video (1-2 minutes). Please record and upload this video to YouTube before you start this application.
- TEDxWilmington has a very rigorous process and includes many deadlines along the way. Please read the disclosure at the end of this application which has more details about the materials due.

Before starting your application, you must verify that your idea is within TEDx Content Guidelines. To do this, please review the following link from TED:

http://storage.ted.com/tedx/manuals/tedxcontentguidelines.pdf

- We strongly encourage you to visit www.TED.com and check out TED and TEDx talks that might have similar ideas to your proposed TEDx talk. Be prepared to share with us why your proposed talk is unique and different.
- Last, but not least, all applications must be completed by the speaker, and not a third party.

Email address_____

First Name *_____

Your answer_____

Last Name *_____

Your answer_____

How would you like to be addressed? *_____

(First name, Nickname, Last Name, etc)_____

Your answer_____

About You

Tell us a little about yourself!

Gender*

- ○ Male
- ○ Female
- ○ Other

Race *

This will not affect the speaker selection, but it must be answered.

- ○ American Indian or Alaska Native
- ○ Asian
- ○ Black or African American
- ○ Native Hawaiian or Other Pacific Islander
- ○ White
- ○ Hispanic or Latino
- ○ Other:

Date of Birth *_____

Cell Phone Number *_____

Alternative Phone Numbers Where You Can Be Reached_____

Mailing Street Address *_____

Mailing City *_____

Mailing State *_____

Mailing Zip *_____

Country of Residence *_____

Position/Title and Employer *_____

How would you like to be described on promotional materials? (For Example: Assisant Director of Joe Company, Inc. or Software Developer at TechStartUp, LLC) If student, please write your school & grade, if retired please write "retired.." followed by your previous career. Please DO NOT use "Self-Employed" or "Public/Keynote Speaker"

_____

Have you ever given a TED or TEDx Talk? *
Please include where, when, and the title of your talk(s)

_____

Have you ever attended any TED or TEDx events in the past? *
Please list any and all you have been to, including TEDxWilmington.

_____

Have you ever been to any TEDxWilmington events, specifically? *
Please list their names and dates, if possible.

_____

Do you personally know any of the previous TEDxWilmington speakers?

_____

How did you hear about TEDxWilmington? *

_____

Give us a short biography of yourself in 120 words or less. *

_____

Do you plan on having a speaker coach? If you already have one, what is their name? *

Video Submission (1-2 minutes)

Before you can submit this form, you are required to attach a video link that distills your Idea Worth Spreading for your proposed TEDx talk. Below are the required guidelines:

1. This video should be between 1 and 2 minutes long, but NO LONGER than 2 minutes. DO NOT use more than 2 minutes, or your application will be disqualified.

2. It SHOULD BE filmed for the sole purpose of briefly and concisely summarizing your message to TEDxWilmington and give our "Speaker Curating Committee" a snapshot of how you come across, in person, with your Idea Worth Spreading. Be specific as possible.

3. Make sure you have energy and passion in your tone of voice, body language, and words.

4. This video should complement the written portion of your application and give us more specifications of your idea. Do not repeat what you have already said in the written portion.

5. This SHOULD NOT be a reused video from any other previous media appearances. Feel free to film from a computer or smartphone since the video does not need to be fancy. You will be disqualified immediately if you send a video clip that was not created specifically for this application.

6. While you can use either YouTube or Vimeo for your video, we had less problems when people have submitted via YouTube. Please make sure it is not set as "Private" and make the video "unlisted".

7. Label your video as: "Your Name—TEDxWilm2019", (example: "Sarah Smith—TEDxWilm2019") and paste the link below.

Keep in mind that we receive hundreds of applications so TAKE THE TIME TO PLAN exactly what you are going to say.

The video you submit will have more weight than any other single factor when the curating committee decides who to extend an invitation to.

Please Paste Video Link Below *

_____

About Your Talk

In the following section, you will be answering questions specifically about the TEDx Talk you wish to give. Some of your ideas may change in the future, but please answer relative to how it stands currently.

Are you giving this talk with someone else? If so, include their name and email. Each person much complete a separate application. *

_____

What would you like the title of your talk to be? Something short and catchy to grab audiences and viewers. *
Come up with something short, clever, and catchy to grab audiences and viewers. [Your title must be 100 characters or less TOTAL, including spaces, vertical slashes, and the following format: "Title | Name | TEDx-Wilmington*event*" for instance "Dating is Dead | Kevin Carr | TEDxWilmingtonSalon" - 49 characters] Usually shorter is better, but make sure to use wording that would be easily searchable on the internet.

_____

What is the desired time length of your TEDx talk? (Maximum: 12 Minutes) *
The shorter talks often get more views. Feel free to write in any other unlisted specific amount of time between 2 and 12 minutes, in the "other" section. Be aware that you may not always get the full time you request. TED has recently stated publicly that 12 minutes is the optimum length of a TED or TEDx talk in order to receive the most viewership.

- ○ 5 Minutes
- ○ 10 Minutes
- ○ 12 Minutes
- ○ Other:

What is your one "Idea Worth Spreading"? In reference to Chris Anderson's "TED Talks: The Official TED Guide to Public Speaking", the throughline is the connecting theme that ties together each narrative element. What is the precise idea you want to build inside your audience? (in 50 words or less) *
Think of an overarching message you would want the audience to take away from your talk.

_____

I affirm I have purchased Chris Anderson's "TED Talks: The Official TED Guide to Public Speaking" and have read at least Chapter 4: The Throughline. *

- ○ Yes I have
- ○ I plan to do so very quickly

Why are you the right person to speak on this topic? Please list any job titles, passions, or credentials that qualify you as an expert. *
_____

What "Call to Action" do you have for your audience? What will they be motivated to do after hearing you speak or how can they take action? (in 50 words or less) *
_____

Under which of the following categories would your TEDx talk be categorized? Your talk must fall under one of these topics as they are set forth by TED when uploading the final videos. *(Please choose one)* *

- ○ Art
- ○ Business
- ○ Design
- ○ Education
- ○ Entertainment
- ○ Global Issues
- ○ Health
- ○ Humanities
- ○ Life
- ○ Science (Hard)
- ○ Social Sciences
- ○ Technology

At which event would you like to speak? *

- ○ One of the upcoming TEDxWilmington events (Subject to receiving approval from TED)

Please list 3 of your favorite TED or TEDx talks and why you like them. *
_____
_____
_____

Please list any websites you are affiliated with.
Not including social media websites like Facebook.
_____

Why do you want to give a TEDx talk? *
_____

Please tell us something intriguing, remarkable, unusual, or unexpected about yourself that you have not yet shared shared with us? *
_____

Social Media

Much of our marketing and promotion is done through social media. Please answer the following questions to the extent that they apply to you.

Facebook Name
_____

# of Facebook Friends
_____

Twitter Handle
_____

# of Twitter Followers
_____

LinkedIn Name
_____

# of LinkedIn Connections
_____

Instagram Name
_____

# of Instagram Followers
_____

TEDx Wilmington Disclore

Please carefully read the following before submitting your application.

Please note that there is no compensation paid to any speaker giving a TEDx talk. Travel & Accommodation costs are also the sole responsibility of the speaker.

When invited to speak, you will have to sign an agreement that holds you responsible for the electronic delivery, according to a given timeline, of many materials regarding your talk including, but not limited to:

- A Professional Headshot Photo
- A Biography (and an additional shorter version for program guides)
- An Outline of your talk
- 3 blogs about the process (~300 words each)
- 2 Video drafts
- 2 Powerpoint Drafts (optional)

Please do not apply if you feel that you will not be able to meet given deadlines with these deliverables.

Please direct any questions or concerns about this nomination form to ajitgeorge@tedxwilmington.com

Your Official Invitation to Give a TEDxWilmington Talk in November

Ajit George <ajitgeorge@tedxwilmington.com>
Tue, Sep 25, 2018 at 12:56 PM
Cc: Elissa Ben-Eli <Elissa@tedxwilmington.com>

Dear Karen,

Subject to approval by TED for TEDxWilmington to host the 2018 TEDxWilmingtonWomen Conference, the TEDxWilmington tribe is delighted to inform you that you have been officially selected from a large pool of applicants to give a TEDx talk at our 3rd Annual Women Conference on Friday, November 30, 2018!

Women all over the world are no longer accepting the status quo. They're rising up, breaking out, and pushing boundaries. Whatever their focus and talent—business, technology, art, science, politics—these pioneers and their allies are joining forces in an explosion of discovery and ingenuity to drive real, meaningful change.

TEDxWomen will celebrate how these dynamic and diverse people are showing up to face challenges head on, all while empowering each other to shape the future we all want to see.

There will be **four 90-minute sessions** throughout the day, **separated by one-hour breaks**, as well as **one streamed** session from Palm Springs, California TEDWomen.

The following documents are attached:

- Official Invitation (has your time allotment)
- Speaker Agreement (describes the process and expectations)
- Speaker Release (required by TED)
- Table of Deadlines (everything is due on a Wednesday)
- Speaker Coaches (highly recommended)
- TEDx Speaker Guide
- Speak Like A Pro article
- Promotion Video (see Speaker Agreement)

Please thoroughly review all the attachments. When reading the article Speak Like A Pro, please substitute the word speech(es) with talk(s). TEDx and TED talks should never be referred to as speeches, like the article does. Since the information in the article is extremely useful, we want to send it to you nevertheless, and thus this disclaimer.

The official invitation document will give you instructions on what to do in order to accept the invitation. Please note your **first deadline** is **Wednesday, October 3, 2018.**

Please search and watch any TED Talks (https://www.ted.com/talks) and TEDx Talks (https://www.youtube.com/user/TEDxTalks) that come up using keywords that may be associated with your TEDxWilmington talk as well. This will ensure that your talk is different from any TED or TEDx talk that's already available to the public.

We highly suggest reading a couple blogs from past speakers to get an understanding of what the TEDxWilmington process is like before accepting our invitation: http://www.tedxwilmington.com/blog/

Please watch video of No Apple Presenter Speaks for Longer Than 10 Minutes, and the Reason Is Backed by Neuroscience:

> https://www.inc.com/carmine-gallo/apple-follows-this-10-minute-rule-to-keep-you-glued-to- product-presentations.html

In the next 10 days we will send out hotel accommodation information for you and your guests to reserve a room at a special rate.

Congratulations on your invitation and we look forward to hearing back from you! As always, please don't hesitate to ask questions or express concerns.

In the spirit of ideas worth spreading,

September 25, 2018,

Dear Karen:

Subject to approval by TED for TEDxWilmington to host the 2018 TEDxWilmingtonWomen Conference, TEDxWilmington is honored to extend a formal invitation to you to give a TEDx talk that does **not exceed 10 minutes** at the 3rd Annual TEDxWilmingtonWomen Conference on Friday, November 30, 2018 in Wilmington, Delaware. The theme of this event is **Showing Up**. You were carefully selected from a list of **over 200 applications.**

Please **carefully read through the deadlines set forth in the Speaker Agreement** and mark them down in your calendar. They are all very important and essential to you giving a TEDx talk at this TEDxWilmington event. A spreadsheet of all the deadlines is attached. **We recommend printing it out**.

To accept your invitation, you will need to initial the last 4 pages of the speaker agreement starting with the page entitled "Acceptance of Invitation to Give a TEDx talk", sign, scan and return it via e-mail on or before **12:00 pm, New York Time, Wednesday, October 3, 2018** to my Assistant Producer, Elissa Ben- Eli, at elissa@tedxwilmington.com. Please also sign, scan, and return the TED required speaker release form. Please do not announce publicly that you are a speaker until you are listed as a speaker on our website on or after Thursday, October 4th.

The **first deadline** is **Wednesday, October 3rd**. You will need to send us your signed and initialed agreement, signed release, headshot photograph, working title of your talk, and 2 versions of your biography, your professional title and connect with me on Facebook as listed in more detail in the Speaker Agreement. **If you miss this deadline, we will assume you are not interested in giving a TEDx talk.**

Upon receiving your signed acceptance of this invitation together with the speaker release, we will send you more resources by e-mail that will help you prepare for this TEDx talk. We and previous TEDxWilmington speakers highly recommend watching this playlist from TED of 9 talks to watch before public speaking: https://www.ted.com/playlists/226/before_public_speaking

TEDxWilmington will arrange, at its own expense, for each talk at this TEDxWilmington Conference to be professionally videotaped with three cameras, edited and uploaded to the TEDx Talks YouTube Channel, subject to the review and final approval by TED.

Our team looks forward to working closely with you between now and November 30, 2018 to help you with your Idea Worth Spreading via a TEDx talk.

Sincerely yours,
Ajit Mathew George
Organizer & Executive Producer TEDxWilmington
P.O. Box 69 | Wilmington, DE | 19899
Ajit George, Organizer: ajitgeorge@tedxwilmington.com
Elissa Ben-Eli, Assistant Producer: elissa@tedxwilmington.com

x = independently organized TED event

3rd Annual TEDxWilmingtonWomen Conference: "Showing Up"

Your Official Invitation to Give a TEDx Talk

TEDxWilmington
Friday, November 30, 2018

This event will be held at **The Mill Auditorium**, 1007 N Orange St, Wilmington, Delaware. Doors will be open to the general public at 7:30 am. Our program begins at 8:00 am and will end by 5:00 pm. There will be 4 Sessions. Each session is 90 minutes long with an hour break between the sessions.

We will do a FULL rehearsal on **Thursday, November 29** starting at **8:30 am** that will go **until 6:00 pm** at **The Mill Auditorium**. Please **arrive at 8:30 am** so we can start rehearsal on time. (You will need to arrive for the time of your session, which you will know the week prior to rehearsal).

Immediately following rehearsal, you will be joining all the speakers and members of the TEDxWilmington Tribe for a *"Speakers Dinner"*, as guests of TEDxWilmington, on **Thursday evening**, November 29, 2018.

Our speakers and audience are all encouraged to attend the entire event so that the diverse group of people present, both speakers and attendees, will be able to learn from one another, and leave the conference inspired to act on the ideas that will be shared.

For more information about TEDxWilmington please visit www.tedxwilmington.com and follow us on Facebook, Instagram, Twitter, and LinkedIn.

Your TEDxWilmington talk

Beginning

TED and TEDx presenters might make their talk look effortless, but hours of preparation go into making a great talk - thinking, practicing, revising slides, memorizing, more practicing... We expect the same.

Developing your content

Like the best TED Talks, your TEDx Talk should be focused, sharp, and go deep rather than broad. It can include aspects of your personal experience or projects, but these examples should be powerful, illuminating, and succinct.

Please purchase and carefully read the book *TED Talks: The Official TED Guide to Public Speaking* by Chris Anderson, who is the head of TED. We will be sending some additional resource materials after you accept our invitation. Please carefully read all the information we send to you.

Many TEDx speakers find it beneficial to hire a speech coach to help them with their TEDx talk. We think it is money well spent. Please find attached a list of 3 speaker coaches recommended by past TEDxWilmington speakers.

Practice

Great TED presenters are passionate and engaging. They speak slowly and clearly, as well as deliver their talks by memory.

Our timeline gives you some key dates to work towards, but the key is to rehearse again and again.

Visuals

Less is more.
A single, strong, graphic image or succinct line of text will tell your story better than a crowded collage or packed paragraph. Remember, people need to process everything you're saying while simultaneously absorbing your slides. Rather than one complex slide, use several slides, each with one idea, image or data point. Eliminate 'headline and bullet-points' slides; they are tiring to read.

Ask for help

Please don't hesitate to ask us any questions, however trivial they may seem—we're here to help.

Speaker Resources

Visuals: our technical specifications

Remember that your slides will be included in your online video as well. If you are going to use slides in your presentation, we require your final slides and final title no later than **12:00 pm, November 14, 2018**. Please *do not* include a title slide, as we use TEDxWilmington template slide for every speaker. If you have any questions regarding the technical aspects of your presentation that are not answered below, please do not hesitate to contact Elissa Ben-Eli via e-mail at elissa@tedxwilmington.com.

Your presentation will run off of our laptops and projected onto a screen behind you. There will be a "confidence monitor" on the ground in front of you, showing ***only*** exactly what is on the projection screen behind you.

You will need to deliver:

- Your presentation slides in PowerPoint format ONLY.
- Separate files of any embedded videos.
- A list of all the images and videos used in your slideshow, showing that you have received permission, with details of their source.
- A PDF version of your final slides in addition to your final PowerPoint file.

Slide Dimensions

Please ensure your presentation display size conforms to a 16:9 aspect ratio (*not* 4:3).

Font Size

You rarely need more than 6 lines of text on a slide - often a line or two will do, if any. Sans-serif fonts (e.g. Helvetica) are easier to read at a distance than serif fonts (like Times New Roman). Bold text whenever possible and keep it away from the edges. Minimum font: 28pt

Slide Background

A simple background keeps your text readable. Please avoid template backgrounds and try to use a dark or black background. Our title slides have a black background with red and white font.

Graphs, Graphics and Photos

Use visually arresting images, data, and large words to serve as a mnemonic device so the audience has higher visual recall. Use high-resolution pictures and graphics. Full- quality photos from a digital camera will look better than images from the web.

Keep in mind that finding an image on the internet does not give speakers permission to use the image in their presentation. You can find free public images on Flickr (http://www.flickr.com/search/advanced/) if you select the "creative commons" box, ensuring you have an appropriate license. Depositphotos.com, Pexels.com, Unsplash.com, and istockphoto.com are other sites where you can find free public images.

All slides with images downloaded from the Internet need the URL displayed on the slide. If the URL (web address) if lengthy, we recommend using bit.ly.com or any other service that shortens the length of the address for you.

Please provide a list including each and every image, along with the rights/source that grants its inclusion. You must properly license all images for TED's use in worldwide video and web distribution. Only photos and images that are listed with appropriate rights can be included in your slides.

Additional Media

Please embed any multimedia in their respective slides and supply us with separate files in a standard format (mp4 and mp3). Please ensure that your presentation ***does not require WiFi or internet connectivity*** on the day of your talk.

Useful examples. These presentations worked really well at TED and online:

- John Doerr—Profit and Salvation in Greentech (2007) www.ted.com/talks/view/id/128
- Bill Gates—Innovating to Zero! (2010) www.ted.com/talks/lang/eng/bill_gates.html
- Larry Lessig—Creativity and the Law (2007) www.ted.com/talks/view/id/187
- Rives—4a.m. (2007) www.ted.com/talks/view/id/148

ACCEPTANCE OF THE INVITATION TO GIVE A TEDx TALK

I accept your invitation to be a speaker at the 3rd Annual TEDxWilmingtonWomen Conference and agree to be available on **Friday, November 30, 2018** to give my TEDx talk within the time allocated in the invitation cover letter.

I agree to attend the rehearsal on **Thursday, November 29, 2018**. I also agree to attend the dinner, as a guest of TEDxWilmington, in honor of all the speakers on **Thursday evening, November 29, 2018**.

I acknowledge that I will receive no consideration in exchange for giving this TEDx talk and I am not obligated to contribute any money to TEDxWilmington on account of the 3rd Annual TEDxWilmingtonWomen Conference. **I acknowledge that as a speaker I will receive one ticket, for myself only, to this TEDxWilmington event which is nontransferable.**

I promise to:

- Execute and return this **agreement** on or before 12:00 pm, New York Time, **Wednesday, October 3, 2018** to elissa@tedxwilmington.com;

- Execute and return both pages the attached **Speaker Release** agreement to elissa@tedxwilmington.com on or before 12:00 pm, New York Time, **Wednesday, October 3, 2018**;

- Purchase and carefully read or listen to the book *TED Talks: The Official TED Guide to Public Speaking* by Chris Anderson, the head of TED;

- Provide at least three high-resolution professional **headshot** photo (at least 300 pixels per inch) to elissa@tedxwilmington.com on or before 12:00 pm, New York Time, **Wednesday, October 3, 2018**;

- Provide my **professional title** and **name** for marketing materials EX: Jane Doe, VP of Development, Awesome Productions (Name, Title, Company) to elissa@tedxwilmington on or before 12:00 pm, New York Time, **Wednesday, October 3, 2018**;

- Provide an updated copy of my **bio** in 3rd person in a **Word document** on or before 12:00 pm, New York Time, **Wednesday, October 3, 2018** in **two different lengths** to elissa@tedxwilmington.com. One bio will be a summary that **does not exceed 120 words** for the printed program guide. The second bio will be more detailed (over 120 words) for marketing purposes including posting on the TEDxWilmington website;

- Provide an updated **working title** of my TEDx talk to elissa@tedxwilmington.com on or before 12:00 pm, New York Time, **Wednesday, October 3, 2018**;

- If I am on **Facebook**, I will "like" the **TEDxWilmington Facebook** page and send a friend request to **Ajit Mathew George** by **Wednesday, October 3, 2018** so TEDxWilmington can tag me in their efforts to promote me when I am announced as a speaker and when my talk has been uploaded to YouTube.

- Work collaboratively with TEDxWilmington to develop the topic;

- Craft a talk attendees wouldn't have heard before;

- Present a detailed **outline** (not a script) in a **Word document** of my talk in writing to elissa@tedxwilmington.com on or before 12:00 pm, New York Time, **Wednesday, October 10, 2018**;

- Provide a **60 second promotional video** to elissa@tedxwilmington.com on or before 12:00 pm, New York Time, **Wednesday October 10, 2018** for TEDxWilmington to use as it sees fits on its website, social media channels, and any other marketing vehicles. Key language will be outlined in the **attachment** titled **TEDx Promotional Video**.

- Provide a **300 word blog** in a **Word document** reflecting on this experience so far on or before 12:00 pm, New York Time, **Wednesday, October 17, 2018** to alessandra@tedxwilmington.com which blog will be published at http://www.tedxwilmington.com/blog/ and various social media sites. Use link to find examples of blogs posted by previous presenters labeled Meet the Speaker;

○ Respond to communications from TEDxWilmington promptly;

○ Keep my talk within the allotted time and not exceed it;

○ Provide a **video** of my entire talk **standing up** with full length of body shown (taken on a smartphone, camera, or computer) that is uploaded to **YouTube** and marked as **unlisted** or public on or before 12:00 pm, New York Time, **Wednesday, October 24, 2018** to elissa@tedxwilmington.com. You may read from notes while filming this video. If any video issues arise, contact our Video

○ Producer, Jake Voorhees at hello@jakevoorhees.com;

○ Provide elissa@tedxwilmington.com with a draft version of my **slide deck** (if any) and list of **image/media rights** on or before 12:00 pm, New York Time, **Wednesday, October 24, 2018**;

○ Implement feedback given to me from the Speaker Curating Committee on the video submissions;

○ Provide a second **300 word blog,** which will be labeled the TEDx process, in a **Word document** reflecting on this experience so far on or before 12:00 pm, New York Time, **Wednesday, November 7, 2018 to** alessandra@tedxwilmington.com which will be published at http://www.tedxwilmington.com/blog/ and our various social media sites;

○ Provide a **list of stage props** I am proposing to bring with me (stage props are optional) on or before 12:00pm, New York Time, **Wednesday, November 7, 2018** to elissa@tedxwilmington.com;

○ Provide a **video** of my final talk **standing up** with full length of body shown and **without notes** (taken on a smartphone, camera, or computer) that is uploaded to **YouTube** and marked as **unlisted** or public **AND** send video link to elissa@tedxwilmington.com on or before 12:00 pm, New York Time **Wednesday, November 14, 2018.** If any video issues arise, contact our Video Producer, Jake Voorhees at hello@jakevoorhees.com;

○ Email the **final title** of my TEDx talk on or before 12:00 pm, New York Time, **Wednesday, November 14, 2018,** to elissa@tedxwilmington.com;

○ Provide elissa@tedxwilmington.com with a final version of my **slide deck** (if any) and **finalized list of image/media rights** that you were granted on or before 12:00 pm, New York Time, **Wednesday, November 14, 2018** recognizing that a great TEDx talk minimizes the number of slides used. To the extent I plan to use a slide deck with my presentation and if I do not provide the final version of my slide deck on or before

12:00 pm, **November 14, 2018,** I agree to pay TEDxWilmington a late fee of $800 per day for every day that I am late;

- Carefully review the Illustrated TEDx Speaker Guide;

- Rehearse my talk sufficiently so that I can give my TEDx talk without reading any notes or using a podium;

- Be present **Thursday, November 29, 2018,** at **8:30 am**, New York Time, for a full rehearsal;

- Be present on **Friday, November 30, 2018 between 7:30 am and 5:00 pm**, New York Time, for the 3rd Annual TEDxWilmingtonWomen Conference**;**

- Provide a final **300 word blog**, which will be titled Reflecting, in a **Word document** on or before 12:00 pm, New York Time, **Wednesday, December 5, 2018** reflecting on the entire experience from submitting an application to giving this TEDx talk to alessandra@tedxwilmington.com which will be published at http://www.tedxwilmington.com/blog/ and shared on our various social media pages;

- Provide all descriptors of my talk necessary for **YouTube**, including a title, tags, and short description on or before 12:00pm, New York Time, **Wednesday, December 12, 2018** to elissa@tedxwilmington.com. All required material will be explained in a separate document, which will be sent after the conference;

- Not use third-party copyrighted materials in my presentation, without a written release;

- Not use the TEDxWilmington stage to promote a person, political agenda, religious agenda, a business, or an organization;

- Never refer to this talk as a TED talk, but only as a TEDx talk.

If I do not honor any of the above promises on a timely basis, or if TEDxWilmington learns that I materially withheld or misrepresented information about myself or my proposed TEDx talk in my application or any subsequent questionnaire that I was required to fill out or if TEDxWilmington learns from any other reliable source that I materially withheld or misrepresented information about myself or my proposed TEDx talk in my application or any subsequent questionnaire that I was required to fill out, my invitation to give a TEDx talk at the *3rd Annual TEDxWilmingtonWomen Conference* **on Friday, November 30, 2018 may be revoked unilaterally by TEDxWilmington at any time.**

Speaker's Signature_____ **Date**_____

Name (Printed)_____
Thank you for contributing to the TEDx Community. Our goal is for your upcoming TEDx

Talk to be widely distributed across a range of media platforms around the world. In order to do so, please review and if agreed, sign the **speaker release** below. Please note that if the materials in your TEDx Talk are not properly licensed, the Talk may be (i) rejected for publication, (ii) taken down from the TEDx YouTube channel by a copyright owner, and/or (iii) targeted for legal action due to infringement. **Please complete this form, make copies for your records and email to your TEDxWilmington contact: [Elissa@tedxwilmington.com]**

Scope. TEDxWilmington will be recording all the presentations at the TEDx event to be held [November 30, 2018] (the "Event"). The Event is operated under license of TED Conferences, LLC located at 330 Hudson Street, 11th Floor, New York, NY 10013 ("TED"). This release (the "Release") represents our agreement concerning your participation at the Event. In consideration for the platform provided to you and in support of the goal of "ideas worth spreading", you agree that: (i) you have created your own presentation; (ii) the materials used in your presentation are owned by you or licensed appropriately for use; (iii) you grant TEDxWilmington, TED and other entities authorized to do so—e.g., broadcasters—(collectively, the "TED Parties") the right to record, stream, film and photograph your presentation at the Event (the "Presentation"); and (iv) you grant TED exclusive, unrestricted rights to display, distribute, perform, reproduce, edit, create derivative works from, and/or otherwise use the Presentation anywhere around the world, in whole or in part, alone or accompanied by other material, in any and all media without any further approval from you, in perpetuity. This includes the ability to translate your Presentation into any language, and the right to sub-license the Presentation as necessary to third parties that TED deems appropriate.

Personal information. You understand and agree that by contributing to TEDxWilmington, that you consent to have your Presentation published worldwide, and grant full consent to TEDxWilmington and TED to process, manage, store and transmit personal information collected from your Presentation, including supporting information, such as your name, voice, photograph, likeness and biographical data (collectively, "Supporting Information") to third parties for permitted use. Examples of permitted uses of the Presentation and Supporting Information include TED's right to display the Presentation on the TEDx YouTube channel or on TED's website (TED.com) on television and distributing the Presentation on mobile phones, films, and other video distribution channels, such as iTunes, or through other third party organizations (such as airlines, hotels or corporate partners).

Public distribution. You understand and agree that TEDx Talks selected for publication may be shared under a "Creative Commons" license, CC BY – NC – ND 4.0 as long as appropriate credit is given, not edited or distorted, nor used for commercial purposes.

No conditions. You understand and agree that your involvement is for the opportunity to present an idea to a wide audience and to support the TEDxWilmington and TED mission, as good and valuable consideration. You agree that there are no other conditions required and that: (i) TEDxWilmington and TED aren't obligated to use, publish or distribute the Presentation or Supporting Information in any way; (ii) you won't receive any form of payment in connection with the use of the Presentation and/or Supporting Information; and (iii) except as required by law, you may not revoke the rights granted in this Release.

Ownership. You affirm that: (i) you have the full power and authority to grant the rights set forth in this Release; (ii) you are the sole author of the Presentation;
(iii) you have not violated the intellectual property rights of another party and have permission to include all material in the Presentation, including, but not limited to, all copyrights and trademark rights; and (iv) you will advise TEDxWilmington in writing of all third-party material contained in the Presentation (and provide copies of licenses or permissions securing all necessary rights).

Legal claims. If any third party claims arise stating the use of the Presentation violates their rights, you agree to hold harmless and to cooperate fully with TEDxWilmington and TED to defend against or otherwise respond to such claim, pay license fees, if applicable, and provide written evidence of ownership of any portion of your Presentation if required.

Entire agreement. This Release contains the entire understanding between the parties and may not be modified except in a writing signed by both of us. This Release is governed by New
York law, without regard to conflict-of-law principles. If you are under the age of 18, a signature from your parent/guardian is required below.

Name (Signed)_____
Name (Printed)_____
Date_____

Parent/Guardian Name (Signed)_____
Name (Printed)_____
Date_____

Deadlines
TEDxWilmingtonWomen Conference
November 30, 2018
* Details of requirements are in your Speaker Agreement *

Item Due	Deadline
Accept the Invitaton by signing and returning the Speaker Agreement	3-Oct
Speaker Release	3-Oct
Headshot in JPG; high resolution	3-Oct
Professional Title	3-Oct
2 Bios	3-Oct
Working title of talk	3-Oct
Friend Ajit Mathew George and Like TEDxWilmington (Facebook)	3-Oct
Outline of TEDx talk in Word Document	10-Oct
Promotional Video	10-Oct
1st blog in Word Document	17-Oct
1st video	24-Oct
PowerPoint draft (slide show is optional)	24-Oct
Drafted list of image and media rights (if using PowerPoint)	24-Oct
2nd blog in Word Document	7-Nov
List of props you will be bringing (stage props are optional)	7-Nov
Final title of talk	14-Nov
Final video	14-Nov
Final PowerPoint (slide show is optional)	14-Nov
Finalized list of image and media rights (if using PowerPoint)	14-Nov
REHEARSAL	29-Nov
DAY OF EVENT	30-Nov
Final blog in Word Document	5-Dec
YouTube information	12-Dec

There is an endless amount of ways to create an outline for a TEDx talk. One thing to keep in mind is that curators will be giving feedback to make sure the speaker is on the right track for their TEDx talk. If a speaker writes an outline that only makes sense to them, or one worded bullets, it doesn't help them get the best feedback and help possible. Here are a few examples of clear, concise outlines from Shavon Lindley, Tiffany Gwilliam, Frankie Bonilla, and Dominick Quartuccio.

Speaker Resources

Outline

- Personal story of when I experienced exclusionary behavior and remained silent
- Ask audience about their reaction when they witness exclusionary behavior
- Personal story of when I addressed exclusionary behavior for the first time
- Introduce four steps to address exclusionary behavior
- Personal story of when I made an exclusionary comment and how to use the same four steps to confess exclusionary behavior
- Explain brain science behind why people freeze when they experience exclusionary behavior
- Explore the backlash of remaining silent or calling out exclusionary behavior publicly
- Call to action that by harnessing the courage to address exclusionary behavior, we disrupt the tendency to normalize that behavior

Outline

- My daughter's story: Juvenile Arthritis
- My father's story: non-Hodgkin's lymphoma
- My story: melanoma
- Lessons learned from medical challenges in my life:
- Build trusting relationships with doctors
- Medical errors
- Make women aware
- Mobilize women, make them advocates
- Women have purchasing power in healthcare
- My experience with thyroid cancer
- My experience with an avoidable hospital readmission
- The magic phrase that will get a doctor to listen to you
- Conclusion
- Repeat the issue: miscommunication leads to medical errors
- Repeat the solution: trust with doctors; patient advocacy
- Call for action for women to join you

Outline

Poverty and necessity forced me to be creative! But it's been technology that has driven me out of poverty and necessity.

Let me start by not deceiving you, though. I wasn't always the tech type. I used to be a hater. I condemned the internet, technology, social media, and I even hated Drake. Nowadays, I be like…. (Break out into dance)

Kiki, do you love me? Are you riding?
Say you'll never ever leave from beside me

My transformation wasn't overnight, though. It started 10 years ago when the iPhone 3G came out. I was teaching 11th grade Spanish and I couldn't get one kid to look up at me. I was as frustrated as I've ever been as a teacher. So, I did what any good teacher would do, I thought, well, if I can't beat 'em, I might as well join'em… I went out and got an iPhone and that thing was AMAZING! I got on Facebook, where I reconnected with my college crush, married her, we now have two beautiful boys, Ezekiel and Isaac and the rest well, it's history.

Today I focus my educational philosophies to the multisensory expression of academics through creativity, by combining traditional methods of communication like rhythm, spoken word, dance and the written language along with apps like Keynote, Garageband, iMovie and YouTube.

But I would be doing all of us a disservice if I didn't also discuss some of the neurological setbacks that come with today's technology. For example,

> I can't get around without my GPS.
> I only know my own phone number, I can't remember the rest.
> All these shortcuts have caused us to use our brains
> WAY LESS!
> Digital dementia is real, as the research suggests.
>
> So, what now, what's the solution,
> do we destroy all our tech?
> Or do we just give in,
> just consume and use our brains less?
> Nah, we elevate, we create, we rewire our minds.
> With these five steps that I've designed:
>
> Mindfulness, Movement, Play, Create and Reflect.

These are the steps that will help our minds Protect From Consumer to Creator:

Turning digital dementia into creative brilliance.

We're the creators of technology, it's our brain that possesses optimal resilience.

The answer to digital dementia is simple and quite great.

It's to supplement the loss of basic usage with our ability to create.

The first and most important step to Creative Brilliance is Mindfulness. Mindfulness is simply being aware that it's possible and that you can achieve it.

As a child, every time I was down and having a hard time, my mom would ask me "Who Are You?" to which I would respond "Frankie Bonilla."

"Who Are You?" — "Frankie Bonilla"

"Who Are You?" — "Frankie Bonilla"

These simple affirmations of my name and identity are a major reason of why I can stand today before you without doubt or fear. Our brains are malleable! Our neurological wiring can change through the introduction of new habits and behaviors. WE HAVE THE POWER! Neuroplasticity is real. We can literally change our minds. Norman Vincent Peale famously said, "Change your thoughts and you change your world." Believe that you can create, and you will.

The second step to Creative Brilliance is MOVEMENT. Neuroscientist Daniel Wolpert claims that our brains have evolved not to think or feel, but to control movement. A test conducted at the University of Illinois used brain images that read neural activity following sitting and walking for 20 minutes. The results were of polar opposites. The ones for those sitting had low levels of neural activity. While the ones for those walking displayed higher brain activity. This may also help to explain the correlation between uber successful people like business mogul Sir Richard Branson, Ikea founder Ingvar Kamprad, and JetBlue founder David Needleman who have all been diagnosed with Attention Deficit and Hyperactivity Disorder. The inability to be still for long periods of time causes the brain to be at continuous high levels of neural activity. A moving body will lead to a boundless genius.

The third step to Creative Brilliance is PLAY. Albert Einstein famously said: "If you want your children to be intelligent, read them fairy tales." Much like the fairy tales of old, games have the ability to transform us into everyday heroes. We all desire to be the "Chosen One," regardless of our race, age, gender or socioeconomic status. The "Chosen One" answers the call to greatness. Games allow us to retake control. We are able to take risks and experience fear in a controlled environment. That continuous repetition of simulated challenges rewires our minds to react differently to situations that may have brought about defeat in the past. It affords our minds a world by which we can attain total control of our destinies by defeating our greatest nemesis, our previous personal best. Games empower us to create our narrative of choice.

The fourth step to Creative Brilliance is to CREATE. Poverty made me Creative. Necessity is the mother of creativity. I saw my mother design, cut and sew our outfits because it was cheaper to buy fabric. I saw her buy loads of used name brand clothes just to remove the tags in order to attach them to our no name attire so that I wouldn't get bullied at school. Her creativity came out of need, and that's how I learned it. But those days are far gone. I no longer live in survival mode. Adrenaline doesn't infuse my need to react and I don't have the luxury to wait for inspiration. I've created a framework; I look for 10 awesome people or relatable things that I like, and I give myself 20 minutes to unnecessarily recreate some variation of it. When it leads to your own creativity, imitation is the greatest compliment.

The fifth step to Creative Brilliance is REFLECTION. I mean, we do it every day to the point of obsession. We look in the mirror daily to see a face that we recognize as our own. We use the mirror's reflection as a tool to help us decide if we chose the right color, shade, pattern or length or if the strategy has to be changed. Our frontal lobe is what differentiates us from all other species, it makes up 40 percent of our brain. It's where our conscious resides, it's what allows us to observe our actions, observe our thoughts, pay attention to our feelings, and then decide how we are going to change who we are. The practice and art of paying attention allows the brain to work into more synchrony, balance and coherence. Through reflection, we're inventing new possibilities & speculating new outcomes.

True Education is the Knowledge of Self.

End

Every time I've turned my nose up to the "new" and "harmful" ways by which our young people are "destroying" this generation, I am reminded of one of my favorite students of all time, Mr. Nyri Poole. Several years back, I caught Nyri watching footage on YouTube of someone else playing video games. I was appalled. The following conversation ensued:

> "What's wrong with y'all? Why are you watching someone else play video games. That's so weird, you're supposed to play video games, not watch 'em."

"Mr. B, did you catch the game last night?"
"Yeah!"
"Did you play in the game?"
"No."
"It's the same thing Mr. B."
He turned back around and continued watching one of his favorite players play a game that he loves. As the author of the book of Ecclesiastes famously said, "There is nothing new under the sun."

Briefly summarize idea and points:
Productivity is intentional and deliverable. Mindfulness, Movement, Play, Creativity and Reflection are tools in simplifying the approach for us to viably reach a mental state in which we are not scripted thinkers, but innovators within our fields and careers. Technology is not our enemy; it is a tool that will level the playing fields between the disenfranchised and the affluent. It is a vehicle for progression and innovation. The aforementioned five steps were put together as minimalist and low risk habits that, if taken seriously and practiced with consistency, can lead to drastic changes in our neurological connections, to inspire countless others to take control of their destiny through their creative outlets. Everyone is a creator! It is not a gift for the few; it is a learned skill for the many!

Call to Action:
When we inhale, we consume the oxygen created by plants through photosynthesis, and it allows us to LIVE. When we exhale, we create the carbon dioxide that is absorbed by plants in photosynthesis allowing them to LIVE. Every consumption is fuel for creativity. I create so others can inhale. So today I urge you, please exhale your creativity, give life to life, we desperately need you to.

Outline

The Big Idea: *We can end toxic masculinity by providing a clear path to Higher Ground.*

Part One: The Problem
My Story
- I've spent an inordinate amount of my life's energy trying to become more attractive to women (like many heterosexual men)
- I built an entire life centered around attaining the external validation of women which, subsequently, won me the respect and acceptance of men
- On the surface, I was living the dream
- Below the surface, I was lost, alone, and living what Henry David Thoreau describes as a "life of quiet desperation."
- Culminating in the most humiliating moment of my life — entering Sex Addicts Anonymous in 2013, where I would spend the next four years

I'm Speaking to a Very Specific Man
- The man who oriented his life around one way
- Has discovered that way no longer works
- Wants to find higher ground but doesn't know how to begin
- I am speaking to YOU

Part Two: Clear Path to Lower Ground (Why Toxic Masculinity Persists)
The Origins of the Problem:
- In Denmark, to "be a man" means "not to be a boy."
- In the United States, to "be a man" means "not to be a woman."
- We naturally reject traits typically associated with femininity, no matter how powerful: vulnerability, feeling emotions, asking for help
- This is reinforced by countless examples of lower ground: fraternities, male-dominated work environments, athletic teams

Speaker Resources

Lower Ground:

- Toxic masculinity persists because it provides clear and present benefits to those who embody it: Belonging, Social Status, Sexual Validation
- The path to Higher Ground is ambiguous; Inaccessible communities of evolved men, resistance to showing weakness of exploring emotions, unclear payoffs, risking becoming a man without a nation

The Call: To do the most courageous thing asked of any modern man—to begin the journey of stripping away all of the bogus social conditioning and finding out who you really are.

Part Three: Building the Path to Higher Ground

Call to Action: Become a Man Amongst Men: The Modern Day Explorer

- In every man is the desire to explore
- Every inch of the external world, the physical terrain, has already been explored and discovered
- Modern day exploration happens internally—the untold realms within you
- YOU HAVE NO IDEA HOW GOOD IT CAN BE

Success Story—My Story:

- The demons I battled
- The pain I experienced
- The freedom I've attained
- The new communities of women and men I've forged
- The payoffs: financial abundance, deep-lasting relationships with men, loving intimate relationships with women

It's time for you to blaze the trail to Higher Ground.
There's a whole new world waiting for you.
I'm waiting for you.
The women in your life are waiting for you.
Will you answer the call?

CHAPTER 14
Legacy

I had made a decision by the end of August 2017 that I would most likely retire from organizing TEDx talks by the end of 2018, if not sooner, to create Second Chances Farm. I could not transfer the TEDxWilmington license to someone I designated as the license from TED was non-transferrable.

To continue the legacy I helped create at TEDxWilmington, I encouraged various members of the TEDxWilmington tribe when we met as a group on September 23, 2017 at TEDxGlobal Day to consider applying for a new license from TED in their own name. I felt it was best if one or more members of the TEDxWilmington tribe could create their own event so that they could establish their own style without having to follow the footsteps I left as an organizer of TEDxWilmington.

Rhianon Husmann was the first member of the TEDxWilmington tribe, having worked with me since June 2015. She was also the associate producer of TEDxWilmington, and had done virtually everything that was involved with organizing a TEDx event. I had organized TEDxYouth@Wilmington at Ursuline Academy in 2017. For all these reasons, I encouraged Rhianon to submit an application to TED to organize in 2018 a new TEDxYouth@UrsulineAcademy. I offered my support and recruited members of TEDxWilmington tribe to help Rhianon if and when TED granted her license.

TED approved Rhianon's application to organize TEDxYouth@UrsulineAcademy, and she did a great job organizing her first event on May 20, 2018. Here is a list of the speakers that gave TEDx talks at Rhianon's inaugural event.

Joyce Short's TEDx talk at the 2018 TEDxYouth@UrsulineAcademy was cited in an article in the New York Times on April 23, 2019.

https://www.nytimes.com/2019/04/23/well/mind/is-sex-by-deception-a-form-of-rape.html

May 20, 2018

Joseph Larasha
TEDx Title: How I Learned Confidence from a Lion

Dorcas Ntindai
TEDx Title: Education Has No Age

Mia Gifford
TEDx Title: Twenty-Two a Day, No Way!

Lilly Ridgely
TEDx Title: The Journey of Meditation

Alondra Posada
TEDx Title: Spanglish is a Language Too!

Annabel Gioffre
TEDx Title: You Run the Day, or The Day Runs You

Joshua Gunter
TEDx Title: A Day In the Life

Abigail Wilson-Kageni
TEDx Title: Autism, the Creative Arts and You and Me

Shanea Higgin
TEDx Title: The Art of Patience, from a "Rookie"

Auriela Garcia
TEDx Title: What it Takes to Become a Super You

Alex Sharpe
TEDx Title: AP Teacher Diversity: The Unspoken Issue in our Schools

Cyntiche Deba
TEDx Title: The Ugliness of Beauty

Erin Pudlo
TEDx Title: Don't Be a Teacher

Justin J. Shaifer
TEDx Title: How to Speak 'Generation Z'

Abby Sager
TEDx Title: Advocacy in the 21st Century

Chidi Wosu
TEDx Title: Yay I Failed!

Joyce Short
TEDx Title: When "Yes" Means "No:" The Truth about Consent

I was thrilled that Justin Schaifer's TEDx talk has attracted more than 169,000 views as of June 30, 2019.

Based on the success of her inaugural TEDx event, Rhianon applied and received approval from TED to organize TEDxYouth@UrsulineAcademy in 2019. This event attracted 24 speakers plus a chorale of 53 students and a teacher. There were students from nine different schools including MOT Charter, Avon Grove Charter, Design Thinking Academy, Stuart Country Day School, Mount Pleasant School, Concord High School, Newark Charter High School, Charter School of Wilmington and Ursuline Academy. Two speakers flew in from California, while one speaker came from London, United Kingdom.

Here is a list of the speakers who gave TEDx talks at Rhianon's second event.
March 31, 2019

Fran Tusso
TEDx Title: Being Donor-Conceived & Normalizing Nontraditional Families

Stephanie Petrone
TEDx Title: Sticky Act of Kindness

Lexi Goff
TEDx Title: The Power of a Compliment

Whitney Grinnage-Cassidy
TEDx Title: Why Microaggressions Aren't so Micro

Alizcelie Romero
TEDx Title: Keeping up with the Support

Avery Laur
TEDx Title: Expression Through Poetry

Sahana Mathiarasan
TEDx Title: Misogynistic Microaggressions

Naheem Watson
TEDx Title: Words are Weapons

Jus-Tina Garcia
TEDx Title: Stringing Your Way Through

Jordyn Arrington
TEDx Title: Scary Socials

Jason Kageni
TEDx Title: Autism is not a Death Sentence

Julia Friedman
TEDx Title: Dear Diary

Immnauel Fowler
TEDx Title: Looking Through a New Lens

Kayla Grant
TEDx Title: Grief for the Greater Good

Kate Krukiel
TEDx Title: Building Impact: How Business Must Give to Create Change

Dr. Lauren Conrad and Chorale
TEDx Title: CHS Chorale Sings for an Unclouded Day

Renée Piane
TEDx Title: The Power of Your Love Lineage & Role Models

Finley Walshe
TEDx Title: The Jobs of Tomorrow: Where Dreams Become Reality

Tony Hsieh
TEDx Title: How to Challenge Yourself Out of Your Comfort Zone

Noelle Picara
TEDx Title: Dismantling White Supremacy in Education

Andrew Ellis
TEDx Title: Students are more than Report Cards

My role at the 2019 TEDxYouth@Ursuline Academy was to sit in the audience on March 31, 2019 and truly enjoy all these amazing TEDx talks. This is how I know the legacy of TEDx talks in this community is continuing without my involvement.

If you want to see a truly remarkable end to a TEDx talk, please watch Fran Tusso's TEDx talk entitled, "Being Donor-Conceived & Normalizing Nontraditional Families."

I continue to hope other TEDxWilmington tribe members will apply and get their own TEDx licenses and continue the tradition of showcasing ideas worth spreading in this community.

CHAPTER 15
Second Chances Farm: An Idea Translated into Action

Second Chances Farm's vision is to be an indoor vertical farm that hires exclusively men and women returning to society after serving their time in prison. All crops and produce will be fresh, organic, nutritious, completely free of pesticides and herbicides, and grown within 150 miles of anywhere it is available for consumption, seriously cutting down long-haul shipping costs and pollution. Crops will be fresh and available 365 days a year, no matter what the weather brings.

For me, the road to Second Chances Farm was truly an accidental journey. I had neither served any time in prison nor even visited any prison. I didn't know many people personally who served any time in prison.

I had gotten to know the late Chef Matt Haley, who had won the 2014 James Beard Humanitarian of the Year Award when he helped orchestrate an amazing Farm to Table Dinner, one of 44 events that I organized as Chairman of the 2014 MidAtlantic Wine + Food Festival. My wife, Sarah Brown, and I had attended the star-studded James Beard Award ceremony in New York's Lincoln Center on May 5, 2014 in New York to witness Matt getting this prestigious award, which in the culinary world is the equivalent of getting an Oscar.

To the best of my knowledge, Matt is the first and only Delawarean to win a James Beard Award. His moving acceptance speech about the restaurant community that embraced him after he overcame addiction to drugs and alcohol and time in prison earned him a standing ovation.

Matt attended the black tie gala dinner for the 2014 MidAtlantic Wine + Food Festival that I hosted in the Gold Ballroom of the Hotel Du Pont in downtown Wilmington, and he invited me to meet him at his house in Rehoboth on June 4, 2014 to discuss how he

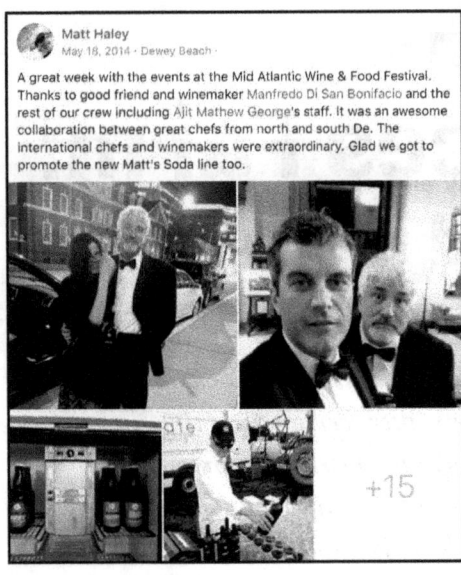

could help me with the 2015 MidAtlantic Wine + Food Festival.

When I met him, he shared how he started doing drugs and alcohol, and how his behavior got him kicked out of 13 schools in 12 years. At age 30, he was sent to a detention center following a drug arrest. Cooking became part of his rehabilitation, and the culinary arts became his way to recovery. He eventually bought a restaurant in 2001, and then created what has become SoDel Concepts, which in 2014 hired about 1,000 people during the summer. Based in Rehoboth Beach, Delaware, SoDel Concepts is an award winning, chef driven restaurant group on the Culinary Coast of Southern Delaware. As the founder of SoDel Concepts, Matt hired returning citizens and gave them a second chance.

Matt wanted me to help organize an event as part of the 2015 MidAtlantic Wine + Food Festival inside a prison. To say I was surprised is a gross understatement, as I started to think about the logistical challenge of bringing visiting chefs with knives and having paying guests get through security. Knowing Matt and what a powerful personality he was, I felt it was impossible to turn him down on the spot. I told Matt if he could get approval from Delaware Governor Jack Markell and secure all the permissions from the Delaware Department of Corrections, I was happy to work with him. I honestly did not expect that we would get any of these approvals.

Much to my surprise, I got a call from Matt later that week saying that Governor Markell was very supportive, subject to getting approval from the Commissioner of Prisons, who turned out to be a good friend of Matt. I began to realize everyone was a friend of Matt. A meeting was scheduled with Rob Coupe, Commissioner of the Delaware Department of Corrections, and his entire leadership team in the Commissioner's office in Dover on July 30, 2014. This was my first ever meeting with anyone who was involved with Corrections, and it was quite a meeting. Matt was there with his leadership team and Michelle Freeman, president of Carl M. Freeman Companies, one of the largest real estate development companies in Southern Delaware. Laura Stimson, who was working with me at the MidAtlantic Wine + Food Festival, joined me.

At that meeting, Commissioner Coupe approved doing an event as part of the 2015 MidAtlantic Wine + Food Festival in May 2015 within Baylor Women's Correctional Institution, the statewide women's prison in Delaware, located in New Castle. The only condition that Commissioner Coupe imposed was that we could not serve alcohol inside the prison, so Matt offered instead to serve his new line of Matt's Homemade Root Beer. Since Matt was going to start a 6-week trek through northwestern India and Nepal in mid-August, we agreed to meet in September 2014 inside Baylor, after Matt returned to Delaware to begin planning the logistics of what was bound to be a very complex event. I left this meeting feeling very excited and scared. I surely had no idea what was involved in doing a complex event inside a prison.

I had invited Matt, in my capacity as the organizer of TEDxWilmington, to give a TEDx talk at the 2014 TEDxWilmington Annual Conference on August 6, 2014 at the World Café Live at the Queen in Wilmington. Matt 's TEDx talk, which was entitled, "Taste of the World: Adventurous Business," was eloquent and powerful. I encourage you to take 18 minutes of your life to watch Matt's TEDx talk at https://youtu.be/i_WsTFtXmoA.

Little did I know when he gave his TEDx talk that he was unknowingly giving the farewell address of his life. At age 53, Matt died doing what he loved to do on August 20th, driving a motorcycle in the mountains in northern India on his way to deliver stoves to a Nepali village.

According to an article written by Patricia Talorico in *The News Journal* after Matt died,

"Haley had a banner year in 2014. He also was recognized for his humanitarian work by the National Restaurant Association in Washington, D.C. and the International Association of Culinary Professionals in Chicago. Haley later picked up a Jefferson Award for Public Service at Wilmington's Hotel du Pont."

Matt's death had a profound impact on me. I had celebrated my 60th birthday earlier that year on May 10th. In his TEDx talk, Matt talked about having love, compassion and the importance of having purpose in life. This planted the first seed that helped grow the idea of Second Chances Farm.

Later that year, I invited Jon Brilliant to give a TEDx talk in November 19, 2014 entitled, "The Creation of a Social Impact Fund: A 'Connect the Dots' Story." Jon, who is a very successful venture capitalist, had created one of the first B corporations in Delaware and made a compelling argument for for-profit companies solving non-profit problems. Please view Jon's TEDx talk at https://youtu.be/_pqL0Ehat-M. This planted the second seed that helped grow the idea of Second Chances Farm. Jon is now a managing member and chief financial officer of Second Chances Farm, LLC. One should never underestimate the long-range benefit of giving a TEDx talk.

Even though Chef Haley died in a tragic motorcycle accident in August 2014, I decided in January 2015 to honor my promise to Matt and do a dinner as part of the 2015 MidAtlantic Wine + Food Festival in May 2015 within Baylor Women's Correctional Institution. With the tremendous help of the entire leadership team at SoDel Concepts and the Delaware Department of Corrections, led by Commissioner Coupe, combined with the assistance of Warden Wendi Caple and her team at Baylor Women's Correctional Institution, I organized and hosted "Breaking Bread Behind Bars" on May 14, 2015 at Baylor.

Breaking Bread Behind Bars was an elegant, gourmet five-course dinner that was prepared by the culinary team of inmates at Baylor, which included Amanda Lemon, with a great deal of help from the SoDel culinary team. Before the dinner, there was a reception at Baylor with Governor Markell, who had approved Matt's request to do this dinner in June 2014, along with the Baylor culinary team and all the paid guests, which included some of the top business leaders including Chip Rossi, Delaware market president of Bank of America, and Vance Kershner, founder and CEO of Labware.

During the reception, I played Matt's TEDx talk for everyone in attendance to watch before we went outside to have dinner on a long table with elegant lights that seated about 60 people in the prison's quadrangle. If it weren't for the barbed wire that you could see in the fading sun at the perimeter of the quadrangle, you would have thought we were having an elegant farm to table dinner on the grounds of a luxurious estate.

At the end of this dinner, Warden Caple thanked the assembled audience and made a plea to help build a greenhouse in the prison quadrangle so that her inmates could grow

plants year round and used by the prison's culinary program. I was standing behind the podium with my very good friend U.S. Senator Chris Coons, and I asked Senator Coons to join me at the podium to see if we could make Warden Caple's dream a reality. Senator Coons and I raised $20,000 in less than three minutes to build this now built greenhouse at Baylor.

I told my wife that night as I left the prison that this was the high water mark of all my experiences with the MidAtlantic Wine + Food Festival, and if I never did another Wine + Food event again, I would consider Breaking Bread Behind Bars as my legacy event that I could be very proud of. This event planted the third seed that helped grow the idea of Second Chances Farm.

With the continued support of Commissioner Coupe and Warden Caple, I organized a TEDxWilmingtonSalon with the theme of, "Second Chances and Redemption" within Baylor Women's Correctional Institution on July 31, 2015. This TEDxWilmingtonSalon

featured 12 TEDx talks, including talks from six inmates including Amanda Lemon, who gave a TEDx talk entitled, "Second Chances and Redemption." I first met Amanda at Breaking Bread Behind Bars, and after her TEDx talk, I had asked her to connect with me after she was released from prison. Amanda Lemon planted the fourth seed that helped grow the idea of Second Chances Farm. Upon Amanda being released from prison in 2018, she was invited to become part of Second Chances Farm. You can never tell what the benefit of giving a TEDx talk might be.

Two or three days before this TEDxWlmingtonSalon in Baylor, I was contacted by someone at the White House about the possibility of a small group of people coming from Washington D.C., led by the then Second Lady Dr. Jill Biden, to attend this event. President Barack Obama had just visited a Federal Prison a few days earlier, making him the first sitting President ever to visit a prison. This involved meetings with the United States Secret Service and coordinating security arrangements with Delaware State Police and the Department of Corrections internal security service. Dr. Biden's presence attracted a large media presence, especially since she sat at lunchtime without any reserved seating, with inmates and paid guests. While everything went without incident, it surely added an interesting dimension to what was already a very unusual event. I had asked Ashley Biden if her mother, Dr. Biden, would be kind enough to personally sign a printed photo book from this event to distribute to all the speakers, including the six inmates who spoke. Dr. Biden was kind enough to do it, and I got to distribute this photo book as a holiday gift in December 2015.

I had to process security clearances for every guest who entered Baylor for this event (as well as Breaking Bread Behind Bars). The true highlight of this TEDxWilmingtonSalon was meeting a guest who paid $100, and when I looked at her security clearance form, it was clear that she was from California and indicated that she knew no inmate at Baylor. It begged the question why she flew to Delaware to attend this event. At lunchtime, I got to meet this mystery guest. Her name was Delia Cohen.

Her LinkedIn profile describes Delia as a vision architect who specializes in turning extraordinary ideas—involving the arts, cutting-edge technology and new media—into reality. The common theme: making the world a better place. Her current and most ambitious social justice project was inspired by Bryan Stevenson, and includes organizing TEDx events in prisons around the United States. The whole event is collaboratively planned and curated by a team of prisoners, prison staff, victims, and community influencers. At each TEDx prison event she curates, half of the attendees are community leaders, and half are inmates.

Previously, Delia was the U.S. prisons coordinator for Eve's Ensler's One Billion Rising for Justice Campaign. Before then, Delia was the executive director of the TED Prize project "Pangea Day," charged with using the power of film to connect the world. She built the organization from the ground up in 15 months—from a staff of one to hundreds all over the world, and raised a budget of $10 million. By May 10, 2008, millions of people in 180 countries participated in the event. Prior jobs have included being the first communications director for the Clinton Global Initiative and as Special Assistant to President Clinton, running an 11-office department in the White House handling public communications. I knew nothing of Delia's background when we first met, but we became instant friends and she promised to keep in touch, a promise she kept.

Between Breaking Bread Behind Bars and this TEDxWilmingtonSalon inside Baylor, I became a regular visitor to this prison. For someone who never visited any prison who didn't know many people who served any time in prison before 2015, I got to know the staff inside Baylor, and I also became well acquainted with many of the inmates and their backgrounds. I learned about the very high recidivism rate in Delaware, but I had no idea how I could personally make a difference in reducing recidivism. The four seeds that were previously planted began to slowly germinate, but had not become an idea yet.

On December 22, 2015, I received an invitation from Delia Cohen, which read as follows:

Dear Ajit,

I am delighted to invite you to attend **TEDxSanQuentin**, Friday, January 22, 2016, 9:00 a.m. to 2:30 p.m. I hope you'll be able to make it!
    We are gathering an eclectic and thought-provoking mix of activists, artists, philanthropists, and felons. :)
    To learn more, please take a look at this wonderful, four-minute promo our incarcerated marketing team created: https://www.youtube.com/TEDxSanQuentin promo.
    Organized and curated by a team of incarcerated men, in cooperation with the California Dept. of Corrections and Rehabilitation, half of the attendees will be high-profile community leaders, and half will be incarcerated residents of San Quentin.
    TEDxSanQuentin speakers include an incarcerated veteran, the warden of San Quentin, a former U.S. Treasury secretary, an incarcerated grammy-nominated musician, a woman whose husband was murdered by a man now on San Quentin's death row, a prison guard, and an incarcerated Shakespeare group, among others.
    Richard Branson attended the only other TEDx prison event in Calif. Afterward, he blogged, "I am fortunate to enjoy all kinds of experiences, but few have been as transformative and moving as TEDxIronwoodStatePrison." http://www.virgin.com/richard-branson/infinite-possibilities-at-californias-first-tedx-inside-a-prison.
    This is going to be an unbelievable event. As Bryan Stevenson says, it's all about proximity.
    There are only a few seats open—if you can attend, I'll need the following info:

Full legal name as it appears on your driver's license
Driver's license number and state that issued it
Date of birth
SSN

NOTE: This event is by invitation only. All invitations are non-transferable without prior approval.

The United States accounts for five percent of the world's population, yet incarcerates a staggering 25 percent of the world's prisoners, with a disproportionate number of black men and boys behind bars. Roughly 90 percent of these 2.2 million prisoners—and another seven million out on probation or parole—will return to society and become our neighbors. If we want healthy and safe communities, we must pay attention to and influence what is happening in our prisons.

Historically, prison has been a place of separation and punishment. Influential community members and public policy shapers don't know how to get involved with a closed and nearly impenetrable criminal justice system.

The goal of TEDxSanQuentin is to bridge the divide between society and prisoners by inviting community influencers directly into prison to interact with prisoners in a powerful day of "ideas worth spreading," and by bringing prisoners' voices to a global audience.

We believe that when we bring together correctional staff, prisoners, victims, law enforcement, innovative thinkers, and influential people from all walks of life, we will be better able to create solutions to our nation's failed policy of mass incarceration.

Outside speakers:
Robert E. Rubin, Co-Chairman, Council on Foreign Relations; former U.S. Treasury Secretary
Neil Barsky, Founder and Chairman, The Marshall Project
Robert Barton, Inspector General, State of California
Dionne Wilson, Board of Directors, Insight Prison Project
Pete Worden, Chairman, Breakthrough Prize Foundation

Incarcerated speakers and performers:
Ronald Self, Founder, Veterans Healing Veterans
Curtis "Wall Street" Carroll, The Oracle of San Quentin State Prison hailed as stock-picking guru
David Jassy, grammy-nominated artist and songwriter
Shakespeare at San Quentin
and much more!

Attendance is by invitation only and requires pre-clearance by the California Department of Corrections and Rehabilitation.

Hope you can make it!

Delia

How many times have you received an invitation and declined it because it required an investment of time and treasure that is always precious and in short supply? I read this invitation and struggled to rationalize investing the time and money to fly across the country to California and attend a TEDx event inside the notorious San Quentin prison. As I struggled to accept this invitation, I remembered that Delia flew from Los Angeles to come to Wilmington to attend my TEDxWilmingtonSalon in Baylor. I felt I ought to accept this invitation and send in the security clearance form to the California Department of Corrections and Rehabilitation.

After I accepted this invitation and was pre-cleared by the California Department of Corrections and Rehabilitation to attend TEDxSanQuentin on January 22nd, I was invited by Delia Cohen, Eric Ryan and Zak Williams to attend the TEDxSanQuentin Speakers Reception on Thursday, January 21st. This reception is where the seeds to grow Second Chances Farm took hold and began to grow into an idea, after I met Beverly Parenti, who together with her husband, Chris Redlitz, founded The Last Mile Program in 2010.

According to Wikipedia, "The Last Mile provides coding and technology training to the incarcerated population across the United States. The program, a 501(c)(3) non-profit, originated in 2010 at San Quentin State Prison, California, United States with the California Department of Corrections and Rehabilitation, and works with the

TEDxSanQuentin Speakers' Reception

incarcerated population at men's, women's, and young adult correctional facilities to help them build relevant skills in technology and other areas so that they can more easily transition to productive employment once they are out of prison. Participation in the program is restricted to incarcerated people who have worked hard to improve themselves intellectually and emotionally. The program is now available in four states (California, Indiana, Kansas, and Oklahoma)."

The Last Mile started as a six-month entrepreneurship program that provided the skills to create a business that would be demonstrated at an annual Demo Day. It later transitioned to become a program that trained incarcerated people on various types of technology and digital communication, as well as participate on Quora. Participants do not have direct online access, and their handwritten or typed answers are uploaded by program volunteers. Participants have reported on Quora that the program is highly beneficial to them, and their Quora answers in particular have received attention in a lot of media coverage of the program. The entrepreneurship program ended in 2015, folding certain aspects of the program into the new coding program.

In 2014, The Last Mile launched Code.7370 in San Quentin State Prison, the first fully inclusive computer-programming curriculum available in a U.S. prison. The students in Code.7370 learn HTML, CSS, JavaScript, and Python, all without internet access. The program consists of two tracks, a beginner track focusing on foundations of computer programming, while the advanced track takes a deeper dive into JavaScript, Node.js, etc.

Originally, students coded projects with pen and paper because internet access is not allowed in prisons. In 2017, four students at The Last Mile at San Quentin State Prison created an offline database of class resources, by the name of JOLT, which allows the students to perform necessary tasks to learn to code. The program curriculum has expanded within California and to other states including Indiana, Kansas, and Oklahoma. There are classrooms operating in San Quentin (2014), Ironwood (2015), Folsom Women's Facility (2016), California Institution for Women (2018), Pelican Bay State Prison (2018), and Ventura Youth Facility (2018). In April 2018, they opened their first out-of-state location in Indiana's women's prison.

In 2016, The Last Mile created the first-ever web development shop operating inside a US prison, The Last Mile Works. After participants complete one year of extensive training, they have the opportunity to apply to TLM Works, where they build real websites for private clients, earning a market wage, honing their skills, and enhancing their portfolio. To date, they have built websites and web applications for clients such as the Coalition for Public Safety, *San Quentin News*, and Dave's Killer Bread Foundation."

What really impressed me was The Last Mile program has a zero rate of recidivism for students who graduate from their program (https://thelastmile.org). This conversation with Beverly Parenti planted the fifth seed that helped nurtured the idea of Second Chances Farm.

Attending the inaugural TEDxSanQuentin turned out to be one of the smartest decisions I ever made. In addition to meeting former US Treasury Secretary Robert Rubin, the truly transformational moment for me was listening to Curtis "Wall Street" Carroll, who is known as "The Oracle of San Quentin State Prison," and hailed as stock-picking guru.

His TEDx talk entitled, "How I Learned to Read—and Trade Stocks—in Prison," is now a TED talk that has attracted 4,790,784 views as of June 21, 2019. If you watch this TED talk, and promise not to blink, you may see me twice sitting in the audience behind California Governor Gavin Newsom. I hope you will be inspired as much as I was by: https://www.ted.com/talks/curtis_wall_street_carroll_how_i_learned_to_read_and_trade_stocks_in_prison/

"Wall Street" Carroll overcame poverty, illiteracy, incarceration and a lack of outside support to become a stock investor, creator and teacher of his own financial literacy philosophy. According to TED, here are the reasons why you should listen to this TEDx talk:

"The media calls Curtis "Wall Street" Carroll the "Oracle of San Quentin" for his stock picking prowess and ability to translate financial information into simple language for his students. Carroll grew up in Oakland, California surrounded by poverty. In 1996, at 17 years old, he committed a robbery where a man was killed. He turned himself in and ended up an illiterate teenager in prison with a 54 years-to-life sentence. While in prison, the stock market captured his attention, but due to his illiteracy he couldn't learn more about it. Motivated by the lure of financial gaining, he taught himself how to read at 20-21 years old, and then started studying the stock market. Carroll's role models changed from drug dealers and sports figures, to Bill Gates and Warren Buffet. He wanted others to learn this new way of making money. When Carroll arrived at San Quentin in 2012, he met Troy Williams, who helped him start the Financial Literacy Program. Together they created the philosophy, F.E.E.L (Financial Empowerment Emotional Literacy), that teaches people to recognize how their emotions affect their financial decision, and how to separate the two."

Curtis's TEDx talk clearly was the tipping point in my journey to Second Chances Farm. This talk planted the sixth seed that helped me decide to do something about recidivism that led to the idea of Second Chances Farm.

Curtis used to co-teach a class with Zak Williams, the son of beloved comedian Robin Williams. Zak, who received his MBA from Columbia, spends a good amount of his time studying behavioral finance and valuing tech companies. After his father's death, Zak says he explored prison rehabilitation programs, looking for ways to give back. In the process, he formed a friendship with "Wall Street." The duo taught a financial literacy class every Thursday at San Quentin. The class educated inmates on what was going on in the economy smart investment strategies, and how inmates can develop skills applicable to life outside prison.

I had met Zak Williams the previous night at the reception he hosted with Delia Cohen for the TEDxSanQuentin speakers, and I got to speak to him at more length during lunch at San Quentin. Like Chef Matt Haley, who had talked about the importance of having purpose in life, I felt Zak's ways of giving back was giving him a purpose in life.

Talking with Zak and understanding his passion for giving back planted the seventh seed that helped me decide to do something about recidivism, which led to the idea of Second Chances Farm.

In February 2016, John Legend gave and sang a powerful TED talk entitled, "Redemption Song." According to TED, he, "is on a mission to transform America's criminal justice system. Through his Free America campaign, he's encouraging rehabilitation and healing in our prisons, jails and detention centers, and giving hope to those who want to create a better life after serving their time. With a spoken-word prelude from James Cavitt, an inmate at San Quentin State Prison, Legend treats us to his version of Bob Marley's "Redemption Song."

This TED talk served as theme song and message for me to do something about recidivism. Please watch https://www.ted.com/talks/john_legend_redemption_song/

What made this talk extra special is when John Legend interviewed James Cavitt, who was part of the Last Mile Program. I have copied below verbatim the transcript of this TED talk, as it planted the eighth seed that propelled me to decide to do something about recidivism, which led to the idea of Second Chances Farm.

"At FreeAmerica, we've done a listening and learning tour. We visited not only with prosecutors, but with legislators, with inmates in our state and local prisons. We've gone to immigration detention centers. We've met a lot of people. And we've seen that redemption and transformation can happen in our prisons, our jails and our immigration detention centers, giving hope to those who want to create a better life after serving their time.

"Imagine if we also considered the front end of this prison pipeline. What would it look like if we intervened, with rehabilitation as a core value — with love and compassion as core values? We would have a society that is safer, healthier and worthy of raising our children in.

"I want to introduce you to James Cavitt. James served 12 years in the San Quentin State Prison and is being released in 18 months. Now James, like you and me, is more than the worst thing he's done. He is a father, a husband, a son, a poet. He committed a crime; he's paying his debt, and working hard to build the skills to make the transition back to a productive life when he enters the civilian population again.

"Now James, like millions of people behind bars, is an example of what happens if we believe that our failings don't define who we are, that we are all worthy of redemption, and if we support those impacted by mass incarceration, we can all heal together."

James Cavitt: "Thanks, John. TED, welcome to San Quentin. The talent is abundant behind prison walls: Future software engineers, entrepreneurs, craftsmen, musicians and artists. This piece is inspired by all of the hard work that men and women are doing on the inside to create better lives and futures for themselves after they serve their time.

"This piece is entitled, 'Where I Live.'

"I live in a world where most people are too afraid to go. Surrounded by tall, concrete walls, steel bars, where razor wire has a way of cutting away at the hopes for a brighter tomorrow.

"I live in a world that kills people who kill people in order to teach people that killing people is wrong. Imagine that.

"Better yet, imagine a world where healed people helped hurt people heal and become strong. Maybe then we would all be singin' "Redemption Song."

"I live in a world that has been called, 'hell on Earth' by those trapped inside. But I've come to the stark realization that prison — it really is what you make it. You see, in spite of the harshness of my reality, there is a silver lining. I knew that my freedom was gonna come, it was just a matter of time. And so I treated my first steps as if they were my last mile, and I realized that you don›t have to be free in order to experience freedom.

"And just because you're free doesn't mean that you have freedom. Many of us, for years, have been battling our inner demons. We walk around smiling when inside we're really screamin': freedom!

"Don't you get it? We're all serving time; we're just in different places. As for me, I choose to be free from the prisons I've created. The key: forgiveness. Action's my witness. If we want freedom, then we gotta think different. Because freedom, it isn't a place. It's a mind setting."

John Legend: "Old pirates, yes, they rob I. Sold I to the merchant ships. Minutes after they took I from the bottomless pit.

"My hands were made strong by the hand of the almighty. We forward in this generation triumphantly.

"Won't you help to sing these songs of freedom? 'Cause all I ever had — redemption songs. Redemption songs.

"Emancipate yourselves from mental slavery. None but ourselves can free our minds. Have no fear for atomic energy 'cause none of them can stop the time.

"How long shall they kill our prophets while we stand aside and look? Some say it's just a part of it, we've got to fulfill the book.

"Won't you help to sing these songs of freedom? 'Cause all I ever had—redemption songs. Redemption songs."

Listening to this impassioned plea by John Legend planted the eighth seed that helped me decide to do something about Second Chances and recidivism that led to the idea of Second Chances Farm.

It was soon thereafter that I experienced the Eureka effect, which is the sudden, unexpected realization of the solution to the problem of recidivism that I could be part of. In late February of 2016, I read a small article about Jack Griffin, who was involved in creating Metropolis Farms, an indoor hydroponic vertical farm in South Philadelphia. Prior to reading this article, I knew very little about indoor hydroponic vertical farming. I contacted Jack Griffin via Facebook and arranged to take a tour of Metropolis Farms. I became fascinated by the idea of creating indoor vertical farms in urban areas like Wilmington.

I invited Jack to give a TEDx talk at the 2016 TEDxWilmington Annual Conference on August 24, 2016. His TEDx talk was entitled "Building the World's First Vertical Farming City," and can be viewed at https://youtu.be/7K-FPkhSF6Y. The Philadelphia Inquirer reported that, "Griffin was hailed as a visionary for his plan to transform Philadelphia, "into the world's first vertical farming city. He delivered a well-received 2016 TEDx Talk in Wilmington, where he said he could put an end to food deserts and bring "green collar" jobs to blighted neighborhoods."

I would be remiss if I didn't point out that Jack Griffin is no longer involved with Metropolis Farms, and Metropolis Farms has been taken over by its investors, many of whom I have gotten to know over the last three years. Without casting any judgment myself, here is the web address to an article published in The Philadelphia Inquirer in June 2018 with the headline "Metropolis Farms' CEO Jack Griffin is either the farmer of the future or a fantastic fraud." https://www.inquirer.com/philly/business/metropolis-farms-jack-griffin-south-philly-start-up-marijuana-20180604.html

Nonetheless, learning about indoor vertical farming as a result of this TEDx talk planted the ninth seed that led to creating Second Chances Farm.

I was first introduced to Saad Soliman by Ken Grant, my very good friend and TEDxWilmington tribe member, in early 2016. We met for the first time on April 15, 2016, and we immediately bonded and became great friends. Saad is a convicted felon who was working at that time for the federal probation office. His experience, both in prison and in reentering society, has helped him contribute to the remarkable turnaround in employment figures for people returning to society from incarceration. In June 2013, Saad became the reentry specialist with the U.S. Probation Office in the District of Delaware. He has created programming based on evidence-based practices, which has helped increase the employment rate of ex-offenders, while reducing the recidivism rate. Saad has a unique understanding and insight into the criminal justice system, including typical obstacles and ways to overcome them. He has innovated and created successful initiatives that benefitted the U.S. Probation Officers he worked alongside, the U.S. District Court, and the citizens of Delaware. Utilizing these unique and opportune circumstances, Saad sought to assist

in positively affecting change in the lives of those reentering the community to enhance public safety and enrich the communities to which these men and women return.

I invited Saad to give a TEDx talk at the 2016 TEDxWilmington Annual Conference about being successfully rehabilitated into society after being in prison for a long time. His TEDx talk entitled, "The Abstracts of Justice," can be viewed at https://youtu.be/16x3jfso7Bw.

Listening to Saad's testimonial in his TEDx talk planted the tenth seed that helped me make it clear how I was going to fight recidivism with the idea of Second Chances Farm.

It was at the conclusion of the 2016 TEDxWilmington Annual Conference that the idea of growing organic food locally in indoor vertical farms 365 days a year, while helping returning citizens get a second chance, became the genesis of what we now call Second Chances Farm. Saad and I met on a regular basis to figure how we could create a for-profit model to battle recidivism. Saad subsequently left his job at the U.S. Department of Justice and founded Peace by Piece, Inc., whose re-entry team is providing a variety of services to returning citizens. If it were not for TEDxWilmington, it is unlikely I would have meet Saad Soliman, or for that matter, Jack Griffin. Second Chances Farm has entered into a formal agreement with Saad's Peace by Piece, Inc. to help recruit, counsel and mentor returning citizens who will be part of our first indoor vertical farm in Wilmington. One can never tell what a TEDx talk could lead to. Just ask Saad!

I remained intrigued by The Last Mile Program at San Quentin, and Delia Cohen shared contact information for Beverly Parenti, executive director for The Last Mile program. We connected in January 2, 2017 by mail and arranged to visit San Quentin Prison again on March 13, 2017 to better understand The Last Mile program and how it could be brought to Delaware.

After visiting San Quentin, I had dinner with Beverly, her husband and co-founder Chris Redlitz, and they offered to make Delaware the first state outside California to have The Last Mile program, if I could raise the necessary funds to cover the out-of-pocket costs and get permission to operate inside one of Delaware's prisons.

I consider myself a progressive conservative, in that I am socially progressive, but fiscally conservative. I am not a big proponent of big government programs, and frankly, I am a big advocate for public-private partnerships to address core problems. I consider myself a compassionate capitalist. It is for this reason that I continue to be enamored with The Last Mile program.

Here is how The Last Mile shares its story via their website: "In 2010, Chris Redlitz entered San Quentin State Prison for the first time. Because of his background in venture capital, he was invited to speak to a group of men about business and entrepreneurship. He was so impressed by the men's level of business knowledge and desire to learn that he began to nurture the idea of creating a technology accelerator inside the prison. His wife and business partner, Beverly Parenti, was not immediately enamored with the idea, but they agreed to immerse themselves in the issue of incarceration in America and find a path to help resolve this daunting problem. Beverly agreed to join Chris on a journey to create The Last Mile. Since its inception, The Last Mile has generated a groundswell of support for criminal justice across America. Never before have we experienced such a cooperative, non-partisan effort to curb the problem of mass incarceration. Imagine if we could break the cycle of incarceration, and instead of spending tax dollars for prison, we could spend these tax dollars on higher education and provide educational opportunities for youth in underserved communities. This would enable them to choose a different path than one of crime. With education and career training opportunities, we could break the generational cycle of incarceration. There's plenty of proof that the impact of one man's incarceration is felt by families and communities for decades."

The Last Mile is in 12 facilities located in California, Indiana, Kansas, and Oklahoma. They have served 460 students since 2010, of which 60 returning citizens are all full-time employes or in higher education, and their returned citizens boast a zero percent recidivism rate. I was truly inspired by what they achieved using private capital.

I was weighing in the spring of 2017 whether or not to accept the invitation from Beverly and Chris to raise private capital to bring The Last Mile program to Delaware, or start Second Chances Farm, a vertical hydroponic organic farm that would exclusively hire returning citizens. I was torn between following in the footsteps of an established program like The Last Mile, which clearly carried less risk, or creating a brand new start up like Second Chances Farm.

Unfortunately, there was a prisoner riot inside Delaware's largest prison on February 1, 2017, and it was clear to me the timing of bringing a program like this to Delaware was terrible and I had to concede that I had to find a way to work outside the prisons if I wanted to have any reasonable chance of success. Without completely giving up on The

Last Mile program, I decided to pursue Second Chances Farm and see if I could replicate the remarkable success that The Last Mile program had achieved since 2011.

One of the unintended outcomes of this prison riot is the fact that I got introduced by Angela Jo Manieri to her good friend, Patricia May. Angela Jo is a member of the TEDxWilmington tribe, and Patricia was the one person held hostage by the inmates—who kept her safe during the whole ordeal. She retired from Department of Corrections in March 2017. I first met Patricia on July 24, 2018, and she is now the restorative justice program coordinator for Second Chances Farm. I continue to believe that everything happens for a reason even though it is unlikely to be clear immediately.

After a great deal of prayer and consideration, I decided to incorporate Second Chances Farm, LLC on April 24, 2017. My very good friend, Rhianon Husmann, who was not only the associate producer of TEDxWilmington but also a very talented graphic designer, subsequently created the logo for Second Chances Farm.

I invited 63 people to help celebrate my 63rd birthday on May 10, 2017. I used this celebration to share my vision for creating Second Chances Farms as my legacy project that would create 70 capitalists by the time I was 70 by giving a second chance to, and hiring exclusively, returning citizens from prison. I was referring to the span of our lives in *Psalms 90*, which states that "the days of our years are three score years and ten," which is 70.

A few years ago, I was certified as a Dream Builder™ Life Coach by my mentor, Mary Morrissey, who subsequently gave a TEDx talk at TEDxWilmington. I had shared with Mary about my vision to create Second Chances Farm. Mary invited me to attend her Alpha Omega 6-Day Immersion Retreat between August 21 and 26, 2017 at the luxurious Ritz Carlton Laguna Niguel, in Dana Point, California. Thanks to a generous scholarship from an anonymous friend who believed in my vision, I was able to accept this kind invitation from Mary. This intense retreat helped me focus intensely for six days on my vision and build on my dream in a concrete way. At the end of this retreat, it was very clear to me that if I wanted to launch Second Chances Farm as a commercially viable entity sooner than later, I would most need to retire from TEDxWilmington at the end of 2018 so I was free to devote all my time, talent and treasure into Second Chances Farm.

Evan Bartle joined me as a Public Ally in mid-September 2017, working about 75 percent of his time on TEDxWilmington, and the remaining 25 percent of his time on Second Chances Farm, which was still an embryonic idea in my mind. Having Evan help me with TEDxWilmington opened up some significant time for me to explore the field of indoor vertical farming in depth.

I got a pleasant surprise in early January 2018 when I learned that Opportunity Zones were added to the Internal Revenue tax code by the Tax Cuts and Jobs Act on December 22, 2017. An Opportunity Zone is an economically distressed community where new investments, under certain conditions, may be eligible for preferential tax treatment. Localities qualify as Opportunity Zones if they have been nominated for the governor of a particular state, and that nomination has been certified by the Secretary of the U.S. Treasury.

Opportunity Zones are an economic development tool—that is, they are designed to spur economic development and job creation in distressed communities. Opportunity Zones are designed to spur economic development by providing tax benefits to investors. First, investors can defer tax on any prior gains invested in a Qualified Opportunity Fund (QOF) until the earlier of the date on which the investment in a QOF is sold or exchanged, or December 31, 2026. If the QOF investment is held for longer than five years, there is a 10 percent exclusion of the deferred gain. If held for more than seven years, the 10 percent becomes 15 percent.

Second, if the investor holds the investment in the Opportunity Fund for at least 10 years, the investor is eligible for an increase on the basis of the QOF investment equal to its fair market value on the date that the QOF investment is sold or exchanged. A Qualified Opportunity Fund is an investment vehicle that is set up as either a partnership or corporation for investing in eligible property that is located in a Qualified Opportunity Zone.

It quickly became clear that if Second Chances Farms could be located in Opportunity Zones, it could attract more capital. I invested a considerable amount of time and energy learning everything I could about Opportunity Zones and Opportunity Funds. The U.S. Secretary of Treasury designated 25 Opportunity Zones in Delaware, eight of which are in Wilmington. There are over 8,000 Opportunity Zones throughout the United States, and I kept getting calls to establish Opportunity funds throughout the United States.

My idea of creating perhaps one or two Second Chances Farms to create 70 compassionate capitalists by age 70 suddenly grew much larger than I could ever imagine. There was no question that I could not organize any more TEDxWilmington events after 2018 if I were to take advantage of Opportunity Zones to establish Second Chances Farms. I also realized that I could not do this on my own.

When his term as a Public Ally ended on June 30, 2018, I asked Evan Bartle to join Second Chances Farm, LLC as my partner on July 1, 2018 and help me transform this idea into reality. Evan and I met John Legaré Williams, an attorney, who gave a TEDx talk at

TEDxWilmington in 2017, on Delaware Series LLC to see if it made sense to convert Second Chances Farm, LLC into a Delaware Series LLC, and followed John's recommendations in this regard. Once again, the ideas worth spreading from giving a TEDx talk have a long shelf life.

Evan and I then worked very closely to identify potential locations for Second Chances Farm number one in Wilmington. We spent a lot of time looking for locations, primarily but not exclusively in Opportunity Zones within Wilmington with about 10,000 sq. ft. that we could rent.

On July 25th, 2017, we met with a large non-profit entity that had a surplus building just a few feet outside an Opportunity Zone. This building was close to downtown Wilmington and had approximately 10,000 sq. ft. of space per floor. Even though the building was not within an Opportunity Zone, the non-profit that owned this building was willing to contribute it at no cost to a joint venture with Second Chances Farm. It was impossible to say no to a piece of real estate that was essentially free to us.

When we contacted the City of Wilmington to determine if the zoning of this building permitted us to install an indoor hydroponic vertical farm, we were advised to apply for a variance to the zoning code to put in an indoor hydroponic vertical farm at this location. The building owner submitted an application for this zoning variance. On November 12, 2018, the City of Wilmington Board of Adjustment denied the requested use variance to allow operation of a vertical farm at this location. Even though this building was essentially "free" to Second Chances Farm, it had no value if we could not operate a vertical farm.

After numerous meetings with the Zoning Administrator and the Planning Department of the City of Wilmington, I learned that in order to put an indoor vertical farm anywhere within the city limits of Wilmington, we would need to get the City Zoning Code amended first by the City Planning Commission, and then by City Council. This process is like adding something to the 10 Commandments!

Meanwhile, on or about October 15, 2019, Second Chances Farm had the opportunity to apply for a grant, in collaboration with our non-profit partner, from the Welfare Foundation. On December 5th, we were notified that farm number one was awarded a $175,000 grant. We are very grateful to Chris Grundner, president and CEO and the trustees of the Welfare Foundation for their vote of confidence. Chris had given a well-received TEDx talk at the 2014 TEDxWilmington Conference.

I was invited to pitch the idea for Second Chances Farm at the Fifth Annual Reinventing Delaware Dinner, hosted by the Pete du Pont Freedom Foundation, on December 5th. The purpose of this foundation is to identify bold ideas that create jobs and make Delaware a better place to live, work and raise a family. Much to my surprise, Second Chances Farm was voted as the top idea of the evening, which resulted in the foundation contracting with Social Contract to help Second Chances Farm finalize its business plan from January through April 2019.

Jon Brilliant, a very successful venture capitalist, suggested we get together for dinner. After several follow up messages from Jon, we set a date to get together on December 29th. Jon had given a TEDx talk in 2014 at the very first TEDxWilmingtonSalon that I organized. In his TEDx talk, he argued the merits of having for-profit solutions to non-profit problems. Following this dinner, Jon and I met several times in January 2019, and based on these discussions, he agreed to join Second Chances Farm, LLC as a fellow managing member and our CFO. What a great way to start the new year.

In early February 2019, I was contacted by Peter Osborne, the new editor of *Delaware Business Times*, who decided to write an article on Second Chances Farm based on its being voted as the Best Idea at the Pete du Pont Freedom Foundation's Reinventing Delaware 2018. What started as a small article turned into two full pages in the print edition of the *Delaware Business Times*. Here the URL of the on-line version of the article: https://www.delawarebusinesstimes.com/vertical-farms-envisioned-as-path-out-of-recidivism/

This article attracted a lot of attention from potential investors, including Nicole Black, a TEDxWilmington speaker based in California, who became one of the first investors.

I was invited by Abby O'Neal, organizer of TEDxRoadtown, British Virgin Islands, to give a TEDx talk on Second Chances Farm at TEDxRoadtown on March 23, 2019. Even though I had organized 32 TEDxWilmington events that featured 490 speakers, giving a TEDx talk on the red carpet on this subject was one of the hardest things I have ever done. I then spoke on April 5th at the Delaware State Chamber of Commerce to a packed audience. I was also invited to give a presentation at the 4th Virginia Urban Agriculture Summit between April 23and 25th. Like an evangelist, I gave presentations on Second Chances Farm to anyone who listened.

On May 1, 2019, the U.S. Department of Treasury published updated proposed regulations for Opportunity Zones in the Federal Register. These regulations clarified a lot of rules governing Opportunity Zone Businesses like Second Chances Farm, enabling us to move forward later in the summer of 2019 to create one or more Opportunity Funds to raise capital from investors for Second Chances Farm.

While waiting for the City of Wilmington to amend the City Code to allow vertical farms within city limits, we focused our energy on finding a home for farm number one within an Opportunity Zone. We located a 47,500 sq. ft. building owned by Opportunity Center, Inc., at 3030 Bowers Street, that was initially available only for leasing. We persuaded Opportunity Center Inc. to sell the property, and on May 7, 2019, we entered into a Letter of Intent to acquire this property, which is within an Opportunity Zone. This idea worth spreading finally found a home where it can grow and become a reality.

I invited about 150 people to my 65th birthday on May 10, 2019 to formally announce my retirement from TEDxWilmington, and share how so many TEDx talks and people I met because of TEDxWilmington inspired to me start Second Chances Farm. We concluded these celebrations on May 10th with Jon Brilliant, Evan Bartle and me executing various documents formalizing our relationship with Second Chances Farm, LLC.

I had submitted on May 30, 2018 a Hemp Grower Application and Site Registration Form to the Delaware Department of Agriculture. On June 11, 2019, I received a letter from the Hon. Michael T. Scuse, Secretary of Agriculture in Delaware, that read in part as follows:

> "The Delaware Department of Agriculture is authorizing Ajit Mathew George to grow hemp (Cannabis sativa L.) in accordance with 3 Del. C. 1301 to 1313 and in accordance with the provisions of Section 7606 of the Agricultural Act of 2014."

I am not sure exactly what to think about all this. After celebrating just over a month ago my 65th birthday, this license was not on my list of things to get when I was younger. But I am grateful for being afforded this opportunity to grow hemp as part of Second Chances Farm.

On June 18th, the City Planning Commission approved the recommendations from the City Planning Department to amend the City Zoning Code to permit, as a matter of right, indoor commercial horticultural operations in all relevant zoning districts. On June 20, 2019, the City Council formally introduced an ordinance to implement the recommendations of the City Planning Commission. The City Council unanimously approved the zoning amendment, and the Mayor signed the ordinance on July 17, 2019.

We look forward to building a prototype vertical farm at 3030 Bowers Street in the fall of 2019 now that we took possession of the property on September 1, 2019, so that we can show potential investors and anyone who is curious what an indoor hydroponic vertical farm looks like.

Here is a summary:

SECOND CHANCES FARM

Second Chances Farm, LLC ("the Company") is a mission driven, for-profit organization that is tackling some of America's most pressing challenges through social innovation and providing innovative business model solutions to some of society's most urgent social problems.

The Company is offering a game-changing answer to clearly identified needs and holds out the promise to benefit multiple individuals in different communities through a clearly articulated strategy, as well as create significant value for the Company's investors.

OUR MISSION

To nurture people, plants, and our planet, one green thumb at a time.

OUR VISION

To solve the world's food shortage and eliminate food deserts by replacing recidivism with compassionate capitalism and turning entrepreneurs-in-residence into "Agri-preneurs."

OUR TRIPLE BOTTOM LINE INVESTING PHILOSOPHY

To attract investors who are interested in financial return, economic activity, job creation and positive social impact on distressed communities in Opportunity Zones.

THE PROBLEMS WE PLAN TO SOLVE

1. While the United States has less than five percent of the world's population, it accounts for 25 percent of the entire world's prison population, with over 2,300,000 people in prison. According to the Bureau of Justice, 76.6 percent of individuals released from prisons in the U.S. are re-arrested within five years of release. Recidivism is defined as, "the tendency of a convicted criminal to

reoffend." It costs more than $43,000 per year to house a prisoner in Delaware, which translated in 2017 to over $282 million to keep prisoners incarcerated. Amongst all 50 states, Delaware represents the bottom third on a cost-per-inmate basis. It is a revolving door, not just in Delaware, but nationwide.

2. Citizens returning from incarceration face many barriers that often lead them back to criminal activity, such as homelessness, lack of job skills, limited education, mental health issues, substance use disorders, lack of transportation to get to work, and difficulty finding work due to their criminal history.

3. By the year 2050, it is estimated that the world population will reach 10 billion people, 80 percent of which will be living in urban areas. This substantial growth will require a 70 percent increase in crop production, and 2.5 billion new acres of farmland, an area larger than the size of Brazil. We are quickly outgrowing our green planet and need a new farming solution fast.

4. In addition, most produce is transported long distance—1,500 miles for the average American—adding to our carbon footprint. Natural disasters like drought, flooding, pollution, and hurricanes are disrupting the food supply.

5. There is a tremendous lack of pesticide-free, herbicide-free organic food available in the Delaware Valley.

6. Two days before Thanksgiving Day 2018, the Center for Disease Control warned Americans not to eat romaine lettuce due to contamination. There have been 40 outbreaks of food related illness traced to leafy greens in the past 10 years. A major source of E.coli contamination comes from organic fertilizers, the polite term for manure. Triple washing does not effectively remove E.coli bacteria.

7. There are numerous buildings and lots in economically distressed communities that are vacant, which adversely affects these communities. Furthermore, most of these distressed communities are also food deserts, lacking access to affordable, healthy and nutritious food.

8. According to a paper published by Brookings on or about March 14, 2018, "about half of ex-prisoners have no reported earnings in the first several years after leaving prison; among those who do find work, half earn less than $10,090 a year, or less than a full-time job at minimum wage." The Brookings research paper found that "ex-prisoners fare poorly in the labor market. In the first full calendar year after their release, only 55 percent reported any earnings, with the median earnings being $10,090. Of those with earnings, four percent earned less than $500, 32 percent earned between $500 and $15,000, and only 20 percent earned more than $15,000."

THE SOLUTION

Second Chances Farm plans to battle recidivism while commercially growing local, organic produce in economically depressed areas and breathing new life into functionally old buildings. We are supporting not just alternatives to this revolving door in the criminal justice system, but also reducing the impact of climate change by growing food locally, protecting the environment by eliminating the use of toxic chemicals, and using much less water than traditional soil-based farming.

We are a for-profit answer to a non-profit problem. By creating an innovative cooperative corporate ownership structure, we are offering a transformative, equitable, and scalable game-changing solution to benefit multiple returning citizens in underserved communities all over the U.S. We have a simple formula in mind to address the issues we face:

**SECOND CHANCES + VERTICAL FARMS =
GREEN COLLAR JOBS + COMPASSIONATE CAPITALISM**

SECOND CHANCES FARM #1 ("FARM #1")

Farm #1 will be the first farm established at the Property. It will use a footprint of approximately 19,400 sq. ft. of the total 47,500 sq. ft.

For more information, visit www.secondchancesfarm.com

The publication of this book will mark the final chapter of my life called TEDxWilmington, and begin a new chapter entitled Second Chances Farm. I am thrilled to take an idea worth spreading and make it an idea translated into action!

This journey was truly unplanned with no clear destination in mind. It has been full of detours and surprises. Thanks to all my fellow travellers.

Onward and forward.

CHAPTER 16

101 Tips

by Evan Bartle, Elissa Ben-Eli and Dana Dobson

1. You MUST read the book, "TED Talks: The Official TED Guide to Public Speaking" by Chris Anderson.
2. If you don't read the entire book, "TED Talks: The Official TED Guide to Public Speaking," focus on Chapter 4: Throughline.
3. If you don't read the entire book, "TED Talks: The Official TED Guide to Public Speaking," or Chapter 4 in its entirety, at least read this section: "a throughline requires you first to identify an idea that can be properly unpacked in the time you have available. You should then build a structure so that every element in your talk is somehow linked to this idea" (p. 39 Throughline).
4. Always say TEDx never TED, when referring to your talk.
5. Always refer to your talk as a talk; a TEDx talk is not a speech.
6. Your "Idea Worth Spreading" must be your own and may not address political/religious agendas or directly promote a company, business, or product.
7. We strongly encourage you to visit www.TED.com and check out TED and TEDx talks that might have similar ideas to your proposed TEDx talk.
8. If your idea worth spreading is similar to a TED or TEDx talk already out there, how is yours different?
9. Don't apply just to be on a TEDx stage — apply to make a difference.
10. If the organization where you have been invited to give a talk does not have deadlines or a strict structure, create your own.
11. If there is a speaker agreement, please read it thoroughly to make sure you understand your obligations.
12. If you apply and don't get accepted, don't stop preparing and apply again.
13. Hire a speaker coach if you can afford one. Please check how many TEDx speakers that coach has helped.

14. Practice, practice, practice.
15. Stick to one idea.
16. Keep old drafts of your talk. Sometimes you will want to keep old parts as you keep editing.
17. Record yourself practicing, watch how fast or slow you talk, your movements, hand gestures, and check the time it took you to give the talk.
18. Practice your talk with pauses where the audience may applaud, laugh, etc.
19. Rehearse in front of a diverse group of people that will give you constructive criticism.
20. Rehearse in front of people that do not know your topic.
21. Watch TED and TEDx talks to see how they use a throughline.
22. You will need hours of preparation. The shorter the talk, the more time needed to prepare.
23. Your first draft will not be your last. Please be prepared to revise your draft often.
24. Be yourself but be flexible.
25. Have a mentor.
26. If you plan on showing your creative side with music, dance, singing, etc. make sure it fits your idea worth spreading.
27. If you are required to submit video drafts of your talk, make sure you are in a well-lit room, your entire body is in the frame, and that you speak clearly.
28. Meet all deadlines set by your TEDx organizer.
29. In a PowerPoint presentation, a single, strong, graphic image or succinct line of text will tell your story better than a crowded collage or packed paragraph.
30. Don't add a PowerPoint if you don't need one.
31. People need to process what you're saying while looking at your slides. Make it simple.
32. Use a simple background for your slides, not a template. Black usually stands out best and makes the text pop.
33. Use large font in your PowerPoint (minimum 28 pt.).
34. Sans serif fonts are easier to read than serif fonts.
35. If you have slides, make sure to run through your talk in full using the slides and a clicker.
36. Do not make any major content changes to your talk the week leading up to your talk.

37. Do not turn around to look at your PowerPoint.
38. If using video clips, keep them short.
39. Less is more when it comes to visuals.
40. Make sure you receive written permission for all images used in your talk.
41. Just because an image was found on the internet does not give a speaker permission to use the image in their presentation.
42. There are free public images on Flickr (www.flickr.com/search/advanced), pexels.com, unsplash.com, and other sites. Use high resolution images whenever possible.
43. If you plan on using props, make sure they aid your idea and do not hinder the audience from focusing on your talk.
44. If you use props, think out where you will place them if you are not using them the entire time.
45. Make sure your props are large enough for the audience to see.
46. Stick to the time allotted given by your TEDx organizer for your TEDx talk.
47. Have transitions that flow.
48. Make sure you have energy and passion in your tone of voice, body language and words.
49. Longer isn't always better. Try to stick to 10 minutes rather than 18 minutes, unless you have a compelling message that keeps the attention of the audience for 18 minutes.
50. Have a 'call to action' for your audience. Motivate them to do something after hearing your TEDx talk.
51. Since the talks are viewed globally, English may not be the viewer's first language. Speak slowly and clearly.
52. Make sure all terms are stated in full, not by acronyms.
53. If you use any research or statistics, make sure you cite your sources.
54. Do not memorize your talk word for word; it will show when you talk.
55. Be a storyteller.
56. Make a connection to the audience.
57. You will not be able to please everyone. Make sure you have a targeted audience in mind when giving your talk.
58. Know your talk in and out so that it sounds like you are talking to a friend, not giving a lecture.

59. Move around the stage, but try to stay on the red carpet.
60. If you have a serious topic, add some humor to lighten the mood.
61. Have a powerful ending.
62. Don't think that you can just "wing" your talk. Make sure you are fully prepared.
63. Even if you have given this talk in lecture form or another setting prior, still prepare for this specific talk. A TEDx talk is very different than other talks.
64. Typically, you will not use a podium while giving your talk. Prepare to give your talk without standing behind a podium and stand in the middle of the stage on the red carpet.
65. If you are giving a talk with one or more persons make sure the talk is cohesive.
66. Do not wear dangly earrings, necklaces, or bracelets, the mic will pick it up and affect the audio in your video.
67. Try on your outfit prior to the day of event.
68. Have backups clothes in case one clashes with the stage.
69. Make sure your outfit is microphone accessible.
70. Many organizations use microphones that need to be clipped to the person's clothing. It is important that if you do not want any wires showing, you wear clothes that will hide the mic transmitter.
71. It is important that the mic is securely fastened to your clothing and will not move.
72. Get a good night's sleep before the event; drink plenty of water.
73. Engage the entire audience.
74. Leave the audience inspired.
75. RELAX.
76. Try not to cram everything into your talk.
77. Be specific and detailed.
78. Make your story relatable to the audience, as if the story were about them.
79. If you have audience involvement in your talk, think about how it would look on video.
80. Show emotion, but don't get out of control where it affects you giving your talk.
81. Have facial expressions that match the tone of your talk.
82. Smile.

83. Use pauses for emphasis. Pauses enable the audience to catch up. Pauses are your friend.
84. Be geographically specific. In the United States, people on the east coast will know where Philadelphia is, or Delaware, but other parts of the country or world need more description. When giving your talk, if you bring up a specific area, make sure you give the location. Instead of just saying Philadelphia, make sure you say, "Philadelphia, a city in Pennsylvania on the East Coast of The United States.
85. Don't look at your shoes when you give your talk.
86. Don't discriminate with your gaze; look all around the audience during your talk.
87. If you stumble or mess up on stage, don't stop or say 'sorry,' just continue.
88. If you've completely lost your place, start at the next part of your talk that you remember.
89. BREATHE.
90. When telling a story, use their names. Don't just say, "a friend."
91. For anything questionable, give a short explanation or definition to make sure the audience understands what you are talking about.
92. Change the tone of your voice to prevent monotony.
93. Your talk is your gift to the world.
94. Be confident when you enter and exit the stage.
95. Summarize your idea worth spreading in your conclusion.
96. Make sure the audience knows when your talk is over. End with "thank you."
97. Don't rush off the stage after you finish. Enjoy the moment and receive applause.
98. Make sure your TEDx title is something short, clever, and catchy to grab audiences and viewers. Your TEDx title must be 100 characters or less. This includes spaces, vertical slashes, your name, and the name of the TEDx organization. "Title | Name | TEDx Organization" Example: "Markevis Gideon | Find Your China | TEDxWilmington" (50 Characters).
99. Make sure your TEDx title has keywords that are searchable on YouTube.
100. Share your TEDx video with friends, family, colleagues, in your email signature, etc.
101. Have fun!

ACKNOWLEDGEMENTS

I had grossly underestimated how much time and talent it would take to write a book like this. Bringing this book to fruition within six months would not have been possible without the encouragement and support of well over 170 people who helped me create *The Magic of the Red Carpet*.

TEDxWilmington existed because of the sweat, love, and unwavering commitment of a large group of volunteers, partners and sponsors. Many thanks to everyone who has had a hand in bringing TEDx to life in Wilmington, Delaware.

This book would have remained in my imagination if Elissa Ben-Eli had not entered my life as a Public Ally from September 2018 to June 30, 2019. Elissa has been patiently working with all the 137 speakers who contributed in more than one way to this book. This book could not exist without Elissa's invaluable help.

I am very grateful to Dana Dobson for several things, including editing and proofreading this book under great time pressure. I had invited a cross section of past TEDxWilmington speakers to share their insight, and I was pleasantly surprised to get detailed responses from 137 speakers. I then asked Dana to go through all these responses and curate all these responses with a view to highlighting the very best in Chapter 6. Many thanks, Dana.

While Alessandra Nicole is our primary photographer, she accepted my invitation a couple of years ago to curate the hundreds of blogs that speakers who gave TEDx talks at TEDxWilmington wrote. She is a brilliant editor, and I couldn't resist asking her to review the over 600 blogs from speakers posted on our website and select a cross section of these blogs in Chapter 7. She selected 96 blogs from 42 different speakers that are very revealing. Any prospective TEDx speaker should read all the blogs we posted at www.tedxwilmington.com to gain a true insight into what our speakers experienced before, during and after they gave a TEDx talk.

I will forever remain grateful to Steve Harrison from Bradley Communications Corp. for offering me the professional assistance of his team, especially Deb Englander and Martha Bullen to help me with this book. I cannot say how thankful I am to Martha Bullen for introducing me to Christy Collins, who is singularly responsible for laying out this book so that it could be published. I am truly in their debt.

Thank you Geoffrey Berwind, Jake Voorhees, Matt Urban and Sheryl Winarick for sharing your wisdom by writing one chapter each in this book. You have enriched this book with your writings.

I asked the talented graphic designer, my good friend and long-time TEDxWilmington associate producer to design the beautiful cover for this book. Designing a cover is much harder than I could ever imagine. So many things go into the front and back cover that I now wonder how anyone who ever published a book made it through the design process. Many thanks Rhianon Husmann.

Evan Bartle, who started out with me in September 2017 as a Public Ally and now works with me as the chief growing officer of Second Chances Farm. I asked Evan to help Elissa compile 101 Tips that I hope readers will find helpful.

I invited 10 TEDx organizers from around the world that I respected to share their pearls of wisdom in this book from their own experiences organizing their own TEDx events. Five of these organizers were from the United States, while the others came from a diverse group of countries such as British Virgin Islands, France, China, Guatemala and India. I was blessed to serve as a fellow TEDx organizer with Randy Bretz, Abby O'Neal, Alysia Dahir, Ben Sabry, Jimmy Tan, Kat Haber, Mark Lovett, Mark Sylvester, Pablo Guzman, and Viiveck Verma.

I also invited 10 members of the TEDxWilmington tribe to share their experiences about being part of this special group that organized 32 different events. Thank you, Angela Jo Manieri, Bob Turner, Dana Dobson, George Waterman, Jake Voorhees, Jeet Patel, Julie Vernot, Ken Grant, Laura Harrison, and Lynne Williams.

There are well over 600 pictures in this book. We have over 16,000 pictures from our various TEDx events that can be viewed at https://www.flickr.com/photos/tedxwilmington/albums. Special thanks to our talented photographers Alessandra Nicole and Joe del Tufo, who took all these amazing pictures. A few photos were taken by Joel Plotkin and Sam Ellis at some MidAtlantic Wine and Food Festival events that I organized.

Special thanks to the 137 speakers who gave a TEDx talk at TEDxWilmington for collaborating with me on this book. I am grateful to Adebisi Adebowale, Alisa Morkides, Allan Ting, Allington Creque, Amy Ogden, Anisha Abraham, Anne Jolles, Annie Norman, Areeba Khan, Arianne Missimer, Arthur Brodsky, Arthuretta Martin, Bill Haley, Bill Jensen, Bill Walshe, Carlyn Montes De Oca, Carolyn Bennett-Sullivan, Cassandra Pavolic, Charlotte Blake Alston, Christy Whitman, Cindy Bo, Claudia Six, Clint Rogers, Cornelius "Nippy" Betz, Cyndi O'Meara, Daniel Lieberman, Dave Nassaney, David Raymond, David Woessner, Debra Laino, Diana Capaldi, Dinette Rivera, Dion Kenney,

Donna Duffy, Dune Thorne, Ellie Laks, Eric Okdeh, Errol Ebanks, Felicia Clark, Galit Goldfarb, George Chanos, Glory Crampton, Greg Plum, Gudrun Penselin, Gustavo Grodnitzky, Harold Lathon, Jalaal Hayes, James Lee, Jaya Jaya Myra Godfrey, Jen Kluczkowski, Jennifer Myers, Jill Murrary, Joan DelFattore, Jody Wood, Joe del Tufo, John Jeremiah, John Livesay, John Quinlan, Joia Nuri, Joseph Geraci, Kalvin J. Evans, Karen Mayo, Kate Kirkwood, Kevin Carr, Kevin Rose, Kien Vuu, Kris Younger, Laura Wellington, Lauri Robbins Ericson, Liane Hansen, Linda Arrey-Mbi Nkwenti, Linda Farquhar, Lindsay Page, Lisa Mims, Marianne Ryan, Marie White, Mark LoGiudice, Markevis Gideon, Martin Rayala, Mary Morrissey, Massoma Alam, Maureen Rabotin, Melissa Root, Michael Morgan, Michelle Nagel, Michelle Yep Martin, Mikki Williams, Mindy Tatz Chernoff, Nicole Black, Otto Borsich, Patrick Wright, Paul Dixon, Paul Rosen, Peter Atwater, Peter Hillard, Phil Spampinato, Pina DeRosa, Rachel Hutchisson, Rani St. Pucchi, Renae Baker, Renee Jones, Ria Story, Rita Wilkins, Rob Bentley, Robert "Dusty" Staub, Robert Ward, Robyn Howton, Rod Wallace, Sara Blanchard, Sara Crawford Jones, Sean Douglas, Sean Kennedy, Seth Rainess, Setrag Khoshafian, Shane Coen, Sharon Livingston, Shavon Lindley, Stephanie Diggins, Stephen T. Lawless, Sunil Robert, Susan Bremer O'Neill, Susan Heitler, Tamsen Webster, Taria Pritchett, Teresa Rodriguez, Terri Levine, Therese Jornlin, Tiffany Gwilliam, Tiffany Stallings, Tom Devine, Tony Selimi, Tonya Fitzpatrick, Vicky Kelly, and Vincent James.

Finally, I wish with all my heart and soul to thank my wife, Sarah, for her patience in putting up with all my adventures, especially TEDxWilmington, including having literally hundreds of TEDxWilmington speakers come to our house for dinners following various TEDx events and having boxes of program guides and supplies delivered to our house before each TEDxWilmington event. Sarah reluctantly tolerated all the mayhem that was created at our house which acted as the headquarters for TEDxWilmington from 2011 to 2018.

Soli Deo Gloria

ABOUT THE AUTHOR

Ajit Mathew George is a serial entrepreneur, opportunity maker, creative marketer, TEDx organizer emeritus, food & wine aficionado, philanthropist. He has over 40 years of experience in creative marketing, strategic planning, and business development in various arenas from broadcasting and events to non-profits and real estate development.

Ajit is the founder of Second Chances Farm, LLC, (www.secondchancesfarm.com) an organization focused on hiring and giving turn key entrepreneurial opportunities to people returning from prison after serving their sentences through the creation of indoor, hydroponic vertical farms – or "plant factories."

Through Magic Dust, LLC, he helps organizations and individuals build their dreams, accelerate their results, and create richer, more fulfilling lives through Life Coaching, strategic marketing and event planning. Over the years, Ajit has sprinkled his "magic dust" to create some magical events such as First Night Wilmington, Meals From the Masters Celebrity Chef's Brunch, Evening With The Masters, Cellar Masters Wine Auction, Evening of Style, Black Tie Monopoly Tournament, Virgin Islands Winemakers Dinners, MidAtlantic Wine + Food Festival and TEDxWilmington.

As the founder of TEDxWilmington (www.tedxwilmington.com) Ajit organized and produced 32 TEDx events between 2012 and 2018 including a very special TEDx Salon inside a prison in July 2015. These different TEDxWilmington events featured 490 speakers from around the world who gave 469 TEDx talks. As of August 6, 2019, the TEDx talks given at TEDxWilmington had over 22.5 million views on YouTube.

Ajit was also the founder of the MidAtlantic Wine+ Food Festival, which in 2015 consisted of a series of 33 acclaimed food and wine events in four states over four days featuring 60 chefs plus 23 winemakers from six continents. He organized this annual Wine + Food Festival for four years.

In 1989, Ajit became the founding chairman of Meals On Wheels Delaware. He launched the highly successful Meals From The Masters Culinary "Weekend in Delaware," starting with the Meals From The Masters Celebrity Brunch in 1998 and added The Evening With The Masters and Cellar Masters Wine Auction. When he retired from Meals On Wheels Delaware in 2007, these three events had raised more than $4.2 million for Meals On Wheels in Delaware to ensure that Delaware was one of the few states in the United States where senior citizens did not have to join a waiting list for home-delivered meals each weekday.

Together with his wife, Dr. Sarah Brown, Ajit created "An Evening Of Style" for YWCA Delaware and co-chaired this event in 2006 and 2007. In addition, Ajit was actively involved in developing a $3.7 million project to double the capacity of the YWCA's Home Life Management Center which assists homeless families achieve self-sufficiency.

Ajit was also the coordinating chairman of First Night Delaware which attracted over 30,000 people at the inaugural New Year's Eve celebration of the arts. In 2006 and 2007, Ajit served as chairman of the American Red Cross Delmarva Chapter's highly successful "Black Tie Monopoly Tournament." He has served as chairman of the Governor's Council on Family Services, general convener of Delaware Futures, co-chairman of the first Delaware Mini-Grand Prix of the Arthritis Foundation, president of the Kiwanis Foundation and the Kiwanis Club of Wilmington. He is also a member of the Rotary Club of Wilmington, Delaware.

Prior to going into the private sector in 1980, Ajit was director of marketing and membership services for WHYY Inc. in Philadelphia, Pa., where he raised millions of dollars for public television and public radio through direct mail and on-air fundraising.

Over the years, Ajit has been recognized for his many philanthropic activities. He received the prestigious 2007 Award for Outstanding Philanthropic Service from the Association of Fundraising Professionals, Brandywine Chapter. Ajit also received from the Rotary Club of Tortola in 2006 the Paul Harris Award by Rotary International. In addition to being the recipient of the 1994 Governor's Outstanding Volunteer Award in Delaware, Ajit was the recipient of the Jefferson Award in 2002 for his work with the YWCA and the Jefferson Award in 2003 for his work with Meals On Wheels. Ajit also received in 1999 the National Volunteer of the Year award from the Meals On Wheels Association of America.

Ajit is the recipient of the 2019 Wilmington Award for Community Service. This award by the Mayor of the City of Wilmington honors Wilmington citizens for outstanding accomplishments, community service, and life-long achievement.

He attended the University of Delaware and received his undergraduate degree from Antioch College and a graduate degree in organization development from Antioch University. Born of Indian parents and brought up in Kuwait, Ajit moved to the United States in July 1970.

Ajit resides in Wilmington with his wife and their red standard poodle HRH Maharani. They have a long tradition of hosting a monthly Seven Course Wine Dinner in a wine cellar at their house in Wilmington, Delaware where they have mementos from their travels around the world. Ajit is a passionate gardener who has planted over a 1,500 plants over the years at Sunset Watch in Virgin Gorda, British Virgin Islands (www.sunsetwatch.com).

www.ingramcontent.com/pod-product-compliance
Lightning Source LLC
Chambersburg PA
CBHW080436170426
43195CB00017B/2800